PAMELA STEPHENSON

Treasure Islands

SAILING THE SOUTH SEAS

in the wake of

FANNY AND ROBERT LOUIS STEVENSON

headline

First published in 2005
by HEADLINE BOOK PUBLISHING

First published in paperback in 2006
by HEADLINE BOOK PUBLISHING

1

Cataloguing in Publication Data is available from the British Library

10-digit ISBN 0 7553 1286 4
13-digit ISBN 978 0 7553 1286 3

Typeset in Palatino by Avon DataSet Ltd, Bidford on Avon, Warwickshire

Designed by Ben Cracknell Studios

Maps by ML Design
Integrated black and white photographs © The Writers' Museum, Edinburgh

Printed and bound in Great Britain by Clays Ltd, St Ives plc

Headline's policy is to use papers that are natural, renewable and recyclable
products and made from wood grown in sustainable forests.
The logging and manufacturing processes are expected to conform to the
environmental regulations of the country of origin.

Headline Book Publishing
A division of Hodder Headline
338 Euston Road
London NW1 3BH

www.headline.co.uk
www.hodderheadline.com

To Scarlett, my venturesome valley-girl: for braving the squalls, saluting the sunrise, sword-dancing in the *maneabas* and gliding with sharks.

CONTENTS

ACKNOWLEDGEMENTS

It was my husband who made this trip possible, despite his unshakeable belief that boats are prisons with the possibility of drowning. I will be forever grateful for his loving support and generosity. Indeed, my whole family was challenged to put up with me in ways that were, at times, quite difficult (especially Scarlett, who, as she puts it, 'moved to the middle of the ocean for a whole year'). I appreciate them all the more for their understanding.

Many other people who inspired and helped me are mentioned within these pages: sailors, storytellers, teachers, guides, historians, preachers, divers, librarians, traders, elders, fishermen, diplomats and drivers. My research was aided, in particular, by: Ann Kindred, curator of the Robert Louis Stevenson Silverado Museum in St Helena; Elaine Greig of the Writers Museum in Edinburgh; and Chris Quist, curator of the Stevenson House State Historical Monument in Monterey, northern California. The Huntington Museum provided essential microfilm, and Felicitas Macfie most kindly welcomed me into Robert Louis Stevenson's former home in Heriot Row, Edinburgh. I owe special thanks to Togi Aifa'i Patu Tunupopo, Chief Librarian at the National University of Samoa, and to many other librarians in various campuses of the University of the South Pacific throughout the Pacific region, particularly in Pape'ete. I am also grateful to the librarians at the Pacific Room in the Apia Public Library, to those in the Office of Archives in Pago Pago, to Sisters Eileen and Aileen at the Sacred Heart Convent in Tarawa, and Lufilufi Rassensen at the Robert Louis Stevenson Museum at Vailima, Samoa.

The colour photographs, apart from those I took myself, were taken by my daughter Scarlett, Jock Edwards, Professor Eli Coleman and *Takapuna* crew members, especially Susan Rann who took the front cover photo in the Marshall Islands and Kayt Williamson who snapped the candid back cover shot as I was rowing away from the island of Arorai. In addition, I would like to thank everyone who contributed to the pictorial sections of the book.

That we safely and punctually completed the voyage itself is a testament to the skill, dedication and professionalism of Captain Mike Dailey and the entire *Takapuna* crew, past and present, who also supported the writing of this book in innumerable other ways. I am endlessly thankful to them all. I am grateful, too, to Steve Brown, Natalie Portelli and all at Tickety-Boo for their administration and organisational help. Others I would like to particularly thank are Samuel 'Salty Sam' Stephenson and Robert Brooke, as well as Allan Alo, Martine and Paul Hicks, John Jacobs, Jurek Juszczyk, Dr Duane MacKay, Malcolm and Nadine Millar, Dr L. Puni, Dr Alan Spira, Natan and Tebi Teewe, Dr Joshua Trabulus, and Jeanmarie Williams.

Throughout the trip, my thoughts were with Val Hudson, Publishing Director at Headline, who was undergoing a different kind of challenging journey during the year. I am immensely touched that she was nevertheless able to offer me her precious time and guidance. My very grateful thanks are also due to Editor Jo Roberts-Miller for her patience, dedication, unswerving support and hard work; indeed everyone in the superb Headline team has earned my appreciation and gratitude.

Finally, it was the people of the islands of the Pacific Ocean who really made this book possible; the boatmen who ferried me ashore and the residents who welcomed me and shared the treasures of their lives, stories and ancestral spirits. Thank you, *gracias, koutai, merci beaucoup, fa'afetai lava, metaki ma'ata, mauruuru roa, ko tab'a, kommool tata, tank yu tumas.*

LIST OF CHARTS

LIST OF ILLUSTRATIONS

THE ROUTE OF THE TAKAPUNA

Hawaiian Islands

Pacific

Marianas
Islands

South

Marshall
Islands

Caroline Islands

Line
Islands

0° Equator

Namorik
Ebon
Jaluit
Abaiang
Majuro
Butaritari
Marakei
Tarawa
Abemama
Nonouti
Beru
Kiribati

Aranuka
Nikunau
Tamana
Arorae

Phoenix
Islands

Ose

Solomon
Islands

New
Guinea

Nanoumea
Nuitau
Ellis
Islands
Nui
Funafuti

Tokelau
Islands

Pukapuka
Manihiki
Penrhyn

Atafu
Nukunonu
Fakaofo
Swains

Samoa
Savai'i
Upola

Nassau

Suwarrow

Cook
Islands

Vanuatu

Viti Levu
Vanua Levu

Tutuila
American
Samoa

Society
Islands

Tahiti

New
Caledonia

Fiji

AUSTRALIA

New
Zealand

120° E

150° E

180°

150° W

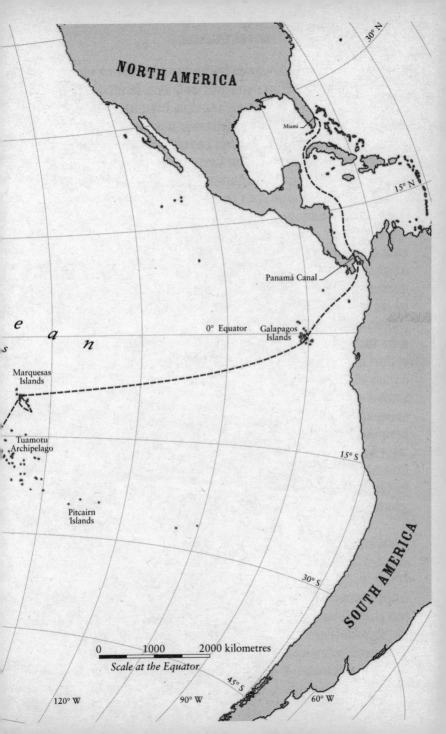

NORTH AMERICA

Miami

30° N

15° N

Panamá Canal

0° Equator

Galapagos
Islands

e

a

n

s

Marquesas
Islands

Tuamotu
Archipelago

15° S

Pitcairn
Islands

30° S

SOUTH AMERICA

0   1000   2000 kilometres
Scale at the Equator

45° S

120° W   90° W   60° W

CHAPTER ONE

FANNY AND ME

Saturday 22 November 2003

It's strange how a seemingly rogue thought can suddenly enter one's mind and initiate the abandonment of one's entire universe. An epiphany occurred at 7.10 this morning as I was sitting on the bed in my Auckland hotel room. I was beginning a day just like most others – an egg-white omelette, followed by sixteen hours of relentless juggling, from which I would retire worn-out and resentful, only to repeat the same mistakes the following day. This morning, quite unusually, I paused for a moment. Staring out at the glistening harbour, I traced the cat's cradle pattern of eager boats with well-trimmed sails cutting confidently through the waves. Of those on a starboard tack, sunlight simultaneously caught each filled sail in the same quadrant, a thrilling synchronicity that seemed more art than nature. Those pearly triangles seemed to hold a rare potential for joy, optimism, adventure and clarity of purpose – all elements from which I had become disengaged in my present life. As I gazed beyond them to Rangitoto, the green-peaked volcanic isle familiar to me from my early childhood, I grasped a terrifying reality. *I'm drowning. I am gasping for breath. Splashing furiously just to stay on the surface. No life jacket.*

An instant later, a female spectre clad in pale Victorian garments floated up from my unconscious realm. I recognized her immediately. It was Fanny, the wife of Scottish author Robert Louis Stevenson. I had just been reading about their fascinating voyages around the Pacific Ocean in the late 1800s, through which Fanny had helped her ailing husband become infused with health, energy and a new zest for life – exactly what I need myself. Fanny was a wild pioneer woman, a legendary dynamo and singular adventuress. She faced her mortality on the beaches of dangerous archipelagos, amid violent squalls at sea, and beneath the night-crawling of giant ship-rats. I had been particularly struck by one image of this delicate-framed Victorian woman – perched on a boat with a silver revolver in each hand, shooting at sharks with deadly accuracy. A dark-skinned beauty in a necklace of human teeth, Fanny was a mistress of pragmatism.

'You are truly awash,' she declared, poking me with her umbrella. 'Label it what you will . . . existential angst, creative illness, mid-life crisis . . . you must take action!'

From that marvellous moment on, Fanny became my accomplice, co-conspirator and inspiration. If that petite, corseted woman could turn her husband's life around through a series of perilous adventures on the high seas then, in spirit, she could do the same for me. The notion of following in her wake began to crystallize in my mind's eye. My cousin Elizabeth's husband is a boat-builder.

'Robert!' I called him and skipped the pleasantries. 'How can I get a sailboat?'

'I'll build you one,' he offered.

'How long will it take?'

'Couple of years.'

'But Robert,' I shook my head and turned to face the sea, 'I don't have that kind of time.'

*

Over one hundred years earlier, in 1888 to be exact, my near-namesake, Robert Louis Stevenson, sat on Pioneer Hill, his favourite vantage point in San Francisco, and gazed with longing at the passage of sailing boats through the magnificent, misty-grey harbour below him. Absorbed by their beauty, their ease of movement and their thrilling zigzags, he was distracted from the pain in his body, the terrifying constriction in his lungs that prompted constant coughing, his struggle with his latest book and the overwhelming fear that it would be ill-received.

'I am dying.' He knew that to be true, as did Fanny and his doctors. 'I need fresh air, optimism, and adventure.'

When I met with my cousin-in-law and sketched out my evolving plan to retrace Fanny's voyages through the Pacific, then continue on around the world, his eyes lit up.

'We planned to take off, too,' he said wistfully, 'but then Elizabeth got cancer.'

The number of years I have now lived on Earth form a nasty maths equation: when subtracted from my life expectancy, the remainder is hardly a big fat chunk of prime functioning. 'If you don't do it now,' said Robert, shaking his head, 'you never will.'

With this sober warning reverberating in my head, and Fanny spurring me on, I set out on what I was convinced was a life-saving mission: to find a sailboat.

Tuesday 20 January 2004

It is hardly a revelation to state that I'm no Ellen MacArthur. Sailing for me is adventure, not a sport. On the other hand, I am even less of a gin-palace queen. I enjoy luxury, but I will never have a fancy motor yacht moored off Cannes. I love leaky, old rust-buckets and fat, hard-working tugs. I love creaky wooden barges and clanking cargo ships. I love smelly fishing boats and staunch, jolly ferries. At sea you never have to worry about location, location, location; no matter what you're floating on, just cast off and the horizon is yours. I wanted to find a solid, reasonably comfortable sailing vessel, large enough to accommodate my whole family of nine – should they wish to come aboard. After a two-month search, I found a ten-year-old Valdettaro cutter-rigged sloop. No sleek racer, she would hardly cut a swathe on the dock at San Tropez, but at 112 feet and 130 tons, with steel hull and an enclosed pilot house from which to view an unsettled horizon, she's sturdy enough to face the oceans of the world, then return home and start again. I've renamed her *Takapuna* after my birthplace, the New Zealand beachside city that sits across a gentle stretch of greenish blue from Rangitoto. *Takapuna* is a Maori name, meaning 'high place by the water', associated with an ancient legend about romantic longing.

'The hard part is over,' I thought after selling our house amidst family objections. Have boat, will travel.

In my developing, Fanny-led fantasy, I should now sail off happily upon a silvery sea with my willing husband and other loved ones in tow; but, unfortunately, it's not going to be that easy. My sudden, dramatic announcement that I am running away to sea has shocked and bewildered my entire coterie of family, friends and colleagues, and has especially horrified my husband (you know Billy – funny guy, vomits on boats).

'There's fucking pirates out there!' he stormed, followed by: 'We don't *belong* on the ocean. There's big, bitey things just *waiting* for us to fall in.'

In an interesting reversal of our usual roles, Billy is now seen by most observers as the long-suffering one, and I as the madcap renegade who threatens our family stability with my crazy scheme. It's oddly liberating, but also painful. I remain, however, resolute, ready to fight for the prize that a mere two months ago I hardly dared desire: the rest of my life.

*

Fanny was a poor sailor who hated the sea. Despite that, my heroine urged Louis, as she called her husband, to seek a better climate in the South Seas. Fourteen years earlier a New Zealander, appropriately named Seed, had implanted in Louis an interest in Samoa, insisting that his path to improved health lay in abandoning Europe and moving to the Navigator Islands. At the time, Louis could not entertain a fantasy that involved leaving Edinburgh but the idea of escaping to the Pacific remained dormant. After achieving success as a writer and becoming a celebrity in North America, Louis was finally in a position to charter a yacht, with the intention of cruising to the South Pacific region, recuperating and writing more adventure stories.

It was Fanny who found the boat. In May 1888, while visiting family in Northern California, she telegraphed her husband: 'Can secure splendid sea-going schooner yacht *Casco* for seven hundred and fifty a month with most comfortable accommodation for six aft and six forward. Can be ready for sea in ten days. Reply immediately.'

'Blessed girl.' Louis was delighted. 'Take the yacht and expect us in ten days.'

Fanny was infallibly resourceful. When it came to adventure, she frequently took the initiative. That was second nature to her – she was a frontierswoman, raised in Indiana. Her father, Jacob Vandegrift, was a handsome, blue-eyed man of Dutch descent who settled in Indianapolis in 1836 and married Esther Keen, who bore him seven children. Francis Matilda was the oldest, born on 10 March 1840. Fanny, as she became known, inherited her father's profile and piercing gaze, although her eyes were not blue, but jet black. Her mother bequeathed her a petite frame, dark curls and an exceptionally strong will. Esther was said to have once held a mad dog's jaws closed with her hands to protect her children until help arrived, and, true or not, the story provided Fanny with a model of courage and practicality that certainly came in handy when she grew up.

As a child, Fanny was a dark-skinned, high-spirited tomboy, who roamed around the countryside with her cousin Tom. In vain, her mother rubbed lotions on to her face and sewed a gingham bonnet into her hair to protect her skin from becoming any more swarthy than it already was. Fairness was fashionable at that time and some even believed that dark looks and a wicked temper went hand in hand.

'She is that colour by nature,' lamented her grandmother. 'God made her ugly.'

Her mother, more kindly, called her a little tiger lily, which led to Fanny's lifelong affection for that particular flower – a striking, curly-petalled emblem of her exotic beauty.

Fanny showed early talent in painting, drawing and writing, and she had an exceptional ability to engage people with her compelling story-telling and re-enactments of daily life. Jacob exerted little discipline upon his children, believing that their innate characters should be nurtured, rather than changed or controlled. Thus Fanny grew up with a striking originality, an ever-flourishing self-confidence and ability to be quite independent.

When Louis met Fanny, he was enthralled by her New World charisma. The 'Wild Woman of the West', as he called her, was certainly not the kind of lady he was accustomed to meeting. Most women of his class and society were the antithesis: pampered and protected. One might speculate that they bored him . . . or perhaps that such a physical weakling as Louis was unlikely to win the hearts of healthy women his own age. Anyway, he had gravitated towards the company of Edinburgh's earthy tavern women: whores and barmaids. Fanny, though eleven years his senior, was an ideal partner because her captivating side was balanced with a thoroughly capable, caretaking nature. When she met Louis at a French artists' colony hotel, she was unhappily married to Sam Osbourne and had given birth to three children. Isobel and Lloyd were then seventeen and eleven respectively, but she was in mourning for the very recent death of her youngest, Hervey, at only four years old.

Louis, who had been a semi-invalid for most of his life, responded well to the warmth of older, kindly women. Earlier on, he had fallen in love with another dark-haired Fanny, Mrs Sitwell, who was twelve years his senior, and she in turn had helped him with his career. His many letters to Fanny Sitwell reveal an all-consuming attachment to her that was no more than gently tolerated by the object of his boyish passion – unless there is more to the story than the available letters reveal. Mrs

Sitwell had been separated from her clergyman husband and, if that were not scandalous enough for those times, she was often seen in the company of a successful London literary editor, Sidney Colvin, whom Louis viewed as both mentor and rival.

Throughout Louis's childhood in Edinburgh, his self-centred and somewhat distant mother Margaret may have taken second place in his affections to his doting nurse Cummy, with whom he had a very special bond. It was Cummy who told him thrilling stories, who soothed him night after night when he was feverish or sleepless with terrible imaginings. Fanny most probably reminded him of both Cummy and Mrs Sitwell, and, for Louis, that was a powerful combination. Fanny, on the other hand, needed to be admired as the uniquely talented and unusual beauty she was – for not everyone saw those qualities in her. It had been particularly hard for her to maintain her marriage to Sam Osbourne, a man who engaged in numerous affairs with classically attractive young women. Fanny was drawn to Louis for his intellect, his brilliance, his personal style as an aristocratic bohemian – and most particularly because he was fascinated by her.

Wednesday 25 February 2004

I'm beginning to understand why people say the two happiest days of your life are the day you buy the boat and the day you sell it. The *Takapuna* has now undergone an extensive marine survey and it's been recommended that the mast should be removed and inspected, two new generators should be fitted, and the mainsail and staysail replaced. In addition, there's new navigational equipment to be installed, a global satellite system, and a number of security measures. Once crew members are hired, she'll be sailed to a shipyard in West Palm Beach, Florida, where she will spend the next few months being refitted. Ker-ching, ker-ching. It's making me very nervous. Things were much the same in the nineteenth century. Dr Merritt, the Californian physician who owned the *Casco*, was probably very glad to be able to charter her to the Stevensons and recoup some of his running costs. The charter price was a significant amount of cash in those days, but Louis, who had been short of money for most of his adult life, had recently managed to make a decent living from his writing, largely through the popularity of *Treasure Island*. In addition, he had received an inheritance from his late father. These windfalls gave him the confidence to go ahead with such an extravagant programme.

Wednesday 3 March 2004

Some of my friends (those who suspect I barely know one end of a boat from the other) think I'm mad enough to take a crash course in sailing then skipper my own vessel round the world. Well, OK, I am tempted, but I'm not a total lunatic. I'm going to have some professional sailors aboard who really know what they're doing. In the meantime, however, I've decided to hone my sailing skills down in Marina del Rey with a contemporary pirate named Gary.

A short, yapping Irishman with an enormous beer gut, Gary sat me on a plastic chair in front of a whiteboard in an open-air, dockside classroom and set to work with a dry-erase marker. He drew crude diagrams of the points of sail, types of buoys to be found in the harbour and maritime rights of way. There are three months of training ahead of me and so far I'm the only one taking this course. Considering the howling gale blowing round my ears, I assume that either this is the off-season, or everyone else who wants to learn sailing theory in winter is smart enough to do so indoors.

After lunch, we set off in a small, rudimentary sloop to put my new learning into practice. Gary is a child of nature. He doesn't much care for the American Sailing Association manual, but prefers to teach me to read the ripples, feel the wind and sense the weather. That's all fine and well, but just when I've managed to achieve oneness with the elements, and I've got the boat zipping along on a beautiful close reach course for Santa Monica, he'll break into a low, nasal sea shanty without warning: 'What shall we do with a drunken sailor?' It's hard to believe I'm in twenty-first-century California.

That became easier, though, when Gary told me he's also a screenwriter. (I doubt there's anyone who *isn't* here in LA.) He's angling to have me sweet-talk my husband into starring in his next, as yet unfunded, movie. While I attempted to get the hang of a tricky, man-overboard manoeuvre, he pitched me the convoluted story-line, until I ended his spiel – and the lesson – with an accidental jibe (a sudden, unplanned change of tack that can cause a boat to capsize).

Frankly, I'm disappointed that so far I don't seem to have much aptitude for nautical skills – except when it comes to tying knots. I am quite the bowline-queen and can tie a clove hitch faster than Gary can sing 'Yo, ho, ho and a bottle of rum'.

In Fanny's time, sailing was a skill that was largely denied to women. A female mariner who wanted to sail or race a dinghy would have to adhere to the prevalent rules of proper attire: a tight corset and long petticoats under a dress that covered her ankles. If she capsized, she would be sure to drown; it was impossible to swim in that getup. Besides, it was considered bad luck for women to be at sea. They rated in the top three guarantors of ill-fate, right up there with rabbits and bananas. Nevertheless, Louis planned to bring three women on the proposed voyage: as well as Fanny there would be his mother Margaret, a dour fifty-nine-year-old Scottish widow who always dressed in a long, black dress with whalebone corset and starched white Dutch cap, along with her French maid, Valentine Roch, who was in her early twenties. Fanny's son Lloyd, a sensitive, bespectacled twenty-year-old, who planned to take a photographic record of the journey, would complete the party.

The *Casco*'s Captain Otis was gruff, taciturn and practical. Initially, he was unwilling to take on the job of ferrying a sickly man and four other effete passengers 3,000 miles away to the South Pacific Ocean. For a start, he'd heard on the grapevine that Louis, despite being a celebrated author, was a little crazy. Fortunately, Captain Otis's mind was put to rest after meeting him – or perhaps he was just offered the right price. Whatever swayed the Captain, he remained concerned about Louis' physical stamina to survive the journey and made a mental note to stow gear for burial at sea.

Wednesday 10 March 2004

I drove to San Diego to view a wonderful collection of early maps. The best charts were those with striking errors, such as California depicted as an island. Compass roses delight me – the more ornate the better – and some seventeenth-century European charts I saw today have colourful monsters, mermaids and Neptunes painted in the oceans. How marvellous that people had the courage to venture into the unknown! I'm desperate to sail right round the world. What is *wrong* with me? There is practically no one in my life who approves of what I'm about to do, and that fact alone has catapulted me into even more stress than I was experiencing before. I'm a married career woman with two grown children and three teenagers – the youngest, Scarlett, being sixteen. I have moments – even days – of self-doubt. My heart, though, tells me this journey is more important than I can know.

Perhaps this is all Joseph Conrad's fault. His essays on the sea in the library of the Sydney Church of England Girls' Grammar School sowed a seed that has now grown to overshadow all other urges. 'Escape,' remarked some wise person, 'is the only way to stay alive and to continue dreaming.' That's certainly what it seems like from the inside of my city-frazzled, teenager-whipped, career-addled brain. I have been a caretaker, mother and wife for over 20 years now and I'm sooo ready for adventure. Rousing sea-shanties are howling in my ear, my tolerance for the ordinary has entirely waned and I'm sick of seeing the world from airport lounges. The precarious-ness of mid-life supersedes the threat of typhoon, tsunami, or a twelve-bore rifle in my well-padded ribs, and I don't care what anyone says – Fanny would understand – I've made up my mind and I'm off.

Saturday 20 March 2004

My husband was right about the pirates. The seas are indeed being overrun by entirely unromantic scoundrels with balaclavas in lieu of eyepatches. But risk is a highly subjective concept and there are choices to be made. Shall I chance the icy Norwegian Sea? Cross the Atlantic by the northern route? 'Anyway,' I reminded my husband, 'we're about to be empty-nesters. It's the perfect solution to the painful prospect of being abandoned by one's children: leave them first. We're gonna be dead soon, anyway, right? Might as well go out with a boom-break on Bora Bora.'

'I've got two words to say to you,' said Billy: 'Bermuda Triangle.'

Truthfully, the enormity of what I am contemplating has begun to sink in, especially in the wake of Scarlett's desire to accompany me. While I believe it would be a thrilling piece of experiential education for her, it has sobered me to contemplate putting her at risk, too – if indeed there are significant risks involved. Is it really more dangerous than being on land? I wonder if it's not simply the fear of the unknown that makes people so nervous about the ocean. Here in southern California we live with the possibility of earthquakes, violent crime, car accidents, horrible diseases related to the poor air quality, yet we think of sea travel as far more hazardous.

Today, in a purple velvet armchair at Starbucks, I thought through the various risks ahead; at least those that I, with my limited maritime knowledge, can imagine. I listed them all on an eco-friendly, recycled brown paper napkin: 1. Weather, 2. On-board Emergencies, 3. Medical Emergencies, 4. Law/Customs, and 5. Attack!

First, there is the sea itself, its power and relentlessness – and its fickleness. A huge, unexpected storm or hurricane could arise and threaten our lives. So could a rogue wave – a prospect that terrifies even the most unflappable mariner. Lately, I have heard more and more about the way those gigantic anomalies can come from nowhere and crack huge ships in two in the space of a minute. Hmm. Then we could have an out-of-control blaze on board. We would have to abandon ship and take our chances of being rescued. We could make a navigational error and hit, say, a reef, that could put a hole in the hull. Or we could run into an object that was not detected by radar, like a half-submerged container. Our mast could break, the rigging could fail, or the loss of other essential equipment could disable the boat. The thought of having to slide into the sea on a cold, dark night to await the possible arrival of a rescue vessel makes me very afraid. My coffee sat unsipped. Someone on board could have a life-threatening medical emergency, or become psychologically unstable and a danger to the others. I imagined getting the worst possible toothache while miles from relief. I put down my pen, sat back in my chair and tried to breathe.

A famous sitcom actor I know very slightly jogged into the coffee queue, all headphones, Prada baseball cap and New Balance runners, with the weekly script tucked ostentatiously beneath his arm. I ducked my head and forced myself to focus on a different drama.

We could all be thrown in jail for no good reason in some

inhospitable country. The yacht could be impounded and we could face an insidious melange of corruption and conspiracy. We could be attacked by pirates on the high seas. Scoundrels in fast powerboats with tarpaulins over the identity plates could approach us with AK47s at the ready, board the *Takapuna* with grappling hooks, and force us to hand over money, goods, essential navigational equipment, and even hostages. It is a fact that many victims have been killed, most notably the famous New Zealand sailor Sir Peter Blake who was shot dead by pirates in the Amazon a few years ago. Last year there were around 500 recorded attacks worldwide, with 92 crew members murdered or missing and 359 taken hostage. One is more vulnerable in certain hotspots of the world, such as the Malacca Straits and the coasts of Thailand, Africa and Indonesia, but a yacht was recently attacked at sea between Panama and the Galapagos, which is right on the early part of our planned route. One of the worst areas for pirates is the Gulf of Aden, just near the Red Sea where I hope to venture after following Fanny through the South Seas.

A pair of tanned legs appeared in my line of vision. 'Hey, wassup?'

I stared into the famous hazel eyes, surveyed the pouty, sensual smile. 'Nothin' much,' I said shakily. 'I'm, er, just about to spend our life's savings on a boat and sail round the world risking cyclones, tsunamis, fire, toothache, jail, pirates and divorce, in a death-defying bid to salve my mortality-awareness.' He stared at me suspiciously for a second while his smile faded to a silent 'What's she smoking?' whistle.

'Cool,' he nodded nervously, turning on his heels. 'Have fun then!'

Friday 26 March 2004

I have begun to wonder if, between the weather, the hazards of sailing and the human threats, I am prepared to take these risks, either for myself, or for anyone else who might be aboard. I have spent the last five days in a funk, playing out more terrible scenarios in my head, and even considered abandoning the whole venture. My husband is obviously right. I am a 'bampot' – that's Scottish for heedless, suicidal maniac.

Tuesday 30 March 2004

I have calmed down enough to face the fact that, yes, this kind of adventure comes with significant attendant risks, ones that might not only threaten the enjoyment of the journey, but could even prevent me from surviving it – but that's just like any old day in Los Angeles. If I stay at home, I could be hit by a ricocheting bullet from the gun of a twelve-year-old gang member at a Hollywood gas station, run over by a coked-out movie star in a purple pimpmobile; ripped apart by a mountain lion during a power walk in Malibu; get over-filled with botox and paralysed beyond the life of the next party. Life's dangerous, wherever you roam. I shall prepare the boat and myself as best I can, then let fate take its course. I have decided to address the various threats in order of their perceived magnitude.

First, then, the risk of piracy to yachts around the Red Sea is roughly one in a hundred – too high for me. There are shocking narratives all over the internet: 'Six men armed with guns and knives boarded our vessel'; 'Five bandits, brandishing three pistols and two shotguns, bound and gagged us and proceeded to tear apart the boat'; 'We were attacked by three old ships' lifeboats, crammed with what appeared to be very frightened Somalian people.' I also read of a Spanish sailboat held up by masked pirates armed with pistols, machetes and an Uzi; a hijacked German yacht whose crew was kidnapped; and an Australian yacht shot at when it failed to stop after being threatened by pirates posing as police. There are hundreds of similar reports, some ending in fatalities. When I analysed these attacks, I noticed that most victims did little to defend themselves. There is a debate in yachting circles about whether or not one should carry weapons aboard for self-defence. Most, it seems, believe that it's a no-no – and there are all kinds of potential problems when entering ports where firearms are prohibited. Yet the high seas are clearly wild, lawless territories, and I've come to the conclusion that if I don't have the means to defend myself, I'll be a sitting duck.

I have never kept weapons in my home, even during the 90s riots in Los Angeles when most of my anti-gun friends caved in and took themselves off to the Beverly Hills Gun Club. But this is different. It's not just about protecting property; it's about not being vulnerable to ruthless bandits who expect little resistance from a private sailing vessel. I have decided to learn to handle weapons safely and confidently.

'You'd better watch out,' said one of my girlfriends, herself an excellent markswoman. 'Playing with guns can make you cranky.'

'Oh, that's OK,' I gave her a dark grin. 'I'm *already* cranky.'

Fanny knew well how to overcome the obstacles of both man and nature, and how to survive in a tough environment, having been taught the way of the Wild West from childhood. She eventually became a crack shot and, I'm thinking, I could use her now – as co-conspirator, fellow voyageur and pirate-shaker. We could have been blood-sisters: two short, playful, bossy women who became endlessly protective of wonderfully interesting but vulnerable Scottish husbands, and even wrote about them. A couple of zingaras in red ballet slippers, each of us escaped a stultifying aridity of childhood and couldn't wait to travel the world. Each of us became resourceful, controversial and darned handy with a hammer.

I want to have Fanny's hand on my shoulder as I retrace the voyages she took with her husband through the South Pacific:

the Marquesas, the Cook and Society Islands, Samoa, Kiribati, and on. Like me, Fanny loved the sun. I covet her olive skin, her black eyes 'full of sex and mystery as they changed from fire to fun to gloom to tenderness', as Sidney Colvin wrote. I shall resurrect her to share my own journey. Together we'll lament the tide, invite the wild and throw caution to the trade winds for a bonnet-gripping ride.

CHAPTER TWO

PIRATES AND PAHRUMP

Thursday 27 May 2004

In a Florida shipyard, near a palm-lined manatee haunt that draws retiring sun-seekers with wads of cash to condo-encase themselves for the rest of their days, the *Takapuna* is undergoing her final preparations. Without her fresh-shined jauntiness, she is a sad carcass of a boat – filthy, disorganized, with wires hanging out of her bulkheads and navigation station. Beside her on the dock sit two colossal, rough-wrapped boxes that contain our new generators. Hauling myself on board this morning I was greeted by Neal, a freckly young Englishman in a navy T-shirt and shorts, who baffles me with a rapid oscillation between cheerfulness and gloom.

'Mast's OK,' he announced.

I caught my breath. 'Thank God for that.'

As interim Captain, Neal's job is to see the boat through the yard work. A few weeks ago I made the mistake of asking him to give me his opinion of a worst-case scenario. His answer, one that aligned with the pessimistic side of his nature, chilled me to the core. 'Well,' he said thoughtfully, scratching his ginger curls, 'the rigging could be condemned.'

Before any boat undertakes a major journey, it is prudent to have it thoroughly inspected and overhauled. Neal has been ordering new parts (including spares to take on the voyage) and initiating works to satisfy the requirements of the insurers and the recommendations made during the marine survey. Fortunately, the *Takapuna* has surveyed well. But beyond the basics, I am also driven to upgrade her in any way that will increase her navigability, communications and safety. I scanned the teak deck. A cursing, perspiring group of workers was hoisting two large satellite domes to their perch above the stern, while, on the bow, a sunburned youth in overalls and bandana was craning over the forward anchors. Two Jamaican men wearing protective masks were applying varnish to the cap rail, the handsome mahogany strip that runs over the bulwarks. While Bob Marley wailed from a boom box on the foredeck, I perched against the sturdy stainless-steel side rail and took stock. If true love is possible between woman and sailboat, I am engaged to mine, a pearly vision designed by Laurent Giles, with lines so well proportioned that from afar one cannot accurately discern her size or volume.

Her on-deck pilot house is one of her best points, I think, a comfortable, weather-protected room with a seating area, table and navigation station. Beyond it is an open aft deck, where one can feel the wind, bask in the sun, or glimpse a falling star. A few steps down the stern a small launch platform, for swimming or landing fish, is the threshold for the lazarette, a garage that stores dive compressor and scuba equipment. I noticed that the latter was open, with buckets, rags, oxygen tanks and two pairs of shapely female legs protruding from its mouth. I gazed up at the rigging. From below, the top of a 137-foot mast is a dizzying sight. I tried to imagine the three massive sails – mainsail, staysail and genoa – unfurled and filled with lusty trade winds. If only that could be tomorrow! I allowed myself to daydream until Neal wrenched me back to the safety issues at hand.

'You'll want to replace the life vests.' I sighed and listened to his discourse on Personal Flotation Devices. No matter how big your boat, no matter how luxurious or well-equipped, in an angry ocean you're a tiny, tiny dot.

Neal and I went below to discuss the yard progress. We sat in the cool of the main saloon, a mid-ship communal space in two parts. To port, a circular seating area around a curved coffee table faces an electronics cupboard and a computer workstation. The starboard corners are fitted with bookshelves by two handsome, varnished dining tables that double as worktops, while a swing door leads forward to the galley, engine room, a cosy crew mess and five crew cabins.

After my meeting with Neal, I stepped down into the aft companionway that leads to the six passenger cabins. I inspected the end two, which can be turned into one large cabin by removing the dividing bulkhead. I pondered the options before deciding to keep the bulkhead, and mount computer desks and a bookshelf on either side so that Scarlett and I can both work in peace. Thus, each of us shall have a personal work-and-sleep space measuring roughly six feet by ten; pretty darn good for a sailboat. A well-designed vessel is compact and everything must be properly stowed. I fancy that will take some getting used to – I am the mother of all clutter-queens.

In the companionway, 'Lucky Mike', a talented carpenter who crewed on the boat some years earlier, was busy securing wine-glasses in nests of felt-covered wood. He had invented an ingenious fastener made of wire and painted clothes pegs. Sneaking in beside him, I openly admired his system.

'I sailed round the world on my own thirty-seven-footer,' he told me. 'I took two crystal glasses with me and kept them safe the whole way using this trick . . . well, until I hit a whale just off the Maldives. Broke the mast and cracked the hull. That was the end of my trip.'

Whales. Now that's a hazard I hadn't thought of before. I consulted my cruising manual: 'Treat them with caution and respect, as they've been known to attack boats in the past. It's a good idea to put a jerry can of diesel into the water if you spot a group of whales. It gets in their blowholes and sends them packing.' Whatever happened to 'Save the Whale'?

In preparation for her cruise aboard the *Casco*, Fanny, too, was pitched into a fever of activity. Like the *Takapuna*, the schooner was well appointed, with accommodation for six crew forward and six passengers aft. The Stevensons were enthralled with her interior, far more lavishly decorated than the *Takapuna*. The cabins were fitted with silk and velvet, while her luxurious saloon was decked out with gold and white panels, Venetian mirrors, a mahogany table, a Persian rug and plush crimson cushions. From afar, she was a graceful vessel, only slightly shorter than the *Takapuna*, with white sails on her two masts, pearly decks and well-polished brass work. Before long, the people of the South Pacific would name her *Pahi Muni*, or *The Silver Ship*.

And what did our heroine stow on board as protection against pirates and scoundrels? Three revolvers and a large quantity of ammunition.

Sunday 30 May 2004

It is 4.35 am, I'm wide awake and shaking inexplicably. I'm wondering about the oysters I ate at dinner, but, no . . . this is a different kind of stomach-churning. My thoughts turn to last night in the Seafood Bar. The ginger Captain sat opposite me, his mood even more sullen than usual. On my right was Andre, my long-time unarmed-combat instructor who taught me years ago that I didn't need to be nice, that my well-bred compliance kept me unsafe, that when the going got tough, it was best not to wait around for some gallant man to come along and save me. He taught me that if I ever needed to defend myself or my children I could wrap my thumb and third finger round an assailant's eyeball, jab my nails deep inside his clavicle to steal his breath, or grab his testicles and hang on. He taught me the crab-walk, the throat-hold and the full-throttle bollocks kick, and I love him for it. For the past two days, Andre has provided me and the crew with an intense training workshop. He drilled us in danger-recognition, fighting techniques and weapon defensiveness, which has left us all exhausted, raw and pumped with adrenaline.

Andre was raised in South Central, the gangland of Los Angeles. From early childhood he witnessed street violence, gang beatings, murders and the whole gamut of criminal activity. He'd learned self-defence the hard way, and was subsequently inspired to empower others to protect themselves. He, too, was unusually silent.

On my left sat Charlie, a troubled young man who was not long out of the covert Special Air Service, or SAS. Now a specialist in anti-piracy plans for yachts, his eyes held horror, loss, grief and that quality of longing that is unique to the inconsolable.

Andre cleared his throat. Normally softly spoken and peaceful of face, his dark eyes glistened with apprehension.

'Since I'm notorious for bringing up subjects no one wants to talk about,' he said, 'let's discuss weapons. On board, or not?' Nobody spoke.

'Why don't they just let it out?' I thought to myself. 'I know what they're thinking.'

'Probably best that no one have a weapon if they don't know how to use it,' someone ventured, quite pointedly.

'Agreed,' I muttered, in a pissed-off twelve-year-old, 'please lemme use my catapult' kind of way.

Monday 31 May 2004

I had arranged to meet with Charlie at 10 am so he could summarize his assessment of our risk level and propose some safety procedures. When I drew in to his hotel to pick him up, he was waiting for me on the street in jeans and T-shirt.

'I'm a bit hung over.' He rubbed his unshaven chin.

'Yeah?'

'Went out for a drink with the crew last night . . .'

'With the crew?' I was twelve again, left out of the party.

'Yeah. Good way to get to know people, getting drunk with them. My head's a right mess.' I had thought the idea was that *you* stay sober and take note of what *they* do and say when they're disinhibited. I kept that to myself.

'And?'

'They're a good bunch of guys. You've got a great crew there.'

'So?' I said, changing the subject. 'What's your assessment?'

He outlined the safety plans over coffee. The Somerset Maugham ambience – white wicker rocking chairs and formal gardens – made talk of stealth attacks upon the high seas seem remote and ridiculous. 'Crew's not happy about the prospect of having weapons on board,' said Charlie at last. Here was the nitty-gritty of last night's bar-room badinage. 'Unless they're in the hands of trained professionals.'

'Ah,' I said. 'You mean they'd rather not be shot in the backside in the middle of the night by a paranoid owner who doesn't know the difference between pirate attack and nocturnal bowel movement?'

'Something like that,' he smiled sheepishly and looked away.

'Listen,' I said, 'I'll take your advice in all general security measures. We'll have our safe room and hire armed guards for the trouble spots as you suggested . . . but I have to think a bit more about the prospect of not being able to defend myself and my daughter in a worst-case scenario when everything's going horribly pear-shaped and there's no one else around to protect us. I haven't made up my mind yet, but I want you to know it's still on the table.' I was getting my concealed weapons permit the following weekend.

'Fair enough.' He quickly switched to a discussion of the type of weapon I should purchase. 'I like the SIG P228,' he said. 'No safety catch, but very reliable weapon. I know lots of blokes who got shot while they were fumbling with the safety catch, so these are tops. I used them all the time in the Service.' He was trying another approach, and it was working. Not having a safety catch seemed like a terrible idea.

Thursday 3 June 2004

Los Angeles.

I'm leaving this month. Oh, God. I'm leaving this month. My last day in my psychotherapy office was bitter-sweet. On one hand I felt enormous relief – for I badly need time off – but there was also unexpected sadness. One patient I've been seeing for ten years, who was undergoing chemotherapy for an advanced, small-cell carcinoma, put into words the fear in my own mind.

'I'm thinking you may be the first person I'm saying goodbye to . . . for ever,' he said. Tears rolled down both our cheeks.

'You're in good hands with Dr K,' I said. My colleague, herself a cancer survivor, would see him to the final door.

At the end of that session, my last for a long time, I stood up and looked around the room. I began to put a few last personal items in my bag to take home: a candle, a small statue of Hippocrates I'd bought in Athens and a willow-pattern china teapot. I became aware that the room itself held the stories, the pain and the laughter of the people who'd sat in here with me. The fabric of the couch seemed rank with secrets. I got in my car and began to drive. When I stopped suddenly for a pedestrian, the teapot smashed beside me. 'That's it,' I smiled. 'Time for a break.'

Friday 4 June 2004

Miami.

The phone rang early in my hotel room, waking me from a restless sleep. It was my friend and colleague Dr Dennis, whom I had invited to accompany me for some handgun training sessions. 'I'm like an excited kid,' he announced, obviously a lot wider awake than I. 'All my childhood I played cowboys and Indians, double holster, quick-draw games. I just can't wait to unleash that stuff for real.' It was hard to imagine. An utterly mild, softly spoken leader in my professional field, he'd previously spent nine years in a Catholic seminary training for the priesthood.

We drove out of the city to an indoor weapon range. On the way I remembered to take out a small tube of cream and squeeze half an inch on to the soles of my feet.

'It's testosterone,' I explained to Dennis. 'Great stuff. Makes me horny and mad.'

He eyed me uncomfortably. 'Guess I'll be giving you a wide berth.'

The American Indoor Gun Range was located inside a trade mall in one of the ugliest suburbs of Fort Lauderdale. Across the road, at the cheap-assembly furniture outlet, scores of Hispanic men worked feverishly with their nail staplers, while the proprietors of the Cuban hamburger cafe looked distrustfully though the window. After the hundred-degree heat we were grateful for the air-conditioning within the Gun Shop shed. A toilet just inside the door was marked 'Men', but there was no 'Women' to be seen. The walls were lined with shooting accoutrements: earmuffs, holsters and waist packs that rip open for a quick front-draw. A two-dimensional, steel cartoon cut-out of a pistol-raising cowboy stood in a corner for sale. 'What a horrible piece of art,' I thought to myself, until I realized it was a standing target, presumably one you take home to your ranch and plant among the cacti for convenient, twenty-four-hour slug practice. 'Guns for Rent' said the notice above a wall of Lugers, Berettas and the Czech pistols known as CZs (short for the manufacturing company Ceska Zbrojovka). We produced our driving licences and were provided with weapons and 400 rounds each of 9-millimetre ammunition.

'Hi, I'm Randy.' A podgy, Cuban-looking man with over-attentive eyes, wearing a black T-shirt and jeans, was our combat instructor. He turned out to be an ex-pat, ex-army British man who's been living in Florida for three years. He coaches US citizens through their Concealed Weapons Permits and instructs travellers headed to Eastern Europe and other hostile environments how to avoid being kidnapped. He led us up a bare stairway to a small, windowless classroom, illuminated by strip lighting. I soon realized I'd made a huge mistake in letting him know I was interested in buying the firepower on Charlie's list: three SIG P228s and couple of M16s.

'Yeah, this Irish chick turned up here a few months ago, and bought a bunch of M16s,' he said suspiciously. 'Turned out she was shipping them back to the IRA.'

I looked at Dennis and rolled my eyes. Randy faced me off, with one hand on his holster. 'So, what's your story?'

'Um . . . well, I'm going on a trip on a boat,' I said weakly. 'I'll be travelling in waters where the incidents of piracy are growing and I'd like to be able to defend myself.'

'Let's see you check the chamber of this,' he said nastily, sliding his Luger towards me. I picked it up and tried to open the slide. It was too stiff; I couldn't get it to budge. He took back the weapon and gave me a despising half-smile. 'Yeah,' he snarled, 'some people don't even have the basics.'

I sat there, smarting with rage and humiliation. 'You think I can't defend myself, don't you?' I thought. 'Well, I could take you out in a second with my bare hands, you fat prick.' Perhaps I had overdone the testosterone.

Randy did not soften his attitude towards me until we went downstairs to the gun range and he watched my first two shots land right through the paper target's brain. Unfortunately, my expression probably revealed that it was a surprise to me, too. He grudgingly drilled us in fast-draw target shooting at a variety of distances, 'double-tapping' style, from standing, seated and kneeling positions. We practised Russian sequences involving single-handed shooting and firing at paper hostage-takers from behind cover. Dr Dennis turned out to be an excellent shot and was far more comfortable with Lugers than I. I preferred the smaller CZ, and discovered that, as Charlie had said, not having a safety-catch was an advantage. I just kept wondering when I was going to shoot myself in the leg, especially when I struggled with a particularly difficult draw.

After only a hundred rounds my arms and hands were aching, my thumb was bleeding from being held too close to the hammer, and my face and eyes were set in permanent wincing mode from the power of the recoil and the flash of the explosion. Empty cartridges sprayed all round us. To our left was a group of ten neophyte security officers taking their target exams. Next to them, a Florida family was having a nice day out with their gun collection. Their ten-year-old youngster, wielding a huge Smith and Wesson, was busy making lead patterns on a large paper portrait of Osama bin Laden. Even with our earmuffs, the noise from multiple rounds was unbearable.

Gradually, over the next twenty-four hours, the loading, firing and holstering became fast routines, and our precision shooting improved. 'Congratulations,' said Randy at midday on Saturday. 'You've now had more shooting experience, and can hit more targets, than most Florida police officers.'

After lunch we moved back upstairs to talk about unarmed combat, and tried a few moves. After nearly dislocating Randy's arm, Dennis gently informed him he had a black belt in Do Jong, which gained Randy's immediate respect. I, on the other hand, was told my punches were weak and my knees wobbly. We moved on to improvised weapons. Randy had an entire armament of household-articles-turned-lethal-weapons.

'I got this from Sears,' he said, wielding a spatula. 'Their tool department's a whole smorgasbord of "doing damage".' He proceeded to give us a lecture entitled 'How to explain away concealed weapons'. 'These knuckledusters are illegal in Florida,' he said slyly, 'but it's OK to have them, 'cos they're just paperweights.' He produced an instrument of torture that was a kitchen fork with prongs bent in several different directions. 'Anyone catches you with these, they're just forks,' he smiled. He showed us how to 'drop' someone with a Maglite torch, a rolled-up magazine, a crunched Coke can and a plastic coffee-cup lid, then introduced the wire saw, the petroleum-soaked cottonwool ball and the pocket cosh. After half an hour of this, I wanted to vomit. It was one thing to fire at paper heads with pointy bits of lead, fast-ejected from a smoking cylinder; but here, laid out before us, were the true instruments of thuggery. 'See them commercials on TV for pens that are so sharp they can pierce a soda can?' he said. 'Sweet.'

As the afternoon wore on, Randy showed us some weapon-blocking techniques, where to stand in a darkened room to avoid detection and how to place nightlights outside your bedroom door to create a silhouette of a would-be attacker. He provided tips about where to sit defensively in a restaurant, how to know if you're being followed, how to behave if you're kidnapped and how to stop an entire SWAT team from catching you in a building. For dealing with unwanted guests, he demonstrated strong-arming techniques, utilizing an impressive array of painful holds. 'Always be polite,' he told us in a sing-song kind of voice. 'Just because you're hurting someone, doesn't mean you can't be nice.'

Eventually, we returned to a discussion of potential pirate attacks. 'If something goes down out there,' he said, eyes loaded with meaning, 'and you drop one or two of them – don't let the rest of 'em get away. They'll come after you, or their friends will. You gotta kill everybody, then sink their boat. A few twelve-gauge slugs in a wooden hull should do the trick.' The room suddenly became entirely airless.

Afterwards, Dennis and I drove back engaged in conversation about everything except the unthinkable.

'To friendship.' Dennis raised his glass. Back at the civilization of our hotel on Saturday evening, the two of us, freshly showered and changed, were sipping Mojitos just a few yards from a dance floor where a women in a red evening dress was executing a polished tango with a man in a white forties-style suit and panama hat. Dennis raised his voice a little to be heard above the band and leaned forward conspiratorially. 'I've got a hypo-thetical for you,' he said. 'You're on the boat and you've been attacked. You've returned fire and three of the pirates are dead, but there's a couple more wounded guys lying incapacitated on the deck. Could you do what Randy advised?' He glanced round to make sure the waiter was not nearby. 'Could you execute them point blank then sink their boat to make sure no one could come after you?' He had put into words a question that had been weighing heavily on my mind since the afternoon.

'I guess it would depend where we are,' I said, after a long pause. 'It appears some of the piracy, especially around the coast of Africa, is government-sponsored, so I wouldn't like to take my chances with either local militia or their prisons.' Silence. 'Here's one for you,' I said. 'A Somali boat tries to ram you. There's two AK47s mounted on the foredeck and half a dozen men are firing at you, but inside their boat you see fifty or sixty terrified refugees being smuggled to a "better" place. If you return fire, you'll likely hit innocents.'

'I guess I'd have to weigh up my own safety and that of the people on board *Takapuna* against the possibility of doing . . . collateral damage.'

We were both feeling extremely uncomfortable and neither

was willing to commit a definitive answer to either scenario.

'Can you believe we're actually having this conversation?' I said at last. 'I mean, you and I both spend our professional and private lives taking care of people. Is it not utterly extraordinary that here we are, entertaining the thought of not only killing someone in self-defence, but *executing* them?'

Sunday 6 June 2004

Late this afternoon, at the end of our third day of training, Dennis accompanied me on a quick trip to West Palm Beach to visit the *Takapuna* in the boatyard. Considering how many famous, pricey boats were sitting in the yard, I was shocked to find that the entry gate was open and no one seemed to be on site. We wandered round in search of the *Takapuna* and finally saw her dark bottom hauled out of the water, not ten yards from Jimmy Buffet's pristine pale jade fishing boat and Ivana Trump's pearly motor-monster. We climbed the yellow rolling ladder up the side of the hull and picked our way amid an unholy mess of tools, canvas, pieces of wood, tarpaulins and rubbish lying on deck. The companionway entrance was locked, so we slid under the forward tarpaulin and unscrewed the crew hatch leading down a narrow ladder to the galley floor. Below, there was an even worse shambles. At least the generators had been craned on board. They sat in the ravaged saloon, waiting to be lowered into the engine room. There was no hint of the beauty and spaciousness of the comfortable yacht I'd purchased. Untamed wires snaked out from every part of the unlined saloon walls, and everywhere there were piles of clothing, charts, books, bottles, cushions and plastic bags. We tiptoed around for a while, aghast at the mess, until Dennis faced me with the question that had been on my own lips.

'You're leaving in three weeks?' he asked, incredulously.

*

Fanny's chartered boat the *Casco* was not ready to sail within the promised ten days after her telegram. However, one month later, on 28 June 1888, the Stevenson party – Louis, Fanny, Margaret, Valentine and Lloyd – waved goodbye to Belle and a small gathering of friends in San Francisco Bay. Captain Otis pointed his vessel on a course for the Marquesas Islands, roughly 3,000 miles south-southwest. It was hurricane season in the North Pacific and they were likely to face doldrums as they neared the equator, so it is hard to understand why Otis hired such a small and inexperienced crew: one Russian, one Finnish and two Swedish deckhands, plus a renegade Chinese cook who, for some unknown reason, pretended to be Japanese. Only the

Captain knew how to navigate, so if anything should happen to him in the stormy, unpredictable and largely uncharted waters of the Pacific Ocean, the rest would most likely perish. Either Louis didn't understand the risks, or else he didn't care. 'This is an old dream of mine which actually seems to be coming true,' he wrote, 'and I am sun-struck.'

Tuesday 8 June 2004

Los Angeles.

I went to visit Dr Spira, whose consulting rooms are a traveller's den of Chinese furniture, Nepalese pennants and photos of Balinese rice fields. His mother worked in the adjacent shop, which carried mosquito nets, fast-dry underwear, and maps of Paris printed on silk headscarves. I discussed our need for medical supplies, as well as a defibrillator and vital signs monitoring capability, including an ECG machine.

'Tell your husband he owes me a signed photograph,' he said in parting, 'and he needs a rabies booster. Someone in Scotland just died from a bat bite.'

Later in the morning I had dental surgery, which meant a whole precious hour of anaesthetized slumber. The oral surgeon, a lanky, bleached blond dude with a surfboard decorating his waiting room wall, sent me off with a mouthful of dissolvable stitches, a bottle of antibiotics and an even larger bottle of Vicodin. The experience increased my concern about facing serious dental or health issues at sea, so I went online and researched emergency medical systems. I found the Tempus 2000, a wizard of an on-board electronic device that connects to the Medlink remote medical service. It is capable of relaying vital patient information, such as ECG data, to a hospital in Arizona. It can even send visual images of, say, a wound, via a wrist-mounted video camera. Then the Arizona doctors can prescribe medication and talk people through any necessary treatment. I emailed our business advisor to find out if we could afford this device, as well as all the security equipment on Charlie's list, and received the following reply:

Dear Dr Connolly

I have received and noted the contents of your email relating to the purchase of weapons to repel invaders from your boat. I should inform you that I am in the process of obtaining statements from various friends and acquaintances of yours, and the evidence gathered so far is more than sufficient to have you committed to an asylum before the boat leaves port. However, in the unfortunate event that one of your crew, in a drunken rage, massacres your entire family in their beds, I suggest that you purchase the best medical equipment that money can buy.

Steve Brown

My friend Mimi Kennedy called in the evening to ask me to attend a peace rally.

'No, I'm sorry,' I replied. 'I'll be in Death Valley learning how to handle an AK47.'

Wednesday 9 June 2004

There must have been a long-acting stimulant in the dental surgical cocktail because, unable to sleep at 2 am, I sat up, sighed, turned on my computer and set about ordering the protection equipment Charlie suggested we put on board: bullet-proof flotation vests, ballistic shields, military-grade night vision goggles, pepper spray canisters, personal alarms and smoke hoods. Do we really need all this? Some items could not be legally imported from the foreign websites Charlie had identified, so I had to find the US-made equivalent. Surely there must be an FBI file on me by now?

At 10 am Neal phoned to say the welder who came to do a small piece of work on the mast expressed his concern about a section near the gooseneck that he said was bent. This could be very, very serious. I cannot believe that, among all those people who've inspected the mast lately, no one noticed it before. I tried to study for a sailing exam I'm taking tomorrow, but instead I kept worrying about the mast. I had particular difficulty remembering all the shapes and markings on beacons and buoys. I'd better get it down, though. A mistake entering a rocky harbour in heavy swell could bring down the mast as quick as you can say the mariners' mnemonic, 'Red, Right, Returning'!

Thursday 10 June 2004

After all that, I had to postpone my sailing exam because I woke with a fever and half my face as swollen as a chipmunk – a complication from my dental procedure. Then Neal called again with terrible news. 'Turns out the mast's definitely got a problem. I just don't know exactly how serious. It's going to mean either a major repair, or maybe a whole new rig.' It took me quite a few beats to respond. I felt like I'd been punched in the chest. Was this the end of my trip? I had to face the possibility that it might be. I tried to think through what this might cost in terms of scheduling, finances and family, but without further information it was impossible to know. I alternately panicked and brooded most of the morning, then called Andre to tell him the news.

'I hear the disappointment in your voice,' he commiserated. 'It's as though they postponed Christmas.'

As afternoon arrived, however, and despite being chock full of medication, I decided I'd better get on the road and drive out to my next combat course. The training site was at least five hours away in the middle of Death Valley, Nevada, but I thought I'd probably make it by nightfall. What the hell was I thinking? In retrospect, this was an insane, Vicodin-induced decision.

Driving inland from Los Angeles on Interstate Highway 10 East, one quickly leaves behind any semblance of lushness. The vast reserves of water that soak the unnaturally green lawns and gardens of those Los Angelinos who can afford it are largely withheld from the vistas of the outer suburbs, so one is very abruptly aware that the entire inland sweep is really all desert. As I drove, I half listened to the Mojave Desert highway report and half fretted about the mast. I hadn't heard the latest from Neal and my cell phone did not work out here. A sickly grey haze filtered my view of the pale plains and ridges that stretched out all the way to Las Vegas and beyond. Massive electric towers rose in formation through every valley, every piece of flatland. Now and again a town would appear, each one a dry, gaudy, tired place – occasionally having its own bizarre claim to fame. 'The largest thermometer in the USA' was Barstow's. My fellow road-warriors were Vegas weekenders, school camping trip bus riders, and big-rig drivers galore. 'Truckers: Free Drinks!' was a billboard's written invitation to patronize the 'Mad Greek' restaurant in Baker. Instead, I pressed on to Peggy Sue's truck-stop diner, slid out of the car and tried to make my legs walk inside. 'If the door's open, so are we . . . so get in here!' said the painted lettering above a wooden door. I managed to obey.

Inside the hangar-like building a sign instructed 'Please seat your beautiful selves!' while 'King of the Road' blared out from a distorted loudspeaker. Another sign invited people to book early for weddings, bar mitzvahs and retirement parties.

'People get married here?' I quizzed the manager. Mistaking me for a potential bride-customer, she ushered me out the back door onto a tattered veranda decorated with plastic wisteria that overlooked a couple of filthy puddles. Two or three forlorn-looking ducks were trying to swim amid the rubbish.

'We had a *surprise* wedding in here last week,' she said proudly. I looked at her sharply and realized she was serious.

'What is that?' I was almost afraid to ask.

'Everyone in the wedding party knew about it in advance – except the bridegroom.'

'How'd he take it?' I inquired.

'Well,' she said, 'I guess he spent most of the party sitting down.'

To the left of the entrance hallway was a Five and Dime store, so jam-packed with 50s kitsch and Hollywood memorabilia, one could barely walk to the cash register. A soda fountain offered ice-cream scoops and soda floats, served to customers seated on retro chrome barstools. 'If you think you have reservations,' said a sign, 'you're in the wrong restaurant.' A pile of flyers sat on the counter. 'HARLEY COW' was the heading on one, and underneath 'FREE BBQ, Live Bands and Door Prizes'. In smaller letters halfway down was the nitty-gritty: 'Come Meet Bikers for Christ. Guest Speaker: Pastor Big Mike.'

To my right in the entrance hall stood Elvis Presley's gold-caped torso, mechanically animated, in a glass case. He spoke to me as I approached, reverberating loud and clear. 'Hey you . . . yeah, you!' he commanded in his idiosyncratic drawl. 'Get over here, and let the King give you a hunka hunka burnin' wisdom.' The wooden slot took two quarters.

'I wonder if he knows about the mast,' I thought savagely, slamming in my change.

'Your destiny is not a certainty,' he crooned, 'but a chosen path.'

'Oh, yeah?' I said sourly. 'Is that it?' As if in response, a small, yellow cardboard rectangle slid out towards me. It was headed *Your Fortune*.

My cheek was throbbing again. I tucked the card into my pocket, slunk into the diner, and ordered a Doris Day Omelette. A morose man on a counter stool beside me was tucking into a TV dinner. Every item on his plate was the same colour, a brownish-grey. The signs on the walls around me were designed to amuse. *If your standards are too high for this establishment, lower your standards*, said one. *Hey, teenagers!* said another, *sick of your parents? Why not move out, get a job and pay your own bills while you still know everything?* I must say, that one did strike a chord. When my omelette arrived, I took out Elvis's proclamation and began to read: *You have a very sympathetic nature. You devote a great many hours to the welfare of others.* 'Right so far, I suppose,' I mused. *You have a very fine mind and, if you cultivate it properly, you will be very successful.* 'Bit late for that, isn't it?' *You are very fond of sports.* 'Wrong there!' I thought triumphantly. *And you love to dance . . .* 'Well, OK . . .' *You have a graceful walk and a determined step.* 'You obviously didn't see me getting out of the car.' *People respect you for your determination.* 'Nah, right now they think I'm crazy.' *You will endure some hardship in the near future.* 'Oh, here we go, the mast's totally wrecked and we're not going to get out of port until next year!' *But eventually, everything will turn out for the best and unending happiness will be yours.*

Exiting the diner, I happened to look back above the inner door and noticed a sign I'd not seen when I entered: a mural of a flounce-skirted, smiling waitress, expounding her wisdom for all travellers: *The joy is in the journey*, she was saying, *not the destination*. Such a sentiment seemed particularly true when I pulled up to the Saddle West Hotel, Casino and RV Park in Central Pahrump, after a humbling two-hours' drive through the stark, empty and vapourless magnificence of Death Valley: its dry lakes, saltbush plains and silhouettes of granite mountains, its evening primrose, Joshua trees and sunset of peach and lavender over shadow-scribbled sand dunes. The neon-lit resort turned out to be a pan-handler's paradise, a Vegas-loser's hide-out and, alas, an internet-seeker's defeat. Frosty, the mullet-sporting receptionist, greeted me at the check-in desk in a back corner of the casino. He provided me with an exterior room in a dark corner of the property where my car would be lucky to survive the night. I put Randy's lessons into practice by booby-trapping my motel room door, so an intruder would get nothing but the screech of my personal alarm, followed by the click of my Glock pistol, and fell asleep to the whirring of ten-cent slot machines and the moaning of low-rider choppers.

I slept poorly and woke at 4.30 am. The dingy bathroom mirror revealed that my face was still swollen, my internal stitches undissolved and my shoulders fully hunched. I pulled on a pair of cargo pants, and the only T-shirt I'd brought, which unfortunately said 'Dog' on the front. It did label me quite accurately at that particular moment. At 6 am, after donning cap and boots, I stumbled out into the already-sweltering desert air and was relieved to find my car intact. I loaded two gallons of water in the passenger seat, and tried to swallow a banana and protein bar. I drank a pint of Gatorade to replace lost electrolytes in my body, but regretted it when I needed to pee fifteen minutes further into Death Valley. The desert was utterly empty and had already reached ninety-two degrees, even at this early hour. I stopped the car and stumbled into a sparse bed of creosote bush scrub but was discouraged from lowering my pants when I heard an ominous rustle. I froze, whirled round and just caught a glimpse of a greyish, diamond-patterned snake a short distance away. As I leapt back into the driver's seat, my eye caught a picture of that same reptile on the cover of my Death Valley guide map. *The Mojave rattlesnake*, it said, *blends in easily with this habitat. Aggressive and highly venomous . . . it is most active at night and early in the morning.* I took off, smiling to myself as I remembered that Fanny had narrowly escaped being bitten on the leg by a similar reptile near the Reese River in Austin. Hearing its rattle behind her, she whipped out her pistol, whirled round and shattered its head as it prepared to strike. Oh yes, she could take care of herself.

Further into the searing landscape I saw a sign to the training site, and turned off on to a well-maintained private track. *You are now leaving publicly designated roads,* warned my talking GPS system. After another five miles or so, I spotted the entrance of a large compound protected by a high, barbed-wire perimeter fence. Its gates were manned by armed, uniformed guards in black-and-grey military-style outfits. They checked my ID, then waved me on to an unshaded parking lot that was already occupied by scores of other students' cars.

'Sign in over there.' Uniformed officials were organizing people into groups. I was directed to a supply store inside a sweltering hangar to buy ammunition.

'Five hundred rounds?' asked the clerk, an automaton in blue mirror shades.

'Will that do me for the whole four-day course?' I asked.

He looked at me pityingly. 'Just about get you through the morning.'

The next stop was a dressing area, where an official saw that my weapon and cartridges were holstered according to Institute rules: on a sturdy, well-anchored belt, no shoulder or thigh carrying allowed. The dry heat was already sapping my energy. Sipping from my water bottle, I stepped inside a huge white tent where an orientation lecture was about to begin and glanced around at my fellow students. Mainly men, they were big, beefy and loud, most with super-short hair, wearing paramilitary camouflage pants and T-shirts with overt symbols of bravado, such as open cans of 'Whoop-Ass'. Many wore heavy belts strung around with leather holsters, knives, spray canisters and survival gear. I searched around for any sign of racial diversity but found none, except a couple of Hawaiians on my far left. That was a worry. It began to dawn on me that I might have unwittingly found myself in the middle of some kind of crazy militia cult, the seat of white supremacy USA, a vortex of voodoo and violence.

'Hi, Pamela!' I jumped, until I remembered that the man at the first desk had taped my name in huge letters across front and back of my baseball cap. The man handed me a welcome pack, inside which was a series of lecture notes and a liability release. Obviously these people wanted to protect their investment. They had even background-checked every student prior to arrival. Whoever *they* were, they seemed to have big plans for the place. On a large screen to my left, a recorded news segment on the Institute was constantly being looped. It featured the chiropractor-turned-firearms guru, and founder of the place, who still calls himself 'Doctor'. Along the back wall, wooden easels supported a series of artists' impressions of how the 'future community' will look: an upscale city with Spanish haciendas, condos, schools and shopping malls.

'This will be the safest community in the USA,' said the spokesman during his monotonic welcoming lecture. I sat there with mounting apprehension. He reminded me of Arnold Schwarzenegger's nemesis in *Terminator II*, the terrifying humanoid with the eyeshades. 'Our purpose is to affirm and support second amendment rights,' he told his attentive audience. 'And we're planning a celebrity training centre!' Yeah, yeah, yeah. The last speaker was the founder, a short, intense man, who gave a pep-talk to the 300-strong class. 'Today, you're all gonna be part of a movie we're making,' he said excitedly, 'to promote the Institute. It's gonna be incredible.' Most of the class seemed impressed.

'Great,' I thought. 'Just what I need, being caught on film participating in activities at Camp Kill Bill.'

We drove out to our respective target ranges. There were thirty-two people in my group, divided into two relays. A former marine was our range master.

'How many of you are marines?' he asked. There were grunts and whoops all round. Several were on leave from Iraq. 'How many law enforcement?' More than half the class. I noted that, of the five women in my group, three were police officers. Two of the male officers had brought their sons with them, pre-teen children swaggering round with sizeable handguns and cartridges of live ammunition in their holsters. A massively overweight police officer began challenging one of the line coaches on a point of protocol. I surveyed the target area and realized that we would all be shooting side by side together, without protective barriers. I began to feel queasy, and it wasn't just the sun.

For a civilian like me, at least, this was boot camp. The temperature was now above 100 degrees and there was little shade. There was no food, but water and powdered Gatorade could be pumped from plastic containers. Three portable toilet stalls were constantly in use. People did not socialize and I was far too intimidated to talk to my neighbours, although I was fascinated that most of them carried guns for a living. Still no sign of racial diversity. I worried that the two lesbians I'd spotted in the early lecture were taking a big risk in what seemed to be a pretty intolerant environment.

When the detailed gun-handling and target shooting instruction began, however, I was immediately impressed by the precision and clarity of the teaching style. My earlier problems with wrenching open the slide disappeared, as my range master gave me an alternative method to check the chamber. Each drill, whether loading, unloading or firing, was broken down into precise sections, accompanied by explanation and rationale, and taught to perfection. But, the biggest problem remained: I was truly terrified to be around these people and their weapons. By noon, and 104 degrees in the shade, I was beginning to experience heat exhaustion, signified by a piercing headache and mounting dizziness. When we returned to the tent at lunchtime, I had to wonder, was I anywhere near ready for primetime paramilitaryism? I fled to my car, hiked up the air-conditioning and allowed myself to sob uncontrollably. After a lifetime of opposing the carrying of weapons, I had now crossed a line. I had voluntarily chosen to bear firearms. I was now one of *them*.

Back at the Saddle West that evening, Frosty the receptionist handed me a message from Neal. *Still no definitive answer. They can probably fix the mast, but the work would be quite extensive. If we go ahead it will take at least two months.* I allowed this to sink in for a moment, but without consulting my cruising guides I had no idea what this loss of momentum would do to our narrow time frame to get through the Pacific before the hurricane season began. I called home and discovered that, for several days, my husband had been trying in vain to reach me from Europe. 'Where's your mother?' he'd asked our daughter. 'She's in a motel in Death Valley with a guy called Frosty,' she'd replied. All things considered, I thought it best to return home toute de suite.

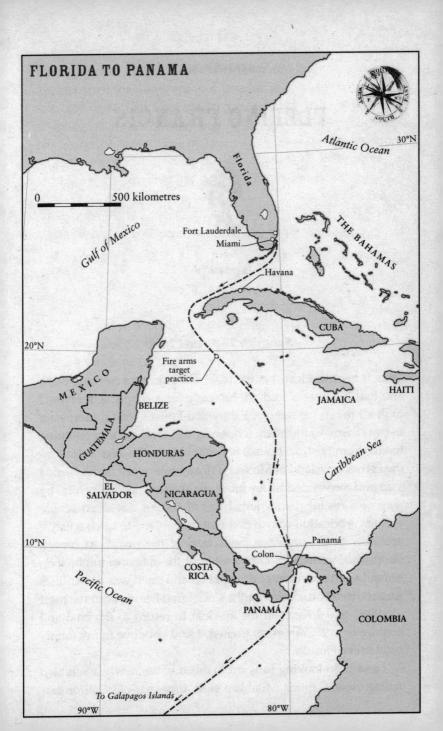

FLORIDA TO PANAMA

Atlantic Ocean

30°N

Florida

THE BAHAMAS

0 — 500 kilometres

Fort Lauderdale
Miami

Gulf of Mexico

Havana

CUBA

20°N

Fire arms
target
practice

JAMAICA

HAITI

M E X I C O

BELIZE

GUATEMALA

HONDURAS

EL
SALVADOR

NICARAGUA

Caribbean Sea

10°N

Colon

Panamá

COSTA
RICA

Pacific Ocean

PANAMÁ

COLOMBIA

To Galapagos Islands

90°W

80°W

CHAPTER THREE

FLEEING FRANCIS

24°34.4' N
081°09.2' W

Saturday 28 August 2004

Once it became clear that the mast did indeed need some work and that the boat would not be ready for a couple of months, I took off to retrace some of Fanny and Louis's land routes, from the northern Californian forests to the Nevada silver mining towns; from the townhouses of Edinburgh to the leper colony on the Hawaiian island of Molokai. Meanwhile, work in the Florida shipyard proceeded at an infuriatingly slow pace. In July, by way of a useful distraction, I completed an advanced scuba-diving certification course that will prepare me to catch a fish's-eye view of the undersea landscapes of the world. At several points during those months I thought the *Takapuna* might soon be ready, but the summer dragged on and on. It was not until 26 August, two and a half months since I first heard about the mast problem, that I received the all-clear to return to the boat and prepare to sail. Cautiously excited, I said goodbye to my family and left for Florida.

I had been looking forward to meeting the newly assembled sailing crew. Captain Mike is a slim, fifty-year-old Californian, with a perfectionist bent and cynical outlook, who has been at sea since he was seventeen. His blond, moustachioed good looks make him the perfect sea captain of romantic fiction. Dick, his First Mate, is a self-assured young Australian from a pioneering family of fishermen. His curly hair, freckles and cheeky grin are counterbalanced by his well-targeted, sardonic humour, while on deck he is a miracle of balance, precision and unshakable confidence. Kayt, a sweet-natured twenty-six-year-old with an open face, limpid eyes and a comforting, matey way about her, will cook meals and take care of the boat's interior. The dual role of deckhand and ship's medic will be filled by Jock, a rugged, forty-year-old Welshman who grew up in Zimbabwe. Daragh, the son of a family friend, is a delightfully naive seventeen-year-old, who will help out both on deck and below. In contrast to the others, our Swedish engineer, Rolle, is a crazy, unpredictable, shaggy-headed Viking. He is also charming and child-like, with a disarming honesty that took me by surprise when I cheekily suggested his lungs must be quite black from his chain-smoking habit.

'Yes,' he nodded wryly. 'Dey match my black heart.'

Many people who own boats never actually travel on them. They fly in and waltz aboard for a week or so in fancy ports like Capri and St Maarten. But I never planned to be a passenger; lounging in a deckchair drinking champagne is not my idea of having an adventure. I have now undertaken several types of marine training so I can actually participate in sailing the *Takapuna*. While respecting the fact that the professional sailors I have hired must be allowed to do their jobs unhindered, I will stand watches with everyone else, do chores, drive the tender, and generally help out as much as possible – with the exception of cooking, since I firmly believe that life's too short to stuff an aubergine. All right, I confess – I'm a terrible cook and there would be a mutiny if I tried.

The day after I arrived in Florida the crew and I began a three-

day, on-board medical emergency training course. Sitting in a
Fort Lauderdale conference room we learned how to hook
someone up to an intravenous drip, fill a syringe and administer
injections. My classmates and I practised on each other as far as
possible; but for invasive procedures we had to get creative. If
there are any frozen chicken legs out there that need stitches, I'm
your man. I pray I'll never be called upon to use the defibrillator,
oxygen, or even just the blood-pressure gauge. The very thought
of having a medical emergency at sea makes me very anxious.

Our nurse instructor habitually related everything to her
poor husband Barney, who seems to have had most of the
diseases and conditions we are studying. I was on the verge of
hysteria several times, but when Barney's haemorrhoids became
the focus of one lecture, I had to dart out of the classroom like a
giggling eight-year-old, missing the segment on splinting a
broken arm. Fortunately, I've been able to acquire the Tempus
2000. We have already done a dummy run with the device,
during which I had to hook up Dick to ECG electrodes, CO_2
finger clip, blood-pressure gauge and thermometer. When it was
my turn to practise relaying information from a live doctor
without scaring the bejesus out of my 'patient', I thought about
it for a moment and took a deep breath.

'You've got an alien inside you,' I explained, in my best
bedside manner. 'In forty minutes he'll burst through your chest,
splattering little bits of you throughout the ship.'

I'm afraid all this talk of medical emergencies is scaring me
almost more than the thought of pirates. It was particularly sobering to imagine having to deal with the casualties of a gun battle.

At one point I put up my hand. 'It's not in the manual,' I said,
trying to keep my voice level, 'but what would we do about
bullet wounds?'

'Ah, yes, very nasty,' replied our instructor. 'My Barney . . .'
This time several of us had to leave the room without the full
details of how Barney survived shooting himself in the arse
during a particularly violent haemorrhoid attack.

At the end of our last medical class, I went on a panic-buying spree and threw into two supermarket trolleys everything I thought I might need over the next couple of years. After all, who knew what would be available in Nuku Hiva? As I watched myself pile up such items as Day Nurse, Mentos and those foam things you put in between your toes when applying nail polish, I reflected on my attachment to these most trifling of creature comforts, and the futility of my attempt to quit hoarding. I hope we push off before I get another chance to go shopping.

In the nineteenth century there were few places to buy provisions in the South Seas so, before Fanny left, she was faced with the task of laying in enough food and necessities to keep eleven people on board the *Casco* happy for a whole seven months. For meat, she stowed enormous quantities of corned beef, dried beef, hams and bacon. The larder was filled with staples of flour, sugar, rice, beans and butter, as well as a variety of tinned goods, syrup, dried fruits and wine. Beyond foodstuff, there had to be a typewriter so Lloyd could prepare Louis's manuscripts, packets of books and medical supplies for Louis, as well as his manuscript trunk, portable writing case with pens and bottles of ink, and his beloved flageolet, or musical pipe. Lloyd would bring his new camera and his own musical instruments: banjo, fiddle and guitar. There had to be a pack of cards, lots of tobacco, knitting supplies for the women, shady hats for everyone and hundreds of gifts 'for the natives'.

Before leaving San Francisco, the *Casco* passengers paid some considerable attention to finding suitable cruising attire. Louis couldn't resist throwing in a couple of his signature velvet jackets, but he also acquired a yachting cap and some striped pyjama suits, the costume of South Seas traders. Fanny, Margaret and Valentine decided on a wardrobe of 'Mother Hubbards', or *holakus*. These are the shapeless tents missionaries foisted on bare-breasted Pacific island women, in a culturally inappropriate attempt to encourage 'moral fortitude' in the new,

Christian societies. The women ordered a number of these flounced garments in fine, light fabric from Yee Lee in San Francisco's Chinatown, along with several *muumuus* (voluminous robes with puffed sleeves that originated in Christianized Hawaii). This new style of dressing must have felt liberating for the Victorian women, after lives spent in tight gowns that required the wearing of corsets. In fact, Fanny found the *holakus* so comfortable she never really gave them up. Once south of the equator, she even abandoned her boots and stockings, and wandered around bare-footed. With her hair cropped short and a cigarette never far from her mouth, she would have raised some eyebrows back in Edinburgh.

Wednesday 1 September 2004

I went aboard early to try to reduce the amount of stuff I'd stashed in my cabin, but failed miserably. Captain Mike had growled at me about bringing so much on board and even produced a list of items he thought I could do without, including a collapsible ballet barre for Scarlett (she is a dedicated dancer), a couple of large wicker baskets and a silverwork bowl depicting a triumphant Neptune, triton held high, riding through the waves on the dorsal flanks of leaping fishes. All right, these were ridiculous choices, and so were the six business suits I tried to stow in the bilge. It is harder than I thought to let go of the trappings of a professional life. No matter how much the skipper complains, however, my books are non-negotiable. I'm beginning to think I may now have a disapproving sea-husband, one who will join my long-suffering land-husband in a resounding, 'Pamela, what *possessed* you?'

At 9 am the boat shoved off without me so the crew could spin the compass. I went back to my hotel to mail off the few items I'd removed from the boat then realized I had even more paraphernalia sitting in my hotel room ready to be boarded and stowed. I tried hard to eliminate some of it, but apparently my packratishness is well entrenched. On my hotel-room television, an approaching hurricane named Francis was getting a great deal of air play. Over the past three days it has grown to the size of Texas and is heading this way. The Captain is doing everything he can to ready us for a fast escape, but our electronics are not yet up and running, and the rigging has not been tuned since the mast was replaced.

Once the *Takapuna* returned to the dock, Dennis (who is going to ride with us as far as Panama) took our bags down to the mooring and managed to sneak my extras aboard without attracting too much attention. When challenged, he gallantly referred to my largest bag as part of his own kit. All right, I'm just a stupid landlubber. Am I really ready for this life? I stowed the remaining things as best I could, then spent some time trying to connect up my computers. While I was doing so, I suddenly noticed I was feeling disconnected from my surroundings: a state of *derealization* in the terminology of psychologists. It happens to people under unusual conditions of stress. The air on deck was stultifying, with the kind of heavy tension you get right before a big storm. I ate a salad, then sat in the coolness of Dennis's cabin and talked to him about pre-psychotic states, one of which I thought I might be entering. At 1 pm I had a brief chat with Charlie, who'll be joining us as far as the Galapagos Islands, then left the boat again for a walk with Dennis to avoid hyperventilating over the fact that the 'expert' trying to hook my laptop up to our new satellite system didn't seem to know what he was doing. We were supposed to go out for a sail this afternoon to tune the rigging, but there was still no sign of our being ready for that.

The Captain estimated a crack of dawn departure tomorrow but, meanwhile, Hurricane Francis is advancing at an alarming pace. Everyone in town is as jumpy as a busted evangelist. Dennis and I sat in the bar at the Hyatt Hotel and leapt to attention whenever there was a weather bulletin, i.e. every five minutes. People are predicting a direct hit just north of us, with shocking water disturbance in a huge radius. At 3 pm came the announcement that the Fort Lauderdale harbour will be closed by noon tomorrow, after which no boats will be allowed in or out. I took a long gulp of my cappuccino and thoughtfully licked the froth off my upper lip.

'The Captain knows what he's doing,' I muttered, as much to myself as to Dennis. 'I trust him to make this decision.'

But further news coverage revealed that the good people of South Florida have entered a siege state – buying up water and boarding up their houses. Price hiking is the order of the day, and everyone has a theory about just where and when Francis is going to hit. Right now, in the Bahamas, the winds have reached a speed of 140 mph and the hurricane is gaining strength as it draws close to the Gulf Stream and the warmth of the Florida landfall. Dennis and I ordered more coffee, and watched a steady flow of business travellers running past with rolling suitcases, gesticulating wildly as they let off steam in the direction of the hotel concierge. At this stage, it is impossible to get a flight out. A team of construction workers appeared with planks of wood, preparing to board up the lobby windows.

At 4.30 pm we walked back to the boat and saw exactly the same chaos we'd left. Now there were two men working on the electronics, one of whom was actually reading a manual and scratching his head. In all of this, I continued to feel strangely separated from reality. Anything could happen in the next few hours. The *Takapuna* could set sail and be safe, set sail and be caught in the storm, stay here and be safe, or stay here and be destroyed. My head was spinning.

'I'm going for a kip,' I announced, deciding to be an ostrich. 'Don't wake me, even for food.'

At 8 pm, and fast asleep, I was half-woken by a furious banging on my cabin door. It was Dennis.

'What?' I snarled.

'We're getting ready to shove off!' he said.

'OK,' I said, and went back to sleep. But a few minutes later I woke again in a state of agitation and lay there wondering: 'Perhaps we're not just going for a rig-tune . . .' There had been a sense of urgency in Dennis's voice. I looked out of the porthole. We were pulling away from the bridge. I dressed hurriedly and clambered on deck. 'Are we going for a sail, or GOING?' I whispered to Dennis, afraid to ask such an ill-informed question of anyone else.

'Oh, we're GOING,' he said, dialling his wife for an excited goodbye. It was only then that reality caught up with me. Tears slid down my cheeks. All the frustration, fury and disappointment of the past ten months, since I first dreamed of departing these shores on a sailboat, dissolved into one moment of head-shaking, silent thanks. I stood at the stern and watched the egg-moon rising, and the Miami skyline fade to angry purple.

The boat began rolling heavily in a bad swell, but I was relieved to find my sea legs were more or less in place. Dennis retired early, looking very green. I, on the other hand, found that a bowl of lukewarm chicken curry never tasted so good.

'It won't ever get any rougher than this, will it?' asked Daragh. The experienced crew members glanced uneasily at each other. Rolle shook his long blond mane and rolled his eyes.

'Not dis afternoon,' he cackled. It was way past sunset.

'Well,' said the Captain as we stood together at the helm, 'it may be a bit of an anti-climax, but we're off.'

' "We're off" is a big fat orgasm as far as I'm concerned,' I replied. 'Congratulations!'

'Congratulations yourself,' he returned, adding, 'frankly, we're not ready, but we had to get the hell outta Dodge.' A highly capable and experienced seaman, Mike had already survived one hurricane at sea and was in no hurry to do it again. The Casco's master, too, preferred to take no chances with an angry wind. Ten days out of San Francisco, Captain Otis noticed the rapidly falling barometer and feared that a cyclone was on its way. He altered the Casco's course to the west, estimating that he would thus bypass the centre of the approaching storm. It was a smart move. Although the schooner experienced strong winds and choppy seas for the ensuing thirty hours, she was spared the fate of another ship, the *Tropic Bird*, that left San Francisco in her wake but failed to alter course. She sailed headlong into the storm and suffered the consequences: injured crew members and damaged sails.

For many hours that first night I sat on deck, trying to take in the fact that we had actually left.

'I've run away to sea,' I breathed, smirking at the stars. I stared at the radar screen, watching illuminated red stripes, indicating the courses of all the other boats frantically trying to outrun the hurricane.

'C'mon, you old tub,' said Dick.

'On behalf of the *Takapuna*,' I said, 'I am deeply offended.' At ten years old, she is a relative youngster, although it's true that among the newest mega yachts of the world she's hardly a bright young thing.

A little later, Dick softened his judgement. 'Yeah,' he said, 'she's a bit wide in the middle and in the past she hasn't had all the TLC she deserves, but she's really a good girl who's going to get you where you want to go, no worries.'

At midnight I tried to get some sleep, but the boat was pitching so much it wasn't until hours later that I figured out how to chock my torso into an immobile state with a couple of well-placed pillows and wedge my feet strategically against the nightstand. I stupidly opened a cupboard in the middle of the night and everything fell out. I must acquire the fine art of stowing.

Thursday 2 September 2004

I awoke to calmer seas. In fact, it is a beautiful day. Rolle and Daragh, who'd had night-watches, looked pretty rough and were on their way to bed. I wandered into the galley, where Kayt handed me a cup of coffee. Life is good, I told myself. After lunch it was my turn to do a four-hour watch. Dick trained me to fill out an hourly log, recording our position, wind speed, boat speed, sea and sky conditions, and barometer reading. I attempted to get to grips with our new pilot-house navigation screens, capable of displaying charts of our destinations, our current and projected courses, the direction of wind and currents, and the proximity of other boats, storms and landforms we might encounter along the way.

Our satellite phones are not yet hooked up because the Captain was forced to throw the technicians off the boat before their work was finished, so neither telephone nor internet is working; however, I managed to reach my husband on my cell phone.

'I'm going to have a skull and crossbones necklace made for you,' he said gaily, chomping on crème brûlée in a London brasserie. I didn't mention that we're not yet out of harm's way. Francis is catching up and is now set to hit the Florida Keys where a massive evacuation is taking place. There's no telling where it will whoosh after that. Ideally, we should head due south to safety, but the Captain says we're forced to veer west. 'There's a big thing called Cuba in the way,' he explained. At 224° 25′ north and 81° 38′ west I lost network coverage on my cell phone.

At around 6 pm Dick unfurled both mainsail and genoa, and we had a beautiful sail as the sun retired; perfect sunset sky, perfect temperature, perfect warm wind on my skin. The *Takapuna* is designed for pure sailing, motoring, or both (known as motor-sailing), and I have discovered it's a much smoother ride with the sails up. I ate dinner on deck, enjoying the early evening with Kayt and Rolle. Everyone looks happy to be out of the boatyard – except poor Dennis, who is still a little queasy. At 8 pm I noticed lightning over the stern. Francis is obviously moving faster than I thought. After a few minutes we were treated to a fantastic light display as two storms played off each other. I sat at the stern, transported from stars to lightning, overshadowed by huge, billowy clouds with hearts of pure platinum fire.

So this is how fast things change at sea: I went below for five minutes, luxuriating in the coolness of my cabin, and when I returned, the storm had caught up with us in all its sopping fury. The crew had thrown on life jackets and harnesses, and as I emerged I heard Dick swearing as he tried to reduce sail amid a hydraulics failure. A huge gust of wind with a torrent of rain entered the pilot house, taking the charts with it. I lunged for them and lay prostrate across the navigation table while Daragh leapt below to alert Rolle to the hydraulics problem.

'Do I have to do everything my fucking self?' Dick was trying to manually winch in the mainsail, without much luck. Kayt and Daragh took over the winding and feeding of the winches while Dick shouted directions. Everyone was wet and terse. Rolle appeared from his bunk, sleepy and disgruntled, muttering something about 'overload'. The crew anxiously tried to gauge the extent of the storm and what would happen if the mainsail was left out like that but, fortunately, Rolle soon revived the hydraulics. It was all over within thirty minutes, after which I retired to my cabin and chocked myself into my bunk.

The tropical zone has long been known to be beset with squalls and calms. Thirty days out of port, when the *Casco* was nearing the Marquesas Islands, she encountered a freak squall unlike anything Captain Otis had ever seen. Louis wrote:

> The squall, which was black as a cat, first passed the yacht to leeward; when well off the quarter, it suddenly turned and came down upon us, like the dropping of a cloak. All whips were let go, and the wheel was put hard down; but before the *Casco* could be brought into the wind, she was struck and knocked down until the wind spilled out of her sails, and the edge of the house was under water, with the sea pouring over the cockpit like a torrent.

Neither Fanny nor Margaret had paid heed to the Captain's instructions that the portholes should be kept closed. The open deadlights dipped to eighteen inches below the surface, and water poured into the cabins with extraordinary force. The *Casco*'s Master had little time for either of the women; he barely tolerated Fanny and, when asked what he would do if Margaret were washed overboard, he replied dourly, 'Put it in the ship's log.'

Friday 3 September 2004

At 5.45 on our second morning at sea, someone knocked on my cabin door to wake me for my 6 am watch. Mascara seemed to be the bare necessity. 'Wonder how long that'll last?' I pondered, thinking of my beauty regime. On deck, the Captain seemed pleased, if a little surprised, to see me. 'Bet he thought I'd back out of my watch,' I thought to myself. I took a squint at the log. It had gradually become calmer through the night, the waves now being only four feet high. Dawn was just breaking to port, and there were few other boats in the area.

'Where are we?' I peered at the electronic chart tracker.

'Few miles north of Havana,' replied the Captain. Havana! I visited the city last year for a professional conference, without any idea I would soon be sailing right past it. Rolle took me into his domain to teach me how to do an engine-room check, a necessary part of my watch duties. We couldn't talk in there, for the throb of the engines, so he communicated everything by hand signals. It was more complicated than I thought it would be, reading the gauges for temperature, pressure, water tanks and so on. Besides, it's scary in that grinding, groaning, workplace, with areas of extreme heat and the risk of being thrown against a moving part, or breaking a limb on one of the heavy compartment doors. I lost my footing inside the auxiliary room.

'Dat's de propeller shaft,' grinned Rolle, pointing at a nasty hole beside me. 'You fall in dere, it vill chop you up.'

The Captain was fiddling with our electronics system all day. He was clearly frustrated, trying to get internet access through our satellite system. I finally managed to make a phone call out. Then, at 4.30 pm there was a commotion on deck when both fishing lines we'd put out over the stern started whirring at once. On the end of one was a nice mahimahi for our dinner, reeled in by Jock. On watch for the second time today, from 6 to 10 pm, I had the benefit of observing the sunset while plotting our course down the west coast of Cuba. We have finally been delivered beyond the ravages of Francis.

When I woke on Saturday morning, I had become so accustomed to the boat's movement I couldn't figure out why I was no longer rolling around in my bunk. I peered through my porthole and, instead of white-caps over blue, I saw a shimmering plate of sea-glass. Climbing on deck, I stared at an unblemished horizon.

'Come forward.' Jock led me to the bow and instructed me to lean over the side, pointing out my own reflection in the perfect surface. The sky was cloudless and there was nothing looming on the radar. With such plain sailing ahead of us, I had thought it would be a lazy day, devoid of excitement, but I was quite wrong. This afternoon, Charlie unpacked our considerable armoury and proceeded to tow some floating objects off the stern so we could test our weapons and have some target practice. The non-shooters lined themselves up on the pilot-house roof and observed, Daragh with clear envy, as we slammed 900 rounds into a few cardboard boxes, about 200 yards off the stern.

'Savage!' cooed Daragh.

'Can I have a turn?' asked Kayt.

Dennis, finally over his seasickness, was in his element, and I was impressed by the Captain's prowess with both rifles and handguns. Soon shell carcasses were littering the decks. In the 100-degree heat, the weapons became searing hot in no time, especially the rifles.

When it was my turn to fire the AR15, I picked it up, slammed in a magazine and, true to my desert training, very aggressively fired twenty fast rounds, double-tapping each target. My adrenaline was soaring. After depleting my first magazine, I dropped to my knee and performed a tactical reload, releasing the clip, picking up another and jamming it in as I rose to deliver another twenty rounds.

'Not bad,' I said to myself, critiquing my accuracy. 'That should chase 'em off.' I lowered my weapon and turned round in time to see my audience, open-jawed at my startling, primal display. As I safety-checked my weapon, I heard the Captain say, 'Remind me never to piss her off.'

I was hot and exhilarated. 'Let's have a swim!' I cried.

'Well,' drawled Dick, 'I guess we do have to perform a Man Overboard drill.'

A few miles on from our place of carnage, we stopped the engines and flopped, dived, or slunk into the warmest, pale indigo water I've ever known. Daragh and Jock took it in turns to run full pelt over the pilot-house roof and plunge in headlong, just clearing the side-decks. 'All my mates are goin' back to school today,' said Daragh exultantly in his Dublin accent, 'and here I am swimmin' in the sea!' I'm sure everyone *thought* about sharks, but no one brought it up – until I sadistically inquired if anyone else had seen the movie *Open Water*.

After our swim we tried to pick up speed, setting a course south down the coast of Mexico to Belize. It would have been nice to use the sails but there was just no wind. I had never imagined that one could be beyond sight of land, yet without a single ripple within the entire circle of an unbroken horizon. I reflected on the *Rime of the Ancient Mariner*, and could truly understand how eerie it would be if one were stuck out here, becalmed without the graces of a decent engine.

Seventeen days out of port, the *Casco* hit the doldrums. With little wind, their progress was halted to thirty-five nautical miles a day, about a sixth of the speed they'd managed at the start of the journey. The seas were flat and glassy, the cabins became unbearably hot, and the Pacific swells and currents rolled them from side to side with very little headway. Unconcerned, Louis happily dangled a fishing line over the side while Fanny watched, thrilled to see him so relaxed and well.

This afternoon, a little hitch-hiking friend came on board the *Takapuna*, a tiny, round migrating bird of unknown species, with fluffy, dark brown feathers and an ivory throat. I watched him wobble here and there, quite exhausted, and take short flights round his new, floating island. He gratefully drank fresh water proffered on a saucer by Daragh and Rolle, and eventually huddled in a corner of the pilot house and fell asleep.

The *Casco*'s voyage was followed by several types of birds, particularly two species described as 'pilot' and 'boatswain birds' that scavenged food from the slop buckets thrown overboard after meals. Just before sunset we were joined by a school of small dolphin, playfully bow-riding in the transparent water.

'Speaking as your cruise director,' mocked the Captain, 'I'm not sure if I can top today.' I had been wondering the same thing. The day had been blissful, and it wasn't yet over. When the stars came out, the brightest canopy so far, I lay on stern cushions and gazed high into the universe. One, two . . . three shooting stars followed close upon each other.

'All the seafarers of the world,' I thought, 'they know about this and they keep it to themselves. Bastards. Leave the rest of the people to settle lands, raise communities, govern, while they have days like these. Hah! I know their game and I can play it, too. At last I'm one of them.'

Sunday 5 September 2004

Another fine day. During my early morning watch, Rolle produced a divider to check our route and spotted a mistake in my 8 am position. Damn! You'd think a woman with a PhD would be able to handle a spot of plotting. Later, the Captain taught me the best way to plot a dead-reckoning course and even brought out his own prized instruments for me to use, silver beauties in a velvet-lined leather case. We got talking about early seafarers, and their system of navigation, which he sees as a lost art. 'It's become more of a science now,' he explained.

'But,' I posited, 'the *interpretation* of modern navigational data – that's still an art, is it not?'

'I suppose so,' he said, looking skywards at a couple of frigate birds circling our mast. 'But back then, sailors searching for land would scan the skies for terrestrial birds and watch where they went at sunset,' he said, ''cos they were goin' home.'

After my watch I fell into bed and snoozed until noon. When I awoke, I found that Charlie had landed a wahoo. On the other rod, Daragh had been reeling in a yellowfin tuna when an oppor-tuna-ing shark took half of it. The lad didn't mind; he was pleased to have such a thrilling tale to tell his friends. I suggested he shouldn't tell his mother it occurred in the vicinity of our ocean swim. He laughed conspiratorially and went down to the galley to make bread.

'I think we're gonna get a wash-down,' announced Kayt in her Merseyside accent. At 2.30 pm, sure enough, we received some light rain.

Around thirty hours later, as we commenced our approach to the isthmus of Panama, the radar screen began to fill up with 'bogies', or electronically generated targets representing vessels we would have to avoid as we entered and traversed the harbour. Container docks lay to port, their idle cranes like orange, monochromatic Ferris wheels after the fair is over. A bouillabaisse of sea-peeled vessels darted about the harbour jostling for position; the unofficial race had begun. Some had already received their canal transit times and were smugly waiting for pilots to see them safely through the locks system. Others would wait days for their crossings. We inspected many of the ships at close quarters, peering through the anchor lockers of rusty, square container vessels, with harsh, yellow lights illuminating their exposed engines and pipes, and tired, sunbeaten men standing on deck. Every now and then an open door would allow us a glimpse of a galley, where more men – blubbery, singlet-wearing, hairy mammals – sat hunched over their dinner, reading newspapers and waiting for their watches to begin.

Our Captain turned off the autopilot and hand-steered a dodge 'em course through the busiest part of the harbour.

'He's earning his money all right,' whispered Dennis, thoroughly impressed. The crew stood silently behind him in the dark, with the glow from two radar screens lighting their faces. Half eager to be ashore, half mourning the loss of our world at sea, we all gave quiet thanks for our delivery from the fury of Francis. Now we could smell the land – a sweet, oily, smoky scent of humankind. I ran to the bow and stood to greet it, legs astride, hair flying, soliciting the wind's embrace. I was Francis Drake, Joseph Conrad, Boadicea . . . and, of course, Fanny, whose very first sea voyage brought her right here. I imagined her, a lonely waif, on deck in those early days. Did she feel the same thrill at the first sights, the smells, the sounds of Colon, then known as Aspinwall?

Long before Fanny set off on the *Casco* she had learned how to survive dangerous journeys. Her first husband Sam was a dreamer – an idealist with a perverse sense of priorities. When Fanny married him in 1857, he was a young lieutenant from Kentucky and she was just seventeen. A daughter, Isobel (usually called Belle), was born a year later, but when the American Civil War began, Sam left his family to serve as a Captain in the Yankee army. Fanny's adored childhood friend George Marshall went too. Both were gone for two years, during which time each of them faced some of the toughest combat experiences a young man could have. Consequently, they returned as changed men.

Back in Indianapolis, George married Fanny's younger sister Jo, but he had paid a higher price than he knew for the Yankee cause; the battlefields were rife with tuberculosis and he became gravely ill. In 1863, while Fanny and her pregnant sister Jo waited at home, Sam took it upon himself to escort his friend George to California, where the climate might save his life. In those days, before the east–west railroad was built, a westward journey across America could be undertaken by either of two equally dangerous routes. A stagecoach crossing meant risking attack by native Indians or robbers, so Sam chose the alternative: the Panama route. Tragically, George died at sea in Sam's arms before they even reached Colon.

After burying George on the isthmus, Sam made the surprising decision not to return to his family, but to continue on to California. It is difficult to know exactly why he made that choice. He was in mourning for his pal, and probably not thinking too clearly. He was also short of money and, like many people at that time, was lured by tales of fortunes made in the silver and gold mines of Nevada and California. He wrote to Fanny, firing her imagination with stories of San Francisco prospectors with diamond buttons in their shirts and their women bathing in champagne. Fanny was enthralled by the idea that they might make their fortune by owning a mine, so when Sam wrote to her, instructing her to sell up and follow him to California, she readily agreed. Before she had even left Indiana he had spent all their savings on a worthless mine in the Sierra Nevada; yet, at twenty-three years old, Fanny blindly said goodbye to her family and set off with Belle in tow. Their train journey would take them via Chicago to New York, where they would board the *Iroquois* for a twelve-day passage south through the Atlantic Ocean to Aspinwall on the east coast of the Isthmus of Panama. There they would await a train to carry them across the early path of Inca gold, the Camino Real, to the Pacific Ocean, where another ship, the *Saint Louis*, was due to carry them another fifteen days north. The final part of the journey would be spent in a stagecoach, trundling through the treacherous lands of the Indian wars to the inland mining town of Austin, just east of Carson City in Nevada.

Fanny must have known about the many dangers ahead. Several ships had been lost of late and the isthmus was known for swamp fevers – yellow fever, malaria and dysentery. Nefarious characters inhabited the trail, and Fanny was particularly at risk during this journey because she was short of funds, having sold all her assets to pay for Sam's prospecting forays. In her pocket she carried her uncle's parting gift: a pocket derringer pistol decorated with an ivory cross.

'Watch out for the riff-raff, my dear,' said her uncle. 'The far west is a promising country, but dangerous.'

Though travelling unaccompanied made Fanny especially vulnerable, it also allowed for her to receive protection and privileges from benevolent strangers. Fanny's precocious understanding of the power of her apparent helplessness served her well throughout her life.

A gentleman seated in the same carriage to New York, a Mr Hill, rallied support from other passengers when the ticket collector disputed Fanny's fare payment. He took up a collection for her, which Fanny accepted only after what she considered to be a proper number of refusals and protestations. Mr Hill kept an eye on her throughout their Atlantic voyage, during which she was upgraded to first class and frequently invited to dine with the Captain. Perceiving Fanny to be both needy and resourceful, many went out of their way to help her.

'There goes a brave little woman,' Mr Hill was heard to say. She needed all the bravery she could muster to survive Aspinwall.

Just before midnight, we docked very close to the old Aspinwall, alongside thirty or so other ocean-battered sailboats at the well-guarded, palm-lined Panama Canal Yacht Club. A shabby little marina compared to many, it nevertheless held all the intrepid charm of a true haven for cruising sailors. A few 'mom and pop' cruisers sat in the outdoor cafe eating fish and chips off plastic tablecloths, while the crustier long-distance sailors gave themselves an inside soaking in the air-conditioned bar, itself resembling a Hemingway movie set with decoratively hung ropes and bells, polished wood, neglected helms and torn leather seats. Outside the window, two enormous vultures were poised above a group of rubbish bins. Some of the cruisers we met there had never made it beyond this protected little enclave. The couple scrubbing their forty-four-foot sailboat beside us had been here for thirty years.

Tuesday 7 September 2004

This morning, Dennis and I set off for the centre of Colon. Now-adays, it is a thoroughly dangerous town that even Panamanians think twice about visiting, so the Captain sent Charlie with us for security. He jumped into the taxi with a bulky rucksack.

'How's this for adventure?' I smiled slyly at Dennis. 'We're visiting a full-service, crack den zone, with an armed ex-SAS guard in tow.'

The town seemed true to its reputation. What few decent houses still remained were defended by barbed wire, dogs and gun-toting security officers.

'This area is inhabited by Arabs who have businesses in the Free Zone,' said Carlos, our driver. 'They call it the Gaza Strip.' A few years ago terrorists bombed the Free Zone and killed twenty- five people, most of whom were Jewish.

The people here are under threat at both home and work, so many live in the safer environment of Panama City and commute when necessary. We heard about the recent kidnapping of several employees of a major company. A large ransom was paid but the hostages were killed anyway. We asked about the old port but Carlos refused to take us there. In fact, he looked panic-stricken at the very suggestion. He is still suffering from the terrible memory of the 1989 invasion, when American forces launched a military campaign to end the regime of Manuel Noriega.

'On December twentieth, I came into the city to buy milk for my two-year-old daughter,' began Carlos, who was eager to tell his story. 'I stopped by my brother's office – he had a fish supply business. He asked me to deliver 200 pounds of fish to a large boat, then after I finished at 10 pm I sat around and chatted with him. At midnight the bombing started. They killed a lot of people. The official figures were much lower but I think it was close to 6,000, and many buildings were destroyed. There were gunmen hiding in the grass with night optics and it was too dangerous to move. I had to stay there in the Free Zone for three days. I was so scared. My brother went to the hospital and saw three trucks full of dead people, so many they were buried in a common grave. It was really bad. We'd been living peacefully with America for eighty years . . . how could they kill so many people just to get one man?'

High above us, sleepy, two-toed sloths hung in the *guarumo* trees. We drove past American-built residential blocks, two of which have been turned into a school. Everywhere, there was evidence of the former US presence, from the many mahogany trees they planted (there are 10,000 in Colon and Panama) to the old army training compound that is now a five-star hotel. We passed the soldiers' barracks that have become apartment complexes and the old army bowling alley that is now the *Bolos Espinar*.

'So . . . was your family OK?' I was almost afraid to ask. Carlos slowed down.

'I begged permission to the soldiers to let me go home with milk for my daughter,' he replied. 'I didn't know if my family was safe and no one was allowed out of the city. Then I wrote a letter explaining my situation. I begged a Puerto Rican sergeant to read it, and he said, "OK you can go." But then I said, "If I just walk out you might shoot me. Give me a ride." So they sent me in a Hummer.' It seemed unusual, but one could entirely imagine this feisty little man talking his way into an armoured car. 'On the way,' continued Carlos, 'I saw a lot of people with weapons, looting, stealing everything in the Free Zone. All the stores were destroyed. People you'd never imagine were looting . . . even doctors.'

The old Aspinwall, too, was a treacherous place. When Fanny arrived, she left her luggage piled up haphazardly in the street and tramped across the railroad tracks to the swampy, vaporous cemetery. Sam had provided her with a map, so she was able to find George's grave without too much trouble. She knelt to say a prayer, then dried her tears and hastily joined the hordes of other passengers who were clamouring for seats on the train that crossed the isthmus. But the corrupt railroad company took advantage of the fact that the *Saint Louis* had not yet arrived to transport the waiting passengers to San Francisco and raised the ticket prices. Those who did not secure a place would have to wait even longer for another train, another boat, and risk becoming ill with swamp fever.

Fanny did not have the funds to pay the new, exorbitant fare. At dusk, she made her way to the ticket office to try to barter her wedding ring for a ticket for her and Belle. A man lurking in the shadows offered to pay their way – provided Fanny 'share his hammock'. When she indignantly put him in his place, he grabbed her and tried to force her against the station wall. In an instant, Fanny had her pistol pressed firmly against his throat. She cocked it and told him to clear off, sending him running away into the night.

'Well,' she said lightly to Belle, crouched frozen with fear in the shadows, 'your mother nearly killed a man. Come along.'

Our day in Colon continued to be wet and muggy.

'We have the rainy season all year round,' said Carlos,

driving us to the Mount Hope cemetery to search for George
Marshall's headstone. He had died in 1863, so I was disheartened to see '1908' on the white, arched entry gate. The records
department showed nothing prior to the start of the twentieth
century; however, we managed to find a few earlier burial sites.
As we stumbled around in the undergrowth, a couple of grave-
diggers lay chewing their lunch on a flat, marble mausoleum,
using the headstone for a pillow. Finding George Marshall's
grave seemed an impossible task in that steamy, mosquito-
ridden, overgrown place. If this was the right cemetery, then
Fanny had certainly taken a risk to walk here.

Carlos drove us through the oldest part of town, an area that
had been fashionable in Fanny's day. Several of the spacious,
balconied hotels that once lodged transit passengers headed for
the California gold and silver mines are still there, only now
they are filthy and decrepit. Their exteriors are disgracefully
run down for such fine buildings; blackened with age and
otherwise marred with peeling paint, graffiti and untidy
electrical wires. Finely carved wooden balconies have been
replaced with sheets of corrugated iron and hung about with
washing that will never dry on such a rainy day. I could not
identify the Union Hotel where Fanny rested, and the
neighbourhood was too unsavoury to allow for an inspection
on foot; however, the recently rejuvenated Hotel Washington,
first built in 1870 as the headquarters of the Panama Railroad
Company, beautifully echoes the Spanish colonial style and
location of those early overnight lodgings. Its cool lobby is
adorned with potted palms and decorative ceiling fans, while
its upper balconies, once the prerogative of first class transit
passengers, overlook the Caribbean Sea and the outskirts of the
Bahia Limón. A modern wing of the Hotel Washington boasts a
casino and the new 'Piratas' bar, a smoky den with heavy-hewn
wooden tables and a dance floor with a stage, over which hangs
a skull and crossbones flag. Such set-dressing is based on
reality, for this part of the world is truly pirate territory, the

breeding ground for the original *Pirates of the Caribbean*.

The history of swashbuckling pretty well started here in the sixteenth century, once the English and Dutch seafarers of the time began to notice the passage of Inca gold. It was moved along the Camino Real by slaves and donkeys, then stored in such ill-guarded buildings as the Royal Customs House of San Felipe de Portobelo to await transport to Spain. Among those who attacked both cities and the well-laden Spanish galleons were pirates, privateers, and commanders of the British Navy – although it was sometimes difficult to distinguish one from another.

The restored Customs House in Portobelo, half an hour's drive from Colon, once housed the majority of all gold that made its way from the Americas to Spain, as well as wine, cheeses, glass, silver and tapestries. But Portobelo itself became little more than a hideaway for thieves. Its renowned international fairs drew seafarers, merchants, pilgrims – and pirates. During fair time, the Customs House was permanently guarded by around 250 soldiers, but they were unreliable drunkards who slept on important, sealed documents and urinated wherever they pleased. They were joined by the generals of visiting armadas, who moved in for the interim with their women and servants. It must have been a riot. Eventually the place became a scandal, a twenty-four-hour gambling house. The final straw came when the Council of Portobelo allowed two rich merchants to build houses between the Customs House and the pier, creating a tax-free haven. Complaints were made to the Crown about this nice little earner and the Customs House was relocated.

Considering how little attention was being paid to defence at that time, it's no wonder Portobelo was sacked seven times, by the likes of Sir Francis Drake, Admiral Edward Vernon, William Kinghills and Henry Morgan. Wandering round the Customs House, it was startling to hear British heroes being described as scoundrels.

'That pirate, Francis Drake,' frowned the guide, 'he attacked the city several times.' Beside a picture of the English explorer William Darius was written: TERRIBLE PIRATA.

The palm-lined, cannon-guarded Bay of Portobelo is beautiful, mysterious and serene, yet it has been so bloodied by pirate attacks it once had a chain drawn across it at night to prevent boats from entering by stealth. Sir Francis Drake died there. He is now 'sleepin' there below' the blue-black waters of the Bay, eternally encased in a lead coffin. I suppose the ravaged Portobeleños wanted to make sure he didn't return. It was strange to be reminded of the romantic notions concerning pirates (Gilbert & Sullivan et al), and at the same time confronted with the terrible, tragic realities. I wonder, are the pirates of the Red Sea, Ecuador and Indonesia, which I fear so much, regarded as romantic heroes by their communities?

Fanny did not have to deal with the threat of pirates in Aspinwall, but to be stuck there without the resources to cross the Isthmus would have been disastrous, even fatal, for her and her daughter. Children were known to be particularly susceptible to swamp fever. But, resourceful as ever, Fanny hatched a plan to get her and Belle to safety. She would persuade the benevolent Mr Hill to pay for mules, provisions and a guide to take them via the Inca gold trail, some forty-seven miles through swamps and tropical jungle, and across the River Chagres, to the safety of the Port of Panama and a waiting ship. They must do this secretly. Fanny would warn her companion that if he breathed a word, the price of mules would be elevated beyond his pocket. At two or three in the morning she turned up at Mr Hill's hotel room (in itself a scandalous move at that time), announced her plan and extracted his last 100 dollars to hire mules and provisions. She instructed him to pack and meet her at the cemetery at dawn. How they fared on that overland trip, if indeed she took it, is a mystery. Did the twenty-three year-old, carrying Belle, really manage to hire mules in the three hours between her conversation with Mr Hill in the hotel and the crack of dawn? There are apparently no records of that part of their journey; and of Mr Hill there is no further mention. He does not even appear on the passenger list of the *Moses Taylor*, the ship that eventually carried Fanny and Belle to San Francisco.

It is hard to imagine Fanny, who loved to tell a good story, not recounting her thrilling trek through the jungle by mule – if it occurred. One thing I am sure of: Fanny would have done anything she thought necessary to keep Belle from danger and be reunited with Sam. And who can blame her?

As I sat sipping a pina colada with the Captain in the Yacht Club Bar, our Panama agent turned up, a rotund, perspiring Englishman with a folder under his arm.

'There's a chance you may be able to transit first thing tomorrow,' he said, rather doubtfully. 'Unfortunately, one of the canal lanes is closed so traffic is slow and there are more delays than usual.'

We returned to the boat with this news, only to find that Charlie had organized a taxi for a crew night out at the Piratas Bar. Rolle made quite an entrance, staggering out of the galley freshly showered, and dressed in Hawaiian shirt and Panama hat, with a bottle of beer in one hand.

'You could score in that outfit,' I teased him. But his efforts were in vain because the Captain vetoed the night out, wanting to be sure we were all sober, and in one piece, for tomorrow's early start. It's a bit like boarding school round here.

Scarlett's friend Evan arrived that same evening, a lanky eighteen-year-old Californian who is to join Daragh in helping out on deck and below. He was grilled at Customs by officials who detained him, it seemed, in the hope of extracting a bribe. The teenager, who speaks excellent Spanish, managed to convince them he was just a kid with minimal funds. When I saw his three suitcases lying on the deck, I knew he'd be ribbed by the rest of the crew. He's charming and articulate, but he's got a lot to learn. I hope he gets on with Daragh because they are sharing a cabin. Most of all, I hope we can transit the Canal tomorrow. I'm not keen to spend another night here.

Wednesday 8 September 2004

At 5 am we heard we had a slot so, immediately after breakfast, we headed out to the pilotage area in the Bahia Limón to wait for our pilot captain who would guide us through two of the three sets of locks. It was extraordinary to think we would be crossing the American continent within a space of eight hours. When the pilot came on board at ten, we learned that we were to go through each set of locks tethered to a tug on our starboard side. This is easier than having to attach ourselves to one of the 'new mules', the stainless-steel electric locomotives, costing one million dollars each, that have replaced the animals once harnessed to all boats. These days the largest vessels need eight of these Japanese trains, working in pairs, to correctly align and tow them, and to help maintain their position within the lock chambers.

Our pilot, an impressively solid black man in a tight, short-sleeved uniform and cap, gave me a wide smile. 'Owner not on board?'

'No,' I lied. He looked disappointed, turned his back and walked away, chatting on his mobile phone. It's always best to keep a low profile. As we began to motor towards the start of our first transit leg, the two-laned Gatun Locks, we saw enormously long passenger wharves and container bases lining the Bahia Limón.

'Every year, 1.5 million containers pass through the Panama Canal,' said the pilot, 'and sixty to a hundred cruise ships arrive.' A special arrival port has been built for the latter, complete with souvenir shops, supermarkets and cafes. Hanging about on deck, I spied an alligator lazing by the bank just a few yards off to starboard. He must give the cruise-ship passengers a bit of a start.

The Gatun Locks operate as a water-lift, elevating vessels twenty-six metres above sea level to the height of the man-made Gatun Lake, formed after the Chagres River was sealed off. We passed through the first gigantic, mitre gates and took up our position beside our lock-partner, a Panamanian tug. It was a jolly boat, manned by a couple of overweight, bored-looking men in orange life vests, thick boots and hard hats. Kayt, wearing a wide-brimmed, waterproof hat with *Takapuna* embroidered on it, offered them soft drinks. They happily accepted, then began angling for her hat.

'Sorry,' said Kayt firmly, flashing them a disarming smile, 'we've only just got enough for the crew.' She plonked herself on the foredeck and watched them work. 'If I were a boat, I think I'd be a tug,' she sighed, patting her tummy. Like most women in the western world, she is weight-conscious, but she needn't be. She is remarkably beautiful – athletic and well proportioned.

Daragh threw the first line. It made a perfect arc, landing neatly within the grasp of the portside tugman, a burly, bow-legged man with a gold-tooth smile, who tied it off then strolled aft to receive and cleat the second line, thrown by Jock. When I handled a line it felt as though it had been soaked in detergent, like a hundred-foot dishrag. Into our lock chamber, right behind us, slid a gargantuan, green-hulled Monrovian monster called the *Sanko Rejoice*. The mitre gates swung closed and we began to rise with the gravity-induced influx of 197,000 litres of fresh water from holes in the lock bed. Then began a long wait inside the dark, glistening walls as they slowly lengthened. The sun was relentless. Chugging endless cool drinks, we stood by with fenders at the ready in case one of our neighbouring vessels came loose. Recently, a fifty-foot catamaran was quite badly damaged. It had been sandwiched ahead of a very large ship, whose wash, while moving from one compartment to another, was powerful enough to send a surge of water over its neighbour's decks, breaking some lines, and smashing it against the wall.

As we lounged watchfully on deck, huddled together in the few shady, on-deck places, I heard Charlie, crouched beneath the tender, holding court with the boys about 'jungle ops'.

'Them balaclavas were too itchy for me,' he said. I turned round and saw Evan and Daragh wide-eyed. 'So I cut a couple of holes in my underpants and wore them on my head.'

'Thanks, Charlie,' I called. 'Just a little too much info.' I was aghast at such a shattering of illusions. The SAS had just become a bunch of Keystone Kops. 'And while your underpants were on your head,' I teased him, 'where were you wearing your balaclava?'

Rolle appeared on deck, strutting round in his new straw hat. 'So dis is real cool, yah? I go trew de Panama Canal wearing my Panama hat!'

Charlie ignored us both. 'When we were in Northern Ireland,' he continued, 'they decided we looked too aggressive in black balaclavas, so they changed the colour. Issued bright pink ones instead. I mean, there's people trying to shoot you, and they've given you a glowing head.'

After we were spewed out of the first locks we were delighted to be permitted to nip through the shorter and little-used 'banana channel' to meet our faster lock-partner. While the tug took the usual western route, our course took us in between five or six islands clustered together in the middle of the Gatun Lake. The channels were narrow and quite shallow, so we had a sense of sailing right through a live, vibrating jungle. Scarlet macaws, snail kites and keel-billed toucans nestled above.

'There's monkeys in there, swinging from the trees,' said the Captain, but we didn't see any. Instead, cormorants and other water birds squawked at us from their lookout posts, atop blackened stakes sticking up through muddy banks.

As we approached the next phase of our transit, a new pilot came on board, carrying an umbrella, a life jacket and radio. He looked tired and gratefully accepted a sandwich. In line with us now was a lonely canoeist, seeming all the tinier for the huge dredger and giant crane beside him. Swarthy, moustachioed men waited, weary, hot and starving, to make the last lock. Eventually, we moved into the Gaillard Cut, a stepped, grass-covered gash that was hewn out of the mountain in a monumental feat of labour and engineering. It was humbling to see the place where many thousands of people lost their lives during the Canal construction.

'In those days they were not very good at blasting,' said the pilot. 'The landslides killed many.'

Finally, we reached Miraflores, the very last lock. Its two massive, rivet-studded gates opened into the Pacific Ocean just as the sun was setting. As darkness fell, huge fruit bats began to circle the new mules. Orange lamps cast an eerie glow on a patchwork of waiting containers, while to port, the silhouettes of dockside cranes waved and ducked against a reddening sky. The breeze lifted us. After the oppressiveness of the day, it was thrilling to be spewed out into the fresh breezes of the Pacific. A vee-shaped flock of migrating birds winged overhead calling an evening message, while ahead loomed the Bridge of the Americas. Its single span arch reminded me of the Sydney Harbour Bridge and a tear or two cooled my folded arms.

'I was going to say, "Welcome to my ocean." ' The Captain interrupted my reverie. 'But I guess it's your ocean too.' I smiled at him, but he was staring out at the horizon. 'Things always seem to go better here . . .' He trailed off. I realized then he is a man imbued with longing, a kind I understand.

Later that evening we docked at the Flamenco Yacht Club, across the harbour from the tiara lights of Old Panama and the skyscrapers of the new Panama City. Everyone set to work to replenish the fuel bladder, then stood back satisfied to admire the strange, wobbling alien that would see us through to the Galapagos Islands.

'A full bladder is not usually a positive thing,' I mused. 'Permission to go ashore, Captain?'

I'll never get used to having to ask. Dennis and I took a stroll, then sat drinking Margaritas at a waterfront cafe. 'I'm glad you're having this adventure,' he said wistfully. 'Thank you for letting me be part of it.'

We took a quick taxi tour to inspect Old Panama. Its discoloured, once-grand, balconied residences and Castilian town squares were reminiscent of Havana, and a sharp contrast to the new steel-and-glass towers of the modern city.

'The Miss World Contest was held here last year,' grinned our driver, who had little else to say.

The next day Dennis departed very early for Michigan, leaving a 'thank you' note tucked inside my laptop. I heard the forbidden click-click of his cowboy boots marking the teak deck above my cabin and smiled to myself. I'll be giving him hell for that. The *Takapuna* slipped silently out of the harbour just before daybreak. I half-woke to the now-familiar sound of the rattling anchor chain. I even heard a sail being raised, then some delicious moments of pure sailing before I slid back into my dreams. Galapagos Islands, here we come.

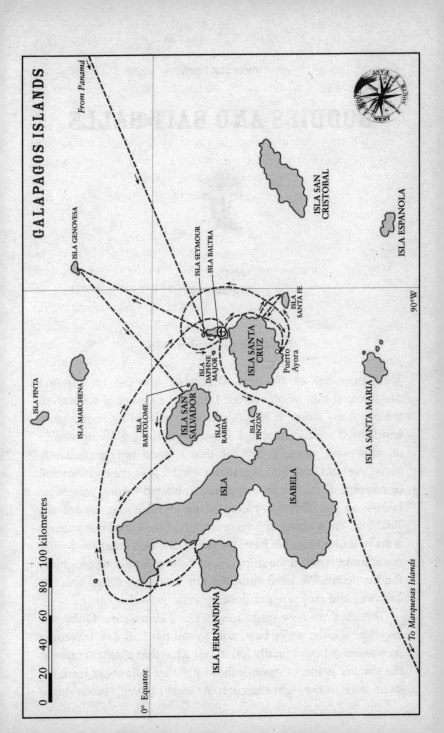

GALAPAGOS ISLANDS

From Panamá

To Marquesas Islands

ISLA PINTA

ISLA MARCHENA

ISLA GENOVESA

ISLA SEYMOUR
ISLA BALTRA

ISLA SANTA FE

ISLA SAN SALVADOR
ISLA BARTOLOME
ISLA RABIDA
ISLA PINZON

ISLA DAPHNE MAJOR

ISLA SANTA CRUZ

Puerto Ayora

ISLA FERNANDINA

ISLA ISABELA

ISLA SANTA MARIA

ISLA SAN CRISTOBAL

ISLA ESPANOLA

Equator

90°W

NORTH
EAST
SOUTH
WEST

0 20 40 60 80 100 kilometres

CHAPTER FOUR

BOOBIES AND BAIT BALLS

08°14.2' N
079°38.3' W

Friday 10 September 2004

This morning, as the last, flickering glimpse of Panama disappeared into smoky cloud, I noticed a kernel of warmth in the pit of my stomach that eventually radiated up to my heart and flowed around my head. It was a swirling, glowing stream of something vaguely familiar that I could not immediately name. Around lunchtime I realized what it was: the combination of happiness, excitement, optimism and adventure, otherwise known as *joy*. There is plenty to be joyful about aboard the *Takapuna*. We're moving further into the Pacific and our journey is truly under way. We have beaten all the odds that we would never make it out of the shipyard, or that we would be caught by the hurricane. We have survived our first sea passage and the *Takapuna* and crew are performing well.

The seas are now quite rough, but I don't care. Given the excellent winds, we've been able to sail hard all day, travelling on a massive heel. I finally found out what that plastic scraper in the shower is for: to swoosh the water that falls away from the drain back in the right direction. At least I haven't fallen out of the shower like Evan did this morning. He forgot to lock the door and was thrown violently into the companionway, covered in soap. He slid all over the place before he managed to grab hold of a railing and haul himself back into the cubicle. The poor kid seems very green compared to Daragh, yet the two of them complement each other; he is as outgoing and articulate as Daragh is shy. It was Evan's turn to swab the galley after lunch and before anyone could stop him he sluiced an entire bucket of water on the floor. Rolle came on deck chortling. 'Is gonna take him all day to mop dat up!'

Both boys overslept by several hours this morning and as a consequence they have been put on the worst night-watches for the rest of the week. I heard the Captain chiding them: 'The boat could have been on fire and you were so sound asleep you couldn't be woken! I'm not comin' in to get you!'

Saturday 11 September 2004

I'm less scared of the engine room now; in fact it seems almost friendly. I can do a full check in there twice as fast as when I started, having learned what to grab to avoid being thrown against something dangerous if the boat suddenly lurches.

Jock reeled in a huge mahimahi for lunch. I like being a hunter in the sea. The boys kill the fish by pouring vodka in their gills. 'A happy death,' says Rolle who, despite the no-alcohol rule at sea, occasionally takes a swig himself during the process. This morning he placed a toy donkey he bought at Disney World on the dashboard of the pilot house.

'Donkey's on watch, yah?' he said. 'If he takes a nose-plant we know we're going pitch-pole.'

'What's that,' I asked fearfully.

'It's also called *ass over tea-kettle*,' explained the Captain.

'I'll try hard to master your nautical phraseology,' I replied.

Later on, I took a deep breath and asked Rolle what a pitch-pole was. 'Ven de boat does a forward front-flip,' he replied. 'I never done it.'

'Good to know,' I sighed.

Dick helped me revise the phonetic alphabet today, as well as the protocol for making emergency radio calls. Henceforth I shall be spelling my name *papa alpha mike echo lima alpha*. The sea is still very rough. A headwind caused the boat to pitch mighty forcefully all day, sending masses of spray flying across the bow on to the foredeck.

'The southeast wind that will take us to the Galapagos gets up here then sweeps right back to Panama,' said the Captain, 'due to the Coriolis effect.' He explained the latter as a deflection of winds and ocean currents caused by the rotation of the Earth. Fanny and Louis had very much wished to head for the Galapagos Islands as their very first stop aboard the *Casco*. It was precisely the type of heavy swell and unpredictable wind patterns we're experiencing now that led Captain Otis to dissuade them from going this far east in the equatorial zone, and to head for the Marquesas Islands instead.

At 5 pm the sea was a series of undulating, silver-splattered hillocks, with a horizon of grey and apricot cloud-lands. Above, a whiskered sun slowly sank behind transparent iron-grey mesh bands. It being the anniversary of the Twin Towers attack, I was glad to be away from news coverage and focused instead on the beauty of the sky. I did, however, ruminate about the recent pirate attack on a vessel travelling on this very route to the Galapagos Islands. A few months ago, very close to where we are now, a yacht was attacked at sea by a 'fishing boat'.

'I suppose,' I reasoned out loud, 'we're still a lot safer than driving on the motorway.'

'Yeah,' agreed the Captain, 'not too many drive-by shootings in this neighbourhood.'

Nevertheless, on watch this evening, I kept the night-vision binoculars handy and frequently swept the surrounding seas for any visitors.

Sunday 12 September 2004

Evan's in trouble again. He was fooling round with the radar and navigation screen and somehow managed to completely re-plot our course. Dick, who was watch-captain at the time, eventually noticed the new route – a complete U-turn back to the Caribbean, not even via Panama, but overland, straight through the middle of the Continental Divide.

'What the hell . . . ?' Dick yelled at him. Evan slunk below and scrubbed the galley floor for penance. Personally, I think it was genius of Evan to figure out how to plot anything on that screen. So far, with regard to that particular piece of equipment, I am utterly technologically challenged.

Tonight, I'm really afraid of the sea. I think about being sucked down deep into a cold, dark, airless place. I lie in my bunk, without a nightlight, battling my fears. Pitching non-stop, I cling fast to my mortality. I am beginning to understand what mariners know: humility, awe and terror of what lies beneath. Land people have it all wrong, thinking sailors are just a rough, randy bunch when they come ashore. No, they crave the *comfort* of a lover's arms and a life-affirming celebration of surviving the inexorable sea.

Fanny's first, death-defying voyage to San Francisco with Belle did not culminate with a loving embrace. Sam was not there to meet her. He arrived at the dock when the *Saint Louis* sailed in, but when his wife and daughter did not appear, he hurried back to attend to urgent mining business in Austin, having arranged for a trusted friend to wait for the next ship and settle them into a hotel. To catch up with Sam, Fanny and Belle had to travel alone once more; this time on the Pony Express stagecoach, 200 miles across the Sierras then onwards through the desert.

The Wells Fargo money travelled with them, which increased the likelihood of their being attacked by bandits. None of the passengers knew where the gold was; probably secreted in the

clothing of one of the Wells Fargo employees disguised as a
hard-up miner. Belle sat inside the carriage but Fanny persuaded
the driver to allow her to ride beside him on the lookout seat. He
forced her to travel hunched over her knees, with the barrel of
his rifle resting on her back. It is hard to know why Fanny put
up with that. Did she plan to draw her own weapon and join
him in fending off an attack? Was that how she would protect
Belle? Eventually she defied the driver and sat bolt upright, with
the barrel of his gun pointing directly at her head.

Fanny was suffering from severe fatigue and stress, and Belle
thought she saw her mother talking to herself. Had her
exhaustion and terror led her into a separation from reality? A
psychotic episode? Fanny would have called it one of her 'little
bouts of brain fever'.

Monday 13 September 2004

We're much closer to the equator, only three degrees off now,
and there's great excitement on board. We should be in the
Galapagos Islands within thirty hours. I wish the swell would
diminish. We've come this whole leg with a headwind, causing
constant rolling and no relief. Our next long sea journey, from
the Galapagos to the Marquesas, is nearly three weeks long. I'm
starting to wonder, can I hack it?

Twenty-four hours later the weather had improved, with
more compliant winds and less swell, although there's a faint
chill in the air. It was thrilling to finally cross the equator, just
after noon. We stood by the navigation screen, watching 0
degrees north become 0 degrees south. Evan and Daragh had
not crossed before and, according to the old hands on board,
they got off very lightly, without having to brave the humiliation
that is usually perpetrated on novices. Dick described a navy
tradition of subjecting first-time equator-crossers to a 'greasing',
a sadistic public ritual that involved having a broom handle

Life's too short to stuff a chicken –
learning to suture a wound

Showing her bottom – the
Takapuna in a Florida shipyard

Just off Cuba – the pot of gold's behind my head

Bring on the margaritas! Exiting the Panama canal

Sailing the trade winds

Inventors of the bouncy castle – Dick and Jock inspecting the fuel bladders

Bag ladies – (left to right) Kayt, Kim and
Scarlett provisioning

Breakfast

Look Ma, no hands! Scarlett at the helm

Male frigate bird   Land iguana   Blue-footed boobie

Above Darwin's Lake, Galapagos Islands – (left to right) Evan, Daragh, Scarlett, Captain Mike, Kim, me, my friend Corki and Champi. *Takapuna* in the background in Caleta Tagus

Giant land tortoise   Hitch-hiking pelican   Sea lion

Wife on the ocean wave –
approaching the Marquesas Islands

Dream lover – Akitini

A favourite haunt of Fanny and Louis – Anaho Bay

Above: Cannibals' larder – the man to be eaten next was kept in the right-hand cave

Left: Modern tikis, Nuku Hiva

Below: Guess who's coming as dinner? Skulls found at the cannibal site, Nuku Hiva

above: Thence we bore away along the shore – in the *Casco*'s wake

right: At the foot of Mount Jacuzzi, Marquesas

below: Bay of Penises, Fatu Hiva

The Dancing Sperm – (left to right) Dick, Eli and Rolle

Long Jane Silver

Halloween in Taiohae Bay

shoved up one's arse. The first time I crossed the equator, at the age of eleven, I was on board a passenger ship travelling from Australia to Britain. My father took part in a competition in which men sat facing each other astride a greasy pole laid across the swimming pool and whacked each other with balloons until the loser fell in the water. Now I know what that game symbolized.

I managed a feeble 'Land ahoy!' on sighting the faint outline of the mist-encircled peak of Isla San Cristóbal. The Galapagos archipelago was officially discovered by a Bishop of Panama in 1535 when his ship was swept off course. Over the years it has been a whaling centre, a penal colony – and a hideout for pirates. By the 1680s, buccaneers such as William Dampier, Edward Davis, and Ambrose Cowley (who first charted the islands) had based themselves in the Galapagos and were regularly sacking the coastal towns of Ecuador and Peru. When we sailed past Buccaneer's Cove on Santiago, it was easy to imagine them hiding out in its well-protected bay and launching attacks on passing Peruvian galleons stuffed to the brim with Inca gold.

We pulled into a fuelling dock on a flat and arid part of the island of Baltra. The air was crisp and the wind chilly. Four enormous oval fuel storage tanks and a modern lighthouse dwarfed an assortment of container sheds and shipping offices. Beside us bounced a grimy turquoise and white fishing vessel, stuffed with nets, floats and oilcans, its main aft deck space taken up with two enormous refrigerated lockers. I leaned over the starboard rail and watched half a dozen sea lions basking on a small pontoon, flapping their tails languidly and warming themselves in the dwindling sun. Baltra was bathed in a harsh, metallic sunset that softened to a peach rosiness over the silhouettes of Daphne Major and Daphne Minor, a duet of crater-topped islets to the west. We shall all set foot on dry earth tomorrow.

Wednesday 15 September 2004

The Captain and I went to the tiny, tourist-targeted airport this morning to pick up Scarlett and her tutor Kim, arriving from the Ecuadorian mainland. We sat in the cafeteria, shooing off a pack of Darwin's damn finches that were trying to scavenge crumbs on our table. My daughter emerged first, towering over her petite, twenty-eight-year-old Chinese–Filipina teacher. Kim is smart with gamine features and a child-like quality that inspires people to take care of her – a bit like Fanny. Once they were settled in aboard the *Takapuna*, we met our Galapagos Park naturalist and dive guide, Luis (nicknamed Champi after an unfortunate haircut that made his head resemble a champignon), and began our tour of the Park.

The Galapagos National Park was created in 1959 to celebrate the centenary of the publication of Charles Darwin's *On the Origin of Species*. We were shocked when Champi told us that they were closing the place down. The Galapagos Islands are beset with political problems, he said, and many people here question whether the Park can be saved. Illegal fishermen and those who are in their pocket are gaining a foothold and, since the Ecuadorian government seems apathetic, the fragile eco-system is unlikely to be sustained.

'If even the Galapagos cannot be kept pristine,' sighed Champi, 'there is no hope for the world.'

The animals here are fearless because they have no predators. 'But don't touch them,' said Champi. 'They will come to you.' Stepping off the dinghy in North Seymour for our first hike, we found ourselves in the midst of a group of sleepy, black marine iguanas, hunched around lava rock pools. One of them spat at Rolle, but Champi explained that was neither an aggressive nor defensive gesture, just, well, a biological need to spit. It's actually more like a sneeze, he said, designed to remove excess salt from their diet. Colossal, sandy-brown sea lions were everywhere, sprawled out on the path before us, snoozing and warming themselves. Huge, gold-orange, 'smiling' land iguanas posed on high volcanic rocks, while small mockingbirds pecked at parasites and foraged for cactus pads. None of the animals bothered to move away from us, so we tiptoed round them in single file. It was astounding to see blue-footed boobies trusting us to be so close.

We walked within a few feet of nesting frigate birds, the pirates of the Galapagos winged community. They position themselves close to nesting boobies so they can sneak food from them right in the very act of feeding their young. Inept at catching fish (because their wings won't stand a soaking), they survive by being thieves and rascals. They are not beyond grabbing a booby in mid-air by its tail-tip and shaking it until it regurgitates its food. It was amusing to see a colony of single male frigate birds, each with a puffed-up, scarlet pouch beneath his beak, gazing skywards in the hope of attracting a female. I imagined it would be hard for them to fly with big red party balloons under their beaks, but we saw some managing it. We even saw fathers sitting on nests while mothers searched for food – a co-operative style of parenting that went unnoticed by Darwin. Of course, he was a Victorian gentleman seeing the natural world through a nineteenth-century filter.

On Genovesa, an arid island north of Baltra, we immediately encountered a living shag-carpet of hundreds of marine iguanas warming themselves right on our path. The wrinkled reptiles like to stretch themselves as flat as possible to expose the maximum back area to the sun. There were so many of them, and they were so well camouflaged against the dark, speckled rocks, I was afraid I might step on one. Above Prince Philip's Steps, a wide staircase of broken lava on the southwest side of the island, the sky was spattered with storm petrels, soaring and swooping above a wild, white-water sea. Below them, a short-eared owl with beautiful brown-gold colouring lay in wait for a petrel to make the mistake of venturing too close. In swirling water off-shore, boobies dive-bombed their targets, sometimes a

whole flock of them plummeting vertically in unison. By
comparison, a couple of neighbouring pelicans seemed third-
rate divers, managing only the clumsiest of belly-flops.

Under the sea we encountered round-eyed, yellow-bellied
triggerfish, schools of silver jack mackerel and polka-dotted
pufferfish. A bumpy-skinned scorpion fish was colour-
coordinated purple and pink with the rocks on which it rested.
Scarlett glimpsed a shy hammerhead shark and a spotted eagle
ray. Oversized, azure parrotfish flashed by, while on the sea bed
slid bright violet starfish. Fantastic.

I was unprepared to be so moved by this archipelago. On
Thursday, while snorkelling at Cousins Rock off San Salvador
Island, we were joined by a group of seven rambunctious young
sea lions who played with us for thirty minutes, while a large
white bull below us fed sullenly on fish he shooed from their
hiding places in the rocky wall. A green turtle was foraging for
food in crevices several metres below the bull, flanked by a
school of crimson soldierfish. I never imagined I would find
myself in the midst of such an extraordinary creature-
community.

Saturday 18 September 2004

On the Isla Isabela's Punta Tortuga, a halved volcano decorated
with stark outcrops of lava rocks, I had a sense of having time-
travelled back aeons to drop in among life in a prehistoric era.
High above us, two grumpy male iguanas fought each other for
territory, facing off precariously on the edge of slippery cliffs. A
solitary pelican stood motionless on a wave-splashed rocky
outcrop, surrounded by orange-red sally lightfoot crabs
scuttling to and fro on the salty lava. Flightless cormorants
waddled nearby, hawks observed us from the sky, and baby sea
lions fed confidently on their dozing mothers. For the first time
I saw some marine iguana swimming – quite a comical sight,

with their heads held high out of the water, paddling furiously like dogs.

For several centuries, mariners have carved the names of their ships on the volcanic cliffs of Isla Fernandina above Caleta Tagus, a placid caldera that forms a near-perfect circle of sheltered water. Unfortunately, modern visitors have immortalised their names with paint, which looks ugly but the lake is still stunning. We hiked up the volcano to its highest point and were surprised to look down on an inner caldera, Darwin's Lake, separated from the outer one by a very narrow strip of land. Charles Darwin is said to have run down from the volcano, eager for a sip of fresh water, only to be disappointed by its brackish taste. There is no entryway for the sea, so the phenomenon of salt water is thought to have been caused by a tidal wave splashing over the dividing land strip just a couple of hundred years ago.

Gazing down on the *Takapuna*, lying all by herself in the indigo caldera, I thought of my initial dream of having a sailing boat; yet I never imagined it would bring me somewhere like this. I am almost numb with the enchantment of the Galapagos, unable to take it all in, and I'm not the only one. After we returned to the *Takapuna*, I caught Evan writing in his journal with tears in his eyes.

'That was probably the best thing I've seen in my whole life,' he said.

A ship of fools came by late this afternoon – a permitted fishing boat loaded with men who actually wanted to barter their fresh-caught lobster for chicken. Hardly believing her luck, Kayt exchanged a box of chicken fingers for fourteen large lobsters. We ate a fantastic meal, while sea lions zoomed around us in the starlight, then finished the evening off with a spooky night dive. The strangest things move about down there in the dark at sixty feet – nudibranchs shaped like short, waving tubes; pale needlefish, translucent gobies and huge white starfish. Frogfish crouched on the bottom, their monstrous eyes fixed imperiously

upon us. Dick reached out too close to a small electric stingray
and received a nasty zap. Pausing for a safety stop on the way up
to the surface, we turned off our torches and 'had a rave', as Kayt
put it, in the phosphorescence – slow-motion, aqua disco-dancing
amid millions of bioluminescent bubbles of light.

Tuesday 21 September 2004

In a northeast bay on Santa Fe Island there are many sea lion
harems protected by large, territorial bulls that can turn quite
nasty if they mistake you for a single male insurgent, attempting
to reach their females. During our snorkel among some young
sea lions this morning, Evan failed to follow the rules about
sticking together. He became separated from the group for an
instant, pausing to take an underwater photograph of an
enormous, bumpy-headed bull – that immediately went after
him and sunk its teeth into his backside.

Evan stuck his head out of the water. 'Hey!' he gurgled. 'That
fucker bit me!'

Champi was trying out our underwater video camera at the
time, so he actually captured the moment in moving pictures.
Naturally, the episode was replayed over and over again for the
amusement of all. Jock dressed Evan's wound, and informed
him that, luckily, he would have only a small scar. Evan was
openly disappointed; he would have preferred a sizable war
wound, an eyesore that would not fail to be noticed by all his
friends back home, and lead to the telling and retelling of his
painful encounter.

Our afternoon walk, amid a landscape of prickly pear, white-
flowered carpetweed, and the pod-hung acacia, led us to a sea
lion bachelors' colony. Here the ferocity of male competition was
particularly evident, as exhausted, bleeding, battle-scared males
cowered in shady bowers, resting-up for the inevitable violence
of their next harem invasion. Inspecting their wounds, we

realized that Evan got off very lightly; a really savage bite from one of those aggressors can do some serious damage. In the aftermath of his attack, Evan has earned the nickname 'Bait'. He was not the only casualty of our underwater adventures, for today, diving in strong currents, Kim was caught in an upward surge that swept her up some twenty feet – a dangerously fast ascent. Kayt managed to drag her down, but she was very shaken. This is definitely a place for experienced divers.

Every island on the archipelago has its own distinctive features. On Santa Fe there are a great many prickly pear cacti, between 100 and 300 years old. They have adapted along with the indigenous, long-necked 'saddle-back' tortoises, so they have evolved bare trunks with leaves just out of reach for all but the 'fittest' of the tortoises. On the top of one cactus tree sat a massive female hawk.

'Those birds practise polyandry,' said Champi.

'What does that mean?' said Scarlett.

'The females are in charge and can choose as many partners as they wish,' he explained.

'I think I'll come back as one of them,' said Kayt.

Friday 24 September 2004

Champi and Dick took Scarlett and me for an extreme dive at a phenomenal site called Gordon's Rock. On our approach, the sea's surface was uninviting; choppy, dark and murky. To avoid being immediately swept away by the current we were forced to descend very fast, to a depth of over a hundred feet, right into the middle of a gigantic bait ball that was vibrating violently within a sunken volcanic crater. It was an extraordinary micro-universe, a pulsing mixture of feeding sea life, composed of schools of tiny minnows being dive-bombed by boobies and penguins from above, while turtles attacked them from each side. At the same time, sea lions attacked the snapper and wrasse that came to feed on the minnows. It was an awesome sight. We became one with the bait ball, diving and darting around it, ignored by the creatures within who were bent only on survival.

Rising up from the bottom of the crater were three underwater pinnacles and the current ripped though the chasms at a terrifying pace. Holding our regulators to prevent them from being whipped out of our mouths, we negotiated our way past schools of hammerhead sharks, yellowtail snapper and king angelfish. The site certainly lived up to its local name of *La Lavadora* (the washing machine), but every now and again we managed to halt for a minute or two, clinging to a piece of rock, to gape at the extraordinary wealth of sea life. A turbo-charged sea turtle almost kissed Scarlett. We are elated to have experienced such wonders.

En route to Santa Cruz we stood on the stern applauding as giant manta rays did back flips in the air beyond our wake, landing with resounding thwacks. Champi says they do that to slough off tiny, unwanted creatures that attach themselves to their skin. Later this afternoon, after we anchored in Academy Bay, Jock was driving in to the landing stage when a small ray back-flipped right next to the dinghy, nearly landing beside him on the seat.

Champi is getting married tomorrow. I had fun at his stag night, at which all the women wore men's clothing and painted-on moustaches. I drank way too much tequila, then salsa-danced furiously for hours with the local people. I think I shocked the crew.

Saturday 25 September 2004

It's many years since I had a hangover and this one's a beauty. Serves me right. I'm contrite today, but not too much so. Anyway, in the aftermath, the teenagers have decided to take salsa lessons, which I am wholeheartedly encouraging. After all, they could be somewhere in downtown Los Angeles doing crack.

Carl, a stocky American southerner, arrived from Florida to check and tune the rigging. He and some of the crew went for a sail and cranked the *Takapuna* up to fourteen knots. I took Scarlett, Evan, Daragh and Kim inland, to hike through underground lava tunnels and a giant tortoise reserve. Meanwhile, Kayt went for a snorkel with a local man whose idea of a date was novel: a fantastic close encounter with sea lions, rays, dolphins and turtles.

'I was so overcome, I felt like snogging him,' she said.

Visiting the Darwin Institute the next day, we found it under siege. Illegal fishermen had turned up with weapons in hand, so the place was being guarded by police in riot gear, while fifty or so Park Rangers were staging a sit-down demonstration against the corruption that threatens the Park. The situation looks very serious. We sat and observed the stand-off for a while, while Evan, wearing an 80s Nike hat, was interviewed for Ecuadorian television. Holding forth in his best Spanish, he offered his views on the developing scene. Unfortunately, being a Californian rebel, he mistook the police for the bad guys, thus hampering the fight for conservation – which was not his intention.

We were still able to visit the Institute. The teenagers were particularly taken with Lonesome George, the very elderly Galapagos land tortoise who is the last of his sub-species. Females from closely related sub-species have been provided to mate with him, but he doesn't fancy them. He does look pretty forlorn. Evan is down in the dumps, too. He has been rationed from his preferred three bowls of cereal per day, because of the amount of milk he consumes along with it. Today he went ashore and bought a whole gallon of milk which he stuck in the fridge labelled 'Evan's milk'. That did not go down too well. The process of having to live in an egalitarian fashion with others is a steep learning curve for him. It seems he's never done his own laundry before, nor been asked to wash dishes with any kind of regularity. He is eager to learn, though, and even showed an interest in sewing when he saw me working on a curtain that will be erected above the stairwell leading to the saloon. Previously, that communal space could not be used at night during sea-voyages, because light bled above to the navigation station and ruined the watch-keeper's night-vision. With an effective blackout, people who are not doing chores will be able to congregate for a movie , play games, or read at one of the side tables.

Wednesday 29 September 2004

We're leaving tomorrow at 3 pm. I bought a nice fat tuna in town and we barbecued it for dinner. The prospect of three weeks at sea led to a party atmosphere on deck tonight, with beers, laughter and terrible stories. Carl turned out to be the kind of party animal who performs set pieces and one of them was actually a Billy Connolly joke. I still found it funny.

At lunch ashore, I talked to Scarlett and Kim over tostadas and guacamole. 'This is quite a journey we're about to undertake,' I said.

'I know,' said Scarlett. 'We're going to be further away from other people than anyone else on the planet – except astronauts in space.' I was astonished. I hadn't known that exactly. But, yes, nine days out of the Galapagos we will be 1,500 miles from the nearest landfall; that's as far from civilization as one can get anywhere in the world. There will be few other vessels along the way. No coastguards, no rescue boats.

'So,' I continued, 'we're all in it together. You and I are essentially passengers, but none of that matters out there in the ocean. We all have to help. We must work hard, do our duties, and support everyone. That's how we survive. No shirking, no princesses.' I said it as much for myself as for them. Compared to most others on board I was spoiled, cushioned, accustomed to comfort. The restaurant music system was playing Eric Clapton's 'Layla'. Scarlett's middle name had been chosen after that very song. I looked at her and tears came into my eyes. She was really just a baby. I knew she was enjoying this adventure, but what if something terrible happened? It was unthinkable. I used to have a dream about drowning at sea and being unable to save my children. But there is no turning back now.

Travelling across America with Belle may have prepared Fanny for a journey that would put another of her children at risk. By the time Fanny was thirty-five years old, having borne Sam two more children, Lloyd and Hervey, and after years of putting up with his unfaithfulness, she left him. She and Belle had attended the San Francisco School of Design, where she was taught by an inspirational teacher, Virgil Williams. Her thirst for self-development had become intense. Her time under Williams's tutelage changed her profoundly, to the extent that she decided to become an artist and study at one of the great schools of Europe. In April 1875, when Belle was sixteen, Lloyd seven and Hervey only four, Fanny set off with them for Belgium. She intended to study at the Academy of Painting in Antwerp, but on arrival she discovered the school did not admit women. Disappointed, she stayed with friends and began to search for alternatives. In the meantime, Hervey contracted a fever. His baffled doctor suggested Fanny take him to a paediatrician in Paris and, under the French doctor's care, he immediately improved. In Paris, Fanny enrolled herself and Belle in the Julian Academy but, before long, little Hervey became seriously ill again, with what was probably scrofulous tuberculosis. Fanny nursed him constantly but he deteriorated over four ensuing months. On 1 March 1876, she sent a cable to Sam: 'Impossible to move Hervey. Come at any price. Come quickly.'

Fanny's decision to take her children to Europe was roundly criticized. It was the kind of decision that contemporary women make with impunity, but in those days the idea of a mother seeking personal growth – or even fleeing a society where she has been publicly humiliated by her husband – was considered selfish and destructive. In April 1876, Fanny received a letter from a long-time friend, Timothy Rearden in San Francisco:

Dear Mrs Osbourne,
This is what happens when a woman, a mother, goes gallivanting around like a young girl! If you had stayed sensibly at home as I advised, none of this would have happened. What an idea, to drag your children around on such an adventure. And now, you've been in Paris for five months, without any money, with a sick little boy whom you cannot care for . . . A fine thing. Hervey must have caught a cold, if not some contagious illness in Belgium or on the boat. Let this be a lesson to you!

    You thought you were being strong to leave your country when you were merely being irresponsible. Between us, my dear, whatever happens you've got it coming. You have confused courage with lack of conscience, and this blindness has cost you dear. Stop your nonsense, then, and save your children.

Dear Mr Rearden,
. . . In one letter you told me to cut my baby's curls and try to make him more of a boy like Sammy. I cut off the yellow curls, and that is all I have left of my pretty boy. You thought him not as manly as Sammy because of his pretty face and the yellow curls. There never was a boy so brave. His death was hideous and a continual torture, and his appearance was so dreadful that strangers could not look upon him, and Sam was afraid of him . . . And my poor brave boy, for he became very precocious in dying, tried to comfort his father, patting his bent head with his little hand, and smiling such a smile that I pray no human being may ever have the terror and misery of beholding.

I did not dare leave him, because every few hours he bled in a new place . . . I only wish he had been unconscious. His bones had cut through the skin and lay bare, and yet there was no word of complaint through it all. The only thing he asked for was that he might see the sky and grass once more, and we both watched every morning eagerly for the bright warm day when it was promised that his father would carry him out to ride.

One awful day I smelled blood and could not find it. I looked all day, my boy growing weaker all the time but I could not find it. At night I burned all the front off my hair looking at his throat with a candle but I could find nothing; he was bleeding internally. He asked that his father should sing a song that he heard long ago. Once he woke and said, 'Lie down with me.' After that he never spoke again.

His father tried to comfort me by saying that he died so peacefully, but I heard him cry, a dreadful moaning cry, just before he died, my brave boy who had never cried before through it all. I knew then that he was dying and that the cry was involuntary. He never would have cried like that if he had known that I heard it. There is no comfort for me; there can be none but to give me back my child.

The weather changed and the first bright day my boy went out to ride as I had promised him, but he rode alone and never came back . . .

He bade everybody goodbye. It is too cruel that my child should die. They try to comfort me by telling me that he is better where he lies, that he would have been deaf and dumb and probably deformed, had he lived. That only makes me feel that he must be tired lying so long on his back, and that I must dig him up and turn him over. Then they talk to me of heaven; what sort of a heaven would it be for my baby alone, without his mother.

Fanny M.O.

I cannot even imagine what it must be like to lose a child, yet I am about to take my youngest daughter to the furthest no-land point on Earth.

Thursday 30 September, 2004

I woke to the news that the plane bringing the rest of our provisions from Guayaquil has been delayed twenty-four hours. Then I heard some of the crew talking about sailors' superstitions. Apparently it's bad luck that we now have to leave port on a Friday.

'Anybody got a St Christopher on them?' asked the Captain, who obviously didn't know the former saint had been demoted. I realized then that he is actually superstitious himself. That must be why the banana bunches remained lashed to the backstays, barely on board.

Peter, an American electronics expert, is still repairing our system, handicapped by the fact that he has managed to drop his only pair of spectacles overboard. Dick and Kayt donned diving gear and searched round for them on the sea bed, but saw only a couple of pufferfish chewing the barnacles growing on our bow.

On Friday there was a lot of furious, last-minute deck-work and the filling of four fuel bladders that will see us through to the Marquesas. Daragh was struggling, having injured his hand when he caught it in a hatch. Jock announced that it was probably broken, and has splinted it accordingly.

I watched Evan take a fuel pipe forward. He seems more confident, focused and aware than he did two weeks ago, his body less awkward moving round the boat. His hair is getting longer, to the point where it is now in his eyes. Come to think of it, everyone's hair is getting long, including mine.

'Could you cut my hair in a mullet?' Evan asked me.

'This boat is a mullet-free zone,' I replied firmly. Although I admit to having sported it in the eighties, the short on top, long at the back look now repulses me. When the provisions arrived at 11 am, the girls and Daragh set to work wrapping cabbages, melons and giant papaya in brown paper, and labelling them with a thick black pen. I disappeared below to organize my cabin while it was still relatively calm, then heard the anchors going at around 1 pm. While I was working, Kim stuck her head in my door.

'The Captain suggests you come on deck and say goodbye to the last land we'll be seeing for a long, long time.' I obeyed. My watch began at 2 pm, so for the next four hours I enjoyed the last views of the archipelago, first sunlit, then rain-drenched. Later it was shrouded in mist, then golden with a late-afternoon glow, and finally bathed in sunset rays. We observed one last manta ray flipping far off our starboard side.

'Dey must be vewy happy fish,' Rolle gurgled, 'yust trowing demselves up in de air all de time. Whee!' He disappeared for a while, then I found him in the galley doing a little dance, wearing four pairs of headphones at varying positions around his head. Just before Scarlett went off watch at 10 pm, the last, eerie little settlement on Isla Isabela winked a final farewell as we disappeared into the darkest, black-cloud night I'd ever known.

CHAPTER FIVE

FIRE!

02°01.3′ S
092°27.7′ W

Sunday 3 October 2004

We're having a competition to guess the time and date of our arrival in the Marquesas Islands. We're also vying to predict the most and fewest number of miles covered on any one day, the number of fish we manage to land and how many vessels we'll sight along the way. There's a hundred bucks riding on it, so people are eagerly calculating fuel consumption, wind direction and speed, and allowing for fishing stops. According to the Captain, the ocean currents are flowing in our favour, which should add around one knot to our average speed per day. The breezes will also sweeten our time, with a probable average of sixteen knots of true wind. With a total distance of 3,000 miles, and figuring that our daily average speed will be around eight to nine knots, I reckon we'll cover an average of 200 miles per day and that we'll arrive on 17 October at 5 pm. Most people, however, believe I'm overly optimistic, especially concerning my estimate of forty-two landed fish and four sighted vessels.

Today I caved in on my earlier stance and gave Evan a mullet haircut. The execution of this reviled eighties look was quite challenging, since Dick insisted my barber shop be located on deck and down wind, to avoid hitting everyone at the helm with flying hairballs. Scarlett watched from the corner of the pilot house, aghast to see her mother doing something so wicked. I had never cut a person's hair before, let alone in a mullet style, but Evan seemed quite pleased with the result, and immediately adopted a 'trailer-trash' character.

'My ma gets off work from the dancehall at five.' His southern accent was terrible, but his performance brought out the snob in us all.

Fanny, too, loved to reinvent herself. But when she took Belle and Lloyd to the Hôtel Chevillon in the French village of Grez, known as an artists' summer retreat, she immediately captured the admiration of the other guests for being exactly who she was: an alluring woman of the New World. Fanny reclined attractively on a swinging garden swing, surrounded by a lively group of devotees that included two brilliant Scottish cousins, Bob and Louis Stevenson.

Monday 4 October 2004

Rolle's been working intently in the pilot house for a few hours, trying to install an on-deck stereo machine. Suddenly, I heard him scream, 'It's a beautiful thing!' at the top of his voice.

'Why?' I inquired.

'I was asking God for twelve volts,' he said, 'and He yust sent me down de connection!' Soon Outkast was blaring all over the cockpit.

We had plenty of wind today, enough to sail without the engine. I love our days of pure sailing; no noise, just a gentle port tack with the sun over our starboard bow.

'Does it get any better than this?' I asked Dick.

'Not much,' he grinned.

'How did I ever get away with it?' I asked myself for the

billionth time, stretching out on deck and allowing the *Takapuna* to rock me closer and closer to Fanny's first South Seas island.

Tonight, with our new sound system, we had a dance-party on deck. We bopped to Prince, Crowded House and Blondie. Oh yeah, we're an eclectic group, musically speaking. Just when I was shaking my tail-feathers rather exuberantly, the Captain appeared on deck and had the gall to address me as the Queen of Hubba Hubba. I was not amused.

I discovered that he joined the navy at eighteen and came out at twenty-three. 'I missed a lot of things, being in a submarine,' he mused, 'Bob Dylan, Watergate . . .'

I imagine that affected his love relationships. I mean, who would have wanted to go out with a man who asked, 'Ringo who?'

There were contrasting perceptions between Fanny and Louis when they first met. His wife-to-be was introduced to him as a tragic, bereaved mother; and she was eager to save another ailing little boy. Not that Louis was immature, just child-like in the manner of many invalids who have, of necessity, been cosseted all their lives. Some say that it was Bob, Louis's cousin, to whom Fanny was initially attracted. She was certainly aware of his striking looks, extraordinary talent and engaging conversation. But on a deeper level, when she and Louis met, 'love at first sight' may be too corny a way to put it, but it was a fait accompli. Deep in their respective psyches, they complemented each other's woundedness. They were bound to be together, once a few minor details were overcome: her husband, her children, her age, his parents, and his friends.

It wasn't too hard. She divorced her husband and he befriended her children. He pretended she was only ten years older than him, not eleven. It sounded better. Fanny even managed to seduce his parents; after all, they were glad to see someone taking good care of him. But his friends – ah, that was a different story. To this day, there is echoing disapproval from 'friends' he never even knew: that she was not good for him, that she drove wedges between him and others, that she was beneath him, temperamental, a hypochondriac, a plagiarist, a liar. Whatever Fanny's faults, and she was far from perfect, she managed to nurse Louis devotedly *and* avoided being absorbed into his shadow. And who, among her critics, could stand having their lives held up to such intense scrutiny and emerge spotless?

Tuesday 5 October 2004

Early this morning, I found an entire shoal of flying fish lying dead on the forward deck, with staring, frightened eyes. Something huge and predatory had terrified them during the night, so they'd leapt into the air and landed on a death-bed of warm teak. In my family there is a story about one of my great-uncles who was blinded by a flying fish while standing on the bridge of his ship. I always thought it was a myth, but now I'm not so sure. Since we first set sail I have often seen the winged, azure-bodied creatures, skimming high above the waves for three, four, five seconds at a time.

Kayt held an open cookery school in the galley today. Scarlett, Kim, Daragh and Evan turned up and were made to scrub their hands and put on aprons before creating a very good apple crumble. Just when a sweet, homely aroma was permeating the saloon, Daragh had a phone call from his mother in Ireland to say his sister had been injured in a car crash. It is hard to hear such news at sea. I imagine his large, close-knit Dublin family is sorely missing him. When he left Ireland for Florida last summer the airport scene he described had all the makings of a modern-day version of the dockside 'wakes' Irish people used to have in the eighteenth century, when their loved ones left for the New World. Daragh has earned his place in the crew – he's a hard-working boy with a cheerful disposition. Dick says he has beautiful, knot-tying hands – and, fortunately, the one he broke has mended well. Tonight on watch, Daragh summoned us all on deck to see a pod of dolphin leaping through our bioluminescent bow wake, sending showers of sparkling foam whooshing into the night air. What sights he's seeing for a seventeen-year-old!

One of our fuel bladders has now been fully drained. It is a relief when one is emptied, for there's always the risk of its bursting, rather like human plumbing. The swell is increasing. I awoke in the morning to find myself being thrown around my cabin. I've got so many bruises already, though, new ones will make little difference. Trying to shower was like being caught in a fast-cycle washing machine. Once again, there's no wind, just a huge swell. Everyone has been suffering: Scarlett trying to do schoolwork without throwing up, Kim trying to tutor her without throwing up and Kayt trying to cook fish in white wine sauce in the heeling galley without throwing up – God knows why, because no one wants to eat.

I must say, I enjoy being in the galley when it's rough. If you high-jump at exactly the right moment, you can have a zero-gravity experience. Sometimes we put on socks and slide up and down the entire beam, or width of the boat, as it rolls back and forth. I was doing that today when Rolle suddenly opened a floor hatch right underneath my path, nearly creating a perfect pantomime trap-door disappearance.

My computer belly-flopped on the floor during the night, but it seems to have survived undamaged. I was typing on deck when Rolle walked by, saying something in Swedish.

'What does that mean?' I asked.

'It shines de light of working spirit.' That sounded nice. Then Scarlett appeared to do her daily check of our surroundings. Standing in the middle of the aft deck, hands on hips, she mutters, 'What can we see today?' then turns herself round in a circle, stopping once at each quarter-turn while she points at the sea and answers her own question: 'Water – water – water –

water.' She landed a tuna this afternoon, bringing our fish count to eight. The rod holder belt looked a little out of place over her miniskirt, but the boys didn't seem to mind.

Sailing into the late afternoon sun, a fine, gold, silken tablecloth of reflected sunlight was spread out from our bow, over a slate under-cloth. It undulated all the way to the horizon, where its edge gave way to a fine-powder haze. Off our starboard side it was a different story. Dissident currents swept the seascape into an uneven crisscrossing of liquid mountains, some milky-topped, some peaking sharply then valleying in a deeper hue. I was lost in this glory when our autopilot broke.

Thursday 7 October 2004

Another horribly bumpy night. I got very little sleep and rose late. Scarlett, on the other hand, was up early and working on her Spanish.

The autopilot cannot be fixed at sea, so we have to hand-steer the boat. All Takapunians will have to take turns during their four-hour watches. It's more complicated than I thought, a bit like flying a helicopter: watching direction and rudder at the same time, balancing it all with the swell and anticipating the boat's movement. It requires such intense focusing I can only manage twenty minutes at a time. The kids, however, picked it up immediately. To them it's just a video game. I'm enormously impressed with Scarlett, who can steer perfectly accurately with her feet while reclining on the helm chair.

Not having a working autopilot is worrying and inconvenient, but I'm secretly glad to learn how it was done aboard the *Casco*. No wonder Captain Otis had to plead with Fanny not to distract the helmsman.

'Today, Mrs Stevenson,' he said, 'I want him to *steer*.' Now I understand how difficult she must have made his job, especially if she did so when the swell or heavy seas were pulling the boat off course.

Today we spotted our first passing ship, a 200-foot fishing vessel some distance off to starboard. Shortly after it appeared on our radar, an American voice came over our emergency channel: 'Enjoying your sail?'

Their Captain chatted to ours for a while. He's usually at sea for sixteen weeks, with twenty-one people on board. He mentioned they'd recently come upon a ghost vessel, a de-masted sailboat with no lifeboat attached, just drifting in the ocean a few miles from our present position. That was sobering.

When they came within half a mile of us, their Captain called again to ask if we wanted any fish. Oh, yeah! It was too choppy to put out our lines today. Two men came screeching over in a powerboat tender – unkempt, crazy people, in a ten-foot swell. A rugged, hairy man in a checked shirt was waving a giant tuna in the air, like a lasso. I thought at first they might be pirates.

They dinged our hull a few times before they managed to hurl the tuna, a wahoo and a massive swordfish on board. Rolle performed some excellent ice-hockey moves, catching the slippery frozen fish like a determined goalie. Rather reluctantly, he reciprocated by handing down a case of beer, at Kayt's insistence.

'Dat's all wery vell,' he scowled, 'but ve can always catch fish ourselves. Dere's no beer in de ocean.'

Nevertheless, after staring thoughtfully at his enormous frozen 'catch', he nodded to himself then let out a little, 'Hmmm.' He disappeared down to the engine room and returned wielding a chainsaw. Grinning gleefully, he proceeded to hack up the fish into freezer-sized portions, sending showers of tiny icicles on to appalled onlookers.

As we moved on, there was disagreement over whether, for the purposes of our competition, the fishing vessel and tender counted as one or two boats. Naturally, I advocated for treating the powerboat as a separate entity. Then there was the matter of the three fish, which had technically been 'landed' and 'caught' by Rolle. The argument over the fine points continues.

The swell did not let up all day, yet the sunset was clear of cloud so we watched for a green flash at the final moment. The crew is divided about the voracity of the elusive green flash – an atmospheric phenomenon apparently caused by sunlight refraction, occasionally seen just as the last portion of the sun sinks below a sharp horizon. Some say they've seen one in the past and others say it's baloney. I think that if you stare long enough at the setting sun, especially in the tropics, you're bound to see something odd while your retina is frying.

Our bananas are ripening faster than we can eat them, so Kayt made a very good banana pie. After dinner, the girls and I watched *Gosford Park* in the saloon. It was strange to see people engaged in such high-context social behaviour. From our point of view, out here in the middle of the ocean, even the less-mannered culture of modern city life seems asinine. Meanwhile, the boys were around the galley table, glued to *Sex and the City*.

'Well, they're getting an education of sorts, I suppose,' I said to Kayt when we wandered in for a cup of tea.

'Which one do you like best?' I asked the boys.

'The dark one,' answered Jock immediately.

'The blonde,' said Dick, ''cos she's easy.'

'Well, I'd go out with any one of them,' said Evan enthusiastically, only faltering as all eyes turned amusedly in his direction, 'at least, if I ever had the opportunity to . . .'

'I don't think you have to worry about that,' said Dick unkindly.

'Well yeah,' agreed Evan, 'I mean, it wouldn't be legal for any of them . . .'

Fanny's being considerably older than Louis did not mean that her role in their relationship was limited to that of nurse and mother-figure. Fanny was sexy. She liked to flirt, and was an expert seductress. At a time when women had little power to shape their own destinies by any other means, she had taken full advantage of the puissance afforded by her sexuality. The time she and Louis spent together when they first met in Grez, and then in Paris where they presumably shared a bed, was clearly a lovers' awakening, and a blissful period of temporary intimacy – before Fanny was forced to keep her promise to return to Sam. Louis railed against her going and Fanny probably knew better than to take an action so contrary to her heart's desire; nevertheless she removed Belle from the amorous attentions of an Irish painter named Frank O'Meara and dutifully took the steamer back to East Oakland. There, once again living in Sam's cottage, she deteriorated both physically and mentally, not just because of the loss of Louis's presence in her life, but because Sam was spending most of his time with a mistress while she was in the throes of a painful mother–daughter conflict with Belle.

Much has been made of Fanny's 'little bouts of brain fever', as she called them. From the sound of her symptoms, she had probably entered a deep depression, at times even bordering on psychosis. It's really not surprising, given her impossible circumstances. Depression is frequently instigated by loss and, at this point, Fanny had lost everything she held dear – Hervey to his illness, Louis by necessity, Belle through her emerging sexuality and adulthood, and Sam through his infidelity and rejection of her. Her dream of becoming a painter was gone, too, and her self-esteem was dwindling.

There was depression, even suicide, in Fanny's family, which may have meant she had a genetic predisposition to mood swings; but one must also consider her mental state in the context of Victorian society. Its rigid demands of propriety left her trapped by Sam and unable to move forward into a happy life with the man she loved. When she was at her worst, she telegraphed Louis. His reply cheered and sustained her: 'Hold tight. I will be with you in one month.' Against his friends' advice, he scraped together just enough funds to travel steerage among the emigrants to New York, then across the continent by train to Monterey. The trip cost him dearly, for as a result he faced a life-threatening health crisis. Racked with malaria, eczema, pleurisy, malnutrition and severe toothache, he arrived on Fanny's doorstep on 30 August 1877, fifteen pounds lighter than she'd last seen him. It was the evening of Sam's regular weekend visit, so she was forced to send her lover away to a nearby guest house.

When Fanny asked her old friend Timothy Rearden, who had become a successful lawyer, to manage her divorce, Rearden insisted that she and Louis must keep a respectable distance from each other until after the case was settled. Sam, who had publicly humiliated Fanny countless times, agreed to the divorce provided he was not embarrassed by Fanny's liaison with Louis. Thus, for many months, Fanny was unable to care for Louis as she wished. That, too, nearly cost him his life, for he could barely even manage to sustain himself with food. At one point he was rescued by the proprietor of a local restaurant. When he failed to turn up for his regular daily meal two days in a row, the man went to Louis's lodgings, broke down his door and found him feverish and delirious. After that, Fanny managed to nurse him in secret for a while, then once the divorce was finalized, she threw propriety out the window and moved him into Sam's cottage.

'I want to be married,' wrote Louis, despite his father's threats to disinherit him if he attached himself to Fanny '. . . The only question is whether I shall be alive for the ceremony.' As an older divorcee and mother, Fanny was hardly the woman Louis's parents had envisaged as a daughter-in-law.

Nevertheless, Louis and Fanny managed to tie the knot in San Francisco on 19 May 1880, and were thankful that Louis' father relented and provided him with an annual income. For the next four years, the newlyweds traipsed round Europe in search of climates, physicians and sanatoriums that might improve Louis's condition. During that time, he wrote some of his best-known works: *Treasure Island, A Child's Garden of Verses, Prince Otto* and *The New Thousand and One Nights*. From 1884 until 1887 they settled in Bournemouth, England. There, Louis produced *Dr Jekyll and Mr Hyde*. After he had completed the first manuscript, Fanny criticised it so roundly that he might have thrown it on the fire.

'It is a magnificent piece of sensationalism,' she said. 'You have completely missed the allegory!'

Louis shut himself away to completely rewrite the story in six days – as the masterpiece that was subsequently published.

Fanny suited Louis in so many ways, as lover, nurse, protector, accomplice, writer, painter, gardener, cook, conversationalist, fellow bohemian, and adventurer. Can anyone really doubt that she was a positive force in Louis's life? She may have alienated his friends by whisking him home early from literati dinners to fend off exhaustion, but she kept him alive. She may have insisted that any visitor must first show the contents of his handkerchief through the window to prove he was not suffering from contagion, but she kept him alive. She may have been Louis's harshest literary critic from time to time, but she kept him alive.

After four years of marriage, Louis wrote to his mother:

My wife is in pretty good feather. I love her better than ever and admire her more; and I cannot think what I have done to deserve so good a gift . . . my marriage has been the most successful in the world . . . she is everything to me; wife, brother, sister, daughter, my dear companion; and I would not change to get a goddess or a saint.

Friday 8 October 2004

I was still in my bunk when I woke this morning, so I must have had a better night. Kayt and I went on to the foredeck early, to have a sneaky workout. Scarlett had brought an Arnold Schwarzenegger workout tape on board for a laugh. We thought we were unobserved, but in the middle of our leg-lifts, Rolle's voice suddenly boomed out over the loudspeaker.

'Arnold says: "Lift dos legs HIGHER!"'

A few minutes later both fishing reels whirred together. Jock took the port rod while I raced to starboard. The mahimahi on my rod was a fighter, so Kayt helped me wind. When my arms began to give out I called, 'Eh, Rolle! Come and give us a few turns.' But Kayt stopped me. 'No,' she said earnestly, 'this is a chick fish.'

Afterwards, Rolle smirked, 'So vat do you tink is better, workout or fishing?'

'I need to work out so I can handle the rod,' I replied ruefully. Even Dick had trouble when he tried to land my fish with the gaff. He lost his grip and it fell over the side. He retrieved it, but two minutes after he got the monster on deck a wave came over the transom and washed it off again, along with most of the fillets he'd just cut from Jock's fish.

Kayt told me the mahimahi tend to be caught in pairs because they mate for life. Evan was aghast: 'It's like some kind of really sick Romeo and Juliet deal,' he said.

If Kayt's story is true, I wonder what mechanism causes a fish to commit suicide once its partner is hooked. In human relationships, difficulties usually arise in a marriage when one partner becomes the other's caregiver. There is often unspoken resentment, as well as a longing for greater parity. Intimacy is often compromised and angry exchanges serve to avoid acknowledgement of the underlying pain and sadness. All this was true of the Stevensons. Fanny had been catapulted into a lifelong nursing role, a position I doubt she had fully anticipated. In France, Louis had been frail but full of energy, so she and the children had barely thought of him as an invalid. Once settled in Bournemouth, and feebler than before, Louis attempted to lead a busy social life with his literary acquaintances. It gave him pleasure, but denied him the rest he needed, leading to frequent haemorrhage and relapse. Then Fanny would put her foot down and stabilize him – until the next time he was goaded by his friends into late-night revelry.

The zeal with which Fanny took care of Louis had an obsessive quality. In her unconscious mind, she seems to have had a deep-seated need to re-enact her last months with Hervey, seeking another chance to 'save him'. This drove her to sacrifice her energy, her mental health and her own physical well-being, without seeking much comfort for herself. Under great pressure, she may have occasionally retreated into psychosomatic illness. Caretakers need nourishment for themselves, and it was not until much later in their relationship that Fanny finally made the healthy decision to take some breaks from Louis.

The weather in Bournemouth was far from conducive to Louis's recovery. On a visit to California, Fanny met up with

Belle, who had married a well-known painter, Joe Strong, and was now mother of a little boy named Austin. Belle's talk of the balmy atmosphere in Hawai'i, where she and Joe now lived, helped to instigate a plan. Within a few days, Fanny had wired Louis about the *Casco*'s availability, and not long after they left for the South Seas. Louis would never see Europe or North America again.

This afternoon it got rougher. The swell formed dark mountains, and a lumpy-edged horizon met a lobelia sky. I staggered into the galley where I found Evan, who seems to have eradicated his mullet, busy creating posters: 'Evan for Boat President'. Apparently we are about to have some elections.

'Be sure to give the Captain one of them,' smiled Kayt darkly.

When Rolle announced that his toy donkey was going to run against Evan, the boy was mortified. He lobbied Scarlett.

'I dunno, Evan,' she said pointedly, 'maybe if you still had the mullet . . .'

'What am I going to do if I lose to a stuffed animal?' he moaned. 'What will I tell my grandchildren?'

On the telephone later, Dennis had a ready answer. 'He'll have to tell his grandchildren he lost to a jackass,' he said, 'and if Kerry loses to Bush he's going to be telling his grandchildren the same thing.' Thus, I was reminded the USA elections are next week. It seems like an awfully long way away.

I went to bed at midnight, but the boat was rolling so much it was hard to sleep, even with the lee cloth attached to my bed. At 1 am I was just about to nod off when I thought I heard a strange grinding sound. I fell back to asleep again for a moment until I was startled wide awake by a chilling sound I had long dreaded hearing: Wah! Wah! Wah! Wah! Wah! Wah! It was the fire alarm. Kayt came rushing down the companionway in a pink negligee and life jacket, knocking on all doors and shouting at everyone to get up on deck immediately. Note to self: don't sleep naked again, just in case. Fortunately, my foul-weather pants and jacket were within easy reach, so I wrenched them on, threw my life jacket over my shoulder and raced up on deck. I could smell smoke. Scarlett and Kim were up there already, both in their nightclothes and both minus life jackets. I gave Scarlett mine. A strong, acrid smell was emanating from the engine room.

The boat had stopped. Dick was at the helm, trying to appear calm, while Rolle and Jock were down in the engine room, fighting whatever had to be fought. Daragh, who had been on watch when the alarm went off, was right behind them with another fire extinguisher. First he'd had to go to his cabin to throw Evan out of bed with an unceremonious, 'Get the fuck up on deck. NOW!'

Evan appeared wearing green frog boxer shorts and scratching his behind. We sat wondering if we would soon be getting into lifeboats. It was a very, very nasty few minutes. I put my arm around Scarlett and held her, but she was wonderfully calm. In that moment I was faced with the full import of what I had done; the responsibility of bringing her and everyone else on this journey. There would be no fast rescue in this corner of the globe.

After an agonizing few minutes, Jock came up to let us know they had contained the problem. The shaft brake on the propeller had come loose and caused the brake pads to overheat and start smoking, which triggered the alarm. Rolle and Daragh emerged from the engine room wearing firefighting gear, faces flushed, eyes wide, their adrenaline still at racehorse speed. The rest of us were equally shaken.

'I had to have a slug of whisky,' confessed Kayt.

The rest of the day was tough. The Captain held a debriefing at lunchtime, which made everyone more wretched, facing a post-mortem on what we should and shouldn't have done in such an emergency. I'm kicking myself for not taking a seamen's firefighting course. I've been so worried about pirates I've neglected to prepare for the far more likely event of an engine room blaze. I felt more cheerful by the evening, though, and was asleep by nine. Shortly afterwards, I was startled awake again with my heart thumping, thinking I had heard the fire alarm again. I grabbed a life jacket and ran up on deck. Jock, who was at the helm, was surprised by my appearance.

'Dick's just reducing sail because the wind's dropped,' he said. 'You can go back to sleep.' I must have been dreaming, or else it was a post-traumatic response. Since I clearly had the jitters, I decided to sleep on deck, fully clothed, wearing my life jacket. In the state I was in, I figured that should save me some running about.

The third and last of the Stevensons' South Seas cruises took place on board the iron-screw cargo boat called the *Janet Nichol*. Before setting off, one of the passengers, an island trader known as 'Tin Jack', went with Lloyd to purchase some fireworks, including ten pounds of 'calcium fire', for entertaining local friends along the way. Lloyd carefully questioned the chemist, a Mr Dawson, as to whether or not calcium fire was a safe item to be carried on board a ship. Dawson replied that it was 'as safe as a packet of sugar', adding that even a naked flame from a match would not ignite it. Perceiving their ignorance, he even asked, 'Will you have it with or without fumes?' Tin Jack, deciding he should get the most for his money, took it with fumes.

The *Janet Nichol* left Auckland that night. The following morning, Fanny was sitting at the saloon table eating bread and butter when a calamity occurred:

A sudden spitting puff . . . soon followed by gorgeous flames, blue and red, a vivid mixture of colours, startled all. I knew in a second what it was, the calcium fire in Lloyd's bunk; so holding my breath I ran into our room and got one of the red blankets that I bought in Honolulu . . . I handed my blanket to the first man I could touch. It was now so thick with suffocating vapour that I could see nothing, and still holding my breath made to a porthole which I opened and put my head out. It gave me a moment's time to think, when, whether I should try to save Louis's papers. I quickly came to the conclusion that if the fire could be got under at all, it would be before the papers could be torched, whereas if the fire gained headway the person trying to save the papers would most certainly be lost. With a sick heart, I took another breath, still loath to give up the papers, and drew in my head . . . I ran through the room. I found Louis at the stairs, so stupefied by the fumes that he had some difficulty in finding the steps . . . And what do you suppose Louis was doing up to the time he made for the stairs? Standing and gazing at the fire overcome with wonder at the varying colours it displayed. 'Why,' he thought, 'should a fire at sea look like a pantomime?' He knew nothing about the calcium fire, and could find no explanation for the extraordinary scene. I was so angry with him for staying there and courting a haemorrhage, as it were, that I was ready to repeat to myself . . . and to him . . . 'I almost wish I hadn't married a . . . genius!' The Captain . . . ran to see what was burning in so strange and violent a manner. He was forced to turn himself on his face and crawl out to keep from suffocating. He then rushed up on deck where a pail of water was standing, shouting as he ran for the hose . . . The

pump was soon set going, and the blanket and shawl being
pressed over the fire the hose was played upon them. One
thing the Captain did not, I think, know, and probably no
one but Lloyd, that the men left the wheel and worked below
with the rest. It was a very dangerous moment to leave the
ship drifting. For we were not nearly out of the harbour! . . .
A steamer passed us about this time, and what she thought
of us can only be conjecture; coloured fire and thick
poisonous vapour belching from our ports must have given
us a very strange and alarming appearance . . . Had the
conditions been in the least degree different, the Captain says
nothing could have saved us. As it is, our loss is pretty severe
. . . A great number of the photographs that cost us so much
time and money were destroyed . . . I have ever since been
in terror lest Louis should have a haemorrhage. If he does
I feel inclined to do something very desperate to the man
Dawson who for the sake of a few shillings put us all in
such deadly peril.

Sunday 10 October 2004

I was feeling calmer this morning, so I stayed in my cabin sorting
stuff and writing. Suddenly, at around 10 am, I heard the fire
alarm yet again. I grabbed my life jacket and, determined to do
everything right this time, ran out down the companionway,
yelling and banging on every door I passed, only to be met by
Rolle, smiling and shaking his head, saying, 'It's yust your
daughter baking in de galley.' I felt so silly. Even worse, I had to
ask him to help unblock my head, as lavatories are called on
boats. 'Sure,' he said pleasantly. 'I come soon. Coffee, cigarette,
den dive into de toilet.' It is impossible to maintain dignity
aboard a boat.

Everyone went on deck at 10.30 am for our halfway party – a
celebration for having come 1,500 miles. We had Scarlett's

cookies (personalized for each crew member) and a little champagne and orange juice. It feels good to be on the home stretch, but I'll be a lot happier when we're in a position to be rescued if necessary.

The boat presidential campaign, mirroring the USA elections, is getting dirty, with some smear tactics now being used by Evan. This morning he got hold of Donkey and photographed his rival in compromising situations – drinking alcohol, gambling, snorting a line of 'coke', and committing the cardinal sin of drinking too much milk. '**Does this look like a Donkey you can trust**?' says the caption.

A little later, when it seemed that Donkey was still gaining ground, another poster appeared with a sinister picture of Evan in his mullet phase, all snarled lip and 'aviator' shades, with the caption, '**Does this look like the kind of sore loser who would urinate on your toothbrush after losing in a meaningless competition? You decide. Evan for President**.' The secret ballot is tomorrow.

I've injured my shoulder wrenching the main saloon hatch open in heavy seas so I am attempting a do-it-yourself chiropractic manipulation by lying flat in the companionway, rolling my legs over my head and hanging from the rails. Rolle says he can fix anyone's back by attaching them to the winch and winding them out like prisoners on a torture rack. Not this soldier.

Today, the Captain and I discussed our possible onward routes. I'd hoped to be in either Australia or New Zealand for Christmas, but it looks like we'll only make it as far as Tahiti or Samoa. I guess either destination is an awful lot better than a poke in the eye with a blunt instrument. He heard via email that just after we made contact with that fishing boat four days ago it got caught in a terrible storm. Lucky we were moving west.

Donkey won the presidency and Evan is sulking. Toothbrushes will doubtless be removed from all heads. We're probably around five days from the Marquesas now. I did six hours on watch, two for Scarlett who cooked dinner with the teens (spaghetti with prawns). When I wasn't steering, I was bopping to Tom Jones and the Beach Boys. Sad, eh? God, I'm tired.

Tuesday 12 October 2004

This afternoon we had a man-overboard drill. When the alarm sounded, those who saw our cardboard box 'victim' fall into the water had to keep pointing at it, loudly summon the others, and launch our flotation devices. We have the technology to pinpoint anyone who falls overboard with a locator, provided he is wearing a transmitter. Still, the Captain didn't mince his words. 'If you go over, you don't have much fucking chance. So stay on board.' Only 112 hours to go.

Wednesday 13 October 2004

Evan reeled in a 200-pound striped marlin – a huge bugger. He struggled with it for forty-five minutes. Jock had to steady him so he didn't fall off the boat, while Dick and the Captain stood by with the gaff. As the marlin neared the transom, I thought it was going to run one of them through with its sword. What a magnificent, brave creature! None of us wished to land it, and we couldn't anyway. Huge waves were towering over the stern and causing it to rock precariously, so in the end we just had to cut the line. We use the kind of hooks that disintegrate in salt water, so he'll be OK. Nevertheless, Evan was very pleased with himself. I think he's actually growing muscles.

The *Casco* must have sailed somewhere near our current position. Fanny saw skies like this, experienced similar weather. I now understand what a terrible risk they took with no engine and leaving California at such an unfavourable time of year in an undermanned boat. Being a poor sailor, Fanny stayed below most of the time, but at sunset all the passengers gathered on deck, just like we do. 'The best part of the day,' said Louis.

Friday 15 October 2004

It's much calmer today, and warmer. The sea temperature is now 28 degrees centigrade, so if anything happens, we could survive in it for longer. Rolle slung a hammock on the aft deck and everyone took turns in it. The Captain half-seriously suggested we rig the rudder there, so we can steer and swing at the same time. Tonight there was a party atmosphere, with loud music on the evening watch. The teenagers were on the aft deck, dancing and chatting under the stars. I sat slightly forward of them, partially hidden in the dark, and I suspect they forgot I was there. I was elated to see Scarlett having such a great time on the boat. If we were in LA I'd be worrying about what time she'd be home, whom she was with and what drugs she was being offered.

Next morning, the teenagers surprised everyone by getting up in time to see the sunrise. They sat silent and awestruck, bathed in virgin light, until somebody suggested bacon and eggs.

Kayt finally caught a 'chick-fish', a nice wahoo to barbecue for lunch. Meanwhile, Dick carved himself a thin handlebar moustache. I told him he looks like a porn star, and he took it as a compliment. We'll be in the Marquesas Islands tomorrow. Strangely enough, the mood on board is bitter-sweet. We long for land, yet we know we'll miss the intimacy of this voyage.

Sunday 17 October 2004

At 4 am Scarlett and I climbed on deck just in time to see a faint pink glow appearing behind grey, dancing nimbus clouds. A lone star hung in the centre of the low eastern sky. Right where the horizon met the ocean, a pale crimson light began to fight its way through a cushioned, violet hedge. I lifted my head and noticed another star, this one very bright, high above our port stern. Slowly, the violet hedge was illuminated from behind, with escaping streaks of bronze radiating out towards patches of egg-shell blue. Overhead, the night was still navy, punctuated with dirty clouds and several dawdling stars, so that the higher canopy seemed to be a negative image of the lower. Next, a trail of grey smoke ebbed from the horizon. The waves beneath the lightened area of sky gained phosphorescent pathways, and, eventually, a golden wash began to bathe a whole quarter of the sky, producing glowing flecks in the east-facing clouds.

In my mind's eye, I flew upwards to a still-dark corner of the sky and gazed down. The *Takapuna* sat in a round penny of a pond, her tiny white triangles flapping in the trade winds. 'This world of ours is small,' I thought. 'It is private, containable.'

Off our starboard bow loomed an unchanging sliver of dark purple. Land ho! The sky was bleaching to a brilliant ivory over a pattern of purple-grey, white and pink, with lengthening slashes of turquoise. The ivory sheen spread higher, revealing that the quadrant of sky below held a premonition of majesty, a veiled fierceness.

The trade winds filled our sails. A fuchsia-edged light-ball began to glow behind the purple hedge, soon brightening to a luminescent orange, while the swell before it became a deep teal with golden highlights. The nimbus clouds, highlighted with a ferocious gold-orange, edged out from their hideaway. Whispers of grey rain cloud floated feebly above, their borders becoming a searing gold. Suddenly the entire hedge became transparent, allowing the pink, orange and gold light to bleed through with dramatic speed. Those parts too dense to be illuminated became darker silhouettes; but even they gave up their stance as the very first glow of the sun's circumference appeared above the horizon. Now a bridge was constructed between two of the

largest banks of cloud, so well-formed it could be a walkway
between two ethereal palaces.

The outer edge of the two banks, where the sun's reflection
was becoming unbearably bright, suddenly shot a straight-
edged vortex of light heavenwards. The edges grew broader and
soon the nucleus became too bright to view. Eventually the
hedge seemed to shift off the horizon a little, leaving a gap
through which rays could escape from the central orb; yet the
orb remained hidden. Finally, there it was; a radiance too intense
to be witnessed except through the luminous path it created in
the slate-tipped sea. At this point we could see signs of verdant
streaks in the mountains of Nuku Hiva. The clouds, all bleached
to the palest ivory, hid the summits of the island, while below
them lay soft brown valleys and green ridges that seemed to
vary with the angle of the rising sun. As we cruised closer the
contours gained texture, and considerably more detail.

'Broccoli Islands,' laughed Rolle.

'Why was it,' mused the Captain, 'that Europeans built
enormous galleons and sailed off to conquer the world, but these
people didn't bother?'

'If you lived there,' I replied, pointing away in the distance to
a small village with thatched houses on the edge of a perfect,
protected lagoon, 'would you bother?'

At 2.40 pm, five minutes off Rolle's arrival guess, having
passed two vessels en route and caught nineteen fish, we sailed
triumphantly into Taiohae Bay. Here cannibals once swarmed
over the *Casco*, staring curiously at the white women, while Louis
wondered if they would all be slaughtered for the dinner table.
The moment we dropped anchor, a cheer went up and there were
congratulations all round. Beers were cracked open, and Rolle
and Dick swung out the boom so that those who'd had enough
alcohol could take it in turns to monkey-swing over the clear,
warm water and plunge howling into its rewarding depths.

This is the place where Herman Melville claimed to have
encountered enchanting, tattooed maidens who swam out to

greet his ship, climbed aboard and draped their glistening bodies over the gunwales. In *Typee* he painted a tantalizing picture of their eroticism, eager dancing nymphs who were fully available for the delectation of the panting sailors. We, of course, saw none of that. Instead, out of the corner of my eye, I noticed an outrigger canoe approaching us on our port stern. As it got closer, we saw its occupant, a striking, half-naked Marquesan man with long hair gathered into a ponytail. His glistening body, as well as half of his face, was almost completely covered in tattoos, while around his neck hung a heavy necklace of carved bone.

As he drew level with us he flashed a lovely smile. *'Bonjour!'* He raised his paddle in a greeting, then glided beyond us headed towards the next cove.

I glanced at Kayt and Kim. Their jaws were low, eyes wide.

'Oo, I might get lucky here!' said Kayt.

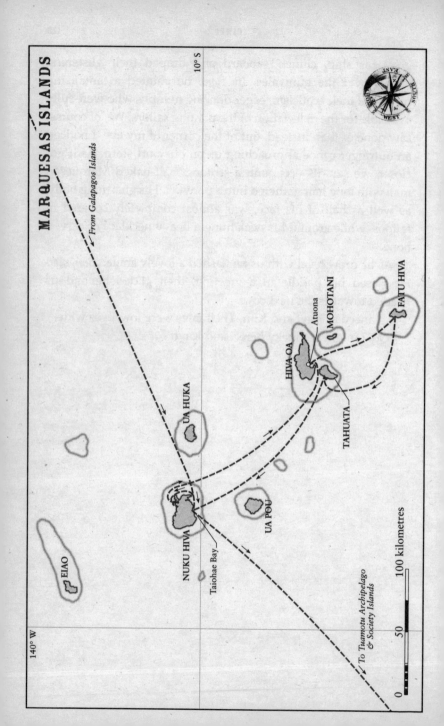

MARQUESAS ISLANDS

From Galapagos Islands

10° S

140° W

 EIAO

UA HUKA

NUKU HIVA

Taiohae Bay

UA POU

HIVA OA

Atuona

MOHOTANI

TAHUATA

FATU HIVA

To Tuamotu Archipelago
& Society Islands

0   50   100 kilometres

CHAPTER SIX

'A VIRGINITY OF SENSE'

08°57.3' S
140°03.7' W

Monday 18 October 2004

I am lost in a flash-flood of sensuality. The beauty of the cloud-encircled peaks before me and the embrace of coconut-scented breezes and bejewelled water – as well as the fantasy of the tattooed canoeist – have seduced me before I've even set foot on land. Goddamn it, Melville might have been right after all. There is a promise over there in Taiohae, beyond the pale, beckoning strip of lava-infused sand.

I went ashore, relishing my first land-steps on the fish-stained, irregular stairs of the *petit quai*. A few smartly painted outrigger canoes and some motorboats sat at the top of a wide slipway, while half a mile away on higher ground I could see the red-and-white beacon tower of the heliport, from which the few tourists who make it here are ferried to and fro from the main airport. I traced the palm-lined, paved road that follows the curve of the bay, in search of some French Polynesian francs. The bank teller wore a mauve sarong, or *pareo* as they call them here, and a headdress of sweet-scented, white *tiaré* flowers.

'*Où est le musée?*' I asked, once flush with over-sized, colourful banknotes depicting garlanded Polynesian beauties, thatched huts and tropical fish and flowers. She instructed me to hitch-hike up the hill at the far end of a beach road adorned with orange hibiscus, golden-centred frangipani and scarlet flame trees.

Despite the heat, I was reluctant to flag down one of the few passing vehicles and chose instead to persevere along the scorching road, past rows of shady bungalows, pensions and a couple of grocery stores, and up the hill to the north. Vanilla vines climbed the palm trees, hummingbirds zigzagged across my path and half-dressed small children smiled and waved from the shade of mauve-canopied jacaranda trees.

At the museum I met Rose Corser, a delicate-looking American who sailed here with her late husband thirty or more years ago and never went back. She established a hotel with a small museum, the latter containing a number of Marquesan artefacts she has collected over the years: exquisite wood and bone carvings, ceremonial masks and jewellery, and miniature canoes. We wandered up to the hotel bar together, where we met the Captain, and sat on the patio discussing American politics. It was difficult to focus on the seemingly remote doings of President Bush, Colin Powell and Condoleezza Rice. Instead I gazed out over the rippling green harbour, trying to imagine what it must have been like for Alvaro de Mendaña, the first European to sight this archipelago in 1595. The Spaniard was on his way to colonize the Solomon Islands when a navigational error led him here instead. Not too terrible. He named these islands the 'Marquesas de Mendoza' after the wife of the Marquis de Mendoza who sponsored his voyage. Fancy having an archipelago named after you! I wonder if he was in love with her.

Ronald, a pleasant, long-haired Frenchman with a broad, medieval face, arrived here on a sailboat twenty years ago. He now provides services for visiting yachties, including fuelling assistance, internet access and a glimpse into what life was like here in the eighties. He gave me a lift to the store.

'What's the story with the roads?' I asked. *'Ils sont terribles!'*

'Ah,' he replied, nodding resignedly. 'Every five years a new French government official turns up from Pape'ete and says, "What you people need is new roads!" And then he goes away and forgets about us – and we forget about him!'

Unpaved, coral sand roads would be better than the broken-up bitumen one encounters on the cross-island trail; yet the traffic is increasing. Seventeen years ago there were just two cars on the island; now there are 400. 'Sometimes Pape'ete makes some money available for new roads,' said Ronald, 'but – *je ne sais quoi* – maybe it's the heat here, the funds just seem to evaporate.'

Taiohae Bay was not the Stevensons' favourite part of Nuku Hiva, in fact they decided that its residents were 'too civilized'. In those days this beach road community comprised the French colonial administrator, whose residence commanded a fine view of the bay, and a few other Europeans who lived in a single row of white houses set back behind the palm trees that still line the shore and a leafy screen of hibiscus shrubs. It was hardly the savage wilderness Louis had hoped for. One inhabitant, though, met with the Stevensons' approval: the elderly Marquesan Queen Vaekehu, who lived above the bay, probably where the hotel is now. She welcomed them into her home and, through a translator, described her early life in Nuku Hiva. Her final words, from the depths of a woman stripped of her former puissance, were infused with bitterness: 'Yes, those were the days before the white people came with their greed, their rum and their diseases, and the yellow men brought their opium to destroy our minds and bodies.'

Considering her outburst, it is a little surprising that she accepted Louis's invitation to join them the next evening for dinner aboard the *Casco*. Clad elegantly in white, she arrived with her son and sat drinking champagne most regally, appearing to enjoy herself, although she spoke neither English nor French. Louis was very taken with her:

> This was a queen of cannibals; she was tattooed from hand to foot, and perhaps the greatest masterpiece of that art now extant, so that a while ago, before she was grown prim, her leg was one of the sights of Taiohae; she had been passed from chief to chief; she had been fought for and taken in war ... And now behold her, out of that past of violence and sickening feasts, step forth in her age, a quiet, smooth, elaborate old lady, such as you might find at home ...

It was during that evening in Taiohae Bay that Fanny, who loved to smoke tobacco, sat down beside Vaekehu and taught her to roll a cigarette. It was a big hit with the tattooed cannibal queen. The Stevensons must have walked back to the quay along the seafront. Strolling along in their footsteps, I found that although the houses facing the bay are no longer uniformly white, most are still set in lush natural landscapes, often with brilliant crimson, blood-orange and violet bougainvillea climbing over wall, roof or garden fence. Sweet jasmine and pink oleander bloom beside the way, and two or three different types of frangipani: pure white, or with either yellow centres or pink edges. I decorated my hair with fallen blossoms, then wandered blissful and blinkered, charmed by the water lapping beside me, the perfume in my nostrils and the breezes on my skin. I was just musing about the indigenous name for the Marquesas, *Te Fenua Enata*, or the Land of Men, when I nearly smacked into one of the Men. He had suddenly emerged from a side path, leading his horse towards the beach under cover of a passionfruit-laden hedge. It was the tattooed canoeist.

We stared at each other for a moment. At around five foot ten inches he was a little smaller than I had thought, but he was perfectly proportioned. His shorts and tank top revealed a great deal of his shining, well-defined, muscular body, most of which was covered in extraordinary tattoo-art depicting tikis, mysterious angular designs and unfamiliar, yet somehow powerful, symbols. He seemed to recognize me as one of the white women from the boat, because he shook my hand, nodding gravely.

'My name Akitini,' he bowed. When his eyes met mine again, I was struck by their profundity. I thought I noticed a little fear, certainly sadness, behind them, and an intensity of gaze that I could not hold.

As I lowered my eyes, my attention fell to a section of tattoo on his right forearm that had been completely shaded, except for a small circle of flesh left in the centre – a brown moon in an unclouded, inky night sky.

'I tattooed myself,' he said. 'It is my whole *histoire*.' Until it was banned by French missionaries, tattooing was an essential part of Marquesan culture, being a means of asserting one's history, status and allegiance to a chief. It was also a means of seduction. Hands, lips and feet that were not tattooed were considered ugly.

The beast beside him stamped a hoof and shook its mane. 'Where are you taking your horse?' I asked, trying to wrench my eyes away from his extraordinarily exotic body.

'To my valley,' he replied, flipping his rope reins beyond the hills on the western side of the bay.

'Are there no roads there?' I asked, stupidly, before remembering there were relatively few cars on the island and the horse was obviously his form of land transport.

'Yes, there are roads,' he shrugged. There was an awkward pause before he broke into a smile. 'Perhaps you will visit me there?' He turned his head to stare out at the bay, presenting to me the right side of his face. Two ornately shaded, interlocking spirals covered his cheek, one arching from a block of Marquesan symbols that lay parallel to his ear, the other winding its way both northward to join a curlew on his nose, and south to a dead end at the corner of his mouth, which was in turn linked to a circular symbol at his jowl. A fan of five, delicately filigreed arches followed the line of his eyebrow and peaked in the centre of his forehead. His long hair being gathered in a ponytail, I could see that his entire neck, and even the area between his ear and nape hairline, was intricately decorated. 'Tomorrow,' he said softly, almost mumbling, 'I will bring you a fish.'

I am a happily married woman with a brilliant, attractive, fine provider of a husband; but at that precise moment it occurred to me that a fish from Akitini sounded rather exciting.

*

Just like Louis, I was eager to see the sites of archaeological interest here on Nuku Hiva, especially the places where cannibal rituals took place. From Hatiheu Bay, Louis climbed up to the *tohua* or set of platforms where ceremonies, including feasts, sacrifice and tattooing, were held. If he climbed alone, he was lucky. Our tour guide was Mathilde, a fat, bourgeois French woman with enormous, low-slung breasts that couched themselves upon the protruding bulge of her misshapen abdomen. She wore a glittery T-shirt and beige shorts, from which extended two jelly-white, swollen legs that ended in ankle socks and tennis shoes. Her dyed, brass-coloured hair was cut short in a harsh, mannish style, with a cropped fringe extending a mere half-inch below her hairline and a full inch from the top of her gold-trimmed, designer sunglasses. When she smiled, her little pointed teeth gave her the appearance of a shark making nice to a killer whale. Overbearing, argumentative and opinionated, she was so far from my notion of the romantic creatures I might meet on Nuku Hiva she put me in a thoroughly bad mood. Worst of all, she knew a lot less than she pretended about the history and archaeology of the place.

Against my better judgement, we set off in her over-scented Explorer, sweltering at first because she was too mean to put on the air-conditioning. Scarlett, Kim, Daragh and Evan had the best deal, travelling behind us in the bed of an accompanying pick-up truck, with loud rap music drowning out Mathilde's high-pitched, grating commentary. We ascended the mountain road from the south side of the island, in a painfully slow single file behind a garbage truck exactly like those in France, with a row of men sitting facing us, all lined up in dark blue vests. Packs of small, wild horses appeared from time to time, swiftly disappearing into the roadside forest of eucalyptus, papaya, avocado and balsa trees.

I hadn't thought it possible but, as we picked our way up towards the jagged crater of the Toovii Plateau, the roads became even worse, with large boulders and potholes making our inland climb a risky rodeo-ride. Beside us the ravaged bitumen dropped off to deep ravines, while the overhanging ridges dotted with loose rocks were far from comforting. SOYEZ PRUDENT (BE CAREFUL) said the road signs, RISQUE DE CHUTE DE PIERRES (RISK OF FALLING ROCKS) and, even more alarmingly, DYNAMITAGE!

White terns swooped close by, while black swifts soared towards the cloudy heights of the antenna-topped Mount Muake, a Mecca for the mad buggers who parasail off its windy cliff tops. We paused for a topside peek at the *Takapuna* lying in Taiohae Bay, and beyond it the misty-purple outline of Ua Pou, known as the Cathedral Isle because of the majestic spires rising from its rocky crown.

The ocean currents here in the Marquesas are cooler than other parts of French Polynesia, so there are very few coral reefs or lagoons. Thus there is a stark definition between sea and headland that I find most appealing. A mysterious steaminess envelops the island. Small guava trees, ylang-ylang and lime trees wafted beside us on the summit, while beneath our feet, a fern that curled petulantly away from our touch reopened a few minutes later.

'Ha, ha! Smell this!' chortled Mathilde, shoving a disgustingly smelly, pale white fruit in my face. 'That's the *noni* fruit,' she tossed it away. 'That's what the Americans drink!' The *noni* juice industry brings big bucks to French Polynesia. The fruit is touted as a natural cure-all and has long been used as such by local people.

We approached the Taipivai Valley, now also known as the Valley of Ten Thousand Coconuts that was the setting for Herman Melville's novel *Typee*. The story goes that Melville arrived here aboard a whaling vessel in 1842. Sick of the arduous life aboard, he and his friend Toby jumped ship in Controller Bay and made a risky run inland. Despite the noonday heat, I walked a short way down the overgrown jungle path that leads to the site of the village where Melville and his friend reportedly lived precariously among cannibals. A sliver of the far-off Kuvee Nui waterfall traced the face of the cliff above, while dragonflies alighted on ferns, cashew nut and pandanus trees. The bushes were alive with the songs of cicadas and every step seemed a suffocating journey into a noisy, green furnace.

Louis must have been secretly envious of Melville. He did not care for his writing – in fact, in one of his letters he called him a 'howling cheese'. Nevertheless, I think Louis would have liked to be the first to write about the Marquesas, and especially to have had the kind of adventures Melville described among real live chomping cannibals. It had been a promising start, when scores of tattooed people had clambered uninvited aboard the arriving *Casco* and settled themselves in every corner of Louis's and Fanny's floating home, peering into mirrors, slouching on chairs and sitting cross-legged on the floor in Louis's cabin while he was trying to write. One woman had even whipped up her dress and swished her bare rump up and down the velvet cushions in apparent ecstasy. Some of the visitors seemed quite menacing and carried knives. Louis confessed to feeling alarm, even repugnance, for the Marquesan people at that point, wondering if the entire *Casco* crew might end up being 'butchered for the table'.

But disappointment followed. He wrote to his friend Sidney Colvin:

> It is all a swindle. I chose these islands as having the most
> beastly population, and they are far better, and far more
> civilized than we. I know one old chief, Ko-o-amua, a great
> cannibal in his day, who ate his enemies even as he walked
> home from killing 'em, and he is a perfect gentleman.

After conducting his own investigations into the lives and culture of Marquesan cannibal societies, Louis became quite scornful of Melville's various inaccuracies and began to doubt the veracity of all his stories. In turn, his own effort to record

Marquesan ethnography was scorned by Fanny, who thought he should be writing adventure stories instead. She was probably right, although I believe Louis was so moved and incensed by what he learned concerning the plight of the Marquesan people after Europeans arrived, he found it hard to do anything other than try to tell their true story. Even today, one is often brought face to face with the underlying sadness of the people here and their struggles, both old and new.

And what was Fanny doing while Louis was clambering up to the cannibal sites? Well, for one thing, she was making pudding. One evening ashore they were served *ka'aku*, a dessert made of baked breadfruit and coconut cream. Fanny thought it so delicious she marched back on shore the very next day, mixing bowl and beater under her arm, to gather the ingredients and try to replicate it. Once accomplished, she declared she now had her first recipe for a South Seas Island Cookbook. Alas, it never materialized.

On entering the cannibal site, we found a magnificent 600-year-old banyan tree standing guard on the path to the *tohua*. Was it just that we were told its root-woven base was a gruesome rubbish dump, a receptacle for bloodstained tools and body parts, or did it indeed hold an eeriness, a sinister power? Our group fell silent in the presence of ancient suffering, violence and taboo. Here and there were petroglyphs, now-faint stone carvings of birds, lobster, tikis and fish. We came upon a tattooing area, with scoops taken out of the stone to serve as pots for the plant-based inks.

On a rock platform that once served as an altar, two prison-wells had been made; a large one that once held five or six victims awaiting their fate, and a smaller pit that housed one unfortunate person who would be the next meal. He was to be clubbed to death and devoured, his eyes being particularly prized hors d'oeuvres, ingested as a means to knowledge. Peering inside a small hut behind the altar, we made a grisly discovery: scores of human skulls were lying in rows on the ground and stuffed into baskets. The teenagers were extremely impressed.

'Cool,' said Evan.

'Savage,' echoed Daragh.

As it happened, an archaeological dig was in process. A little further on, some other, recently discovered, human bones lay exposed in an earth trough.

'They hid these bones from the missionaries,' said Mathilde. 'They didn't want them to know they still ate people after the practice was banned.'

At Hikokuha, we found the graves of the first missionaries.

'You mean they didn't eat these guys?' asked Evan.

'Yes, they did,' replied Mathilde curtly. No one felt like inquiring which bits were left uneaten for burial. Sitting next to a giant stone phallus was a decapitation stone, with a neck-sized indentation.

As we began to descend from the mountains to the northern bays, we were disappointed to find that our view of one of Louis's favourite beaches Hatiheu Bay, was dominated by the *Aranui*, an enormous inter-island supply ship. Her passengers had spilled out of her vast belly in the early morning and ensconced themselves along the narrow beach, the grassy verge, and the stone sea wall in between. All canvas knapsacks, sandals and saggy-bum swimsuits, they were probably recovering from a filling meal at the attractive bayside veranda restaurant run by Yvonne Katupa, the mayoress. As we arrived there, she rose to greet us, the *grande dame* of the island, resplendent in a blue-and-white floral *muumuu*.

'*Enchantée.*' She held out her hand. '*Je suis desolée,*' she murmured, apologizing for being too booked up to accommodate us.

'*De rien,*' I demurred. '*Nous sommes faîtes un pique-nique.*' At the side of the mountain road, we had munched on baguettes filled with questionable ham. While we were eating them, Rolle had driven by in a rental car, recklessly combining beer, cigarettes and a rally-driver style with a top-speed navigation of the precipices, while Jock sat white and shaken in the passenger seat. I force-fed them some of our baguettes, admonished them to slow down, then sent them on their way. I've become everybody's mother.

Yvonne's menu looked very good: grilled lobster with Pacific salad to be eaten in her tropical garden with a view of the bay. As we chatted, the *Aranui*'s yellow crane lifted the last of the tenders on board, her yawning stern closed its mouth and she trundled out to sea with a final fanfare of rude horn-blasts. Once the bay was tranquil, the locals became more visible. Across the road, I spied a young woman minding some children under a frangipani tree. Plump and voluptuous, with a captivating smile, luxuriant hair and playful eyes, I thought she must be a descendant of one of the inspirations for Paul Gauguin's famous Marquesan paintings. While I was admiring her, the Captain radioed me, 'There's a guy here with a fish for you.'

On the way back I was forced to acknowledge that my mood had not lifted since this morning. I had been distracted by the beauty of the island and its dark, intriguing history, yet underneath I was experiencing something else . . . a malaise, a restlessness, a deep ennui. Needing some time alone, I asked to be dropped off at the hotel and checked myself in for the night. In a wooden bungalow decorated with local carvings, I lay under the ceiling fan on the cool, island-print bedspread adorned with a fresh hibiscus flower and contemplated my journey so far. We have travelled over 5,000 miles and, so far, so good. Scarlett seems quite happy, the boat is performing well, we've survived the longest passage . . . but . . . there was something else.

'So, what more do you want?' I asked myself sternly. 'Surely you've got what you asked for, the boat, the journey, the adventure . . . what else will it take to make you happy?'

The answer frightened me.

It must have been nearly midnight when I was startled by an

insistent knocking. I quickly wrapped a sarong around my body and half-opened my door. As a warm, scented breeze swirled into the coolness of my well-fanned room, I stared out at my moonlit visitor, who was proffering a pretty silver fish.

'How did you find me?' I gasped, making way for him to carry it inside. I opened the small guest refrigerator and Akitini slid it inside. 'It's a very fine fish,' I stammered. 'Thank you for . . .' He did not let me finish my sentence, but quickly took my hand and led me out through the wooden-slatted French doors to the moon-bathed balcony overlooking the bay. On the way, I caught sight of my reflection in the half-lit window. I was surprised at my reverse image; it seemed somehow younger, more voluptuous, more carefree than I knew myself to be.

Akitini picked up a fallen frangipani blossom and solemnly offered it to me. I knew it was a test; placing it behind the left ear signals availability, while the right means one is taken. Sighing regretfully, I faced my reflection and watched myself place the fragrant petals firmly behind its right ear. I realized my mistake the moment his strong, warm arms encircled my body, and his dark, tattooed face met mine. His breath was sweet with coconut; he tasted of the sea.

Thursday 21 October 2004

I woke to complete stillness and immediately felt guilty about my dream. Being a psychologist, I tried to tell myself that it was symbolic and not really about Akitini, but later on I found myself daydreaming about him as well.

'Fantasies are allowed and unavoidable.' I kept telling myself what I had often told my patients. 'They are your own. It's *acting* on them that can get you into trouble.' I'm really missing Billy.

It's odd to be ashore. I feel the world is still pitching around me and I'm sure I now walk with a Western roll. But my mood is definitely better today; my 'night visitation' has left me with a secret glow. Checking out of the hotel, I noticed a small advertisement card beside the front desk. *Akitini Tattoos* it said, with a phone number.

'Is that the same man who lives in the next valley who has tattooed himself all over in the traditional style?' I asked the young Frenchwoman who was helping me.

'Ah, Akitini,' she nodded mournfully, her eyes suddenly filled with pain. 'He is a breaker of women's hearts.'

When Fanny saw a tattooed Marquesan chief strip off his loincloth and stand completely naked in front of her aboard the *Casco*, she pronounced it 'a most beautiful sight'. The chief had become a little rum-intoxicated and was responding to a request by the Stevensons to display his tattoos. Both Fanny and her mother-in-law Margaret certainly got an eyeful that day, but then, from the minute they had arrived in the Marquesas, they'd had to get used to seeing near-naked men. It must have been very strange at first, especially for Victorian women. Margaret described their tattooed legs as being like 'open-work silk stockings', while Fanny, in a letter to Henry James, painted a delicious picture of the other Mrs Stevenson 'taking a moonlight promenade on the beach in the company of a gentleman dressed in a single handkerchief'.

Friday 22 October 2004

My colleague Professor Eli has arrived after a series of long flights from the Minnesota winter. Among the brown people who surround us, and even us tanned Takapunians, he seems whiter than any man can truly be and, moreover, it struck me he could easily be a cast member of *Lord of the Rings*. A pearly bald pate tops twinkling eyes and a mischievous mouth with neat teeth, while the rest of his slight body boasts a thick carpet of platinum fur that bestows on him an elfin quality. It's odd, seeing a colleague stripped of his business suit. We'll be doing some joint research here on differently gendered people, known as *mahu*. The crew enjoys his gregarious style and have dubbed him Dr Cool-man.

We sailed through the night to Hiva Oa, one of the southernmost islands of the archipelago, on a terrible heel. No one got much sleep. We arrived close to dawn, when the near-full moon cast ethereal shadows upon the stark contours of the Bay. Atuona was thought by Louis to be the loveliest, as well as the gloomiest, place on earth. Its damp mistiness and towering summits reminded Louis of his homeland. It was here that a mysterious artist, a kind of revered shaman named Mapiao, arrived on board the *Casco*, having been commissioned to make a traditional Marquesan artefact. Unfortunately, he was an excruciatingly difficult guest. He did not speak English but managed to convey his meaning by hand signals. His special requirements included being served refreshments in a very precise manner. If he wanted water, for example, a glass had to be placed in his hand; he would not reach for it. Nor would he eat his food until high noon. Poor Fanny put up with this as long as she could but her patience was severely tried. On his very last day, food and a glass of water were placed right in front of him and, as usual, when noon struck, he signalled for Fanny to lift the glass the last few inches and place it in his hand. I imagine she had finally had enough, because it seems she pretended to misunderstand his signals. With one fell swoop she threw both lunch and water overboard.

Stepping ashore at Hiva Oa, I was lucky enough to hitch a ride into town from a Frenchman who grows vegetables for sale and will supply us with fresh produce in a couple of days. He dropped me at the Gendarmerie so I could formally register our arrival. I was greeted by two young gendarmes, wearing the tiniest, tightest shorts I've ever seen on a policeman. They remind me of toy Action Men. Further along the road there were even more of them – this time of the Jungle Action Series – from the French army training centre, running uphill in step, also wearing ridiculously brief camouflage print shorts with tank tops.

Behind the desk at the mayor's office sat Ernest, a truly grand *mahu*, with a height and imposing carriage that defied his considerable bulk. His hair was cut in a fashionable bob, and his two diamond hoop earrings punctuated a stylish version of the Marquesan tattoo that extended along his cheek like an ornate, ink sideburn. It was his elegance of carriage, though, that impressed me the most. Observing him walking to a filing cabinet, it seemed to me that he bore his weight as effortlessly, and moved as gracefully, as a ballerina. Ernest's duties kept him from talking to me, he explained, until after the dance class he would be teaching at 3 pm.

'May I come along and watch?' I asked.

In the interim I took a quick tour of the grave, replica house and museum of Gauguin, who moved to Hiva Oa towards the end of his life. The poor man was a cliché of the troubled, penniless, anarchic French painter, but I think his work is brilliant, the best of which he painted here and in Tahiti. It seems he infuriated the locals by masquerading as a pious church-goer until he obtained land title deeds from the Church – whereupon he constructed his 'House of Pleasure' and moved in with a fourteen-year-old who soon became pregnant. When the French bishop publicly forbade all young girls to visit him, Gauguin responded by placing outrageous statues around his house, including one depicting the bishop himself. He eventually became ill, exhausted by local politics, and shut himself away until his death in 1903. Ironically, his grave was overshadowed by Catholic images. However, admirers have left offerings: a small watercolour, a photograph and a candle.

Another famous Frenchman, Jacques Brel, lived here in Hiva Oa. He flew around the archipelago in an aeroplane named *Jojo*, which is now housed in a hangar exhibiting its owner's life and music. None of the *Takapuna* teenagers had ever heard of Brel. Their interest was sparked only when I told them the man was once the coolest dude in Europe.

Ernest's dance class was held in a large tin shed opposite the hangar. A group of women and children waited outside, some limbering up a little. I sat on the floor near the back of the mirrored room and watched a couple of eager students practising a routine, following their own movements in one of the cracked mirrors that lined the front wall. Their steps were not those of traditional Marquesan dance, but of the kind of swaying, hip-wiggling, expressive *hula* dance that is common to much of Polynesia. Nevertheless, it was bewitching.

The best of the two dancers was a *mahu* with long orange hair and a lithe, feminine body, wearing a tiny sarong and tight T-shirt. Her hip movements were extraordinarily sensual and strong, while her face carried a shy, coquettish smile that held the attention of all (it is polite to use feminine pronouns when *mahu* are fully presented as females). When the class began, she led the whole room, dancing in the very front and never taking her eyes off her own mirrored self. Behind her, women and girls of all ages struggled to achieve the same oomph. Some of the Polynesian women were accomplished shakers and sensual swayers but, by comparison, the few white women in the class (presumably French residents) seemed stiff and awkward, their hips restrained by centuries of culturally proscribed inhibition and prudery.

But it was Ernest himself who most commanded my attention and applause. At first he just waddled around the class, in and out of the rows of swaying women, giving a verbal instruction here, adjusting the line of an arm there, even clasping a student's hips and physically moving them in the desired direction. After a while he began to move his own arms, head and fingers with a light, graceful and expressive touch I would not have thought possible for such an enormous man. Even further into the class, he began to move his legs, and finally to sway his hips as well, until he metamorphosed before my eyes into the most fluid,

sensual and delicate being in the room. His charisma flamed his
pupils, so that their own bodies seemed to become looser, more
rhythmic, vibrant, passionate, until the hall before us was an
entrancing pageant of brightly coloured human birds, flowers,
canoes and lovers, telling tales of longing, lust, war and loss.

Monday 25 October 2004

'In 1880,' announced our Hiva Oa cannibal site guide, a
Marquesan woman with auburn frizzy hair and tie-dyed T-shirt,
'we were told by the Catholics to stop eating people. But . . .' she
lowered her voice and adopted a confidential tone, 'in 1914 my
mother-in-law, who was six years old at the time, saw the last
old woman eating her grandchild in Tahuata.' She paused to see
what effect this would have, then, sure of her audience, she
continued. 'This is where we sacrificed babies. A sacred dance
was performed, then we offered the heads to the tiki.'

'Only babies were sacrificed here?' asked Evan.

'No, adults too, but they had a chance to escape being eaten
if they won a game. They had to run towards the villagers, who
threw berries at them. If they avoided being hit they would not
be eaten.'

All this led to a series of deep discussions by the teenagers
about morality, taboo and societal safety.

'Well, boys in our society go to war, don't they?' said Scarlett.
'They could be killed . . . but then, I suppose at least they won't
be eaten.'

Evan was more radical. 'I see nothing more offensive about
eating human flesh than eating dog . . . or even cow.'

I imagine there were many discussions on board the *Casco*,
too, about taboo and society. Louis wrote:

To cut a man's flesh after he is dead is far less hateful than to
oppress him while he lives . . . Furthermore, in the eyes of

Buddhists and vegetarians, we consume the carcasses of creatures of like appetites, passions, and organs with ourselves; we feed on babes, though not our own; and the slaughter-house resounds daily with screams of pain and fear.

Wednesday 27 October 2004

The best was kept for last. We sailed into Fatu Hiva, probably the most beautiful bay I've seen so far; a small, curved inlet with steeply sloped, verdant hills rising out of dark jade waters, topped by loftier, misty summits beyond. Dotted around the curve of the bay are towering pitons, rock formations that apparently were the cause of its earlier name, the Bay of Penises; although, later it was changed to the Bay of Virgins. Neither term seems to characterize these intriguing natural sculptures; they seem to be alive, even human, with faces and expressions that change with the angle of falling light. To our right above the bay looms a double-piton I find particularly riveting, for, depending on the time of day or night, the shadows that fall on its many contours create different beings; now a giant with a war club, now a man hunched over a piano. I spent hours today lying on the aft deck gazing at these fascinating guardians of the bay.

A small boatload of fishermen came to our stern this morning and I arranged with the youngest of them, Phillipe, to guide us to the hidden waterfall. He ferried us ashore in his tin boat, gallantly helping the girls aboard. A handsome man in his thirties with red lights in his long, curly hair, Phillipe spoke excellent English and appeared more western in his conversation than most of his compatriots.

We walked up through the village and, after stopping by his small house to see his carvings, we continued up into the hills. Enormously tall palm trees rose into the sky, pointing to misty, shimmering peaks, while closer to eye level grew an orchard of avocado, mango and papaya trees, beside Polynesian chestnuts and all manner of exotic, flowered vines. Phillipe picked us luscious mangoes to eat as we climbed up a narrow, muddy trail with slippery rocks and treacherous drop-offs. Eventually we spied a cascading ribbon falling some 300 feet from the cliffs above. At the base of the waterfall, a perfect, pea-green swimming pool had formed in the rocks. Near ground level, a protruding platform disperses its flow as a wide shower-head does, so that one can sit in the pool and receive a gentle sloshing from above. The water is so deep, it is safe to leap in from the highest surrounding rocks, provided one aims for the centre. The teenagers immediately jumped in and larked about, submerging to try to find the underwater cave beneath the waterfall, and taking it in turns to belly-flop in from an indented, rocky grotto.

I found the water cool, invigorating and inhabited by shrimp, minute silver fish and at least one lazy, immobile eel.

'This is it,' I decided. 'This is the actual "paradise" of fiction, the stuff of Bounty ads, J-Lo videos and hair product commercials.' It was such a cliché of the European notion of paradise, I could barely enjoy it for the breadth of my own cynicism. But after what was probably the most delicious bath of my entire life, Phillipe took some plump pink grapefruit from his knapsack. '*Pamplemousse?*' He peeled them for us, the best I'd ever tasted. I lay back on the rocks, allowing the sun to bake me dry, and decided I was finally happy. Just when I thought the day's pleasures would never end – they did. I began to hear Phillipe's sad story of his eight years in LA, during which time he had become addicted to alcohol and drugs, and subsequently suicidal. His return home saved him, but not before he had slashed his wrists and fallen foul of the American justice system.

By the time Fanny and Louis arrived in the Marquesas, the local population had dwindled so alarmingly, it was believed that it would be completely eradicated within a few years. Louis wrote:

> The Marquesan beholds with dismay the approaching
> extinction of his race . . . Hanging is now the fashion . . .
> This proneness to suicide, and loose seat in life, is not
> peculiar to the Marquesan. What is peculiar is the wide-
> spread depression and acceptance of the national end.
> Pleasures are neglected, the dance languishes, the songs
> forgotten.

The Europeans had brought syphilis, smallpox, leprosy and TB
that decimated the inhabitants of all the islands. The introduction of alcohol and firearms only contributed to the problem.
In 1842 there were around 18,000 people living in the Marquesas,
but by 1926 there were just over two thousand.

Some of the Marquesan people had even been stolen from
their homeland by Peruvian slavers, who used trickery to induce
people to board their boats then set sail with them against their
will. A ship's cook described what happened in December 1862,
after a number of islanders were lured on board the *Empresa*:

> . . . there were about 80 on board. The doctor succeeded in
> enticing eight or nine women into his cabin where he locked
> them in; at the same time the kanakas were all together on
> deck, and the Captain not succeeding in persuading them to
> go below voluntarily ordered the crew to use force. He
> himself, with a revolver in his hand, set the example; but
> only five men followed it, which explains why they were
> only able to seize five natives; who were thrown head
> foremost through the hatches into the between deck. During
> this period the remainder jumped into the sea. The men
> jumped in first, and then the women before jumping in their
> turn threw in their infants.

There still appears to be a general depressive sensibility in the
psyche of the Marquesan people, judging from those I met. It's
hardly surprising, after barely surviving being wiped out

entirely, along with their art and culture, by a bunch of fanatical, white do-gooders – not to mention the blackbirders. Nor is it surprising that the well-equipped *Casco* party were on the receiving end of considerable aggression and scorn when they refused to buy bananas, baskets and other local products at exorbitant prices. 'This is a mighty fine ship, to have no money on board,' they jeered.

Doubtless we court the same kind of resentment wherever we go, either overt or disguised. At 3 pm our crew joined in the local volleyball game with the villagers. I lay in the grass and watched, a proud parent, as Scarlett excelled. After a while, I decided to search for a place to pee. A few local people had set up stalls nearby, selling carvings, tapa cloth (designs or pictures printed on beaten tree bark) and jewellery made from shells, bone and plant materials. I approached a woman to ask if she could point me in the direction of a toilet. She looked at me harshly, through one cataract-veiled eye.

'You buy one tapa cloth?' she asked aggressively. I was taken aback; I had not expected to have to barter for a bathroom visit. But she insisted and soon my need was such that I agreed. She scurried ahead to a dingy concrete cubicle, and when I returned the Mean Old Woman was waiting with a selection of tapas at outrageous prices. I spent the good part of half an hour trying to get out without losing my shirt. When I returned to the volleyball pitch I found that Phillipe had started drinking and was becoming incoherent, so it was definitely time to leave. The latter experiences constituted a harsh jolt back to reality. This is not paradise, but a stunningly beautiful place inhabited by some people who have become disenfranchised, depressed, or otherwise troubled. And as an affluent, visiting Westerner – I suppose I must be part of the problem.

Back on board, from my sunset vantage-point, I nursed my white-man's guilt. The double-piton had become a Madonna with her Child.

'Could I live in a gorgeous place like this?' I asked her at last.

'You want Phillipe and the Mean Old Woman as your neighbours?' she smiled back.

We left Fatu Hiva the next day in the late afternoon for a dazzling moonlight sail to the island of Tahuata. Lying on the aft deck, I read a chapter of Melville's *Typee* aloud for anyone who was interested – mainly the teenagers, although they found the language difficult. We sneaked into the bay at 10 pm.

The wood and stone church in the village of Vaitahu is a beauty, a masterpiece of local craftsmanship, with a large modern stained-glass window depicting a Polynesian Madonna and Child. On Friday afternoon we nipped round to Tuato, the village of master carvers, and went ashore briefly to buy shell jewellery and some beautiful large wooden paddles made of *miro* (rosewood) and *tou* (a dark, grained hardwood), intricately carved with Marquesan designs. When a large cruise ship approached, we quickly departed for an overnight sail back to Nuku Hiva.

On the way I read the second chapter of *Typee* which my audience preferred. It had more relevance to them, being about sailing into Nuku Hiva, and it was also a lot racier. This was the chapter where Melville created, especially for the European male, a fantasy of Marquesan women. Billy is arriving tomorrow; I wonder if he'll be charmed by the local temptresses . . .

Saturday 30 October 2004

I accompanied Kayt ashore at Taiohae to catch the opening of the market at 5 am, but found we had been misinformed, and it had started at four. Almost everything was gone, even the fish. We managed to score a couple of bunches of bananas, a few vegetables, some yoghurt and a bit of mince. Kayt was very upset, but a couple of small supermarkets were open so we're not going to starve. The *Casco*'s Japanese cook was fired three days before leaving Taiohae for drunkenness and going AWOL. In his place, a Chinese man called Ah Fu joined the Stevensons' entourage. Besides being a skilled cook, he became a faithful champion for the ensuing eighteen months. He always wore white, with his head shaved and his traditional Chinese queue gathered with a red ribbon. He had learned English from seafarers, and had little understanding of polite usage. Once, when serving at table he heard Louis describe the notorious pirate Bully Hayes as 'a very bad man'. 'Yes,' nodded Ah Fu, 'him son-of-a-bitch.'

Scarlett and I took the bumpy two-hour drive to the airport to meet Billy. He appeared on the tarmac in tight black jeans, Paul Smith red-frilled pirate shirt, high-heeled cowboy boots and a mad straw hat by Vivienne Westwood with a crown that resembled a risen soufflé. He's a wonderful dandy but it was bizarre to see such high style among the sea of lava-lavas, shorts and flip-flops. He was remarkably tolerant of the terrible road trip across the mountain, but was understandably too tired to join us at the hotel's Halloween party. After he fell asleep on deck, I tucked him into bed, then borrowed his shirt to complete my pirate outfit. I went ashore in the tender with Kayt as a bumble bee with a black Wonderbra on her head, Scarlett as a robot (with wire off-cuts donated by Rolle), Daragh as a Marquesan warrior (everyone contributed to his felt-tip tattoos), the Captain as a tourist, Kim as a cowgirl and Evan as a pantry, complete with vegetables, cereals and canned goods duck-taped to his chest and arms. Dick, Rolle and Eli appeared as a trio of dancing sperm, wearing hooded, white, painters' protection suits. They invented a ridiculous little 'sperm dance' with which they entertained random strangers. We made an odd team of hitch-hikers, thumbing our way along the beach road where Fanny and Louis once walked to dine with a cannibal queen.

A red devil led us to our patio table, where we ate, laughed and danced beneath the stars. At around ten the heavens put on a natural show as a fiery shooting star dashed towards us, tail streaking orange like a fizzling roman candle, before the rising moon drew our eyes to her own silvery path.

The next morning we sailed the boat round to Anaho Bay, while Billy continued to sleep.

'That was hellishly uncomfortable,' he complained, waking after his first night aboard.

'I've found a double hammock,' I smiled. 'Would you like me to put it up for us?'

'Och, no,' he said, 'I don't fancy being flung together like onions in a bag.'

Leaving him to dress, I took a dinghy ride with Dick and the Captain to try to identify Louis's favourite spot. Fortunately, he had left a few clues:

> My favourite haunt was opposite the hamlet, where there was a landing in a cove under a lianaed cliff. The beach was lined with palms and a tree . . . bearing a flower like a great yellow poppy with a maroon heart. In places rocks encroached upon the sand; the beach would be all submerged; and the surf would bubble warmly as high as to my knees . . . A little further, in the turn of the bay, a streamlet trickled in the bottom of a den, thence spilling down a stair of rock into the sea. The draught of air drew down under the foliage in the very bottom of the den, which was a perfect arbour for coolness . . . For in this spot, over a neck of low land at the foot of the mountains, the trade-wind streams into Anaho Bay in a flood of almost constant volume and velocity, and of a heavenly coolness.

I found the place. It wasn't easy, because the landscape has changed somewhat over the years. Fanny and Louis spent many hours here on balmy days, collecting shells or just lounging on the beach. Fanny must have kept her umbrella unfurled beneath the relentless noonday sun – although, in the arbour, the coolness of the trade winds is just as Louis described. There is no longer an abundance of shells, but the maroon-hearted yellow poppy still flourishes, especially in the southeastern corner. What Louis and Fanny did not write about, however, was the presence of the *nonos*, if indeed the highly irritating and aggressive little sandflies existed in their time. Perhaps Fanny was so covered-up in her *holaku* she barely noticed the bloodsucking insects, but I was bitten viciously.

What did cause Fanny alarm was an incident that occurred when a local man appeared from behind the coconut trees and was invited to join them. Louis lit a cigarette and passed it to him first, as was the polite thing to do in Polynesia. The man took a couple of puffs, but when he returned it Louis noticed that his hand was covered in skin lesions, clear signs of leprosy. Hardly batting an eye, Louis took the cigarette, put it to his lips and smoked it to the end.

Afterwards, Fanny had a fit. 'How could you be so irresponsible?'

'I couldn't mortify the man,' explained Louis.

While we were lying in Anaho Bay, Kayt suggested she and I take the sea kayaks around to the next bay at Hatiheu, to get a bit of exercise. I eagerly agreed, although at that point neither of us realized how far that actually was. We set off at a good pace under clear skies, and, noticing the waves pounding savagely on the rocks at the exit of Anaho Bay, we decided it would be prudent to stay well away from them, and to head a fair way out to sea before turning west. But what looked like the end of the bay turned out to be a mere outcrop of surf-beaten rocks that had deceived us into thinking the western side much shorter than it actually was. We persevered and got far enough north to get a glimpse of what we thought was the end of the peninsula we would have to round before entering Hatiheu Bay. At that point the heavens suddenly opened and we realized we were heading into a heavy downpour.

Kayt pulled alongside me. 'This is the point of no return,' she said. I glanced north into the now choppy, squallish sea. I had my doubts, but neither of us wanted to give in.

'I'm up for it,' I muttered, removing my sunglasses and trying to wipe the salt water out of my eyes.

We surged north, straight into the swell. I had not taken this kayak into white-capped waves before, but I was pleased to discover it was reasonably seaworthy. It handled best at a thirty-degree angle across the oncoming wave, which took us in the direction we were headed, i.e. out to sea. So far so good. I glanced west. The rocks to my left were definitely well worth avoiding. The waves were hitting them with a vengeance, and we wouldn't want to risk being drawn on to them and dashed to pieces. My muscles were tiring, though, and it suddenly occurred to me that our left turn westwards could be the most challenging part of the journey, since we'd be travelling at right angles to the waves. Would they break over us and cause us to capsize? We were about to find out.

'Let's go for it!' Kayt took the lead and headed due west. This was a very different experience. Now we were half paddling, half surfing, in eight- to ten-foot waves. Every now and then one broke over the kayak, but I was relieved to see it simply washed though the well-designed cockpit and left us more or less upright. We battled on as the rain continued to pour down and visibility was poor. There was no landing place anywhere along the western promontory and, yet again, we were surprised at the length of it. We had come at least a couple of miles so far and expected to find Hatiheu just round the bend, so it was utterly disheartening to discover that there was another cove or two, extending a distance of another three or four miles along jagged, inhospitable coastline, before we would be in a position to see the cliff-top statue of Mary that dominates the entrance to our destination. I suddenly remembered that Louis himself had been shaken by a terribly hairy whaleboat ride around this exact piece of shoreline.

'Should we radio the boys to come and pick us up in the tender?' I was losing faith.

'I don't think they'll be able to,' shouted Kayt. 'Not in this swell.'

'OK then,' I returned. '*Avanti!*' We had to keep our distance from each other for a while, because the waves tended to pitch us into each other if we strayed too close.

It seemed an eternity, completing that western passage. At the end of it, I could feel my muscles start to spasm and the billowing blisters on my hands. For a horrible moment I wondered if we had really reached the corner of Hatiheu, but there she was; I have never been so happy to see the Virgin, sculpted by Louis's friend Brother Michel, blessing us from her high, rocky perch. Again, we had given the final promontory a wide berth and were quite some distance out at sea. We turned south for our entry to Hatiheu Bay, and now we had the luxury of purely surfing towards it, as the incoming tide and south-flowing waves lifted us towards the calmer water at the mouth. Over my left shoulder I suddenly spied the *Takapuna*, ploughing behind us, on her way to join us in Hatiheu. Now we could relish seeing the boys gaping at us from a distance; I guess they probably thought we'd need to be rescued.

'You want a pick-up?' It was our Captain on the radio.

'No thanks,' we replied. Kayt's seat had broken half a mile earlier, but she wasn't going to give up now. Well inside the bay we high-fived each other and plopped in the water for a restful float. 'Chicks rule,' sighed Kayt.

Not long before the Stevensons arrived here, it was *tapu* (taboo) for a woman to ride in a canoe, a crime punishable by death. Fanny and Margaret were uneasy about the lower spiritual position of most women in Marquesan society, as well as the restrictions placed on them: having to march behind their husbands, not being allowed to eat pork, nor cook from a fire lit by a man, nor walk on roads or bridges constructed by men.

'*Tapu*,' wrote Louis, 'encircled women upon all hands. Many things were forbidden to men; to women we may say that few were permitted.' He was quite the feminist. On the other hand, I heard that in Hiva Oa, all women could have two husbands, a main one and a back-up. The husbands never went to war at the same time, so there was always one at home to keep his wife happy. Makes sense to me.

Early this evening, six young men and women from Hatiheu performed some traditional dances for us at Louis's favourite cannibal site. They wore only green leaves, ingeniously made into skirts, necklaces, headdresses and arm bands. Five drummers created the sonic beat for a fierce warrior dance, while the *cochon*, or pig dance, was performed only to rhythmic grunting. Finally, a young woman danced the *oiseau* (bird), a pretty, sensual solo in which she imitated hopping, foraging and wing-movements. It is sad that so many of the Marquesan dances are entirely lost.

Leaving Eli ashore to complete a research interview he'd begun earlier, we sailed back to Anaho for the night. I sat on the bow at sunset and reread Louis's words on first arriving here at this, their very first stop after leaving San Francisco: 'The first experience can never be repeated. The first love, the first sunrise, the first South Sea island, are memories apart and touched a virginity of sense.'

As night fell, we could see that someone had lit a bonfire ashore.

'They're roasting Eli,' remarked my husband.

Monday 1 November 2004

We sailed back to Taiohae in the company of some huge, show-off porpoises, and caught a nice wahoo on the way. After we arrived, I decided to accept the invitation to visit Akitini's place. My husband said from the sounds of things the poor man was something of a sideshow and refused to come, so I took Kim and the teenagers.

Akitini lives in his own small valley not far from Taihoe. A turquoise bay and ivory beach provide him with fish, canoeing-grounds and a place to bathe. When we arrived, he was dressed only in a tiny loincloth, washing his horse in the gently breaking sea. Sunlight glittered in the droplets of seawater sprayed about his darkly decorated body. It was hard to observe him and retain one's composure at the same time.

'Would you tell me the story of your tattoos?' I asked.

'First, would you like some fruit?' he asked, leading his horse to a tree for tethering. We followed, mostly in silence, with a perfect view of his naked buttocks and incongruous clear plastic sandals.

Daragh and Evan were muttering together. 'I bet he smokes pot all day,' said Evan, 'and bones girls.'

'Yeah,' replied Daragh, approvingly.

Smells of papaya, woodfire, coconuts and kerosene wafted from his house, a corrugated iron roof supported by heavy, carved wooden pillars with a couple of rooms inside. A hammock was strung beneath the awning above a refrigerator, mirror and punching bag. A patio of piled flat stones covered in a woven mat extended beyond the roof line, and below it on the lawn a small carved stone tiki sat on a hewn wooden plinth. Obviously a careful gardener, Akitini had strategically placed palms, hibiscus and local shrubs about a well-maintained lawn.

Behind the main hut was a kitchen area, dominated by a bountiful papaya tree. While Akitini sharpened his knife, Evan was sent to pluck a ripe fruit. As we talked, I realized that something behind my back was causing the corner of Akitini's mouth to crinkle into a disbelieving smile. I turned round in time to see Evan, who had been attempting to climb the papaya tree, fall on his backside. Akitini strode over to the tree and helped him to his feet. Casually grasping the trunk, he gave it a couple of light shakes and deftly caught the ripe fruit as it fell.

We wandered round Akitini's house, admiring his bone carvings, sculptures and the wooden saddle he had carved for his horse. He explained again that he had executed most of his tattoos himself (those in places he could reach), but a friend had begun to do the honours on his back. I could now see the large tiki on his abdomen and the extent to which the artwork covered each limb and even the backs of his hands.

'These are my warrior marks,' he explained, offering his left arm. 'They protect me from danger.' Daragh and Evan, utterly entranced by the man, quizzed him at length about his fighting symbols, his skill in hunting wild boar with a knife (he chases them on foot and stabs them in the heart) and the power of the tiki, which Akitini believes was lessened when Europeans arrived. 'I no like the missionaries,' he said. 'The French changed everything.'

The cause for the lost arts of the Marquesans was taken up by Louis:

> The civil power, in its crusade against man-eating, has had to examine one after another all Marquesan arts and pleasures, has found them one after another tainted with the cannibal element, and one after another has placed them on the prescript list. Their art of tattooing stood by itself, the execution exquisite, the designs most beautiful and intricate; nothing more handsomely sets off a handsome man; it may cost some pain in the beginning, but I doubt it be near so painful in the long run, and I am sure it is far more becoming than the ignoble European practice of tight-lacing women. And now it has been found needful to forbid the art. Their songs and dances were numerous (and the law has had to abolish them by the dozen). They now face empty-handed the tedium of their uneventful days; and who shall pity them?

Louis made the connection between the plight of the Marquesans and that of the Scottish Highlanders, whose kilts,

music and dances were also banned until they were restored by
Queen Victoria:

> Not much beyond a century has passed since they were in
> the same convulsive and transitory states as the Marquesans
> of today. In both cases an alien authority enforced, the clans
> disarmed, the chiefs deposed, new customs introduced . . . In
> one the cherished practice of tattooing, on the other a
> cherished costume, proscribed . . .

As the afternoon progressed, I began to understand why
Akitini had such a powerful effect on me, why I had dreamed
about him and what, in my unconscious mind, he represented.
He struck me as the personification of a free, unfettered spirit,
dwelling in a blissful, natural state. He has not only the
resources and skills to survive, but also the things that are
considered great luxuries by city-dwellers: a gorgeous valley to
himself with a pristine beach, fresh fish and fruit for the taking,
plus the maintenance of health by canoeing and other physically
taxing things he enjoys. Here is a modern lotus-eater, if ever
there is one. Sexual dreams are rarely actually about sex and the
meaning of mine turned out to be my desire to attain a joyful,
simple lifestyle, in whatever form might work best for me.

Predictably, my notion of Akitini, as a being untainted by
western influence, turned out to be illusory. I learned that the
Americans who made the immensely popular television show
Survivor turned up here a few years ago and 'borrowed' Akitini's
valley as the site for one of their episodes. During that time, one
of the female executives on the show fell for Akitini and even
persuaded him to return with her to Wyoming, USA. He showed
us terrible pictures of him dressed in a ski suit in the snow and
giving the 'thumbs up' sign on a flashy motorbike. It had all
gone horribly wrong. She had installed him in her condo with a
hot tub and TV, and went off to work.

'But I needed my woman,' he complained. Fortunately he

managed to find some solace among local Native Americans, who were astounded to see a few of their own symbols among his body-art.

Nowadays, Akitini is waging a one-man battle to restore the early Marquesan way of life, something that is unappreciated by his Christian family members who live in the township. A 'heathen' flag he designed himself flies above his house.

'My family, they try to get me to go to church,' he said, 'but I tell them, me – I worship nature.' He has paid a high price for his individualism, for he seems lonely – almost tragic. A circular graveyard plot was very prominently placed on the beach side of his garden. There was a large headstone and a few bones at the base of it.

'Who is buried there?' I asked. He had mentioned that wild boar had killed some of his dogs, so I expected that to be his answer.

'It is for me,' he muttered, his eyes downcast. 'I wish to rest there.'

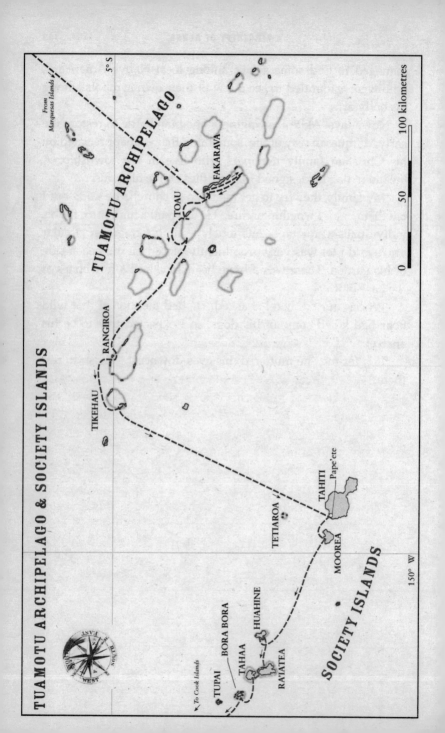

TUAMOTU ARCHIPELAGO & SOCIETY ISLANDS

TUAMOTU ARCHIPELAGO

FAKARAVA

TOAU

RANGIROA

TIKEHAU

From
Marquesas Islands

5° S

0   50   100 kilometres

SOCIETY ISLANDS

TUPAI
BORA BORA
TAHAA
HUAHINE
RAIATEA

To Cook Islands

TETIAROA

MOOREA

TAHITI
Pape'ete

150° W

NORTH
EAST
SOUTH
WEST

CHAPTER SEVEN

NIKI-NAKI-NOO

09°04.5′ S
140°11.5′ W

Monday 1 November 2004

At sunset, the *Takapuna* slid out of Taiohae Bay, carving a blush-pink wake under a glowering, cerise sky. As I watched, the cloudy cathedral summits of Hiva Oa became deep mauve, like the haunts of wicked fairytale queens. I slept for what seemed like Snow White's hundred-year stretch. My awakening prince was a Scotsman who had just seen a complete sea-horizon for the very first time.

'The world's fucking flat!' he cried. Shortly afterwards, when the sea got rougher, he went below to read. Astonishing. He's proved that, despite earlier barfing incidents, he's actually an excellent sailor.

It will be three days' sail to the Tuamotus, our next group of islands in French Polynesia. Spanish and Dutch navigators discovered the archipelago in the early part of the seventeenth century, fifty years or so before Europeans arrived in Tahiti. In Fanny's time it was known as the Dangerous Archipelago, so named for its treacherous reefs that have sliced up many a ship. Low atolls are formed when coral formations slowly appear

around a high island's circumference while erosion and the
subsidence of lava layers cause the collapse of its middle bulge.
Geologically, they are quite different to the younger, high islands
of the Marquesas.

But human design, too, has altered the geology and ecology
of the Tuamotus. We will be visiting only the western part of this
archipelago, since, from 1963 until 1996, the French government
based nuclear-testing activities in the eastern islands. Recently,
politics have become a prime topic of conversation on board and
there is a particular preoccupation with today's US elections.
My own interest was reduced to a head-shaking cynicism;
nevertheless, I called a friend in California to ask who the next
American President was going to be.

The American Democrats on board immediately became
distressed; in fact everyone seems out of sorts. Billy and I had a
disagreement over a parenting issue but, since we were at sea, I
couldn't get away to cool off. Instead, I climbed up on the pilot-
house roof, wrapped myself in a blanket and stayed there till
early morning. The stars were beautiful and the night balmy, but
I felt ridiculous.

'She's not talking to me,' Billy told the smirking crew.

Coincidentally, Louis, too, spent the eve of his arrival in
Fakarava, the seat of government for the Tuamotus, sleeping on
a bench in the cockpit:

A stir at last awoke me, to see all the eastern heaven dyed
with faint orange, the binnacle lamp already dulled against
the brightness of the day, and the steersman leaning eagerly
against the wheel. 'There it is, sir!' he cried, and pointed in
the very eyeball of the dawn.

Louis had been eager to be the first to sight land:

For a while I could see nothing but the bluish ruins of the
morning bank, which lay far along the horizon, like melting

icebergs. Then the sun rose, a piercing gap in these debris of
vapours, and displayed a considerable islet, flat as a plate
upon the sea, and spiked with palms of disproportionate
altitude.

The Tuamotu Archipelago is indeed so flat that our first sight of
it was the very tops of the palm trees on the nearest atoll, a fuzzy
little strip of dark green lining the horizon. The *Casco* lay even
lower in the water than the *Takapuna*, so Fanny and Louis would
not have seen it quite so early, unless they'd climbed the mast.
As we neared the archipelago we were treated to the perfect
screen-saver picture of a white man's paradise: pale, sandy
beaches surrounding emerald, palm-covered strips of land and a
turquoise lagoon.

'Isn't it divine?' I smiled at my husband. Irritated, he looked
up briefly over *Anna Karenina* and dismissed the advancing atoll
with one swat of an approaching jumbo-wasp.

'Och,' he said, 'it's all just Niki-Naki-Noo.' Thus was born the
legendary island-paradise of his Glaswegian imagination;
sufficient sun to turn his skin from blue to pink, enough sand to
lacerate his bum, bitey things in the ocean and, at every turn, a
not-so-loverly bunch of coconuts.

My husband's fellow countryman was far more impressed:
'. . . lost in blue sea and sky: a ring of white beach, green
underwood, and tossing palms, gem-like in colour; of a fairy, of
a heavenly prettiness'. For Louis, the approach to Fakarava was
a once-in-a lifetime experience: 'I have since entered, I suppose,
some dozen atolls in different parts of the Pacific, and the
experience has never been repeated.'

Actually finding the island of Fakarava, though, and
taking the *Casco* safely through the pass, were extremely
daunting navigational challenges in those days. The waters of
the approach were incorrectly charted and treacherous with
unpredictable currents, racing tides and half-submerged coral
heads:

I began to feel sorry for cartographers. We were scarce doing
three and a half; and they asked me to believe that (in five
minutes) we had dropped an island, passed eight miles of
open water, and run almost high and dry upon the next. But
my Captain was more sorry for himself to be afloat in such a
labyrinth.

Captain Otis wisely dropped anchor outside the lagoon and
waited overnight for optimum light, tides and wind before
entering it. Even today, the Admiralty sailing directions advise
against attempting the northern Passe Garuae at night and warn
that low-powered vessels should wait for incoming or slack tide.
Our modern equipment made the daylight crossing relatively
easy, yet we have just heard that a large, luxury motor yacht was
thrown up on the reef at this same time last year. It had been
anchored inside the lagoon when a storm arose without
warning.

'How 'bout that!' Our Captain was horrified to hear that
wind speeds had escalated to sixty knots within a space of
fifteen minutes. The South Pacific hurricane season officially
started four days ago. Our advance-warning weather technology is supposed to give us peace of mind but, in truth, we're
rather too far south to be entirely safe. Under the circumstances,
this is still a dangerous archipelago.

The *Casco* was manoeuvred safely through the pass and her
anchor dropped close to the main village of Rotoava, on the
northeast shore of the lagoon. Standing on deck, Fanny could
make out a coral landing stage with a few stairs, some smart
government residences and a Catholic church with a belfry. That
evening, she and Louis landed by a solitary harbour lamplight.
Slapping at pestering mosquitoes, they strolled along the palm-
lined, coral sand pathway that ran parallel to the beach. They
could hear crickets, and a few voices emanating from one lighted
house, but apart from that the place seemed empty. Louis wrote:

Not a soul was to be seen. But for the thunder of the surf on the far side, it seemed you might have heard a pin drop anywhere about that capital city. There was something thrilling in the unexpected silence, something yet more so in the unexpected sound.

The landing stage at Rotoava is now a substantial concrete container wharf. It seems incongruous on such a small atoll but President Chirac had recently planned to make an official visit so millions of francs were spent on new infrastructure – before he cancelled the trip. Our Captain says that just two years ago there was no pier house, no concrete airport building and no paved roads. A French man with an iguana tattooed on his leg and a marijuana pendant round his neck rented us a motor scooter for a fast, bouncy ride along the causeway. The atoll is thirty miles long but in some places only 300 yards wide from lagoon to surf beach. Burying my face in the nape of Billy's neck, I peeped out at gaily painted houses covered in multi-coloured bougainvillea, gardens of pink ginger flower and passion fruit vine, and a few engaging children. Later, we sat drinking tea on a veranda pier by the utterly still lagoon. There were few people in sight. This entire atoll is silent, hazy and oven-hot. Even the occasional 'plop' of a jumping reef fish reverberates startlingly in this otherwise muzzled isle. It's eerie.

Saturday 6 November 2004

This morning, on an incoming tide, we jumped eagerly into the warm, clear water outside the reef, then drift-dived through the same pass we negotiated yesterday on board the *Takapuna*. It is the very place where Fanny and Louis once leaned over the ship's rails and were smitten by its colour and clarity:

. . . the water shoaling under our board, became changed in

a moment to surprising hues of blue and grey; and in its
transparency the coral branched and blossomed, and the fish
of the inland sea cruised visibly below us, stained and
striped, and even beaked like parrots . . . That exquisite hue
and transparency of submarine day, and these shoals of
rainbow fish, have not enraptured me again.

If only they could have scuba dived, to have seen up close what
we saw, for I guarantee they would then have *continued* to be
enraptured – at least by the variety of the undersea world.
Parrotfish, some with odd, bumpy foreheads, were still in
abundance, which is surprising since the local people like to eat
them. They came in all shades of blue, green and in-between, the
orange blush on their sides flashing boldly as they zoom around
the vivid marine gardens. They pause frequently to chomp on
sprigs of coral, crushing them easily with their strange beaks.
Striped angelfish, black-and-white unicorn fish and electric blue
damselfish streaked above mauve-lipped giant clams.

Swept along by a three-knot current, we were joined by
schools of silvery, striped barracuda and large grey-tipped reef
sharks, all flying in formation with us back inside the lagoon. It
was a relief to discard the thick wetsuits that hampered us in the
Galapagos. Today's conditions are those desired by most divers
– bath-temperature water, fantastic visibility and an abundance
of healthy marine life. No wonder Dick and the Captain are both
talking about living here one day. Me, I'd be worried about the
geographical vulnerability of these low-lying atolls. They've
been hit with hurricanes many times, and there's no escaping to
the hills. As Louis wrote: 'The sense of insecurity in such a
thread of residence is more than fanciful. Hurricanes and tidal
waves overlap these humble obstacles.'

He heard how the survivors of a recent tsunami on one of the
other islands had clung to uprooted coconut palms and ruined
houses. He also noted the presence of sharks in the lagoon and
the danger of eating fish caught there without local advice.

Today's Admiralty book offers a similar warning, for ciguatera poisoning can occur in certain weather, and at certain times in the cycle of days.

The acting Governor of Fakarava, a half-French, half-Tahitian man called Donat, formally welcomed the Stevensons to the Tuamotus. He brought a twenty-one-strong welcoming party on board the *Casco*, to which Fanny served syrup water, ship's biscuits and ginger snaps. Jam was elegantly presented to each person on a plate with a spoon, a touch that was much appreciated; although many guests spooned the jam on to their plates then conveyed it to their mouths island-style – with their fingers.

Donat educated the newcomers about the culture of the local people. Louis must have been especially delighted with his story-telling; just like his old nurse Cummy, Donat had a repertoire of fascinating local legends and chilling ghost stories. With his help Fanny and Louis were able to rent a three-roomed house on Fakarava, where they stayed for several weeks. It was situated near the church and boasted a picket fence and a veranda on two sides. Fanny enjoyed the garden, which was planted with fig trees and flourishing bananas grown in imported soil. She rescued a stove from its rusting-place beneath the house and attempted to create more interesting food than that which was usually on the menu in Fakarava: 'Cocoa-nut beefsteak. Cocoa-nut green, cocoa-nut ripe, cocoa-nut germin-ated; cocoa-nut to eat and cocoa-nut to drink; cocoa-nut raw and cooked, cocoa-nut hot and cold – such is the bill of fare,' complained Louis. These were the days before the supply ship brought the ingredients of gourmet French cuisine. 'When all's said and done,' he wrote, 'there is a sameness, and the Israelites of the low islands murmur at their manna.'

The Stevensons relished the tranquillity of the place. In the coolest parts of the day they combed the beach for shells, and occasionally attended Fakaravan community events, including a funeral, a seance and religious services. Two strands of Western

Christianity were represented there at that time, the Mormons and the Catholics, although their practices and congregation seemed to be interwoven. Louis thought the Catholic service rather Protestant in flavour: 'the Catholics have met their low-island proselytes half-way', he mused. Louis noted that the local people (Paumotans) were rather different from the Marquesans. With the ethnocentricity of those times, he pronounced them 'not even handsome' as well as 'greedy, hardy, enterprising'. Margaret considered the men less attractive than the Marquesans, but also less likely to commit adultery – although it would be interesting to know how she found that out! For all her prim starchiness, she definitely had a twinkle in her eye when it came to black men: 'What wonderful skins they all have!' she enthused. She was particularly taken with Taniera, a catechist and boat-builder, whose services she was inspired to attend twice in one day. After catching him in a skimpy top, she happily noted that his costume left 'an ample stretch of brown satin skin exposed to view'.

Sunday 7 November 2004

In Tetamanu, a ruined village by the Tumakohua Pass that was the capital of the island prior to Fanny's arrival, I found a derelict coral stone church that was built in 1867, and a more intact one nearby, dated 1874. It is unlikely that the Stevensons spent time here, for it is some distance from Rotoava and was a ghost village even then. Only five or six people live in Tetamanu now – two families of fishermen. When I arrived, a woman and some children were lounging in the lagoon, while a couple of men sanded their boat attended by some pugnacious dogs, one of which bore unsightly raw gashes over one side of its body. The sudden, hostile barking was painful on the ears amid the echoing silence of this place.

This afternoon we drift-dived in the nearby pass, which

turned out to be very challenging. The forceful current suddenly switched direction while we were submerged, so without warning we found ourselves being swept back out of the lagoon. In addition, some of the fish we saw proved to be as territorial as the land critters, with surgeon fish flashing yellow fins in our faces and triggerfish warning us away from their eggs. I was, however, excited to see my first Picasso fish: an artist's inspiration in oilpaint shades of umber, aquamarine and gold stripes on a cream background, with yellow lips.

Meanwhile, Billy sat with his cigar on a wooden jetty by a tiny, unattended cafe, peering through the transparent water at a giant Napoleon wrasse, with 'sexy big blue kissy-lips'. It kept cruising by and giving him the eye. He was absolutely entranced. 'I've never seen a fish do that before,' he said.

The *motu*, or single barrier reef island (one of a chain of many that form an atoll), appeared to be deserted, except for a couple of children fishing nearby. I lay on my stomach on the warm deck under an astonishing Peach Melba sky and watched a moray eel position himself between two coral wedges. He waited with mouth agape, hoping something tasty would pop in. He failed so miserably, I actually felt sorry for him.

Yannis, a charming young Frenchman who came aboard as a dive guide, was determined to show us the best of the Tumakohua Pass. At ninety feet a rousing parade of more than 200 grey sharks zoomed by, while scores of giant manta rays wafted gracefully above. In the shallower waters of the lagoon we beheld many splendid varieties of wrasse: brown spotted, pale-blue spotted and a lurking salmon wrasse with its red eyes and grisly, down-turned mouth fitted with rows of tiny teeth. Golden clownfish abounded, each with a dark bonnet tied with a turquoise ribbon. Seemingly motionless yellow trumpetfish were poised against a glorious, pink-spiked coral head.

'I can die now,' I told the Captain.

At sunset I caught Rolle – who doesn't care to dive, or even swim – dangling fish heads off the stern. As if to remind us that the sharks we swam with today are, under certain circumstances, far from benign creatures, we witnessed the astonishing speed with which they shot to the surface to snatch a bite. The Stevenson party saw several large sharks in the bay at Fakarava. Margaret was repulsed by them:

> Two days ago one was swimming round and round us for some time, an ugly fellow indeed; and last night when Lloyd was out fishing with the Captain and M. Donat, he had a very large fish on his hook, and was playing it gently, when a shark came up and carried off fish and hook and line at one fell swoop. I think Lloyd did not much enjoy the fishing after that.

In the evening we went for a barbecue on a small atoll belonging to a charismatic, Tahitian-born man called Manihi. At twenty-five years of age he had visited his Paumautan ancestral home, bagged himself an atoll and stayed. He raised children here and built an elegantly rustic compound, with a wonderful palm-thatched house and surrounding cottages. We landed just as dusk fell. Manihi approached us, bare-chested, wearing nothing but a dusky-pink sarong. He smiled broadly, pink-tinged clouds haloing his movie-star visage. It was a fabulous entrance.

'Is either of those two men your husband?' Once he had met Billy, his seductive style was balanced by his excellent cooking. We sat on rough-hewn banquettes he'd made himself, drinking Tahitian beer while he prepared fish he'd caught this morning. After dinner we danced to Beatles and Stones tapes on a wood floor with fine pandanus matting, while Manihi intrigued my husband with his unusual 'dishwasher': he laid the plates on the coral reef for the fish to clean them off, then gave them a final rinse in rainwater.

We took a dawn ride back to Rotoava for bread and groceries, then sailed to Toau, another gorgeous, largely uninhabited atoll, of which the Admiralty instructions state 'even with radar, the low parts ... are very dangerous to approach'. In order to pick our way through the lagoon's minefield of treacherous coral heads, or 'bommies' as they are known in contemporary sailor slang, Dick was winched 130 feet up the mast in the boatswain's chair, a canvas contraption used to sway a man aloft. Once he was safely balanced on the jumpers, he was able to scan the surrounding water for any colour variation that would indicate shallow shoals. The only difference between this navigational procedure and that of the *Casco*'s crew is that Dick used a walkie-talkie for relaying directions to the Captain instead of a good, old-fashioned holler.

Just before sunset, I conducted a sewing bee to make *pareos* for everyone out of fabric I'd bought in a general store in Fakarava: white hibiscus on a royal blue background. Even Daragh and Evan were eager to learn how to hemstitch, and each impressed the girls by making his own garment. When the group fell silent with the repetitiousness of the work, I read them all another chapter of *Typee* – until Billy turned up and offered a sensitive critique of Melville's prose.

'It's crap,' he hinted.

I wish Billy would come diving with us. I know he'd love it. During his last scuba experience, two years ago in Fiji, he dropped his weight belt with near-disastrous consequences, so he's not much inclined to descend again. This morning, Scarlett and I drift-dived again, in another very fast current. We descended to eighty feet just outside the pass, then found ourselves being swept over rich coral gardens and up a jagged wall to a wide plain of soft coral, sea anemones, brain coral and starfish. Clinging to rock-holds, we scrutinized the fishy freeway for its diverse riders, which included schools of red mullet, and pencil-thin transparent fish called aiguillette. Higher up the wall was another marine playground, where thousands of burnished-red emperor fish cavorted along with a dense school of pale grey, paddletail snapper.

Next, the current catapulted us through gullies filled with Louis's favourite parrotfish. We spun past them so fast they seemed to stare back at us in amazement, beaks agape. At close to four knots, we were truly flying. Scarlett and I caught sight of Yannis and simultaneously began to laugh, a sure-fire way to fill one's mask with seawater. He had become Peter Pan, with arms outstretched and one leg bent – a pose that belonged in the pantomime.

This afternoon we moved to another small *motu* and went ashore to buy lobsters. One large, extended family lives on this stretch of beach, surrounded by shallow turquoise water partially sectioned off with fish traps. At the end of the jetty was the grandfather's house, an open shack with gay Polynesian flower-print curtains, plastic chairs piled up beside a washing bench, a bed and a television set. We turned right past a couple of boatsheds, on which several dozen fishtails were nailed up like trophies, while a dead shark lay rotting on a concrete floor. A teenage girl called off a couple of dogs that seemed intent on taking a bite out of each of us. She told me she'd been at school in Tahiti for eleven years but hated it and was glad to be back here living with her family. Her playmates were two brawny male cousins, with whom she frequently streaked across the lagoon in a tin boat, like LA teenagers cruising Sunset Strip.

We were greeted by the wizened patriarch and a younger man with unkempt hair who had a terrible, open gash on his shoulder. They showed us an oil drum full of coconut crabs – monstrous, maroon-coloured fellows with wicked pincers. They paraded one around our feet, using a stick to keep it within grabbing distance. Smearing the contents of their stomachs on bread is a great delicacy, they said.

Canadian evangelical music emanated from their wooden house, and a woman waved us inside. The living room was pretty and cheerful, full of knick-knacks, delightful shell arrangements, magazine pictures and bright soft furnishings. When she produced a bag of black pearls and invited us to barter them for Coca-Cola, skincare products or DVDs, we radioed the teenagers to came ashore with a few items to swap. Daragh and Evan exchanged DVDs for presents to take home to their mothers, while I acquired a very pretty, gold-coloured pearl for a video and a six-pack of Coke. At the family's request, Jock brought his first aid kit ashore and dressed the man's shoulder, for which he was repaid in black pearls.

Treasures of the sea were presented to Fanny without the need for bartering. Monsieur Donat gave her and Margaret a couple of gold-lined, double oyster shells, each with a gold pearl attached to one side. Everyone in the party received a single pearl, a box of pink coral and another of fine shells, some with coral growing out of them. In return, Fanny sent a gold ring to Donat's wife.

Thursday 11 November 2004

Kayt, Yannis, Billy and I took the tender to the local fish shop, which consisted of a wood-and-wire trap in a shallow part of the lagoon. Teiki, a beefy fisherman in torn T-shirt and grey shorts, came scurrying to meet us accompanied by two youths in a small dinghy with *Better Boat* written on the side. Donning a pair of goggles, he leapt into the water-pen carrying a long spear. He stuck his head beneath the water for a second or two, until suddenly we saw his elbow jerk forward in a swift, well-aimed stab. A frantic swooshing of water followed, and soon the head of the spear was high above his head, with a sorry-looking triggerfish impaled and wriggling on its tip. I had thought the fish would be thrown on the jetty, destined for the frying pan, but instead Teiki tossed the dying creature back into the water outside the corral. He immediately returned to his underwater abattoir and speared another triggerfish, which received the same fate. Mystified, we watched him repeat the routine no fewer than seven times. I finally asked him in French why he was discarding them. He tersely replied that the triggerfish eat the plastic lining of the trap, so they had to go. I tried to glean the point of killing them without either eating them or transferring them to the lagoon, but he was non-committal. Instead, he focused on a wretched porcupine pufferfish that had also got inside the trap. It too was skewered and discarded, producing a last, squeakish moan as its prickly hide deflated. Billy, I noticed, was visibly distressed.

'So why did you kill that creature?' I demanded of the fishmonger.

He shrugged, smiled, and looked away. 'Just because.'

With the worst of the savagery over, or so we hoped, Kayt was invited to join Teiki inside the pen to choose our dinner, although no one's appetite had been particularly enhanced by what we had just witnessed. Kayt selected five parrotfish that were duly speared and chucked into the *Better Boat*. They lay gasping in the sunlight; beautiful, shining things, in variegated blues and greens, flipping sporadically.

We sailed overnight to Rangiroa, a touristy island of black pearl boutiques and over-water bungalows. Leaving the maitais to the others, we wall-dived outside the lagoon in the Tuputa Pass. Several turtles, of hawksbill and green varieties, allowed me to approach while they fed warily on tasty sponges. They remind me of fast-food customers, hunched over their food, eyeing the world suspiciously from a 'super-size me' reverie. *Don't bother me*, as the slogan goes, *I'm eating*. The sea was punctuated with flashing damselfish. One very large tuna cruised alone, and so did a solitary silver-tipped shark. The rest of the pelagic fish were more sociably arranged; a school of yellowfin tuna, another of striped barracuda and a pulsing ball of jackfish silhouetted against the deep-water sunlight.

I was thrilled that Billy at last joined us for an afternoon dive, a very pretty and relatively shallow one near the *motu* Nohi

Nohi, where there's an aquatic park. At times we were entirely surrounded by angelfish and Moorish idols. Some aggressive triggerfish kept us at bay, while the hugest moray eel we'd ever seen displayed its snapping head upon a rocky plinth. A deadly lionfish lurked nearby, a gorgeous, pink-striped creature with poisonous fins that can inflict appalling agony. Billy was ecstatic. He always wanted to be Jacques Cousteau.

Next day, in the Avatoru Pass, Yannis put half a dead fish on a rock and instructed us to wait by the reef, clinging to dead coral, so we could photograph whoever turned up to munch it. Within minutes there were five or six sharks, silver-tipped beauties, two or three metres long, bullying the schools of jackfish out of their way to get first snap at the meat. The monsters cruised close by our posse of cowering humans, even circling us from time to time. The biggest shark of all had a cleaning fish attached to its underside, a sort of on-board groomer. When all Yannis's food was gone, the monsters departed as fast as they'd arrived – a reminder that these predators are not usually interested in eating men.

Sunday 14 November 2004

We weighed anchor at 5 am, bound for Tikehau Atoll, and arrived later in the day at a most gorgeous line of white beaches sparsely dotted with ugly houses. On the off-shore reef we could see some fish traps and a picturesque hut on a mid-lagoon jetty. We immediately set off in the dinghy to buy more fish. It's strange that I have been so wary of reef fish in the past, but ciguatera is now quite low on my list of worries. In Louis's book *In the South Seas* he advises the seeking of local knowledge concerning which fish are poisonous – and that's what we've been doing. I assume the people here catch them at the right time of the cycle and preserve them in the traps so there's always something safe to eat. After peering into one of these traps, Kayt

said there were so many angelfish in the way she could barely
discern the edible species. The vendor, however, skilfully
speared six parrotfish, five jackfish and a dorade, or sea-bream.
While we were loading them into the tender we suddenly heard
a commotion behind us and whipped around just in time to see
the fisherman holding a small reef shark aloft on the end of his
spear. Its magnificent white underbelly spiked and bloody, it
thrashed furiously in vain until it was tossed away into a salty
grave.

In French Polynesia, sharks were not always treated thus, as
Louis noted:

> The chief and his sister were persons perfectly intelligent:
> gentlefolk, apt of speech. The sister was very religious, a
> great church-goer, one that used to reprove me if I stayed
> away; I found out afterwards that she privately worshipped a
> shark.

Monday 15 November 2004

'The cheery announcement that we're going to the sharks' hole
today,' gasped my husband at breakfast, 'is one of the best
laxatives known to man.' Nevertheless, he joined us on our dive
to the home of a clan of gargantuan grey reefers, more than a
hundred feet down in the dingiest part of the lagoon. We clung
to a shelf that formed the eves of their coral grotto and tried to
remain composed. One by one the monsters emerged, first
looming in the mouth of the cave, then gathering momentum
with shocking alacrity as they almost side-swiped our frail little
group on their way upwards for a morning hunt. It was utterly
heart-stopping. Time after time, I was convinced one was
coming straight for us. Yannis said they were all female –
perhaps with young inside the cave, which only added to the
precariousness of the situation.

'Never in my life . . .' cried Billy afterwards, who, for the first time in his entire life, failed to finish a sentence.

Over the following days he surprised himself by becoming quite comfortable around the creatures that had previously filled him with utter dread.

'I never, ever thought,' he said, 'that one day I'd be in a dinghy and come roaring up to a school of them, shout, "Shark! Shark!" and jump straight in!'

When Louis caught a 'fresh chill' in Fakarava, and became quite ill with serious congestion and a risk of haemorrhage, Fanny demanded the *Casco* party set sail immediately for Tahiti where there was a doctor. She feared he had succumbed to a Chilean influenza, a severe strain that had reached epidemic proportions in the Society Islands. They said a hasty goodbye to Donat and presented their Fakaravan friends with a few farewell gifts, including a bag of flour and a handsome carriage clock for Taniera, Margaret's pin-up boy.

Tuesday 16 November 2004

We left early for Tahiti. It was a lovely sail, on a smooth port tack under a sliver of moon and bright stars. We sighted the island at dawn, a jagged, deep purple silhouette against a gold-foil sea. Strips of ivory cloud radiated from the metallic new sun, with blueing sky above, while a shining path of bronze steps connected it to the boat. A horizontal slice of smoky cloud lay near the base of the silhouette and, just beneath it on the coastline, peeped the twinkling lights of Pape'ete.

'We're blessed to witness this,' I thought, leaping below to wake Billy. 'You must come up on deck and see Tahiti!' I cried.

My husband squinted in the early light streaming in from the porthole I'd just opened. 'If it's another bunch of fucking coconuts,' he groaned, 'I'm gonna kill you.'

As the sun rose, a searing whiteness, the island bleached to a misty charcoal beneath chalk cloud fingers and an eggshell sky, while the sea turned a gold-capped navy. To starboard, neighbouring Moorea came into view, with mossy shadowed peaks soaring into brilliant blue. Billy appeared on deck, wearing beige shorts and a Hank Williams T-shirt. Too cool for the world, he was oblivious to everything except the pain in his shoulder.

'There's something uncomfortable,' he winced, 'about flying backwards naked through the shower curtain.' Sometimes I think he's funniest when he's really grumpy.

The sea had been glassy, yet on the final approach to Pape'ete a strong swell caused us to roll like a feverish elephant. But that was not the worst of it. A brownish haze soon became discernible, lying low along the shoreline above the main road, our first sight of city pollution in a long time.

'Wait a minute!' said Kayt, shocked out of a dreamy reverie. 'Is that a factory?' We stared aghast at the sharpening row of ugly high-rise hotels, lining the shore beneath the right tail of the cloud.

There was, nevertheless, mounting excitement about the fact that we'll be docked at the marina, so for the first time since Panama we'll actually be able to walk off the boat. We followed the line of rusty-hulled tankers entering the harbour ahead of us. I smelled something sweet being roasted – and was convinced it came from the copra works – but it turned out to be Kayt baking chocolate coconut muffins.

After we docked, Yannis took us into downtown Pape'ete. It was shocking. The noise, the traffic, the bustle and crowds of people made me very, very anxious. I tried to sit through lunch in a fashionable restaurant but soon became so overwhelmed with a multiplicity of images and stimuli, I had to get out. It's been almost three months since we were last in a city. Could I ever live in one again? Billy, on the other hand, was relieved to be in a metropolis again. 'What were you missing?' I asked. 'Strangers,' he replied.

'I don't much like Tahiti,' wrote Margaret. 'It seems to me a sort of halfway house between savage life and civilization, with the drawbacks of both and the advantages of neither.'

Emily, a short, ebullient Tahitian woman with classic waist-length hair, wearing a *muumuu* that matched the seat-covers of her taxi van, escorted me around the island.

'I don't speak much Polynesian since my mother passed away,' she confessed. Her mother was from one of the Tuamotu Islands, so at five and a half she was sent to the Catholic Mission school in Pape'ete to learn French. 'I lived here with my father,' she explained. 'I saw my mother once a year, in July and August. My father was a taxi driver. He was never home, so in the end my mother decided I would have to go to boarding school.' She pointed to a walled compound behind a line of retail stores, not far from the cathedral. 'I went there for eight years.' The memory caused her to shiver. 'I was scared of those nuns.' Emily married an American soldier, from whom she has picked up words like 'lousy', and moved to Alabama. 'I prefer the lobsters over there,' she said, with idiosyncratic randomness. 'They're much easier to eat. Here they hurt your hands.'

When we pulled up at a seaside public park, I was thrilled to see in its grounds a soaring white lighthouse, adorned with a simple plaque inscribed with Louis's words: *Tahiti 1888. Great were the feelings of emotion, as I stood with mother by my side and we looked upon the edifice designed by my father when I was sixteen and worked in his office during the summer of 1866.* Margaret was more matter-of-fact: 'It is a fine building of grey coral, mixed with a pretty red stone, which looks very well and effective.'

'What's it like living in Pape'ete now?' I asked Emily as we strolled in the lush palm gardens.

'There's a lot of stealing here,' she said. 'They come into your house. They don't kill you, they just take stuff, go in your fridge and look for booze. We have to put bars on our windows, or have high walls topped with bottles or spikes. They steal from Chinese houses the most. They know those people work hard and are never at home during the day.'

*

When Fanny and Louis heard that the southeastern side of Tahiti Nui was not only wonderfully verdant but also inhabited by people who were almost as wild as Marquesans, they became eager to see it for themselves. After spending a month in Pape'ete they were longing for a less civilized environment, and hoped that the climate round there would be conducive to Louis's better health. The *Casco* set sail with a local pilot on board, expecting to drop anchor thirty miles away at Taravao harbour within just a few hours, but they were surprised by heavy seas with extremely strong headwinds. Twelve hours after they departed, they were still battling to make headway and avoid the reefs. With no engine to save her, the *Casco* was in trouble and Captain Otis was forced to execute disquieting manoeuvres, including a dangerous jibe to avoid coming to grief on one lee shore. The foul weather did not let up for another whole day and the expected short trip turned into a thirty-hour ordeal.

After rounding the northeast corner of Tahiti Nui, the yacht was able to point a little better at its destination. But it was soon apparent that, during the earlier part of the journey, the main topmast had become misaligned. Understandably, the crew was afraid to stand watch, expecting the spar to come crashing down at any moment. Captain Otis anticipated disaster as they approached the surf-topped pass to Taravao Harbour, so he readied the lifeboats. Suddenly, the wind died, leaving the *Casco* stranded without the power to cross the reef. This was an extremely dangerous moment.

'We're doomed!' shouted the pilot. Fortunately, a gust of wind saved them, lifting the boat on to the crest of a wave, ploughing her down into its trough, then shooting her safely into the placid harbour. Louis sighed with relief, as did the Captain. Just then, Fanny emerged from below.

'Isn't that nice?' she said, noticing the readied lifeboats. 'The Captain has already made preparations so that we can be going ashore soon.' It is extraordinary to imagine she had no idea of the peril they had just faced.

'Captain,' smiled Louis, 'don't you think that such yachting gymnastics as we just performed accounted to rather a risky sport for invalid authors to engage in?'

'Well, Mr Stevenson,' replied Otis, 'you have known from the very beginning that sailing's not for sissies.'

Once safely ashore, the Stevensons discovered that Taravao was indeed lush with vines and forest trees; yet Fanny was disappointed that the humid climate and prevalence of mosquitoes made it unsuitable as a place of convalescence for Louis, who was deteriorating fast. Hearing that Tautira, a breezier town, lay ten miles away on the northeastern tip of Tahiti Iti, Fanny revved herself into action. Since Captain Otis was unwilling to risk taking the *Casco* on another voyage east before the mast was repaired, she went ashore to find overland transport. Within an hour she had hired wagon and horses, and was back on board ordering lunch for the trip and a mattress so Louis could lie prone during the journey. It was an unbearably hot and bumpy ride. There was no proper road and many streams had to be forded. Upon their arrival in Tautira, Louis was pale, running a fever and coughing up blood.

They were received by Ori a Ori, sub chief of the village, whose fine looks were noted by Margaret: 'over six foot three, and broad in proportion, and he looks more like a Roman emperor in bronze than words can express'. Fanny and Louis were installed in a fine residence by Princess Moë, the King's sister-in-law. She was a charming half-Tahitian matriarch, whose father was an English trader. She had large, laughing eyes, round cheeks with dimples, an upturned nose and an attractive little mouth. Best of all, she offered Louis local healing remedies and brought him nutritious meals several times a day, such as red mullet marinated in seawater, coconut cream, lime juice and red pepper. Under her care he improved so quickly

that soon he was well enough to sit on the veranda, gazing out at 'the garden of the world' as he described the place. 'We are in heaven here,' he wrote home. 'I should prefer living among the people of Tahiti to any other people I have come across.'

I wonder if he really meant 'the people of Tahiti' or, rather, Princess Moë who was the recipient of his undisguised gratitude and affection. In the poem he wrote her, however, he managed to restrain his feelings to a child-like adoration:

> *Upon my threshold, in broad noon,*
> *Fair and helpful, wise and good,*
> *The Fairy Princess Moë stood.*

Meanwhile, Fanny reclined on a pillow at Ori a Ori's thatched smoking room, puffing on native cigarettes. Was she sulking?

'Wouldn't want to do this pissed!' Navigating a perilous channel in the Cook Islands. Rolle on the bow

Instant dry dock – a twin-masted ship thrown into the palm trees, Nassau Island

Dear Dad, please send more money soon…

Attack of the giant flying willy – *Takapuna* in the Society Islands

Pink water rafting – Butaritari lagoon, Kiribati

Scotsman at Niki Naki Noo, and (below) two objects of his affection

Napoleon 'big blue kissy-lips' wrasse

Hot-lips in competition with fresh fish

Woman in need of larger
frying pan

Is that my prostate? A sorry
porcupine fish

'Them as dies'll be the lucky ones…'
Daragh on the spinnaker pole

Bacchus and his *Wahine*, Moorea

Still life with toes and parrotfish

Tarantino fan – Eromango

The garden of the world – Tautira, Tahiti

Heaven's Angel – Marshall Islands Policeman

Fanny's 'dolls house church' on Swain's Island

No need for bath salts – in Fanny's tide pool,
Suwarrow Island

Home entertainment – Maria and her
men, Swain's Island

Vai – Pukapuka Island

No change given – bus driver, Pago Pago

Nukunonu carver making a Tokelau bucket – the type Fanny used as luggage

Outrigger canoeing in Apia Harbour, Samoa

Top: Vailima, Samoa

Far left: The ghost of *Aolele* – in Fanny's bedroom, Vailima

Left: At Louis' tomb, Mount Vaea – Fanny' plaque

Bottom: View from th Vailima veranda

Did she feel her role as nurse, even her position as wife and lover, was undermined by the exotic princess? Louis even engaged Moë's help with a ballad he was writing. Fanny desperately wanted to see Louis well, so I imagine she decided to take a benign view of their liaison; however, her feelings were likely to be expressed somehow. It was about this time that another chief, Tati Salmon, observed that Fanny was 'rude and bossy', that she scolded Louis for overindulging in cigarettes and wine, sent him to bed when she thought he was tired, and interrupted their conversations. Of course, at that time in history, such would have been the culturally designated view of most Tahitian males towards any female who dared assert herself.

As Emily drove me along Fanny and Louis' route eastward, from Pape'ete to the preferred climate of Tautira, she occasionally threw titbits of Tahitian folklore my way. 'You see that cliff? Beneath it is a special grotto. You throw a coconut into the water there and it will come up without a husk.' Nowadays, Taravao is an up-and-coming business district. Tautira, traditionally called Fenua Ehere, or jungle land, remains lush, with quaint, veranda-fronted houses and charming tropical gardens of palms, noni trees, tiaré flowers and ahia, or Polynesian miniature apples. In Fanny's time there were no stores in either place; now supermarkets, photographic stores and snack bars abound. Tautira even boasts a new Complex Sportif. Both towns receive twenty-five TV channels.

While awaiting the return of the Casco, Louis continued to improve and even became quite prolific in his writing. He grew very close to Ori a Ori, to whom he bonded as a 'brother', swapping names with him in the Tahitian way. When Louis and Fanny expressed concern about the lack of news from Captain Otis, whom they only presumed had managed to sail the Casco to Pape'ete for repairs, Ori a Ori embarked on an investigative voyage. He returned a week later, his canoe loaded up with tinned beef, ship's biscuit, jam and rather a lot of champagne. He also brought a letter from Otis explaining that the spar needed to be replaced because it had been undermined with dry rot. There was no suitable replacement in Pape'ete but timbers from a sunken whaling barque could be modified to fit. Thankfully on 21 December, the *Casco* was at last sighted sailing into Tautira harbour. Fanny and Louis threw a farewell village feast, then set sail for Hawaii. They faced 2,300 miles at sea, on a ship with a compromised mast.

Louis and Fanny left the *Casco* in Honolulu. When they heard that the yacht had made it safely back to San Francisco they breathed a huge sigh of relief, for having the financial liability for returning her in one piece had been extremely stressful. Through Belle they were introduced to Hawaiian royalty, in particular King Kalalaua (the 'First Gentleman of the Pacific') and Princess Victoria Kaiulani, who entertained and befriended them. The Stevensons rented a small house on Waikiki Beach, then a quiet, sparsely populated stretch of sand. Louis even visited Father Damien's leper colony at Kaluapapa on the small Hawaiian island of Molokai, and was so moved by what he saw there he wrote letters defending Damien when he was attacked posthumously in the press.

After a time, Fanny and Louis were inspired to return to their cruising life. In June, 1889 they left Honolulu on board the *Equator*, a trading ship bound for Micronesia. Right at the outset, the passengers and crew nearly came to grief – by human design. Two days before their departure, the Stevensons met two Belgian men who asked if they could join them for the trip. Intuition warned Louis and Fanny not to agree, which was just as well; the men turned out to be pirates who customarily inveigled their way on to schooners as deckhands, then poisoned everyone aboard so they could sell the vessels.

Over the next few months Fanny and Louis visited, most notably, Butaritari and Abemama (both now belonging to the Republic of Kiribati), where they spent several months before

finally disembarking in a place Louis had always longed to see: Samoa.

Friday 26 November 2004

In Pape'ete harbour, a seaplane wreck is lying in fairly shallow water. Billy drifted right inside the cockpit and sat happily on the pilot's seat as if he were flying it. 'It's kind of sad,' he said whimsically afterwards, 'when Biggles turns to bubbles.' Outside the harbour, and a short sail across the channel, lies Moorea, or 'yellow lizard' island. Rolle, Yannis and I went for an early snorkel in a shallow part of the lagoon opposite a smart hotel. Semi-tame stingrays leapt all over us like slippery, exuberant puppies searching for food. While hand-feeding one I put my fingers too far inside its mouth and recoiled as it chomped down on my hand. Serves me right for being so ignorant of its anatomy.

This afternoon we went on an island tour with a ghastly ex-pat called Frederick, who could not modulate the insufferably high volume of his in-car sound system. Looking at him, an obnoxious sag-bellied customer with thick-framed spectacles, it seemed unlikely that his story of having three wives in three different houses was plausible. According to him, they were rationed of his favours at a rate of two days each per week, with a rest for him on Sundays. We ended up at a terrible tourist trap called the Tiki Village, with a Polynesian buffet, black-pearl store and live 'cultural' show run by a family of sad, morose people, whose phoney smiles faded the second after we'd passed. During dinner, a tired Tahitian beauty in a coconut bra slunk up and down a catwalk, tying different-coloured *pareos* in a variety of styles; halter neck, culottes, bare-midriff and over-one-shoulder. After every change, she posed, one foot pointed provocatively in front of the other, and blew kisses to an audience of snap-happy tourists. A short, grinning man followed suit with 'male' styles: shorts, cloaks and tunic.

'Now this,' I said to Billy, as we fled the scene, 'you are welcome to call Niki-Naki-Noo.'

Just before sunset we shoved off for a ten-hour ride to Huiahine in a heavy swell. Louis had been keen to visit this island, one of the Leeward Society Isles, partly to escape Pape'ete, but also because he had read about the village of Maeva, where royal families lived side by side in the protection of the sacred mountain of Mou'a Tapu. However, when Captain Otis expressed concern about the island's perilous reefs and the prevalence of mosquitoes, the plan was ditched. When we arrived we found a sweet main village, Fare, a market sea-port with few tourists. Many of the women wore Polynesian floral crowns which made even the weariest face look charming. It seemed silly to put up umbrellas to shelter from the refreshing, light rain, but we did so out of habit. Then we took a late ride to Baie Faie, a stunning lagoon with a thatched pearl farm housed in the middle, perched on a half-submerged coral head.

Wednesday 1 December 2004

In Ra'iatea we dived on the wreck of the schooner *Nordby*, lost some time in the early 1900s. It was lying in shallow water, quite close to a group of over-water resort bungalows. Too late, I noticed the sewer pipe running straight down into the lagoon but it was even more sobering to see the enormous, twin-masted ship lying on her side in the sand, decorated with coral, anemones and tiny clams. Half of one mast had broken clean off and was resting at right angles to its lower half. While Billy inspected the welding, I circled her in horror, taking in the disabled helm, coils of rope and a massive anchor still lying amidship. I wondered what had brought her to grief. Gliding through the wreckage, my fear of disaster at sea came flooding back. Yannis beckoned us inside her three-storeyed carcass. We followed him up to the top of its inverted hull, then emerged with surprise through a disgusting film of dust and oil into a large air pocket that must have been there for a hundred years. I was mentally willing my husband to leave his regulator in place.

'Don't breathe that air, Billy!' I *think* he heard me.

We arrived late Thursday into Bora Bora lagoon. Lights twinkled at us from the base of one of nature's opera sets: a truly dramatic, indigo rock-castle, set against a pale quince sky. The next day we circumnavigated the island in the tender. Bora Bora is largely a series of resorts, but still very beautiful, in true fairy colours: jewel blues and greens, and pearly pink sands, with a peerless lagoon reflected in the clouds. Billy left for New York at five, chic in black jeans, cowboy boots and Voyage shirt, thoroughly optimistic about his forthcoming concerts.

'I wish you could stay longer,' I whispered, kissing him goodbye. 'Don't you think this place is romantic?'

'Och,' he shrugged, slinging his banjo over his shoulder. 'A little Paradise goes a long, long way.'

Saturday 4 December 2004

Outside the reef on my birthday dive there were spotted eagle rays, grey sharks and a huge school of striped barracuda. I glimpsed a moray eel in the act of swimming, a first for me. Since Daragh and Evan are headed home for Christmas this afternoon, and Scarlett is off for a fortnight in LA, none of them could join us underwater (the rules require a 24-hour break between diving and flying to avoid compression sickness). However, Daragh drove the tender and Scarlett came along for the ride. During our safety stop Yannis and I saw the two of them plop into the water above us for a dip, their tanned young bodies splashing around a few metres above a gang of uninterested black-tipped reef sharks. We had a farewell lunch on board, then the boys were sent to clean their cabin. Rolle was a tough inspector, demanding improvements four times before he was satisfied.

When Daragh, Evan and Scarlett left for the airport, there was a wealth of sadness all around. Entering the galley, I saw Kayt and Daragh locked in a tearful embrace. Evan will be coming back after Christmas, but Daragh must return to his academic studies. I told both boys how proud I am of them; each has become so confident and accomplished over the past few months. They jumped into the tender and pulled away from the *Takapuna*. Daragh, carrying his precious new guitar (a present from Jock), looked back with tears in his eyes. Kim has left the boat, too. She returned to LA for Thanksgiving, and has decided not to come back.

This life is not for the faint-hearted, but there are many

rewards. That evening, I lay on deck under the Southern Cross and took stock of my life, a pastime that tends to accompany birthdays. I am happy to say I was able to count my blessings and be humbly thankful that today, a little over a year since my Auckland epiphany, I am no longer a sad, stressed, frantic woman; I am a stargazing Takapunian.

Sunday 5 December 2004

Under the sea this morning, just when I was enjoying the sight of some very large lemon sharks with their mouths open for cleaning, I was startled by the sight of a submarine descending from above. I swam away nervously, thinking it must be a military vehicle, but Yannis urged me to look more closely. It turned out to be a pleasure submersible with tourists inside, peering out at us from transparent walls. I giggled to myself. Who was in the aquarium . . . them or us? I couldn't decide.

A gargantuan cruise ship is moored nearby and some of the passengers were diving in the vicinity. A rather uncoordinated diver caught my attention. He was trailing behind his group, blithely photographing the woman in front of him and completely oblivious to the fact that three massive lemon sharks were shadowing him. I waited gleefully for the moment when he spotted them and sure enough he dropped his camera in fright.

I have finally decided to get a tattoo. Olsen, a quiet, soulful Polynesian artist with beautiful light eyes, works from a small thatched hut beside the ocean guarded by a very young pitbull puppy. Reggae music was playing as I entered.

'What symbols are important to you?' asked Olsen.

'The sea, boats and canoes – and I like sharks, rays, frangipani and tropical flowers,' I replied. I showed him the scar on my lower abdomen – the result of three Caesarean sections – and asked if he could create something attractive to cover it. I was nervous. He told me to lie down. I tried to breathe. His first few cuts were extremely painful but, two hours later, I loved the result: a woven strand of waves, sharks' teeth, turtle, frangipani and hibiscus.

It was Eli's last evening, so we all put on *pareos* and the guys went bare-chested with the bone jewellery I'd given them. Someone put on Motown music and Rolle mixed the drinks. He came out of the galley with blender in hand exclaiming, 'Dere's alcohol in every single ingredient!' Soon a raucous, impromptu dance party began, with Eli in the centre as a flower-crowned Bacchus until we were inspired to dive into the sea to cool off.

Next morning I had my tattoo completed so it now forms an intricate, low girdle completely encircling my lower torso. Again, the process was excruciating. The door was open with people walking by. I wanted to beg one of them to bring me something – Advil, Vicodin, gin-and-tonic – anything – to assuage my agony. Once the endorphins kicked in, however, I could stand it – until the artist moved to a new patch.

I believe I have been improved. Again, Olsen created a wonderful mélange of shark, dolphin, frangipani, fish, and waves, all joining yesterday's lower abdomen curve and culminating in a lovely peak just above my buttocks.

'Tell me what you have done,' I said afterwards, straining to see my rear.

'It's a tattoo,' he said solemnly. Wielding a mirror, I was delighted to see a shark in full glory, undoubtedly my totem animal for it seems to symbolize the facing of my fears. Here in French Polynesia, I have gazed into the jaws of the paramount sea monsters – and found them benign and magnificent.

We left the Society Islands in a grey, tropical haze, a downpour that became ominously worse as we progressed further and further out to sea. Then, at sunset, the grey was relieved by the beginnings of a rainbow off to starboard, complementing the setting ball of orange to port. As we watched, the rainbow grew higher and was joined by another multi-hued section, until it was a full arch. After a few more minutes, we could discern a fainter copy-cat rainbow, slightly higher in the reddening sky. The rain continued; but the double rainbow, ours alone in all the universe, stood sentry to our progress until the tiniest orange crescent took refuge behind a strawberry sea.

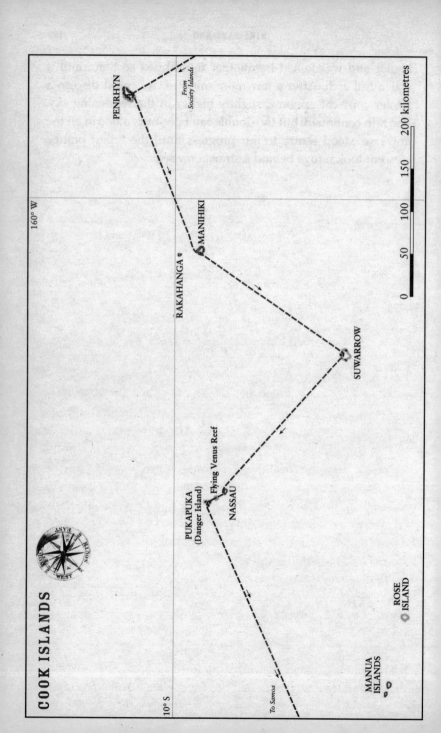

COOK ISLANDS

PENRHYN

From Society Islands

160° W

MANIHIKI

RAKAHANGA

SUWARROW

Flying Venus Reef

PUKAPUKA
(Danger Island)

NASSAU

10° S

To Samoa

MANUA
ISLANDS

ROSE
ISLAND

0   50   100   150   200 kilometres

CHAPTER EIGHT

REEF MADNESS

14°22.8′ S
133°32.3′ W

Tuesday 7 December 2004

We've been pitching all night but making great progress whenever we get a good eastnor'easterly blow. At times we've been doing twelve knots, which is darn hard sailing for this old girl. (I'm talking about the boat.) We're still thrashing about in the ITCZ, or Inter-tropical Convergence Zone, which lies in the equatorial pressure trough between the trade wind systems of the two hemispheres. For the sailor, the ITCZ presents a frustrating band of sudden wind changes and light doldrums, created by a mixing of hot and cooler air masses which produces dense clouds and overcast conditions, with squalls, electric storms and humid murkiness.

Twelve knots! 'We're smoking!' says Dick.

At this rate we should be in Penrhyn within forty-eight hours. Our destination is known to Polynesians as Tongareva, the largest and northernmost of all the Cook Islands. Captain William Sever, the first *palagi*, or European, to discover the island, named it after his ship *Lady Penrhyn* in 1788. I must say, the Admiralty navigational advice for the atoll doesn't look too promising: 'The chart must be used with caution, as it is compiled from sketch surveys only . . . Penrhyn Island lagoon is studded with detached reefs and coral heads.'

The boat seems so quiet without the kids. Weird. Our internet service is down, which is almost a relief, since I seem to be in cocoon mode. At around 6 pm the sun came out and relieved us of the eerie haze we'd seen all day. Then some lapis lazuli sky appeared for a while and a shimmering gold edge to the fading clouds.

After breakfast on Thursday the Captain called, 'Radar ho!' as the first, jagged image of Penrhyn, like a chopped-up, golden flatworm, appeared on one of the outer rings of the radar screen. Shortly after that it was 'Land ho!' as the palm-tree tops of several *motus* came into view, first the triptych of Atiati off our starboard bow, then the table-top of the main *motu*, Mangarongaro. Soon we also spied Moturakina, Atuahi and Ahupapa, and then eventually a crisp line of white sand became visible around the nearest group. These are all classic *motus* of roughly the same geological age as those we saw in the Tuamotus, whose volcanic centres had long since subsided into the sea, leaving only the outer, broken ring of palm-covered beachland. Boobies flew out to meet us. They were mainly of an unremarkable, brownish type and, sadly, not one blue foot to be seen.

'Anyone know what kind they are?' I asked.

'Rolle's the booby specialist,' replied Dick pointedly. 'Brilliant boobologist. He works without any visual aids whatsoever.'

We began to notice a strong, acrid smell. 'It's just rubbish burning off on land,' said the Captain, then jokingly: 'At least I hope it's from the island.' No one laughed. The terrible night of engine room smoke during our Marquesas passage was still fresh in our memory. As we skimmed the deep turquoise swirls on a course parallel to the beach, several blue and white roofs became apparent, as did three or four radio towers and a gigantic satellite dish. We hung around the pilot house taking turns with the binoculars. Kayt made tea and Jock appeared from the bilges, well pleased with himself for having placed a head pillow down by the pump for the comfort of the person, usually himself, who had to squeeze inside.

'I hear de drums,' said Rolle, staring at the near-empty beaches. He was having trouble distinguishing between the English words 'Penrhyn' and 'penguin', and avidly hoped the latter would be found on shore. After passing Mangarongaro we came upon two more *motus*, lined by a high, pounding off-shore surf. This was some reef. The lagoon inside the slash of motus was certainly vast and probably almost as exposed as the open sea. After a large, white A-shaped church roof became discernible, we realized it had been in view for some time, camouflaged by palms and sky.

By all accounts, the lagoon is around a hundred square miles. It is reportedly full of sharks, including a black-coloured variety that is said to be pan-aggressive, and therefore dangerous to divers. I've never heard of a black shark but I am intrigued to imagine such a creature. If it really exists, it must be exceptionally beautiful: a dark, lean, munching-machine. Then again, perhaps it's a myth, promulgated to keep recreational divers away from the pearl farms. I wonder if the locals use scuba gear, or if they still free dive.

No one on board had ever been to these islands. Fanny, though, had a very daunting account of her arrival:

> We entered the lagoon very early in the morning, a most
> perilous and exciting passage . . . Our route until we cast
> anchor was studded with rocks as thick as raisins in a
> pudding. There would be a rock on each side of us, a rock
> in front, and a rock behind, seemingly an absolute
> impossibility to move; yet his unwieldy steamer could twist
> to the right and to the left, back, and dash forward, now fast,

now slow, out of the trap we would come, only to find
ourselves in a new dilemma.

When I showed our Captain Fanny's account of her arrival here,
he wondered aloud if a lagoon entryway might have been
blasted in the reef during the Second World War, to facilitate
movement for the US military who used the island as a stop-off
point for aircraft. He seemed a little nervous. According to
Fanny, the entryway was only two boat-widths across.

'How wide was her boat?' he asked.

'Two feet wider than ours,' I replied. If Fanny's guess was
accurate, that would make the pass approximately fifty-eight
feet; not much room for error.

It was now dead on twelve and, since shallowly submerged
coral rocks are most easily seen with the sun directly overhead,
our Captain had planned well. But there was another factor: the
tide. Attempting that Taruia Passage with an incoming tide
rushing into the lagoon carried the risk of being sucked through
at a headlong pace. The *Janet Nichol* entered the pass early in the
morning, presumably to take advantage of the low solar tide.
We, on the other hand, were approaching it in a north swell, at
just under eleven knots. 'Heavy tide-rips may be experienced at
the entrance,' warned our Admiralty book.

Despite our modern radar and depth finder, the only way to
navigate safely in between the coral heads was to put a man up
the mast to spot them – just as we did in Fakarava lagoon, only
this pass was considerably more challenging. Again, Dick
prepared to be winched aloft, helped this time by his girlfriend
Sarah, who had recently arrived to join the crew. He's undergone
a personality change since she arrived. Vanished are the
occasional acid remarks, sarcasm, and scowling at the
deckhands. Around her he is all satisfied smiles, and he keeps
his Aussie audaciousness to a minimum. With Sarah controlling
his ascent on the winch, Dick began to spider-hop up the mast.
He swung out as the mast tilted, then used his legs to kick

himself away from any encroaching metal and to circum-
navigate the spreaders. Higher and higher. Finally, his arm shot
out with a closed fist – the 'stop' signal. The winch halted, then
began to whir again after he gave another flapping signal that
meant 'a little bit more'. Once in position, he wedged himself
between the mast and the jumpers, just above the third spreader,
and attempted to tie the chair to the latter. It's not easy to execute
a clove hitch with one hand and hold on for dear life with the
other. Once he managed it, his voice crackled over the radio.

'Looks clear. Stick to the middle.' The pass was just ahead of
us, a shockingly narrow gate of pale, shallow water with a
darker, deeper centre, whose portals on each side are a set of
crashing breakers mercilessly flogging a jagged reef. Utter dev-
astation awaits any vessel that fails to navigate the central safety
zone, yet the strong currents are liable to pull her off course.
Everyone came on deck to observe, aghast at our having to take
what seemed to be a monumental maritime risk.

'Vouldn't vont to do dis at night,' said Rolle, bow-riding as
usual.

Our Captain was super-focused, displaying his now-familiar,
under-pressure cool. He gauged the pull of the tide, set the
engine to override any oblique thrust and tweaked the rudder to
compensate for sideways currents. Then he boldly pointed the
bow into the narrowest section and headed through with
impressive smoothness. Hanging over the sides, the rest of us
got a close-up of Fanny's 'raisins in a pudding' – half-
submerged, detached coral heads that spell instant destruction
to any boat that bounces into them.

It didn't take long. Once the big breakers were behind us, we
began to push our way into the rock-studded lagoon.

'Slow starboard turn. Right by that next big bommie. I can see
the guts of it now.' Gashes of treacherous pale turquoise water
thick with brown coral heads were all around us, sometimes
marked with flimsy white beacons topped with triangles,
sometimes not.

'It's like a three-dimensional video game,' said Sarah. We were very fortunate to be doing this at a time of peak visibility.

'Good timing all round,' said the Captain.

'Yeah,' I said wryly. 'Thank heavens I delayed us by finishing my tattoo.'

'Yeah, good job!' Rolle gave me a teasing high five. 'I knew ve could trust in you.'

We turned to starboard, then did a short leg to avoid another bommie with a stick on top, then inched our way to port.

'Hey, the stick on the left is the turn point for a short leftie,' called Dick.

'Roger that,' hollered the Captain.

'It's like a golf course with all these little triangles,' returned Dick.

'Tell him he's buying the drinks at the nineteenth hole,' said Jock.

'There's a few uncharted bommies ahead,' warned Dick.

'I gotcha.'

We passed just five metres off an absolutely enormous coral outcrop. I pictured Fanny and the others gaping at it just like we did. Gradually we began to see the red roofs of the township of Omoka.

'Anchors ready to be dropped, Jock?' the Captain asked.

'Yes, Skipper.' Every metre to our final mooring was precarious. Once we were closer to the town, the Captain began to calculate the swing distance of our anchors, so we could sleep easy without fear of hitting a bommie in the night. 'Tell Rolle we're going to do a spread, three shots aside,' he said (one shot equals ninety feet of anchor chain). 'Gets a bit choppy here.' Now I could see one or two people on shore, motoring along a sandy road on brightly coloured scooters. The palm trees were flattened against the wind, like furry green Ferris wheels, while approaching grey clouds signalled the start of a storm. I wouldn't like to be stuck here in a cyclone.

Once we'd weighed anchor, the Captain and I started ashore

in the tender, but we were immediately challenged by two men in a tin boat. The Customs and Immigration officials, Ru and Pa Taime, motioned us back on board. Ru had received training for his job in Rarotonga, but Pa was still waiting to learn the intricacies of immigration control. They were pleased to be offered beer and wolfed the bowl of Doritos I slapped down in front of them. I was anxious to get ashore but, noticing that the paperwork was proceeding very slowly, I picked up a hose and began to help with the wash-down. The Captain did his best to finish the formalities but Ru and Pa seemed in no hurry to leave. They angled for a tour, so Rolle took them below to the engine room and introduced them to his stuffed animals. They oohed and aahed over the *Takapuna*'s interior and were especially impressed by one of my least favourite saloon features: a circular ceiling panel of the northern hemisphere night sky, achieved by near-accurate placement of tiny globe lights.

There was a plan afoot. Pa introduced the subject of black pearls and let it drop that he had a pearl farm. He opened his briefcase and brought out a selection of low-grade baubles and said he was willing to barter them for sunglasses, new men's shoes and other costly items. We offered T-shirts, baseball caps and a retired food mixer, but he wasn't interested. Partly by way of providing a distraction, I showed the brothers a book containing a picture Lloyd took of Penrhyn Bay. They were fascinated by the photo. They claimed to know the exact spot and agreed to take me there.

'Then let's go!' I cried, trying to get them off the boat. Instead they sat down at the pilot-house table and began taking it in turns to read the book, it seemed, from cover to cover.

'We want to find out how old our church is,' said Pa. I began to worry I'd never get the book back.

'I'll copy the section on Penrhyn for you,' I said at last, firmly wrenching it from them.

Fanny, too, was unimpressed with the 'bartering' attempts of the Penrhyn Islanders of her day:

An impudent young man stooped down and picked up a
worn asperculum, held it out to me grinning and said 'Buy,
one pearl.' 'I could not deprive you of so elegant an
ornament,' I replied with mock courtesy. 'Tie it around your
own neck.' This was at once understood, and received by the
others with shouts of laughter. The lad was a little dampened
by this, but pretty soon came forward again with a dog's
bone. 'Buy,' he said, 'very good, 20 pounds.' 'I could not,' I
said, 'take from him a weapon so suitable for his courage.' I
used pantomime as well as speech. The other young men
pretended, with shrieks of laughter, to be terrified by his
warlike appearance, at which he slunk away, and I saw no
more of him. Several men and women offered pearls of the
most inferior sort for sale at preposterous prices, at which . . .
I jeered at them, and the pearls were shamefully hidden.

Eventually, I went ashore in the brothers' boat, and Ru and Pa
walked me to a place from which the curved aspect of the palm-
lined bay, captured by Lloyd, was once uninterrupted. There
are now more houses and modern boats lining the shore, and
in recent years an ugly breakwater has been built, jutting
straight out from the beach. I was disappointed with the view,
particularly since the area was so untidy, with piles of rubbish
everywhere. After photographing the bay from the spot where
Lloyd once stood to capture thatched houses, palms and pristine
sands, I wandered further down the coral sand road towards a
large blue and white mission house we'd seen from the lagoon.
Along the way, I was surprised to happen upon a western-style,
twelve-piece brass band engaged in a practice session. The
musicians, dressed in shorts, T-shirts and flip-flop sandals, all
played by ear, with not a scrap of sheet music. A woman named
Matapi, in a floral dress, was enjoying the music off to the side.
She and I became the audience, and the only applauders at the
end of each number. Her husband was the bass player. She had
just completed a term of service as a school teacher, but would

shortly return home to the neighbouring island of Pukapuka, so their farewell feast was about to begin. That explained the row of dishes, covered with plastic film, lined up on a low concrete wall. The band played a familiar American crooning song from the forties or fifties that I couldn't quite place.

'How do they learn the tunes?' I asked.

'From tapes brought over from Rarotonga,' replied Matapi. It was bizarre to hear such music here.

Matapi was sad to leave Penrhyn, especially since she was going to miss the island's forthcoming celebrations for the 150th anniversary of the church in Te Tautua, the village on the opposite side of the lagoon, as well as the fiftieth anniversary of the completion of the Omoku Sunday School.

'How old is the church here in this village?' I asked, wondering if Fanny might have seen it.

'No one knows exactly,' said Matapi. Cyclones have destroyed their history, as has the drain of people leaving the island for the larger communities of Rarotonga and New Zealand.

I found the church, a well-kept white building at the end of a coral road lined with graves and family mausoleums. As I continued my walk around the village, I found the people very friendly, many motioning to me to join them for a chat. Some were visitors, Penrhyn Islanders who had moved away to find work in New Zealand or Australia, and had returned for the big celebrations. Everyone was excited about the festivities. A boatload of 200 more guests would arrive within a few days, so the many empty houses on the island would be full for a change. The entire village of Omoku would cross to Te Tautua in aluminium boats. Back at the landing place, I ran into Pa.

'Now I know why you want to know how old your church is,' I smiled. 'You want to plan a big celebration here, like they're having in Te Tautua, don't you?'

'Yes,' he nodded enthusiastically.

'Aren't there any elders here who know the history?' I asked.

'There's no one,' he replied sadly, with downcast eyes. I felt ashamed of having been so irritated by his attention to my book and promised to try to research an answer for him.

Kayt had charged me with the task of finding bread. I tracked down the local baker, Alex, who lives with his wife Christina in a bright turquoise house. Their youngest daughter was named by the older children, who decided on Alestina – a mixture of their parents' names. I asked Alex to bake us six square loaves, then crossed the island to the windy side, where piles of rubbish lay beside an otherwise stunning beach. Three small black-tipped reef sharks were playing in the shallows.

At dusk, I witnessed a wonderful musical group that seemed far more in keeping with this people's heritage than the brass band: a group of men sat by the community hall engaged in a marvellous session of sonic drumming. Some very young children were allowed to join in, experimenting with a variety of percussion sounds on the adults' hollowed-out wooden instruments. After a while, some guitars were added to the mix. As night fell, an eerie bronze electric light cast shadows on the gathering villagers. Adults sat around chatting on benches, while teenagers perched on motor scooters or crouched among the bushes. Children played in the best-lit area, goading me into taking endless digital photos and showing them the results. As the night wore on, a couple of little brothers were put to bed on a mattress stashed in the back of a nearby pick-up truck.

At around 8 pm dancers began to rehearse, a large group of young men and women in colourful lava-lavas. One of the best dancers was Hina, Ru's daughter. The men's performance reminded me of a Maori haka, a warlike dance with loud grunts and chanting, while the women's movements were reminiscent of Tahitian hip-swaying. After three or four numbers, all of them action songs accompanied by expressive hand movements, the session turned into a general sing-song. Lovely, lyrical singing rang out around the village, until the central light was abruptly extinguished and the gathering became a town meeting. People spoke one at a time, earnestly and force-fully, in their local language. I walked alone along the moonless beach road to a pitch-black jetty. Having no torch, I had to rely on the kindness of a seven-year-old boy who gallantly took my hand and led me over the rough coral stones to the pick-up point.

The next day I rose at 5 am to attend an early service. Ru and Pa, who are deacons of the church, warned me to be there before six, for the rules are very strictly enforced. If I were not on time, they said, I would be refused entry altogether.

'And no photography,' frowned Ru.

I had guessed that the women would all be wearing hats and I was right. Hitch-hiking along the road at 5.50 am in an ankle-length dress and straw hat, I was ignored by a lad on a scooter, but picked up by a woman in a small flatbed truck. I climbed in the back with her three, spruced-up teenagers. When we reached the church the entire population seemed to be there, everyone in Sunday best, although this was only Friday. Most women wore the missionary-inspired Mother Hubbards. Smart, coconut-weave hats were perched on the very top of their heads, with their hair in a neat bun at the neck. Older men wore suits and ties, usually with sandals, while the younger men's preference for short-sleeved, open shirts seemed to be tolerated. Men and women sat separately.

As I entered the church, a woman pointed sternly to a vacant spot, nowhere near anyone's husband. During the service, Ru and Pa sat watching for latecomers on either side of the main doors, which were kept open for coolness. Just before each prayer, they rose and closed the doors until after the 'Amen'. It all seemed consistent with the rules Fanny found odd and overly strict during her time on the island:

> The laws are comical in many ways, but excellent in some,
> and are very stringently executed. There is no nonsense about
> the 'remain within your houses,' for remain you must after

nine o'clock. The ship's cook paying a visit was shut in
when the time came and could not get out until the morning.

The preacher did not ascend the stairs to the high pulpit; nevertheless, he preached fire and brimstone from the ground in the
local language. The hymn-singing was spine-tingling. Strong,
pure women's voices rang out first, answered by the men, then
the whole congregation joined in. I felt hairs on the back of my
neck rise at the power and thrill of their music. Here was the
vibrancy, the passion, the optimism that had seemed missing
from the dwindling population of this messy, half-empty village.

Later that morning, the Captain and I walked to the airport a
couple of miles away. It was dreadfully hot, so we were grateful
to be picked up by Alex the baker, who came by in his truck on
the way to his pearl farm. The airport waiting lounge consisted
of a set of wooden benches under a lean-to. The runway was in
a terrible state, with weeds overgrowing it as far as we could see.
The people had been told the air service would be disconnected
if they didn't repair it, but no one did.

We dropped in on Warwick, who runs the meteorological
station. After wandering through his front yard, past oil drums
full of empty drink cans, the Captain reached behind a curtain of
multi-coloured plastic strips and banged on his front door. We
waited quite a while for him to emerge, a grumpy New Zealand
palagi in nothing but a pair of shorts. I guess we disturbed him
in the middle of his hangover. He largely ignored me, but the
Captain managed to humour him a little and eventually
extracted a weather report. A low pressure system is in evidence
– something big brewing over Fiji, moving southeast.

Warwick's demeanour changed when I asked him about his
family. The light finally came on in his eyes as he revealed
fatherly pride in his children, who are excelling in various sports
in New Zealand schools. He married a Cook Islander and has
been living here since 1997. He puts up a weather balloon every
day and generally monitors meteorological conditions, but he

also sells beer, diesel and meat. I wondered why he seemed so glum.

'What's the worst aspect of being here?' I asked.

'Trying to deal with the whims of the local people,' he said grimly. He explained that local trading policies were very tough, the politics tricky, and that there was a lot of infighting. In his opinion, the people here are overly used to receiving handouts. They have never moved on, he says, from the mindset created during the Second World War when American soldiers, who used the place for a base, drove round the island distributing food aplenty. Now the New Zealand government provides massive aid, just as it does for all Cook Islands, but Warwick believes it prevents the Penrhyn Islanders from self-efficacy and ensures that they remain work-shy. He thinks the Penrhyn pearl industry failed not because of the most commonly expressed reasons – algae bloom, the price of pearls and stiff competition from Tahiti – but because the people here didn't want to maintain their responsibilities on the farms. He said the existing successful farms on Penrhyn employ Fijians, who apparently don't mind doing a day's work.

'But if your culture is such that success is defined in terms of family happiness,' I posed, 'and you are surrounded by enough natural produce to keep you healthy, then why would you bother to work?' Warwick conceded that he had no answer for that. I was uncomfortable with his generalizations about the people here, yet I could see that it must be frustrating for him to be a goal-oriented person living among people with such a different set of values. In many ways, he was the modern equivalent of the early traders, a contemporary Tin Jack. Fanny probably would have found him interesting, although he barely spoke to me; the conversation was largely man to man.

I was curious to see Te Tautua, the village on the opposite side of the lagoon, so, in the late afternoon, I asked the Captain to take me across. Ru agreed to be our pilot. He sat in the bow with his briefcase on his knee and pointed out the way. After only a few seconds in the heavy swell, I realized it was going to be a terrible journey. The bow thumped against the oncoming waves with such force I wondered if my back could take it. I tried standing, to take the shocks with my legs instead of my spine, but I barely managed to stay inside the boat. At times we were all entirely airborne.

The palm-lined crescent of a beach at Te Tautua was absolutely gorgeous, the threshold of an utterly clear, turquoise bay with a white-sand bottom. Warwick had told us this village was neater than Omoka, but the first things we noticed were ramshackle modern houses surrounded by piles of kitchen rubbish, cardboard boxes, plastic bottles, old bicycle tyres and sheets of corrugated iron. Pigs wandered freely, as did chickens. As we pulled the tender alongside a coral stone jetty, two enormous nurse sharks came right up to the boat as if they expected to be petted. We learned later that the people here hand-feed them, which explains why they resemble spoiled, fat Labradors. I came very close to leaning out of the tender and rubbing their smooth brown heads.

It was even hotter here than across the lagoon. People congregated in the shade, while children sat in trees drinking soda pop. There are so many mosquitoes here the people often spend the night on another atoll. They say Dengue fever is rife. As we wandered around the village, Ru introduced us to the people, many of whom were visitors here for the forthcoming celebrations. They were extremely welcoming, but I was loath to hang around in such vicious heat. Ru husked coconuts on an old bit of pipe and presented them to us with a top, circular flap sliced open for easy drinking.

The church was practically the only well-maintained place in the village, a blue and white painted building flanked by two large concrete water tanks. As we paused in the shade of a frangipani tree, a woman drove by on a motor scooter, one hand on the steering wheel and one clutching her baby. I was intrigued by an early trader's home, an empty concrete and wood structure with a rusty corrugated tin roof that looked like it had weathered many cyclones.

When we came back to the boat, I printed out photos I'd taken of Ru's wife and baby nephew and said goodbye; but, once again, we couldn't get him off the boat. He plonked himself down in the galley and ate sandwiches for a good hour or two more – until we finally bartered the broken food mixer for a couple of pearls and managed to send him on his way. We left Penrhyn around 3 pm – a little too late for optimum visibility. Consequently, there was a lot of additional anxiety about clearing the pass and avoiding the bommies, especially with a strong flood tide pushing us back into the lagoon.

I learned later that a shameful tragedy occurred in Penrhyn several years prior to Fanny and Louis's visit. In 1863 four evangelical islander missionaries, hoping to raise funds to build a new church on the island, were tricked by Peruvian slave traders into recruiting their congregation for $5 a head. The four were promised $100 per month to act as overseers. Many Penrhyn Islanders, including most of the chiefs, left for Calleo and were never seen again. The incident effectively destroyed the social structure of Penrhyn, for the chiefly line was annihilated. No wonder the people seem aimless.

Saturday 11 December 2004

We sighted Manihiki at around noon and approached it with caution. At first, we saw a long stretch of island on which were a couple of buildings and a radio tower. This atoll has a completely enclosed lagoon and the reef is utterly dangerous, navigable only by people with local knowledge in small boats. The Admiralty book says there is neither access to the lagoon, nor safe anchorage. We could see surf pounding on the reef and a southwest swell breaking on the outer beach. Looking past the reef we could see a number of *motus* lining the lagoon, some developed with substantial buildings. One in particular looked intriguing.

'Wow,' said the Captain, peering at it through binoculars. 'Upscale place over there.' I had a turn at the binoculars and saw concrete structures that looked as though they might have evolved for the booming pearl industry. 'Some dude's got himself a whole *motu*,' he whistled.

Three aluminium fishing vessels, stuffed with people, were bouncing around quite close to the reef off our port side. We approached the beach head-on, towards a place marked on the Admiralty chart as a possible landing place, but through the binoculars we could see only the brown line of a treacherous coral reef, with a huge surf by the shore. We searched for a possible temporary anchorage, described in the chart as being a shallow shelf of 24 metres, but the spot marked as such actually showed 100 metres on our depth finder. While searching for this spot, we came perilously close to the reef.

'It's coming up too fast for me,' said the Captain, quickly turning the boat away. We zigzagged for a while, scrutinizing the depth finder. We had heard that a couple of entryways had been blasted in the reef, but could not find them. Dick and the Captain continued to puzzle over the Admiralty charts, questioning their reliability.

'Looks like there's a jetty close to the end of the island,' said Dick, 'but that's a sketch from bloody last century.' We tried again, closer to the village of Tauhunu.

Suddenly, we caught sight of an aluminium boat emerging from the beach just opposite the village church. The Captain traced its wake through binoculars, until he picked out a narrow band of green that might be the way ashore. We approached it again.

'Sixty metres,' announced Jock.

The Captain sighed. 'Interesting that it's calm here and breaking over there.'

'Thirty five metres . . .'

'That's better . . .'

Still unable to find a place to anchor, the Captain decided to put me into the dinghy to attempt a landing, so at least I could see the island, even if we couldn't anchor. I peered at the shoreline through the binoculars, searching again for that jetty. All I could see was a crisscross pattern of breakers hitting a short coral wall.

There are dry landings, wet landings and mascara-run landings; this one was going to be one of the latter.

'What kinda shoes you wearing?' asked the Captain. 'You're gonna have to leap for your life.' I put my camera in a plastic bag and crawled into the dancing dinghy, driven by Dick. The Captain cast us off. 'No matter what, you gotta come back before dark, OK?' I nodded, then Dick deftly pointed the boat towards what I soon realised was the remains of a jetty. We swooped in between the bommies; not an easy task, for the current and surf were throwing us this way and that, at times horribly close to rocks. Just before the shallows, we saw a man standing on shore, guiding us in with arm signals. He pointed to a channel that provided the deepest possible approach, and we managed to get close enough so I could make a precarious long-jump for the broken-up wharf. I felt lucky to be able to shake the man's hand.

Our benefactor, Jeanmarie Williams, has made far-reaching contributions to the life of Manihiki. He established the black-pearl industry and now, he says, there are 200-odd pearl farms, of varying sizes, on the atoll. At first Jeanmarie was a free diver. He would don helmet and weights, and swing on a rope to a depth of 100 feet or more at a time. After gathering whatever pearl shell he could find before his lungs exploded, he jerked on the rope for a fast ride back to the surface. In 1962, his uncle Tekaki was in the *Guinness Book of World Records* for the deepest recorded free dive, of 206 feet. Nowadays, Jeanmarie uses modern scuba, but he prefers the old way.

'With scuba, you can only do so many dives a day, and then you've got to wait,' he complained.

'Where do you come from?' I asked.

'I was born here,' he replied. I must have shown my surprise at his light colour and European features.

'Ah,' he said, 'I'm a fruit salad.'

Fanny reported that when she landed on Manihiki there were only three white male inhabitants:

> An absconding produce merchant, a runaway marine, and a young Englishman who was a passenger in a vessel wrecked on a neighbouring island. They live upon the bounty of the natives, and although they dislike the diet, seem to thrive very well upon coprah . . .

Fanny herself was something of a curiosity:

> Only once before had a white woman been here . . . At the trader's house . . . all of the population [crowded] into the room. The children were ordered by their elders to take the front row and sit on the floor thus giving those behind a chance to see over their heads. One old woman, who never seemed five steps away from me all the time I was on the Island, apparently neither closed her gaping mouth nor blinked her eyes during the whole period of our stay.

Jeanmarie Williams agreed to show me around, taking me first to the large coral church. Inside it is charming, gaily decorated with turquoise, yellow and red painted pillars, and a very brightly patterned ceiling. My guide, the minister's wife, said it was 200 years old, so it must have been the same one Fanny had visited; however, there was no sign of the ornate carved pulpit with inlaid mother-of-pearl described in her diary. Instead, the plain wooden chancery is decorated with china vases bearing artificial flowers. The word 'Zion' was no longer painted on a pillar but was, however, written above the exterior portal. I was excited to discover that the speak house was still standing, a lean-to with a sloping roof that has become the Tauhunu Sports Hall, right beside a fine volleyball court. I searched in vain for the remains of a pair of shackles Fanny had noticed on a post in that building, once used for punishing wrongdoers.

We strolled down the short lagoon-bound path of white coral sand. On the right side of the path I immediately noticed an extraordinary nineteenth-century colonial building. It was the Royal Palace, a wonderfully elegant but rundown, eggshell-blue structure, with an upper-storey veranda decorated with wooden cut-outs.

'Is there still a king?' I asked Jeanmarie.

'There are two,' he said. 'They're fighting about who should take the throne.'

'Two pretenders!' I was intrigued.

'Yes,' he said. 'Every now and again one of them goes into the palace and tries to sleep upstairs, but he never stays in bed. And the two of them keep having health problems and accidents. I mean, I'm not superstitious, but . . .' He trailed off. It sounded most ominous. Jeanmarie told me the story:

There are two main villages on the atoll. Once upon a time, only Tukao, the village at the northernmost extremity, had a royal family. There were two princes and the older one was a *mahu*, a mixed gender person. After the King's death, the older brother should have succeeded him, but because he was a *mahu*, the throne was bestowed on his younger brother. Outraged and humiliated, the rightful King left the village and wandered past Jeanmarie's village on his way to throw himself into the dangerous waters at the eastern point of the island. One of Jeanmarie's ancestors interceded.

'You have royal blood,' he said, 'and we don't have a king. Instead of killing yourself, come and be ours.' Thus began the royal line that continues to this day.

When Fanny and Louis were on Manihiki, they met the King, as Fanny related:

Lloyd stayed as long as he could to take photographs.
Among others he photographed the King in his royal robes,
a pair of white duck trousers, and a black velveteen coat;
over the latter was a pouch of some sort of black cloth with
gold fringe all around it. Suspended from his neck was a
tinsel star; on his head he wore a sort of crown made from
pandanus leaves dyed red. Later, in the evening, he appeared
in black trousers and a frock coat. He, in common with
most of his subjects, is not of commanding stature.

Jeanmarie led me along a palm-lined, lagoonside road.
Picturesque wooden jetties ran out from the beach into deeper
water, with small shelters at the far end. The houses and gardens
to our left were beautifully kept and I was delighted to see that
some buildings were thatched in the traditional style. A number
of two-storeyed structures were of uniform design and aspect,
with an open-walled lower veranda and an upper room
supported by pillars.

'Those are the cyclone shelter homes,' said Jeanmarie,
'provided by the New Zealand government. We have seventy-
five on the island.'

I stared at the nearest one. 'That thing withstands a cyclone?'
I asked.

'No,' he shrugged.

In 1899, nine years after Fanny's visit, there was a damaging
tsunami here.

'So, where would you take your family in a big blow?' I
asked.

'Ah, I'd put all my possessions up in one of those shelters,
then I'd get in my boat and wait it out in the middle of the
lagoon. Boats are made to move about, but houses aren't. I spent
the last one that way. Nineteen people were killed. By the way,'
he said with a worried tone, 'what are you doing here at this
time of year? The last boat came through four months ago.'

'Ever heard of Robert Louis Stevenson?' I asked.

'Ah,' he said, his face lighting up, '*Tusitala.*' That's the name by which Louis became known in the South Pacific. It is often translated as 'Teller of Tales', but the Samoan writer Albert Wendt says it really means 'Writer of Tales'.

Jeanmarie wanted to show me the new community centre and near-finished hospital. 'But I must warn you,' he said solemnly, 'about the women you'll see there. A new disease has been introduced on to the island.' I faced him in alarm. 'It's called bingo,' he smiled. As we approached the community centre, I could see what he meant. Thirty women were intently focusing on their cards, some with babes in tow, while the local school principal articulated a series of numbers that caused excitement, anxiety or disappointment to each player. I met several of the afflicted, including Jeanmarie's sister.

Manihiki Island appeared to be well organized, with impressive community facilities. Jeanmarie showed me the ambulance boat and a new aluminium transport runner. Many people on the island had scooter bikes and there were a couple of small jeeps. His cousin drove up in a beach buggy loaded with children and presented me with a coconut. I visited the Ruamanu School where Jeanmarie taught, the sailing club where he was treasurer and then I was invited to his home, where two of his seven children were playing in his well-appointed kitchen. On the wall was a coloured poster depicting local fish, one of which was the black shark.

'*Carcharhinus longimanus*', it said. *Mangō* was its Polynesian name, or oceanic white-tip shark. The longest recorded one was 396 centimetres and weighed 167 kilos. This monster eats fish, stingrays, sea turtles, sea birds, gastropods, squids, crustaceans and garbage.

'Have you ever seen one?' I asked Jeanmarie as he handed me a glass of coconut wine he'd made himself.

'Many times,' he replied. 'They're OK if you see them sideways. If they're coming head on, you'd better get out of the water. They'll bite anything: boats, boogie boards, bathers . . .'

Several members of Jeanmarie's family turned up to say 'hello', all handsome, delightful people. Manihiki was once dubbed 'the island of beautiful people' by early whalers. Jeanmarie accounts for his own light colouring as due to the arrival of William Ford, one of the early members of the famous American Ford family, who turned up in Tauhunu and impregnated a member of the royal family.

'Yeah,' said the Captain when I returned, well before sunset as agreed, and recounted the story. 'It was a shagfest round these waters through the 1800s.'

On Sunday, Rolle, Jock, Kayt, Sarah and I went ashore to church at 10 am. Rolle prepared himself for the service by wandering round singing 'Oh Lord, won't you buy me a Mercedes Benz?' at the top of his voice. He was dressed in clean shorts and T-shirt, though, and promised not to smoke during the service. At the Church of the Cook Islands (the CCI) the rules were a lot less rigid than in Penrhyn and many people turned up late. Again, there was wonderful music. The minister's wife sat below the pulpit, facing the congregation, in a lime green suit and coconut-leaf hat. People here seem more prosperous than those in Penrhyn. The woman in front of me wore a finely woven hat with a mother-of-pearl crown and twenty woven frangipani flowers with green leaves round the brim. In the centre of each flower was a stamen fashioned from a wire stalk with a black pearl on the end.

The deaconess, a striking woman with a very loud voice, publicly welcomed us in English. Very touchingly, she said that the people there wished us well on our journey. When it was time for the sermon, the minister ascended the high pulpit above his wife.

'I apologize to our English-speaking friends,' he began, very earnestly, 'that my sermon today has been prepared in our mother tongue; but perhaps the Holy Spirit will enter your minds and translate it for you.'

Rolle, Kayt and Sarah attended the new Catholic church,

designed by Jeanmarie himself, where they were treated to a guitar accompaniment for the hymns, with the words projected on to the wall. The carved pulpit, altar, candlesticks and baptismal font, all beautifully inlaid with mother-of-pearl, had been fashioned by Jeanmarie and his family. After the services, Jeanmarie introduced me to one of his cousins, who turned out to be Arthur Neale, son of Tom Neale who lived alone on Suwarrow and wrote a South Seas classic book called *An Island to Oneself*. I was excited to meet Arthur, especially since we were leaving for Suwarrow later that day. He told me he barely knew his father and tried hard to hide his bitterness about the fact that, in his father's famous book, there had been no mention of his wife and children.

Monday 13 December 2004

I am dreadfully frustrated today. I slept poorly last night, because we were on a port tack which always pitches me out of bed. I woke at 3.30 am in a stew and couldn't get back to sleep. I put on my life vest, went up on deck and lay there in the pilot house through a heavy squall, watching the lightning and listening to the watch keepers, Dick and Sarah, talk on and on about strange marine animals they'd seen while diving, like frogfish and nudibranchs. After the rain stopped, I removed myself to the aft deck and immediately saw four shooting stars, one after another. I wished for a good night's sleep, fearlessness, a Kit Kat bar and world peace – in that order.

I'm fretting about a number of things: I miss Billy and my children, and Jock has announced he's leaving when we get to Samoa to take care of his sister who needs chemotherapy. Our email has been down since we left Bora Bora. I'm eating badly because I'm going for comfort: sugar and starch. I'm sick of falling out of the shower, sick of bruising myself when I lose my footing in bad weather, and sick of worrying about finances and wages. I fell asleep wedged between the pilot-house table and the back of the port bench, then woke up in fright a few minutes later. I went down to my cabin, cried like a wimp for a while, then phoned Scarlett who was having a thoroughly miserable time in LA. We should be in Suwarrow in a few hours.

I'm not the only one who had a bad night in the middle of the ocean:

At six I woke up after a night's struggle with my mat which the wind nearly wrested from me several times, to find that we were just off Suwarrow . . . There are only six people at present living there. Our two passengers, not counting the boy, will make 8 . . . An enchanting lovely little Island. Both Louis and I are burning to be left here. Cocoanuts, all but forty old ones planted by Mr H. cover the Island . . . A great many buildings are gathered together near the pier; indeed, at first sight it looks like quite a thriving little village . . . I went at once . . . across the island to the weather side. It was delightfully cool, but the tide was so high that I had to walk on the shingle. I found a large clear pool where I mean to have a bath tomorrow.

When I went back on deck, at around 10 am, Suwarrow had already been sighted, and we were approaching several of the motus that comprise this still largely uninhabited chain of islands known as the Suvorov Islands. We were pitching fairly heavily. The Captain, at the helm, buzzed the galley.

'Hey, Kayt, we're gonna put away the main so we're turning uphill. Might get a little rolly for a while.'

Kayt made a face, steadied the scrambling eggs and wedged herself into a corner. 'Thanks for letting me know.'

The Captain turned us up into the wind. After the mainsail began to luff and was put away, the boat began to rock alarmingly. Meanwhile Dick was preparing to be winched up the mast in the bosun's chair.

'I hate going up the mast when it's rolling like this,' he groaned. 'I bang into things. It hurts.'

'Pretend you're at Magic Mountain,' I suggested heartlessly.

'Yeah,' said his girlfriend. 'Some people have to wait in line for that kinda ride.'

In fact, I was quite alarmed at the thought of him going aloft in this swell. As he started nimbly up the mast, the boat began to complete swaying arcs of easily thirty-three degrees. He swung way over the ocean, then hit one of the spreaders as he bounced back. Whoo! We all winced. He finally reached the summit, and hailed the Captain on the radio.

'Doesn't look too bad from up here,' he said. 'There is a channel through the bommies. Take it down ten degrees to port.' He guided us through the rock-lined pass. It was broader than the last one.

'Jeez, compared to Penrhyn it's a freeway,' said the Captain. 'What's our depth?'

'Forty metres, Skipper,' replied Jock.

'Then we're in.' The Captain breathed deeper.

We took a starboard turn to the next waypoint. White caps could be seen inside the lagoon as well as outside it. The guide book had said it could be very rough in here.

'There's another shelf,' said the Captain, watching the depth sounder.

'Yeah,' replied Dick. 'Watch out for the nine-metre patch coming up.'

'I'm on it,' said the Captain, turning the wheel first clockwise, then back again, as we skirted a terrifying patch of pale turquoise. 'Well, the sweaty part's over,' he sighed at last. 'What's our depth?'

'Fifty-eight metres.'

'Now, that's deep. Wouldn't want to drop your car keys in there. OK, Dick: last rightie coming up.'

'Roger. I can see the jetty and there's not too many bommies between here and there.'

'Just pick us out a nice glassy spot to anchor in.'

Through the binoculars I could now make out a half-circle of white beach with a volleyball net strung at the point and a thatched roof beside it. The jetty was well maintained: a pristine line of coral wall with a New Zealand flag on a tall pole. I was eager to get ashore. The Captain ferried me to the far side of the jetty and I threw a line around a new-looking stainless-steel stanchion.

'Bye,' I said firmly, as I hopped out. Jeanmarie had said there may be no one there, so I did not want any company. I was eager to experience what it was like to have, as Tom Neale did, 'An Island to Oneself'.

Looking either way, the beach was beautiful. A couple of straggly hammocks were strung between coconut trees. Near the volleyball pitch there was a wooden board announcing 'Welcome to Suwarrow National Park' and a smaller board instructing visitors to *Take but nothing. Leave but footprints*. Beneath it was a collection of oil drums, a rusting anchor, a pile of fishing floats and plastic buckets, and a quarantine notice about not bringing in seeds or leaving rubbish ashore. In recent years, the coconuts Fanny saw on Suwarrow became diseased, and there are strict rules about not taking any piece of a coconut tree from this island to another. A swing seat made from a collapsed orange jerry can dangled from a lofty palm. A little further inland, along a path lined with planted vines, were some rough table-tops thrown over tree stumps. On one was a fingerless glove and a couple of tools. The path led to a decrepit, pale green building with glass shutters and nailed-up doors. We were definitely not expected. No one was, this late in the cyclone season. I peered inside. It was pretty empty, but obviously served as some kind of office or storage space, containing a wheelbarrow or two, an outboard motor and a few cans of paint. Outside, there was a strange sculptured head and a rough stone base on which were carved the words: *1952–77. Tom Neale lived his dream on this island*.

To my right was a much newer structure, one of the buildings I had come to recognize as a New Zealand government cyclone shelter. It had the customary upper storey but the open room below served as the Suwarrow Yacht Club. Painted wooden seats awaited the arrival of a new batch of yachties, while flags from past visitors hung about the ceiling. There was a toilet cubicle and a shower, with the strangly worded notice 'Rare water, shower with friends' hanging conspicuously beside the faucet. Several newspapers lay about on tables: the latest issue being a *New Zealand Herald* from 18 July, five months ago. An enormous spider was weaving a sticky concoction beneath a rusty pipe, while mosquitoes pounced viciously the minute I entered the clubhouse. There was definitely no one here. I suddenly wished the Captain was with me. I was alone on a ghost island and, much as I enjoy my own company, there was something a little sinister about this place.

Some men's shorts and T-shirts were hanging in an outhouse behind the first building, and a yellow hard hat sat in a corner. Perhaps there were people here after all. I walked nervously through the disorganized backyard to another well-marked path that led to the ocean side of the island, a mere fifty yards away. By now, the wind was so strong and the palms waving so furiously, I considered putting on the hard hat to give me a fighting chance if a coconut fell on my head. I glanced round to make sure I was really alone, then ran shamefully, like a scaredy-cat, through to the beach on the windward side. There, the waves were breaking over a wide reef leading to pale green shallows that went on for ever. I scanned the exposed coral outcrops, searching for Fanny's tide pools, then shot on to the beach in excitement. There they were, sitting about a hundred yards beyond the shallows. At first I was eager to wade out and bathe in one, but after reading the ripples I realized that the current was strong. Once again, I was filled with admiration for Fanny's courage. She had done it, why couldn't I? I had almost talked myself into following suit when I saw a sizeable black-tipped reef shark cruising between me and the pools. It was joined by another one and, as I watched, I saw something I'd never seen before: surfing sharks! The two of them entered the wave like champion board kings and whizzed in towards the beach on its crest. It's funny, I thought, I've seen thousands of sharks while diving and felt perfectly comfortable with them . . . but the idea of wading among them in shallow water, even the harmless reef variety, does not thrill me.

Disappointed, I returned to the lagoon and called for the tender to pick me up. Frankly, I was glad to get off the island. There was an atmosphere there I can barely describe, but I didn't like it. For the next couple of hours I told myself that it would be a terrible shame if I did not follow Fanny's tracks and, in the end, I decided to head back and go through with it. It helped that others accompanied me, but what I found this time was a total surprise. The tide had changed. In fact, it had receded quite a way and the ocean side was generally far calmer. Instead of walking across the island, I approached the leeward beach by walking around the point from the lagoon, and thus I came upon what I instantly knew must be Fanny's pools: not the ones I had seen earlier, but four beautifully sculptured baignettes with sandy bottoms closer to the beach. They were beautifully warm – and my favourite even had a steady stream of water bubbling constantly through it. I lay luxuriating in it, as though in a tub with the tap still running. I hope Fanny did take that bath. I can picture her there – in a modest bathing suit, lying supine in the 98-degree water – no doubt comparing it to the freezing porcelain tub that was installed for her at her in-laws' home in Heriot Row, Edinburgh.

After my bath, I felt more secure on the island. I walked around its entire circumference, stopping frequently, in about an hour. Oh yes, Fanny knew a good thing when she saw it. It was the perfect size, I thought, if one was going to have one's own islet. At every turn there was another treasure: the arched bower of pandanus on the southwestern beach, the two horizontal palms further towards the jetty, the thatched hut on the western beach, the tide pool full of sea-cucumbers on the northeastern stretch. Pity the buildings were so in need of housekeeping, but that was probably the fault of the elements. Jeanmarie's uncle, Ioane Kaitara, and two younger relatives live there as caretakers, but they had no doubt been picked up by the petrol boat for a quick trip to Rarotonga. I had a fantasy that I would be Snow White and spring-clean the place before Sleepy, Dopey, Happy and Co arrived home from work. The place definitely needed a woman's touch.

As I sat on the jetty, waiting for the tender, I was entranced by a baby shark, just nine inches in length but perfectly formed, like an adult in miniature, with its tiny black-tipped dorsal fin just cracking the surface of the water. I'd never seen one before. The place must be a shark nursery. It's supposed to be a bird sanctuary but we saw very few birds. One lonely rooster was making a terrible din, possibly because there were no hens.

'Dat poor bird,' said Rolle, 'he's lonely.'

'You feel an affinity with him, do you?' I asked. It must be quite a while since Rolle had a girlfriend, but he didn't understand my question. 'Would you like to rescue him?' I tried again.

'Yes.' He nodded enthusiastically, then smiled wickedly. 'Den eat him.'

I had a good night's sleep, after which I felt revived. At breakfast time, when I went to the galley there was no one there. Propped against the starboard porthole I noticed an Advent calendar, which was a great thrill, for it was a comforting return to happy childhood Christmas memories. I picked it up and saw that today's little window was unopened, so I pressed it apart. Inside was a picture of a plum pudding. It seemed to be a message: Stop over-eating!

We left Suwarrow at 9 am on a starboard tack, bound for Nassau Island. Once outside the reef, the brown and white boobies gave us a send-off, a swooping, soaring escort. For a few horrifying moments we saw a couple of them diving at our fishing lures. It would be horrible if we caught one, but pretty quickly they got wise and lost interest. A white booby flapped above our mast.

'He's got dirty vings,' cooed Rolle. 'Must be an engineer.'

We were headed into a squall.

'Here it comes,' warned the Captain. With Elton John remembering when rock was young in the background, we sprang into action to lower the pilot-house side-flaps. 'Hey, if we get there and can't land,' the Captain said to me, 'we might be able to persuade someone to come out and pick you up.' I looked at him. Nassau was obviously still a challenging destination. The squall came on with a vengeance, and soon the run-off was swirling round my feet inside the pilot house. Rolle did a rain dance.

'Is that to make it start or stop?' I asked, but he didn't seem too sure. After the squall had passed, the wind dropped and the genoa began flapping and banging.

Dick, with mounting frustration, addressed it directly: 'Yeah, I know you haven't got enough wind, big genny, but Jeeez!'

I worked on deck all morning, then just before lunch I went down to the galley and found it in an uproar. Accusations were flying all around as to who had opened this morning's window in the Advent calendar. Apparently, there was a roster. It was Rolle's turn and he'd been looking forward to it for days. I confessed and apologized, but I was secretly glad; now I know what to make him for Christmas: a custom-made Advent calendar – maybe one for the whole year, ending with his birthday.

As it continued to pour, we had a competition to see who could sing the most songs with the word 'rain' in them. Kayt did a marvellous rendition of 'It's Raining Men', while Jock, who cannot carry a tune, gave full lilt to a perfectly dreadful version of 'Singing in the Rain'. Everyone thought I'd made up my song, 'Listen to the Falling Rain', because it's a corny folk ballad. That's what you get for spending too much time strumming old Joan Baez numbers when you're a teenager.

I was on watch from 8 to 11 pm, during which I saw a late sunset: 7.30 pm. I think we need to change our clocks. I danced to old Abba songs to get some exercise.

Wednesday 15 December 2004

I woke at 5 am because the Captain was expecting to make landfall at Nassau around sunrise. The dawn was just beginning to reveal the island, an oval jewel sitting in the middle of an impassable reef. We tried to raise people ashore on our radio, but no one answered. As it got a little lighter, we could see one or two residents on the beach, sitting on an upturned rowing boat. After a few minutes, a small crowd had gathered. Then, as the sun climbed higher in the sky, it revealed something truly shocking: a huge, rusty, double-masted ship stuck in the trees.

'Wow,' I said. 'That gives new meaning to the word "beached" – more like "palmed"!'

We continued to try the radio but there was no answer. We sat around in the pilot house, the Captain looking annoyed and fidgety, until I announced I was going to try things the island way. I went below and grabbed my red lava-lava, went to the bow and waved it above my head, while Kayt scrutinized the beach with binoculars to see if that got a response. Several people waved back, but no one moved towards the boat. I was terribly disappointed. Considering the height of the surf, the lack of information about a safe landing, and the daunting sight of the large ship thrown up into the palm trees, there was no way we were going to risk trying to land a dinghy without local help. I called Jeanmarie by satellite phone. He advised us to wait there, not to attempt the reef because it was far too dangerous. Someone would come out when it was calm enough, he said. The Captain became more and more anxious. We had only a couple of hours in hand; in order to stay on schedule, we had to get to Puka Puka today and leave for Samoa by nightfall.

'If you look at those breakers,' he said, 'they're way too treacherous to navigate now. And there's no engine on that boat those people are sitting on. The tide's too far out. I'd say they're waiting until it comes in a bit. That doesn't leave us any time to do this.'

'But Fanny couldn't do it,' I wailed. 'I *have* to succeed!' Fanny had been extremely disappointed that, since there was no anchorage at Nassau, she was unable to go ashore: 'It was judged too difficult in landing for me and, so to my infinite disappointment I saw the men go off without me.' I assume that it was largely her attire and concerns about her recurring rheumatism that made it 'too difficult'; in reality she was athletic and probably as capable of braving the landing as me.

After another twenty minutes, a group of men came on to the beach carrying an outrigger canoe. I became very excited, because I imagined it would be fantastic to arrive on Nassau in the manner of the early seafarers. Unfortunately, the canoe was never launched, presumably because the waves were so powerful the boatmen had second thoughts. Disappointed, I watched them retreat. Then, after another few minutes, a tractor trailer arrived on the beach and off-loaded a sturdier, aluminium boat with an outboard motor.

'Hurray,' I said. 'That should do the trick.' Several men walked it out in the shallows towards the breaking surf, then skilfully half-rowed, half-motored towards us, timing their movements between the largest of the waves. My heart beat fast when I saw them very close to a couple of jagged rocks with swirling white water all round them.

'How about putting on a life vest?' said the Captain. The crew was alarmed that I was going ashore in such conditions.

'I'd really hate to lose you . . . so close to Christmas,' quipped Sarah.

'You really think I need the vest?' I asked.

'Nah,' said Dick. 'If you fall out on the reef you're a goner anyway.'

'But at least,' said Kayt, 'you'd have something round your neck to bounce off the rocks.'

'I don't think you should go,' said Jock sternly. Ever the protector, he wanted to accompany me. 'It could go horribly wrong.' We watched the men in the boat, still battling the current. Their bow went practically vertical as it hit a crested wall, then slammed down the other side of it and disappeared from view beneath the rise of the next wave.

'I have to,' I said firmly. 'And I think those guys know what they're doing.'

'Hey, if everything goes pear-shaped,' the Captain was tense, 'don't try to hang on to anything, just lie on your back and float.' I already knew one shouldn't try to cling to rocks, but should swim away from them as far as possible. I thought it through further. If I went into the water, my man-overboard alarm would sound and the *Takapuna* crew would have a chance to locate me. But I'd have to get myself to a place for safe pick-up.

The silver boat and crew finally reached the calmer water on our side of the reef, and motored towards our stern. Life vest on, I waved a greeting at six shy, smiling men.

'Thank you so much for coming out,' I said. 'Would you be kind enough to take me ashore . . . and er, also bring me back again?'

'When we come back, can we board your boat and look around?' asked one.

'Of course.'

Jock and Rolle fitted the swim ladder and the local men attempted to line up their boat to it so I could transfer safely. The swell caused both boats to rise and fall on different planes, so in the end I just grabbed one of the outstretched hands and made a leap for the slippery aluminium bow. With my crew watching, I slipped and cracked my thigh, but recovered quickly and gave them the thumbs up.

'I'm in!' I shouted.

I introduced myself to the boatmen as we took off for the reef.

Their Captain, an imposing man in a purple *pareo*, was Poila, the principal of the Nassau school. His crew comprised Palili, Aaron, Mark, Junior and Eddy, who deftly timed our approach to the outer breakers, oars at the ready, so we'd both surf and motor as the waves decreed. I hung on for dear life as the boat see-sawed alarmingly. I watched Poila's face, calm and focused, ready to make the call for the next fast take-off on the crest of a wave. Once we were flying high, the crew would paddle furiously to avoid any nearby rocks and increase the momentum shorewards, essential because the currents seemed to be pulling in different directions. Eventually we entered the shallows and the men hopped out to pull the boat closer.

'Shall I get out?' I inquired.

'No, you stay there for now,' they said protectively. We were still some way from the shore. Eventually Junior helped me out, warning me to be careful of slippery surfaces. He held my hand and pulled me forwards to the sand where around thirty people were waiting. I immediately spotted a *mahu*, looking at me inquisitively while hugging a child. He lowered his eyes when I smiled at him. I was taken aback that the people generally did not move towards me, but continued sitting, one group gathered under a palm-thatched boatshed, and the other around a man on a motor scooter, who turned out to be the chief.

'The people are shy,' said Poila. 'We don't get too many visitors.' I wandered up and introduced myself to the chief, told him I was interested to see the island and thanked him for the ride ashore. I was curious about the way he smiled and nodded, until Junior said, 'I will be your translator.' Hitherto, it had not occurred to me that some of these people would not speak any English; we have become accustomed to easy communication on the previous islands. The chief's name was Tuaine Williams.

'Is he related to . . .' I was going to ask about Jeanmarie.

'Everybody!' replied Poila, before I could finish.

Eddy, a gregarious young man in red shorts, was assigned the task of escorting me around the island. He spoke good English and had visited New Zealand where he had picked up expressions like 'cool' and 'you're the bomb'.

From Fanny's position aboard the *Janet Nichol* she wrote: 'Altogether, from the outside view, and the descriptions given, it is the loveliest of all the low islands.' I think she was right. Nassau is indeed beautiful, and all the more so because it is so unspoilt. I wish she could have gone ashore because she would have found it enchanting. What is more, it has probably changed very little over the past hundred years. The majority of the houses were constructed in the old, thatched style, the *hale pola* that Lloyd photographed – except now they usually have a motor scooter parked outside.

'Do you have any cyclone shelters?' I asked Eddy.

'No,' he said.

'How do these houses withstand big storms?' I asked.

'Ah, some stand, some fall down,' he said, 'but if they do collapse, you can put them back up again in a day or two.' It made perfect sense and they were much prettier than the concrete houses on Penrhyn.

I was utterly thrilled to see people were going about their community life in the old way; here a man was shaving coconut to make coconut cream, there a woman (Eddy's mother), was weaving dry palm fronds to make thatch for her house. The beautiful little children were not the engaging, bold gangs we had seen on Manihiki and Penrhyn. Instead they seemed somewhat afraid and peered at me silently from the shelter of their homes.

'A lot of people here have never seen . . .' Eddy paused in embarrassment. Suddenly I understood.

'A white person?' I finished his sentence.

'Yes,' he said. 'Not in real life. Only in pictures.'

'Roughly how many people here have never before seen a Caucasian?' He looked puzzled by the word. 'Someone like me.'

He thought for a bit. 'I'd say most. The children especially. Some will visit Rarotonga when they get older.'

Fanny had mused about her effect on populations where Caucasians are very much a minority race:

> Natives have said that the first sight of white people is dreadful, as they look like corpses walking. I myself have been startled by the sight of a crowd of whites after having seen only brown-skinned people for a long time. Louis has a theory that we whites were originally albinos. Certainly we are not a nice colour. I remember as a child the words 'flesh colour' were sickening to me, and I remember I could not bear to see them in my paint box.

This last comment is an interesting one from Fanny, since she was always quite dark in complexion.

Eddy took me to a thatched building that served as a community kitchen. Inside, while a naked toddler wandered round with a large knife, a woman was fanning a fire for an *umu*, or oven set in the ground in which lava rocks are heated to slow-cook the food. There was a large bowl of chopped taro root ready for cooking, a basket of lobster and a plate of fish. There are plenty of chickens and pigs on the island, and the latest sea-catch had been several tuna and a wahoo. No wonder the people look so healthy.

'Tell me about the shipwreck,' I said to Eddy as we embarked on a stroll past the school, the volleyball pitch, and a couple of churches.

'It happened around 1988,' he said. 'It was the *Manuvai*, a supply ship. The Captain was drunk, and the person on watch didn't know how to steer.' The ship foundered on the reef, but the forty passengers and ten crew were all rescued.

'It was a day just like today,' said Poila. Some time later, cyclone Sally had put the ship's carcass in the trees.

'We really need to have a passage blasted in the reef,' said Junior.

'And a new trailer,' joined Poila. 'We have asked for these things for a long time now.'

I asked if there were any small things they needed that we might have on board.

'We need books for the school library and some medical supplies,' said Poila. 'And if possible, a photocopier.' He and his wife Teina taught fifty children in two classrooms.

While coconuts were being gathered for me to take back to the *Takapuna*, including some of the *mangaro* variety, which have a sweet husk that can be chewed, a wish-list was compiled and radioed to the *Takapuna*. I was resolved to approach the New Zealand authorities about the larger items. Apparently, the people here share supplies with Puka Puka. They believe that island receives the best stuff, not only because it is more accessible, but because the government representative resides there.

On the return journey over the reef, the boatmen sat me in the centre of the dinghy. There was one particularly worrying moment when we had a false start, surging through a patch that at first seemed to be between breakers, but ending up approaching a very fast-mounting roller head-on. Poila beat a fast retreat then, within seconds, gave the all-clear for a new start. It was imperative that we move swiftly and my heart was in my mouth as I watched him struggle to start the motor just after we made our bid. At the very last moment, it putputted into life and we shot through one wave, only to be spun sideways by a following swell. At the stern, Eddy furiously bailed out the rising seawater as the others used their oars to spin us into line to meet the next wave. I glanced over my shoulder towards the *Takapuna* and grinned triumphantly when I saw Rolle, Dick and Jock watching anxiously from the stern.

Once through to calmer water, we waited for the *Takapuna* to turn and approach us, while we joked and took photos. Back on board, my heroes had a tour of the boat – they wanted to see the engine room first – and drank sodas while books, crayons, felt-tips and spare medical supplies were gathered for them. As they said goodbye, Mark shyly presented me with a small, white cowrie shell.

'Don't forget us,' he said, ever so sweetly. I kissed them all on both cheeks, as Jeanmarie had taught me to do. As they pushed away, the six of them spontaneously burst into a fantastically rousing farewell song, which moved me to tears. I waved until the *Takapuna* slid beyond the corner of the island, and I could see them no more.

A short while after we left Nassau we saw an extraordinary sight. There is an offshore reef known as the Flying Venus Reef, a substantial area of shallowly submerged coral that presents a lurking danger to unwitting mariners. It was weird to see large breakers out at sea. Our radar information showed that the reef was not in the position indicated by Admiralty charts (8°57′ south by 157°54′ west), but rather, was about a mile away, at precisely 11°07. 2717′ south by 165°36.7630′ west. God save anyone who chances upon it at night.

At 3 pm we arrived at Pukapuka, also known as Uluotewatu, or alternatively Danger Island on account of the fact that its west-running current makes it very perilous. Another current runs north and south across the western extension of the reef at five knots with the ebb and flow of the tide, and it's easy to be thrown up and founder on the rocks. The people at Nassau had radioed ahead, so we were expected. As soon as we approached the entry to the pass, a channel that had been created by dynamite, we saw a boat heading towards us. Aboard were two customs officials and Vai Peua, a friend of Jeanmarie, who had agreed to take me ashore and show me round. The channel was exceedingly narrow, only about five metres wide, with a jagged bank of coral on either side and a strong current, but the boat had a good engine and the boatman easily skimmed us through into a gorgeous inner lagoon. The island is a large one, compared to Nassau. We landed on the beach in front of a long tin shed.

'That's the old copra warehouse,' said Vai. There were three families living in it now. When Fanny sighted Danger Island on 4 May, it was governed by a tyrannical King:

None of his subjects are allowed to gather cocoanuts without royal permission, so, as he only lets each person have enough for his food, very little coprah is made. The nuts are dried, contrary to the usual habit, in the shells to prevent the cockroaches from eating them, and consequently make a very fine white coprah; but there is so little of it that it does not pay to keep a trader on the Island. We could see the natives through the glass gathering in great force on the beach. They seemed stricken to stare at the sight of a vessel her sails furled moving rapidly against a strong bad wind; it being the first steamer that touched here.

Vai was keen to impress on me that here there was not the drastic drop in population that had affected other Cook Islands. 'Our people don't want to move away,' he said. 'They like it here, because we have our customs.' There are three villages on Pukapuka atoll, Roto, Yato and Ngake, with an average of around 200 people in each. We walked into downtown Roto, a traditional *marae* or compound, and saw that some of its houses were thatched, while others were fashioned of new materials.

'I like the thatch,' I said to Vai.

'Yes' he said, 'and it's cooler.'

'So why would people choose corrugated iron or concrete over thatch?'

'Thatch has to be repaired every year,' he replied. Sure enough, there was evidence of blue plastic sheeting slung over patches of leaking palm roof.

Overall the island was neat and very nicely set-up, with well-organized community facilities. Vai showed me the school, hospital, coral sand tennis courts, garage, three churches and the taro and sugarcane patches. Their solar panels ran the two large deep freezes, while human legs worked the Singer sewing machines. There were several small stores on the island. I was entranced by a really beautiful, placid inner lagoon, separated from the outer beach by a causeway. The palm trees that lined it were mirrored in the calm, brackish water.

'We catch bonefish in there,' said Vai.

The focal point of the community centre was a sports trophy display. There are many sporting opportunities here for the inhabitants of the island: soccer, wrestling, relays, volleyball, tennis, cricket, even discus throwing. There is a large field, the Niua Ya O Matāliki Stadium, where many of those games are played. The three villages compete with each other 'as though it was war', said Vai. Their teams are called America, Japan and Holland.

'Are the villages friendly with each other, despite such fierce sport competition?' I asked Vai.

'Yes,' he said, beaming. 'And why not? We're all related.'

When I inquired about his children, Vai's face changed. He told me that only three months ago his second son, Terekino Peua, a brilliant athlete who had been chosen to carry the Olympic torch back to Pukapuka from Rarotonga in the last Games, had been found hanged in Australia at the age of twenty-four. Vai, who remains baffled by the reasons for his son's death, managed to raise enough funds to bring his body home to Puka Puka. His son now lies in a white casket in the cemetery.

'When they were bringing his coffin ashore,' he said, 'every team player on the island helped.' At this point we were near Vai's house, so he darted inside and brought me Australian news cuttings about Terekino's death, as well as a copy of the funeral service. When he handed me a photo of his boy, he began to weep inconsolably. I sat with him, as I have done for so many others, until I thought he was ready to talk some more.

'What do you remember most about him?' I asked.

'His love of sports,' replied Vai, in short gasps. 'I wore black for two months, but even now . . .'

'It takes as long as it takes,' I said gently.

When another man came to bring me a fresh coconut to

drink, Vai wiped his eyes and sunk his teeth into it, savagely ripping off the husk to expose the drinking crown. All his disbelief, sadness and fury over his loss seemed bound up in that one ferocious gesture. I drank from the shell he proffered, but the milk seemed bitter.

We should reach Samoa three days from now. Travelling south aboard the *Equator* on the Stevenson's first trip to the Navigator Islands, they were followed all the way by a succession of storms, one of which caused the loss of their foretopmast and staysail, and nearly sent them to the bottom. Had the ship not been steadied by a heavy cargo of copra during that squall, nothing could have saved them.

On watch this evening Kayt told me that while I'd been ashore she'd had a radio conversation with a woman from Hawaii who was skippering a sixty-foot sailboat we'd picked up on our radar. She and two crew members had been around these waters for three months and were headed for Kiribati for Christmas. The boat had no engine, so they were probably doing four-hour solo watches, two each per twenty-four hours. Their fridge had stopped working just out of Samoa so they had to rely on catching fish. They had been unable to stop at any of the islands we'd been to, because they were in a hurry, delivering the boat for the owner. Makes me feel very humble. There are thousands of people who traverse the world, single-, double- or triple-handed, on far smaller, less well-equipped vessels than this. I applaud them all, from the bottom of my respectful, half-envious heart.

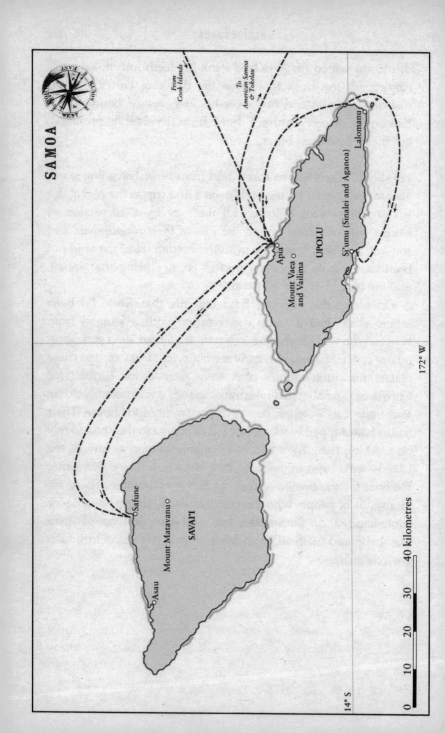

SAMOA

From Cook Islands

To American Samoa & Tokelau

Apia

Mount Vaea
and Vailima

UPOLU

Si'umu (Sinalei and Aganoa)

Lalomanu

Safune

Mount Matavanu

SAVAI'I

Asau

172° W

14° S

0   10   20   30   40 kilometres

CHAPTER NINE

HOME OF FLYING CLOUD

13°43.7′ S
171°38′ W

Saturday 18 December 2004

'Louis and Fanny shagged right here on the balcony,' announced Ian Black, the Australian proprietor of 'Sails', the restaurant that now occupies the upstairs floor of the seafront townhouse where Fanny and Louis stayed when they first arrived in Samoa Then owned by American trader Harry J. Moors, the navy-and-white wooden building is still in pretty good condition, and the uneven stairs up to the restaurant only add to its charm. Tables are dotted around the wide, open-air balcony, which affords a fine view of the harbour, while a spacious bar is situated at the rear of the upstairs parlour. Later in the evening, the thump thump thump of the street-level nightclub drew restaurant patrons downstairs for a sweaty dance in what was probably Moors's trading store. (The following week, Billy joined me for an evening meal at Sails, after he arrived exhausted from a movie promotion tour. I considered wrestling him to the floor of the balcony in a modern reconstruction of the earlier Stevenson scene, but abandoned the idea out of consideration for other patrons.)

*

This afternoon, with the sun on our backs, the *Takapuna* entered Apia harbour on the main Samoan island of Upolu. I have visited Samoa (previously known as Western Samoa) three times before, though never by boat. It was novel to be approaching seashores I already love, inhabited by people I already hold dear. My friend Allan, home for Christmas from his post as choreographer and dance lecturer at the University of the South Pacific in Fiji, was waiting for me on the dockside. His gold earrings and bright green lava-lava flashed in the sunlight.

'*Talofa!*' I greeted him in Samoan. 'Let's go for a drive!' He took me along the familiar sea-wall road to a new cafe in the centre of town, where we caught up on Apia gossip over iced cappuccinos, and greeted passing friends engaged in Christmas shopping. The place is becoming quite cosmopolitan.

Apian 'progress' aside, I found myself comparing this island to others we have visited, and decided it holds its place as one of the most beautiful; a soft, verdant jewel with inspiring mountains and silvery waterfalls. Fanny made similar comparisons.

The mountains, she decided, were not 'so strangely awful as the Marquesan highlands, but very beautiful in outline and in colour'. When the *Janet Nichol* approached the island on 30 April 1890, Fanny and Louis had already chosen Upolu as the island on which they would finally settle, and were in the process of building a house on a 314-acre plot overlooking the ocean. Harry J. Moors had helped them to find and develop the property, and acted as overseer when they were out of the country. This time he had been left to implement several projects, although his taste did not always coincide with Fanny's. She was pretty sniffy about some of his choices when she returned. Nevertheless, she was thrilled to set foot again in her new 'home' country:

> we were burning to go ashore . . . Louis and I got into Mr Moors' boat . . . It was a very strange, dreamlike sensation to find myself walking along the Apia beach, shaking hands, and passing Talofas on every side as we went . . . at Mr Moors' I walked all over the house before I sat down; I was so afraid that I might be dreaming that I wished to get all I could out of the dream before I waked.

Sunday 19 December 2004

I went to church with Allan, who toned down his usual flamboyant dress for the occasion. It is the custom here for the congregation to dress in white from head to toe, the women in elaborate hats and long skirts, and the men in shirts and lava-lavas. As usual, the singing was beautiful with thrilling harmonies. I was amused that the names of everyone in the congregation, with the amount each one put in the collection plate, was read out for all to hear. Allan rolled his eyes disapprovingly and distracted me with a lesson on Samoan fan etiquette; it is apparently polite to waft air in the direction of your neighbour as well as yourself. After the service I was invited to his family home for a traditional Samoan Sunday lunch. So many family members had gathered they had to eat in two shifts, with the second, younger group eating what the elders had left. Much of the Samoan cuisine is prepared in an underground oven called an *umu*. I was treated to baked pork, fish and breadfruit as well as *oka*, or raw fish steeped in coconut and lime juice, and *palusami*, or coconut cream wrapped in young taro leaves.

I am enamoured of Samoan culture, and I am glad the people here are so protective of their traditions. They are gentle, good-natured and generous – with a proud and passionate core. Much of what anthropologist Margaret Mead found in the 1930s is still true today: Samoan people value their families and the clans tend to stay together throughout their lives, unencumbered by the drive to accumulate financial wealth and consumer goods beyond the necessities. Traditionally, everyone in the family plays a well-defined, contributing role for the benefit of all, whether that be child-rearing, fishing, housekeeping or tending to plants and vegetables. In recent years, western influence, especially the arrival of videos and television, has led to family separations and the erosion of some traditions and values; nevertheless, the society seems to me to be a model alternative to our stressful, competitive and family-shattering lifestyle.

Being here makes me acutely aware of the separations we experience in my own family. We are spread out around the world, so much so that I envisage my later years will be spent travelling constantly to try to catch up with them all. How on earth did we get to this point of chaos? And why did we westerners not see it coming, the futility of eighteen-hour workdays, the stupidity of consumer societies, ecological deterioration through waste and ignorance, and the profound loneliness that accompanies city-dwelling? It has occurred to me that Louis, being an only child, may well have had similar feelings of longing, seeing the happiness within the extended families here, all living, working and sharing together. He and

Fanny would probably have been perfectly happy if they'd set themselves up in a traditional Samoan family compound and gathered their family around them – but they chose instead to do the European thing. They created what was to be a grand residence in the Victorian colonial style on a prime piece of property with several streams running through it. They called it *Vailima*, which means 'water scooped into hands'.

In preparation for the Stevensons' arrival aboard the *Janet Nichol*, Harry J. Moors had widened the approaching bridle path, bordered with liana-draped trees and flowering chilli peppers, and erected an impressive gate to the newly constructed, neat little house with two verandas and a separate cook house. This first structure formed the nucleus of the imposing residence Vailima would eventually become. 'Even as it now is,' wrote Fanny, 'it is a garden of Eden, and the most beautiful place in the world.'

Nowadays Vailima is approached via the busy cross-island thoroughfare, roughly three miles up the hill from Apia. The gates are still imposing, leading up a ferny drive to a security booth just before the main lawn. The Stevensons were here during a time of civil war in Samoa. Louis got involved in the struggle and acted as adviser to the chiefs. When some of them were imprisoned, he advocated for them and visited them in jail, bearing gifts to make their incarceration more comfortable. When the chiefs were freed, partly through Louis's persuasion, they showed their gratitude to him by making a proper road to the house for his forty-fourth birthday. They called it Ala Ole Alofa, or the Road of the Loving Heart.

The two-storeyed house itself is still graceful and imposing, while its beautifully landscaped grounds are well maintained. This is the result of the passion and benevolence of Rex Maughan, an American businessman who was a Mormon missionary here in the 1950s. The house had sustained cyclone damage in the early 1990s, after serving as a diplomatic and head-of-state residence for many years. Maughan leased it from the government, restored it and turned it into a museum, which opened in 1994. Although the property is now reduced to seven acres, and is no longer painted the original peacock blue with red verandas, it was thrilling to see the focus of Fanny's toil and devotion. Its exterior is now entirely white, with a red roof. Its spacious verandas catch the cool breezes on three sides, while western extensions that were undertaken in 1897 after the Stevensons left have, to my eye, balanced the earlier eastern wing. I climbed the front steps leading to a wide porch and entered a small L-shaped veranda-room that now serves as ticket booth and gift shop. This room was originally Margaret's. She hated it and complained that it was noisy and lacked privacy. 'It's no better than a maid's chamber,' she whined. Consequently, when she was away visiting Australia in 1891, Louis built her a whole wing. He was smart, though. He did it with her money and included a downstairs ballroom!

Fanny must have gritted her teeth when Margaret complained about Vailima, writing:

I see again she dislikes the life here which we find so

enchanting and is disappointed and soured that she is not
able to persuade us to throw it all up and go to the colonies.
We have given the colonies a fair trial and they mean death
to Louis, whereas this is life and a reasonable health.

Louis had finally reached the very place that Seed had
recommended so many years ago. The New Zealander had been
right; the climate did improve his health. Louis wrote:

It is like a fairy story that I should have recovered liberty and
strength, and should go around again with my fellow men,
boating, riding, bathing, toiling hard with a wood knife in
the forest.

I joined an official tour. Entering the house through ground-
floor French doors, I found myself in the smoking room, also
known as the tapa room because it was lined with the local
fabric. The room boasts a fireplace that was shipped here from
Scotland. The guide solemnly informed us it was never used
because there is no chimney, an explanation that seemed bizarre
under the sweltering Samoan sun. I cannot imagine a warming
fire would ever have been needed. However, it is true that
Samoan builders were unaccustomed to constructing chimneys,
and apparently a trial hearth fire produced a room full of smoke.
Very little of the furniture I saw in the house is original, but
the creators of the museum have attempted to replicate, from
pictorial and written records, what they knew was once there: a
Victorian mirror, framed photographs, and a collection of
cutlasses over the mantelpiece. A mangy lion skin rug on the
floor of the tapa room was described as 'original'. We followed
the guide upstairs to the upper veranda, a gorgeous, breezy
space with superb views of the tropical garden that Fanny
landscaped, and, beyond it, the ocean. They made very smart
choices here, I thought; the place is magnificent. Inside this
second-floor veranda was Louis's study. Another original

fireplace faced the entrance, with his bed warmer beside it. Louis spent most of his time in here, often reclining in a bed along the far wall. A glass case now displays copies of some of Louis's published books that have been translated into other languages. Остров Сокровища caught my eye: the Russian *Treasure Island*.

Margaret's wing is the biggest and easily the best suite in the house, with a four-poster bed facing a private sitting room with a bay window. The Edinburgh widow found the Vailima set-up rather primitive, especially the daily programme. They ate breakfast at 6 am (Louis worked in bed from 6 until 9), lunch at 11 am, dinner at 5.30 pm, and retired early. Margaret preferred being in 'the colonies' – Australia and New Zealand – where she could dine at more civilized hours.

After Belle divorced Joe Strong, she brought her son Austin to live with Fanny and Louis. She helped out by managing household staff, and eventually became Louis's secretary. Austin occupied a yellow-walled bedroom, while Belle's charming boudoir is decorated with a map of her favourite Parisian haunts.

'Her parents met in Paris,' announced the guide, getting it wrong for the umpteenth time. Round the corner I found Fanny's room. It was warm and elegant, the walls lined with Californian redwood panels. Belle must have had a wicked sense of humour. Hung on a corner wall was her comical sketch of the room in disarray, entitled 'Fanny's Messy Room'. Fanny explained the problem:

My bedroom presents a most extraordinary aspect. Whenever a thing is twice lost downstairs I order it up to my room, so that it cannot be taken without my knowledge. Amongst my dresses are hanging bridles, straps and horse ropes. On the camphor wood trunk which serves as my dressing table, besides my comb and brush, is a collection of tools, chisels, pincers, and the like. Leather straps and parts of harness hang from nails on the wall. There are, besides, other

incongruous articles . . . a long carved spear, a pistol and
boxes of cartridges, strings of teeth (fish, human and beast),
necklaces of shells, and quantities of hats, fans, fine mats
and tapas piled up in heaps. My little cot bed seems to have
got into its place by mistake.

One can still see the secret door that Fanny installed to provide
an escape and hiding place during the time of civil unrest:

The war has very nearly begun several times, but now it
seems fairly on its feet . . . There has been a good deal of
vague talk about a massacre of all the whites, and it is well to
be prepared . . .

But war was not the only reason for feeing unsafe in the area.
Newly arrived cannibals (with darker skins than the local
people) threatened both Samoans and *palagis* alike:

The brother of Seumanu's wife has been eaten by black
boys. They are trying to hush it up but I think there is no
doubt about the business . . . they say that they only ate one
of themselves, as though the fact of cannibalism going on at
our door is of no moment unless some of ourselves are eaten.
A number of black boys have been caught already. There
are supposed to be a great many in our bush . . . All those
caught are armed with knives.

Seeing a half-finished dress-and-jacket outfit sitting on a
clothes-horse by a foot-treadle Singer sewing machine, I was
reminded of her doll-like frame. 'People here in Samoa,' said the
guide, 'called her *Aolele*, which means "flying cloud", because she
was always floating around from place to place, from the plantation to the cook house, from Belle's room to the medicine room.'
Fanny created an infirmary at the top of a grand staircase. She
became something of a shamanic healer, using a combination of

traditional and folklore remedies to treat people, whom she often cured, it seems, by the power of suggestion.

> Everybody, white, brown or black, comes to me with full confidence that I am able to cure any wound or disease. I heard a loud weeping as of some person in great pain . . . had just had two fingers dreadfully crushed . . . I really didn't know what to do, except to go to the doctor; but as the wound was bleeding a good deal, I mixed up some crystals of iron in water and his hand was washed with that. To my surprise his cries instantly ceased and he declares that he has had no more pain since.

From the infirmary, a 'Grand Staircase' leads down to a room that made me want to kick off my shoes and dance an eightsome reel: a grand, wood-lined 'Great Hall', where the Stevensons entertained half of Apia with Scottish-style ceilidhs. A piano once sat in the corner with other family instruments, while a mechanical music box still plays 'Home Sweet Home', 'Just One Girl' and 'The Hymnal Galop'. Louis's free-standing safe for money, jewellery and whisky occupied another corner. The room is so *Scottish*. Even the Samoan servants who worked in the house wore lava-lavas made of Royal Stewart tartan – hopefully in summer-weight material.

The running of Vailima was not without its challenges. The local people were very superstitious and believed that Vailima was thronged with devils. Fanny responded to staff fears by insisting that her devils were more powerful than anyone else's, and she was not beyond using simple magic tricks to convince them to work in remote areas of the garden. Many situations required her ingenuity:

> Lafaele, whose wife ran away from him a short time ago . . . tells me that he . . . must attach himself permanently to our establishment. He and his (new) wife will sleep anywhere

and both will 'work like hell'. If the new wife does not suit me in any way I am to just kill her and Lafaele will bear no ill feeling but keep on working like hell.

The main house has no kitchen. A cook house with a wood stove is situated in the back garden, where there was also a pantry and a Samoan *umu*. Fanny's pioneering skills again came to the fore during the establishment of the grounds. After discovering the presence of a fresh water spring on the mountain she designed a pipe-and-reservoir system of feeding water to the house. She planted coconuts and fruit trees and created a cacao, coffee, and vanilla plantation as well as a vegetable garden with peppers, aubergines, avocados, asparagus, rhubarb, tomatoes, lima beans and custard squash. She supervised the building of a carriage house, pig pens and chicken coops. Louis said she had the soul of a peasant. She didn't take it as a compliment but it was true; the best gift a visitor could bring Fanny in those days

was a fine, young boar. The formal gardens were fragrant with gardenia, jasmine and tuberoses; and there was a croquet lawn and a tennis court. A short distance from the house, a natural shaded bathing pool provided a place for the family to dip and take shelter from the tropical sun.

The Stevensons loved to entertain. They hosted traditional Samoan feasts, afternoon teas, evening receptions, dinner parties, balls, paper-chases on horseback, polo, tennis parties and picnics. One of the highlights was a shindig for fourteen sailors from a visiting Australian warship:

Yesterday was perhaps the brightest in the annals of Vailima . . . the band of the Katoomba . . . came . . . with drum, fife, cymbals, and bugles, blue jackets, white caps and smiling faces. Coming up from the mountain they had collected a following of children and we had a picking of Samoan ladies to receive them. Chicken, ham, cake and fruits were served out with coffee and lemonade and rounds of claret flavoured with rum and limes. They played to us, they danced, they sang, they tumbled.

It wasn't all a round of parties. The back-breaking work to tame the grounds of Vailima never ended, and Fanny's goal to make the estate self-sufficient failed. Their third year in Vailima, 1893, began a particularly difficult period for Fanny and those around her. Her moods had become intense and unpredictable – probably hormone-related, since it's likely that, at 53, she was entering menopause. Louis was worried about her. At the same time, he was able to create an extraordinarily objective portrait of her in order to prepare the writer J.M. Barrie for his proposed arrival:

If you don't get on with her, it's a pity about your visit. She runs the show. Infinitely little, extraordinary wig of grey curls, handsome waxen face like Napoleon's, insane black eyes, boy's hands, tiny bare feet, a cigarette, wild blue native

dress, usually spotted with garden mould. In company
manners presents the appearance of a little timid and precise
old maid . . . Hellish energy; relieved by fortnights of entire
hibernation. Can make anything from a house to a row . . .
Doctors everybody . . . cannot be doctored herself . . . A
violent friend, a brimstone enemy . . . Is always either loathed
or slavishly adored – indifference impossible . . . Dreams
dreams and sees visions.

Thursday 23 December 2004

I guess the last-minute Christmas rush happens everywhere,
even in slow-paced Samoa. I ran around Apia frantically buying
stocking-fillers until it was time to go to the airport to greet Billy,
Scarlett and some other family members who were arriving from
LA. I waited at the arrivals gate, wearing a killer red Tahitian
dress with frangipani *leis* for everyone. I thought I was hot stuff
until I began to be mistaken for the Princess Cruises welcome
girl and had to take refuge behind a pillar.

On 24 December we moved the *Takapuna* to the southern side
of Upolu and anchored at Aganua just in time for our Christmas
Eve party at Sinalei. In a thatch-roofed *fale*, or open-air room,
overlooking a peerless, palm-shaded beach, we met at sunset for
a feast of local seafood, fruits and a chocolate dessert. After dark,
a group of young fire-dancers arrived to entertain us. I had been
looking forward to this show. *Siva afi* or fire-dancing is a
traditional Samoan art, in which performers twirl and toss
blazing branches while pirouetting, gyrating, or adopting
difficult poses, including human tiers. Traditionally, the art is
limited to adult males but unfortunately these performers were
children and teenagers. They were excellent, professional
competition-winners and smiled bravely, but my own smile
turned to a horrified jaw-drop when I noticed burns on their
young limbs. I was shocked that they were exposed to the risks at

such a young age and felt terrible for having unwittingly added to their pain by inviting them to perform. Later on, when equally delightful children from the local village choir turned up to sing carols for us, I had concerns of a different nature: the choirmaster switched on a horribly loud, tinny keyboard accompaniment, which drowned out their sweet voices. So much for 'progress'.

Saturday 25 December 2004

Somehow, Santa found his way on board the *Takapuna* without getting his sleigh entangled in the rigging. In the morning there were stockings for all and a good deal of merriment. Dick and Rolle souped up their new radio-controlled toy cars with rubber bands and had a thrilling race around the deck. After a filling lunch (a big mistake in the tropics) we split into dive groups and had a competition to see which could make the stupidest underwater Christmas video. In my group, people entered the water in Santa hats with Xmas stockings over their flippers. I took a pair of scissors and some folded metal foil underwater and cut out a Christmas tree chain at sixty feet. Fortunately someone stopped me stuffing a silver ball in my bathing suit. Even with my limited knowledge of physics I should have remembered that, under pressure, the thing would have exploded.

Our rival dive group attempted a 'Bad Santa' comedy sketch, with Rolle cast in the leading role. I happened to arrive on deck at a crucial moment in the story, just in time to see our engineer, in red hat and fake beard but otherwise naked, dive off the bow pursued by Kayt and Sarah in scarlet cloaks and weird hairdos. Intriguing as it seemed, their video was never finished – in the course of its creation someone managed to put a hole in the tender. The remainder of the afternoon was spent repairing it.

Louis recalled Christmas at Vailima in 1890. It began badly on Christmas Eve when his horse, Jack, kicked him. The excitement continued next day with an odd assortment of guests, including a controversial missionary:

> Christmas Day I wish you could have seen our party at
> table. H.J. Moors at one end with my wife, I at the other
> with Mrs M; between us two native women, Caruthers the
> lawyer, Moors' two shop-boys . . . and the guests of the
> evening, Shirley Baker, the defamed and much accused man
> of Tonga, and his son, with the artificial joint to his arm —
> where the assassins shot him in shooting at his father . . .
> Baker . . . is accused of theft, rape, judicial murder, private
> poisoning, abortion, misappropriation . . .

On Boxing Day we heard that a gigantic tsunami had ravaged coastal areas around Sri Lanka, with effects as far-reaching as the coast of Africa. Our own weather warning system is so reliable, it seems particularly tragic that similar life-saving systems were not in place in those regions. Our compassion for the victims was profound and it reinforced our feelings of gratitude to be afloat; in a tsunami, one is better off at sea. In Savai'i, the larger and less populated island to the northwest of Upolu, we met an Australian geologist who gave us a fascinating lesson in plate tectonics that helped us to understand the geological factors that had led to the creation of the devastating tsunami. Savai'i itself is the site of intense volcanic activity. We explored the black lava fields, created by the eruption of Mount Matavanu a century ago, which cover the northeastern corner of the island, then spill out in messy dark blots through the turquoise shallows. Billy was particularly taken with the church half-filled with lava shaped like thick coils of twine. 'Imagine sitting in your pew when that arrived: "Hail Mary . . . oh my God, it's a plague of licorice!" '

We returned to Upolu for New Year's Eve. Apia was once known as the 'Hell of the Pacific', although that was in the days when it was full of drunken sailors. It conformed to that description this evening, however. Beer-sodden revellers careened in and out of the harbour-facing bars, some becoming dangerously punch-happy as the new year dawned. We did the rounds of a few local parties and nightclubs, but I felt strangely disconnected from the revelry and returned to the *Takapuna* in time for the stroke of midnight. I sat at the bow and reflected a little. It's been quite a year and my life is now so different. When Louis came here he knew he was on borrowed time and enjoyed it all the more for knowing it. I am resolved to lead the rest of my life with a similar sensibility. That, I have decided, is Louis's gift to me.

Monday 3 January 2005

Allan took my family and the whole *Takapuna* team, including Evan who had just arrived back, on an outing to the popular Lalomanu Beach. He installed us in a *fale*, among a cluster of many others. Around us, local people were having a jolly family time, eating, drinking, laughing and playing. Children careered up and down the beach, parents stretched languidly on mats in the cool of the *fales*, and others chatted while cooling off up to their necks in the water. Like everyone else, we ate pork and breadfruit that had been prepared in an *umu*, then waded into the ocean. We felt very underdressed in our bathing suits; for the local people did not remove their lava-lavas but swam fully clothed. In the middle of the beach, a rowdy rugby game began. Since most of the players were drunk, it was great entertainment. One man in particular was feeling no pain at all. From time to time, he would pass out and fall face down in shallow water, usually at a crucial moment in the game. His team mates would rescue him and carry him into his *fale*, but before long he would be upright again and back on the team until the next time he toppled over. Billy told everyone the scene reminded him of one of his favourite jokes about his home town. 'In Glasgow,' he said, 'if you can lie on the ground without hanging on, then you're not drunk.'

A large group of Apian taxi drivers in the next *fale* began their feast with customary speeches and gift-giving. Over time, their oratory became more and more heated, until we feared that there would soon be a full-on brawl. Noticing our trepidation, one of the ringleaders approached us.

'I see from your expressions you think we are fighting,' he said, 'but I want to explain to you that this is our Samoan way of showing respect to the *matai*, or elders, of this village and giving gifts. We are competitive in our oratory and our speeches must be powerful.'

To this my husband also nodded in approval. 'The translation,' he said, when they started up again, 'is, "See you Jimmy"!'

Wednesday 5 January 2005

I had to be Ship's Medical Officer today, now that Jock has gone. Rolle and Kayt asked me to administer their hepatitis A and B booster shots, which threw me into a panic. It is one thing injecting water into a dead chicken and quite another to stab an actual person. I grabbed the Medlink handbook and gave myself a refresher course. I was initially stumped by being unable to locate latex gloves, the sharps container, or even alcohol swabs. I obsessively read the directions over and over. *IM* – that must mean intramuscular. *In the deltoid area* – I had to consult the anatomy chapter to find the deltoids.

'OK,' I murmured. 'So I give this in the upper arm, being careful to avoid bone.' The needles were pre-packaged but I wasn't sure about removing the cap, screwing them in, or whether I still had to eliminate air bubbles. I needed a magnifying glass to read the date on the vials; at least they hadn't expired. I took all the equipment into my cabin so no one would notice my apprehension (I would *act* confident when I emerged) and found my classroom notes. *Resting on elbows, remove the top of the needle with a broad movement*. I donned gloves and managed to prepare the syringes without sticking myself. So far so good. I located the alcohol swabs, rolled up my sleeves, tied back my hair and strode into the saloon with the best brusque nurse impersonation I could muster at the time. Rolle and Kayt were sitting together, nervously waiting for the shots, while the rest of the crew tried to find reasons to be hanging round nearby. I dabbed at Rolle's arm and sized up my target.

'Look away!' I instructed.

'No!' he said. 'I vont to watch.'

'Look over there and breathe in then out,' I insisted, stabbing him swiftly on his exhale. A small trickle of blood made its way down his arm.

'You're shaking,' he told me, with an evil smile.

Kayt was more co-operative and kindly told me it didn't hurt a bit. I left immediately afterwards, bound for the university library to do some research, but soon after began to obsess about whether or not I'd shaken Kayt's compound before I injected it. It was meant to be milky. I could hear her voice on my walkie-talkie from time to time. She sounded a little weak. What could happen to her if I'd got it wrong? I had no idea.

Fanny shared my distaste for playing nurse at sea. Beyond caring for Louis, the general on-board medical responsibilities fell to her. She once wrote to Louis' former flame, Mrs Sitwell:

> In the midst of heavy dangerous weather, when I was lying on the floor in utter misery, down comes the mate with a cracked head, and I must needs cut off the blood-clotted hair, wash and dress the wound, and administer restoratives. I do not like being the 'lady of the yacht'.

At four this afternoon, Allan's friends Fred and Paul and Fred's younger brother Teariki turned up to take Billy, Evan and me for a paddle in a six-man *pa'opa'o*, or outrigger canoe. They are all gorgeous, broad-shouldered Samoan men. Teariki, or Ricky as he's known, taught me to paddle correctly, demonstrating the strokes with precision and talking me through the action with patience and care. The *foe*, or paddle, must be held vertically, with the bottom arm well extended to make each stroke. One foot (on the stroke side) slides forward with each change of side, to take the weight off the lower back. The stroker calls *'Sauni?'* ('Ready?') then *'Alo!'* ('Paddle!'). After another ten strokes or so, the man in the third seat calls out *'Sui!'* ('Change!'). The paddlers stroke one more time, then switch the paddle to the opposite side in perfect rhythm. We tried a few practice rounds, then set off across the harbour. It was brilliant and we went like the wind.

Afterwards, our exhausted fellow canoeists came on board for a tour. Fred and Paul are airline pilots, while Teariki turned out to be a house surgeon at the local hospital. I showed him our ship's medical kit and told him about the Tempus 2000 with much fanfare. Unfortunately, though, I couldn't find it and no one else on board knew where it was. We searched everywhere and finally located it under one of the guest bunks. I opened it and tried to give Teariki a demonstration, but the thing wouldn't start.

'Am I impressing you yet?' I joked. 'I promise you, this is a fantastic piece of equipment. If only I could turn it on.'

'There's no battery in it,' said Kayt, as alarmed as I was. If we'd had a true, life-threatening medical emergency, especially when we were at sea, the consequences of this error could have been fatal.

'You probably forgot to read what it said on the box,' joked Fred. 'Batteries not included!' It was so worrying.

'Teariki,' I said to the doctor at last, 'why don't you drop everything and come with us? You can see we really need you.'

Thursday 6 January 2005

I've woken up with terribly swollen tonsils. God, I hate being sick. Once again, the medical situation was tricky. I had to call Dr Spira in LA to find out which antibiotics to take. I could ride out the infection without them, but I know from past experience I'd be laid up for a couple of weeks. After quite a search I located the Amoxicillin. I'm really quite worried about going up to the North Pacific where there are few doctors or airports, especially with Billy and Scarlett on board.

The next morning I called Teariki at the hospital. He'd just finished his rounds, so he said he would come to Aggie Grey's Hotel to have lunch with me. I was feeling terrible, too sick to get up, but I had to try to persuade him to be our medical officer. Teariki is twenty-six years old, and has been out of med school for a year. When he returned to Samoa, he was immediately placed on the graveyard shift in the accident and emergency department alone, without any on-site supervision. That would explain the grey hairs appearing at the back of his head. I was thrilled when he said he was willing to come on the *Takapuna* for a limited period. He asked his father's permission (Samoan families still respect their parents' wishes long after their eighteenth birthday) and received his blessing. I felt concerned about taking a doctor away from the island, but Teariki assured me there were plenty of new graduates waiting to take his place, and that he would return in three to six months' time. I'm relieved. On Sunday, his family and friends came on board to see him off to Pago Pago. In true Samoan style, they parked their cars around the bay and waited until the *Takapuna* had undulated out of sight into the setting sun. In all my travels, in all my life, no one has ever done that for me. I sat for a while in the dark and allowed myself to be consumed with longing.

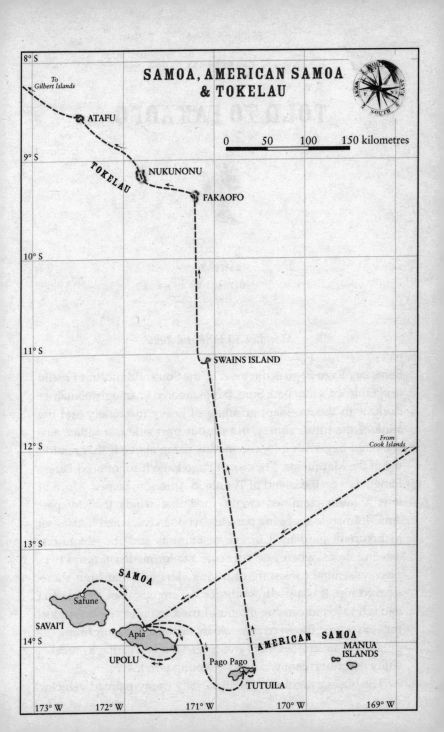

SAMOA, AMERICAN SAMOA & TOKELAU

8° S

To
Gilbert Islands

ATAFU

9° S

TOKELAU

NUKUNONU

FAKAOFO

0   50   100   150 kilometres

10° S

11° S

SWAINS ISLAND

12° S

From
Cook Islands

13° S

SAMOA

14° S

SAVAI'I

Safune

Apia

UPOLU

AMERICAN SAMOA

MANUA
ISLANDS

Pago Pago

TUTUILA

173° W   172° W   171° W   170° W   169° W

CHAPTER TEN

TOLD TO FAKAOFO

14°16′ S
017°40′ W

Monday 10 January, 2005

Some say Pago Pago is the toilet of the South Pacific, but I really don't think it's that bad. Sure, we're moored at an ugly container dock, with the incessant grinding of heavy machinery and the stink of the tuna cannery, but on our port side is a rather nice sheltered bay, with lofty mountains rising above it that remind me of the Marquesas. The city of Pago Pago (pronounced Pango Pango) lies on the island of Tutuila in American Samoa. Much of it is a traffic-crammed circuit road that winds its way past American-style shopping parades, wooden balconied houses set in luxuriant gardens, Chinese restaurants and the ubiquitous 'sewing shops' where one can order a tailor-made *puletasi*, a two-piece ensemble consisting of a long skirt and matching short-sleeved top. It is a useful outfit for the tropics; cool, yet modest enough to avoid causing offence. I tried to order one but unfortunately I used the word *palusami* by mistake, thus informing the giggling seamstresses that I was interested in wearing a parcel of slimy coconut cream wrapped in young taro leaves.

The buses caught my attention, jolly, spray-painted vehicles.

Some of them are themed in 1950s Americana style, like 'Road Runner', a stand-out with yellow and orange flames on a black background. The inhabitants of Pago Pago are all baseball shoes and American Tees, darting in and out of McDonald's and racing in their Chevy pick-up trucks from one end of the harbour-front to another, along the best-maintained roads in the South Pacific. Now and then, in between the trash skips and satellite dishes, one can sneak a glimpse of Old Samoa, such as the handwritten sign indicating that the nearby residents forbid swimming on Sundays. Mostly, though, the New World rules. Outside a traditional *fale* an enormous American eagle sits incongruously upon an impressive plinth. Uncle Sam has sequestrated many boys and girls of this island to fight in Iraq; faded yellow ribbons grace every fence, every compound, every church.

Fanny never set foot on Tutuila but Louis accompanied the American Consul-General, Mr Harold Sewall, on a three-week visit to the island. Here he wrote some lovely passages about the beauty of the 'long-elbowed harbour . . . green like a forest pool, bright in the shallows, dark in the midst with the reflected sides of woody mountains'. Given these inspired words, I was shocked to stumble upon a document in the Office of Archives on which Louis was one of the signature witnesses. It was the land title deed formalizing the sale ('in consideration of the sum of two hundred dollars gold coin of the United States of America') of a large portion of the harbour and surrounding land to the American government for use as a naval base. I suppose Louis's diplomatic hosts expected him to graciously comply, but he must have realized there'd soon be no more 'tongue of water' sleeping 'in perfect quiet'. Instead, cranes dance in the barbed-wire protected shipyards, teasing tiers of containers into the mouths of rusty hulls. Gigantic, sea-stained fishing boats, their nets piled a storey high, wait in line for a tank-load of diesel, or sleep by the cannery until their next long haul.

Despite its aesthetic deterioration, Pago Pago was certainly a useful, well-protected harbour for American naval ships – and we, too, are very glad to have it as a pit stop for the fast welding job we need to have done on our steering equipment. The South Pacific hurricane season is now well under way and we would be foolish to hang around any longer than necessary, even with our long-range weather predictors.

'I won't be breathin' too easy,' says the Captain, 'till we hit seven degrees south of the equator.'

I am hoping I will be able to obtain permission to make a brief stop-off on our way north at Swains Island, once an important copra trading station that was visited by Fanny and Louis aboard the *Janet Nichol*. An American called Eli Jennings, whom Fanny said was known as King Jennings, squatted on the island some years before they arrived. He had been based in Western Samoa, where he married Malia, a chief's daughter, but he ran into trouble there. The *Mao*, a group of *matai*, were fighting an intense battle to move Samoa in the direction of independence, in opposition to the government policies. When Jennings, who was a skilled carpenter, received a government contract to build a war vessel, he created a fifty-man *fautasi*, a transport canoe driven by hand-cranked paddle wheels, complete with mounted guns. After it was completed, however, his commissioners were unhappy with the design. In particular, they found fault with its slow and labour-intensive method of propulsion and refused payment. Licking his wounds, Jennings vamoosed to Swains, which had once been a whaling station. He took over the place, somehow found copra workers and set up a lucrative business.

When Fanny and Louis arrived on the island in May 1890, they met only descendants of the American 'king', for Eli had already passed away. It was still a thriving copra centre and Fanny, who was always impressed with people who knew how to make money, believed the place produced revenue of at least 2,000 dollars per year. Since 1935, the island has been officially part of American Samoa, but it also remains privately owned by the Jennings family. I had heard that permission to visit Swains is rarely given, so I was glad I managed to track down Wallace

Jennings, one of Eli's descendants, working in an Environment Protection office on the top floor of a shopping mall. A congenial man with a familiar Californian style, he listened as I outlined my interest in Eli and the island he developed, then summoned his cousin Alex, who is now the Swains Island *faipule*, or foreign affairs representative. I chatted to them both about the history of the place and expressed a desire to visit it. The men hedged. It seems unlikely that we'll be given permission. Wallace's reasons were that the people up there are worried about diseases we might bring ashore. He told me that, in any case, there were no longer any Jennings family members living there.

'It's not looking good,' I told the Captain later that night. 'I'm afraid I'm not going to like the answer.'

'Whadda they gonna do?' he snorted. 'Take away your birthday?'

When Wallace and Alex Jennings came on board at 4 pm the next day for afternoon tea, we discussed Fanny's Swains Island diary entries. They continued to show interest in my search, but wouldn't give me straight answers to several of my questions, including how many people live on the island.

'What, are you hiding bin Laden up there or something?' I joked. I finally asked them outright if we could have permission to land, but they continued to be evasive. 'Perhaps we could take something up to the residents – food supplies or other goods?' I suggested at last. That seemed to spark a little interest.

Later on, I learned that there is a tricky political situation. Apparently, the people of the nearest northern islands, the Tokelau group, consider Swains their fourth atoll and want it back. According to Alex they have spread rumours about the Jennings family – that Eli stole the island and took people as slaves. Now I understand why the cousins seem so jumpy. I must say, Alex certainly seems sincere in his desire to assuage the ill-feeling. He has a plan to make Swains the 'bread basket' for Tokelau, a place with poor-quality soil.

'It would benefit all,' he said.

Wednesday 12 January 2005

We moved to the shipyard to get the welding job done and found ourselves with a wonderfully decrepit fishing boat sandwiched between us and the dock. Our neighbour is considerably larger than the *Takapuna*, so in boarding or disembarking we have a horribly precarious climb up or down the side of her flaking hull. Nevertheless, I feel a certain affection for the old rust-bucket. She has the aura of a worthy old retainer, a smelly survivor of many storms, a noisy muse of Conrad, Hemingway or Melville. My romantic notion of her diminished somewhat when we returned from dinner ashore last night in pouring rain and a ferocious dog threatened us from a corner of her deck. Teariki and his visiting brother Mana stood guard while we scuttled past to safety. At least we've all had our rabies shots.

This afternoon, Alex Jennings turned up unannounced. He was loath to negotiate the hull ladder in his formal lava-lava (I guess he was afraid the girls would see up his skirt) but, leaning over the side, he gave us the good news that permission to visit Swains has been granted. He and Wallace will bring some supplies on board to take up to the people there. Excellent. We are hoping to leave on Saturday. Not soon enough. I am very bored with Pago Pago and my husband is extremely peeved. It's a depressing, unbearably humid place. Dick dived to clean our hull and complained it was a disgusting business, with little visibility in putrid water. Afterwards, we learned that it was unwise to swim or dive in the harbour because bloodthirsty sharks lie in wait for the cannery waste.

Friday 14 January 2005

There is a pretty side to Tutuila after all. Teariki drove me to Leone Beach and I found it to be much as Louis described it when he circumnavigated the island by whale boat: wind-bent palms on a pale-gold beach, studded with fingers of black lava reaching out into a bewitching blue-green swell. The upscale villas that overlook the beach are set back among foliage screens and there was not a soul about.

Rolle had to switch off the air-conditioning today in order to service it, so my husband is sweltering and irritable. I tried to get him ashore for a walk, without success. He absolutely hates it here.

'I spent my youth trying to escape the shipyards,' he complained, nearly tripping over a welder's helmet that had been left lying on deck, 'and now I'm fucking back.' I finally managed to take him out to a restaurant, where he was awe-struck by the appetites of the local people. 'It's the three-minute warning buffet,' he said uncharitably. Part of the problem is his lack of sleep. 'It's all about pointing in the right direction,' he says. 'At sea, the bed's the compass and you're the needle. All boat bunks should be round.'

Alicia, a Scottish girl invited to join us as a companion for Scarlett, arrived this evening. She is petite and quite posh, so I'm wondering how she's going to manage with our boisterous lot. Evan showed her to her quarters. He pointed down the companionway. 'That's where the decent cabins are,' he said, leading her in the opposite direction. It was the last cabin left, a tiny one on the port bow that will barely hold her bags. 'Yeah, I had a suitcase that size when I first arrived,' said Evan with an evil grin.

Having been advised that we would be departing at 9 am on Saturday, Alex brought some of his family aboard early to help load the provisions for Swains and to see us off. When he introduced me to his sons, I kissed each one on the cheek as I had learned to do on other Pacific Islands. It seemed more awkward than usual and when Teariki shook hands all round without the kiss, I realized I'd made a mistake.

'What's this?' I asked. 'I've just got used to the kissing thing, and now . . . what, is there a different rule here?'

Alex looked at the ground and shuffled his feet. 'Well,' he said, 'here we do things more like in the States. Besides, you have to be careful these days, you know, sexual harassment and all that.' I was appalled. How sad, I thought, that such a sweet and welcoming greeting should become a potential lawsuit. But maybe I've just been at sea too long.

We had a dreadful ride north today, 'goin' uphill' as the Captain would say, and I lay prone for most of it. Poor Alicia was dreadfully ill; her cabin, being forward, is one of the worst in bad weather. She is wonderfully stoic, though, and slept up on deck. Sunday was just as bad, and I was really seasick for the first time this whole trip, probably because I was below deck trying to focus on my computer. Billy, however, was bright as a button. I would have liked to bribe him to take my watch, but we've had to remove him from such duties, in the interests of safety – particularly that of his watch partner. 'The worst thing about standing watch,' he says, 'is other people's music. Belgian fucking jazz . . .'

As a result of the bad weather we arrived at Swains Island five hours later than expected, just before sunset. The entire male population, Palapi, Tolise and a teenager called Rupan, came out in an aluminium boat to take me ashore with the Jenningses' precious gifts of flour and other edibles. Adding Maria and Charlene who met us on the beach, that makes a total of five people on the island, although I gather a number of other residents are away at the moment. I took Alicia and Sarah ashore with me, having first made sure, given Wallace's concern, that neither had a contagious illness.

The little group of Swains Islanders had been waiting all day for our arrival. Maria, a sweet and generous woman dressed in a bright orange and yellow sarong immediately took a wheelbarrow and loaded the supplies off the dinghy. Charlene, a heavy-set young woman in a white T-shirt with *Leone Lions*, a Pago Pago football team, written across her chest, waited with us under a palm tree. I asked her what Palapi's last name was.

'I don't know,' she scowled.

'You live on a desert island with someone whose last name you don't know?' I joked. 'How old is that one, then?' I asked, pointing at the long-haired teenager in board shorts.

'I don't ask personal questions,' she snapped, quite pointedly, coughing loudly several times with a deep-chested sound that usually signals bronchitis. So much for not bringing disease ashore. I resolved to try to give her a wide berth, although on a small island with five inhabitants that was going to be rather difficult.

'How long are you going to stay with us?' asked Maria, 'Overnight?'

'I'm afraid not,' I replied. 'Our Captain says it's impossible to anchor, so we must leave before nightfall.' She looked crestfallen. 'Will you show us the island?' I asked. Fanny had noted a tall copra storehouse, a residence with a veranda, a schoolhouse presided over by a Samoan teacher and a 'doll's church'. She even spied a grazing horse that apparently pulled a carriage. While Louis spent a couple of hours ashore, she stayed on board making salsa. The second time they visited Swains, Fanny went ashore herself. She crossed the island to the inner lagoon and found it to be slightly brackish. While Lloyd swam, she went back with the women to the village, drank many coconuts, then returned to the ship.

Maria and Charlene led us up the short beach, past a couple of thatched lean-tos, into a large grassy village clearing bordered by a few houses, a rundown school and a quaint wooden church with peeling white paint.

'When was that built?' I asked excitedly. Charlene told me it was the only building left here after Hurricane Tusi passed by in the 80s. It was surely Fanny's doll's church, a charming little wooden Victorian structure on stilts, with an aluminium roof and arched windows. The interior was a different story, decorated with mass-produced wall hangings depicting biblical scenes and a cornucopia of plastic flower arrangements. Palapi takes the service here on Sundays.

The abandoned schoolhouse is modern, built on the site of the one Fanny visited. It was a sad sight. Broken brown-paper chains and cardboard mobiles of fish and angels were strung above scattered books, torn wall charts, benches stacked upside-down and a blackboard with its last lesson half-erased. The room has not been alive with the sounds of children since 2000, when apparently there were seven of them in attendance. The tall copra building that Fanny mentioned, the Jubilee Hall built by Eli to commemorate his wedding anniversary, was lost in the hurricane.

Following Fanny's tracks, we walked across the island to the lagoon, led by the wheezing Charlene. Pigs snuffled in the undergrowth, and even at this time of day the heat was suffocating. The lagoon was indeed a little brackish. A small open hut now sits in the middle so that people can cool off in the shallows beneath its shade. Charlene waded into the lagoon and crouched down with most of her body beneath the surface.

'You can take my picture now,' she said. I wondered how she could have adopted a negative view of her body growing up on Swains, but it turned out that in recent years she lived in Seattle while her late mother received treatment for cancer. Charlene, who was Wallace Jennings's niece and therefore distantly related to the original Eli Jennings, had buried her mother only a few months earlier, here on the island. She showed us the grave, a simple slab decorated with plastic flowers.

We made our way back to the thatched hut occupied by Maria and Palapi. While the men cut us drinking coconuts, Maria settled us on a wooden bench beside two beds hung with mosquito nets. Tolise and Palapi took out their guitar and ukulele and all five residents sang sweet songs of the islands, while Maria crocheted three bright woollen ponytail holders. Alicia reciprocated by singing the 'Skye Boat Song' in a pure, clear voice, before we were all decorated with shell necklaces and the ponytail holders as parting gifts. The men loaded coconuts and a basket of coconut crabs into the wheelbarrow to take back to the *Takapuna*, and we made our way down to the beach as the light began to fade. Filled with generosity of spirit, Alicia volunteered to sing one last song for the grumpy Charlene, and launched into another Scottish song, 'Ye Banks and Braes', while her audience of one stood unmoved, with arms folded and feet firmly planted in the sand, glowering into the sunset. Alicia was unfazed. She's a trouper, all right.

We left before nightfall and had a slightly easier sail to Tokelau, a group of three distinct clusters of islets that lie one hundred miles or so north of Swains. Between them they compromise a land area of under eleven kilometres, populated by 1,500 people. There is a long history of fighting between the three islands, and today they are divided by different branches of Christianity, with two of them (Atafu and Fakaofo) predominantly Congregational Church, and the third (Nukunonu) entirely Catholic. Our first stop will be the southernmost island of Fakaofo. My husband has cheered up considerably. He absolutely can't wait to get to a place with a name that is pronounced 'fuck off', or something close. However, a captain in Apia who does the supply-ship run told us that if anything's going to go wrong, it will at Fakaofo. I can't wait.

Monday 17 January 2005

At 11 this morning we arrived at Fakaofo and found it was true to its name, for we were immediately told to leave. My husband thinks it's a comedian's dream. The money we paid to the Tokelau Affairs officer in Apia to have our passports stamped as proof of permission to land has not ensured our welcome. In addition, a satellite failure has hampered communications between Samoa and these islands, so very likely the official notification of our imminent arrival did not get through. Unaware of this, Billy, Evan, Alicia, Scarlett and I set off in the tender and landed at a coral stone jetty by the main village. Heartened by the 'Welcome to Fakaofo' sign above our heads we proceeded past a shallow beachside pen where we were surprised to see pigs swimming and basking like rhinoceroses. We continued through the near-deserted village until we came to a large *fale*, or *marae* as they call them here, crowded with people engaged in a very intense meeting. An extremely worried man came running towards us and said we were not expected. Then an angry Customs official marched up and ordered us off the island. In fact, we were quite glad to leave for there was a strange feeling in that village. We learned that the elections for the new *faipule* were in progress, which may have accounted for the tension.

I decided to give it one more try and made an appointment to meet an island representative in the afternoon. Upon our return we were officially, if unenthusiastically, welcomed to the village by a woman at the council office. Later on we were invited into the current *faipule*'s house where we drank tea with the seemingly benevolent elder, discussing rainwater catchments, food supplies, garbage disposal and other pressing island issues. Given the isolation of the islands of Tokelau, the overcrowding and limited resources, I can understand why the choosing of a new *faipule* would put the people in a bad mood. Nevertheless, I feel very disheartened about our experience today. At sunset, Alicia and Scarlett played soothing flute duets, which improved my mood.

Fanny had a different kind of uncomfortable experience going ashore on this island. There was a heavy swell and her boatmen had a disagreement about the handling of the dinghy, which resulted in their broaching, or turning side-on to a large wave that almost capsized them. Fanny was completely drenched and felt quite chilled by the time she reached the village. She was taken to the King's house where she sat on fine mats conversing with the Queen. Fanny wrote:

It seemed a very languid place, the children soon growing tired of following us. As I felt signs of rheumatism from the chill I had got, I hunted up the trader a pallid Portuguese and asked if his wife could lend me a dress. He said we could find a board house across the Island which was his, and his wife would give me a holaku. As we drew near the house several handsome smiling women joined us and we all sat down on the veranda. The trader was not far behind us, and I was soon clad in comfortable clothes, but it was not in time to save me from a stiff neck. We refused cocoanuts, but accepted brandy and water. I gave the woman a wreath from my hat and a gold ring.

Tuesday 18 January 2005

A man called Mosi was nominated to give me a history lesson. I asked him where the nineteenth-century King's house visited by Fanny might be, but he seemed uncomfortable about the question and excused himself to make enquiries of someone else. He left me waiting in the heat for a very long time but, just as I was about to take off, he returned and led me to a site near the landing stage. There, by a clothes line in someone's back-yard, I saw the remains of stone foundations. Mosi had no further information, and the whole thing seemed a little fishy. I asked him if he knew where the Portuguese trader's house was but he just shuffled off, shaking his head.

The village was neat, with well-maintained houses, coral sand roads and a cricket pitch in the middle of the village square. With the exception of a few shyly smiling children, though, the people were not friendly. Outside the meeting house were two long drums and a rubbish bin that carried the notice 'Use Da Bin PLS'. Inside, people were still in session choosing their new representative. The island maintains a type of chiefly system, but the leaders are now elected more or less democratically. I continued to feel unwelcome and saddened by the general negative atmosphere that pervades the village. It was a relief to go diving in the late afternoon. The reef sharks, striped barracuda, and a huge spotted cod with nasty teeth were all more friendly than the human inhabitants of Fakaofo.

On Wednesday we set off for Nukunonu, our second Tokelau destination. After a lovely, gentle sail we approached a long, uninhabited *motu* with just three tall palms sitting on it. I longed to string a hammock there, rather than facing what could be yet another frosty reception. This time, though, we'd managed to make radio contact, and had ascertained that we were cleared and expected. We noticed immediately that this island seems more contemporary in the western sense than Fakaofo. The first person we saw was a young man jogging along the coral pathway in running shorts and headphones, pushing a baby in a smart stroller. At the same time, though, the material culture is being preserved. In a hut by the shore a man was carving a decorative canoe, and a wooden bucket called a *tuluma* (Fanny used the 'Tokelau buckets' as carry-alls). In a traditional, thatched Tokelauan house, built quite recently for receiving foreign visitors, I was introduced to Pio, the *faipule*, a very bright man with an unsettling nervous giggle. In the absence of a pastor, he is also the lay priest. When I mentioned that the Stevensons had visited the Tokelau Islands he was shocked.

'No one knows that,' he said.

In fact, they had even celebrated their wedding anniversary here. On Thursday 22 May 1890, Fanny and Louis gathered the ship's company together at 4 pm and shared out champagne that had been cooled with wet towels. The passengers took turns doing party pieces. Mounting a makeshift pulpit, one gave a Shakespearean reading, Lloyd sang a song, and Louis delivered a tongue-in-cheek 'sermon', the text of which was an advertisement he found for a product called St Jacob's oil. As an anniversary gift, Louis gave Fanny something she wanted more than almost anything else at that point: a promise to buy Nassau Island. She was ecstatic, and wrote: 'Of Nassau I dream sleeping and waking'. That same night Fanny had a dream that her mother-in-law refused to live at Vailima – obviously more wishful thinking!

Like Fakaofo, Nukunonu is in the throes of the local elections, yet the atmosphere here is far less strained. New Zealand has administered Tokelau since the British government handed it over in 1925, but Pio confirmed that self-government will very likely be in place by 2006. He got very worked up when I mentioned Swains.

'It belongs to us and we want it back. It was taken without the agreement and consultation of the ethnic population. There are people there who are related to residents of Tokelau!' I'm glad we decided not to bring up the fact that we'd just been there. I returned to the *Takapuna* feeling quite anxious.

I had arranged to meet with the elders and historians of the island the next morning, but only one person turned up because a vital council meeting was in progress. Hina, however, was a gold mine. A handsome, intelligent woman in her thirties, wearing a long denim skirt and an orange T-shirt set off with black pearl earrings, she had spent several years in New Zealand and spoke excellent English. Hina was appalled to hear about our treatment at Fakaofo. She had been raised on that island and offered to fill me in on the history I had missed.

I mentioned that Fanny had been drenched while getting ashore and had been lent a dry dress by a Portuguese trader's wife. I was about to ask where the house would have been, but she interrupted me.

'That would have been my great-grandmother.' I stared at her. Suddenly, I could see some Portuguese features in her physiognomy. 'Antonia Vitorino de Perrera, who was known more simply as Jose Perrera, would have been that trader,' said Hina. 'He was my great-grandfather on my mother's side. My great-grandmother was Moiki Perrera. They lived in a two-storeyed wooden house on Fakaofo where the Catholic church now sits. They slept upstairs and used the bottom floor as a trading store, selling corned beef and food staples.'

The Perreras were Catholics. They brought around twenty other Catholics on to the island with them, mainly Samoan and Portuguese. Up until then, the population had been largely Presbyterian, including the *tupu* (king) at the time, so the newcomers drove religious tensions exceedingly high. Finally, Vaopuka, the last King of Fakaofo, who was Hina's great-great-grandfather on her father's side, was shot by a man who worked for Perrera, with Perrera's own gun. That brought the conflict to a head, and shortly afterwards the churches made peace and were able to co-exist. Nowadays, a special celebration takes place annually in Fakaofo, celebrating the end of the religious fighting. It is called *Fuhi O Te Fealofani*, or Tie a Ribbon of Peace.

I asked Hina if she knew where the King's house was on Fakaofo, and recounted that Mosi had acted strangely when I asked him that question. She smiled and shook her head.

'That is because church-going locals are not proud of the fact that, in those days, the King had several houses and quite a few wives. These facts have been erased from official island history. There were about ten royal houses, one of which was really a brothel.'

But that's not the limit of the unpopular history of the King. Some say Peruvian blackbirders (slavers) forced him into condoning the slave trade that almost entirely depopulated the Tokelaus. There are even some who say he worked willingly with the slavers. It must be strange for Hina to have one side of her family implicated in the slave trade and the other side victims of it. Hina's older sister has recently managed to trace some of her mother's family to Cape Verde in Peru, where many Tokelauans were taken.

Fanny and Louis probably had an incorrect impression of the size of the population, for by the time they arrived the islands had been so decimated by slavers that a first sight of any type of arriving vessel prompted a mass exit of all the women and children to the other side of the lagoon. At one stage in Tokelauan history, the islands had been depopulated to the point where only the very young and very old were left.

When I mentioned Fanny's gifts to her great-grandmother, a wreath and a gold ring, Hina's eyes widened. 'My mother still has a collection,' she mused. 'The last time I saw it I was about sixteen years old. I came upon it by accident and she didn't like my seeing it. Among other things, rolled in cloth inside a little wooden box were rings – very old, gold rings.'

'Wouldn't it be amazing,' I said, 'if one of those rings had been Fanny's? In her diary she wrote about another Portuguese trader on Atafu, which is our next stop,' I continued. 'She said his wife was an albino person.'

'Jose probably would have accompanied them to Atafu,' explained Hina, 'but there was another Portuguese trader called Perez who settled here on Nukunonu.' She knew nothing of his wife, although I saw a young girl in church with the same condition carrying her albino brother. I asked Hina about the *tuluma*, or Tokelau buckets that Fanny found so useful. 'They're made from hardwood in many sizes, and were used as locked storage and safes in those days.' Nowadays, small ones are used as fishing hold-alls and jewellery boxes. I managed to locate a big beauty, with inlaid mother-of-pearl. Fanny would have loved it.

While I was ashore talking to Hina, the Captain took my husband manta boarding, a primitive method of rapid deep-diving. This turned out to be a rather risky thrill to offer a Scotsman with a minuscule attention-span. Billy was instructed to hang on to a plank of wood attached to a rope then give the signal to be fast-towed by the dinghy. Turning the manta board at an angle to initiate a dive, he took a deep breath, descended to thirty feet or more for a quick reconnoitre, then whipped back up to the surface just before his lungs exploded. He went scuba diving straight afterwards and wondered why his ears hurt.

Nukunonu's volunteer doctor, a thin, pasty German in his seventies called Klaus, came to dinner with his elegant wife Heike. They had applied to be posted here after reading an article in some German doctors' magazine. The writer had described the Tokelauan islands as a paradise, but apparently that was not the reason they came.

'I have a nice house with a cellar full of French wine,' gloated Klaus, 'and a Mercedes. I wanted to give something back.' They've been contracted for six months, but looking at them after only two, I doubt they'll last the distance. The supply-ship captain told me he ferried them up here – the doctor in hand-made shoes and his wife draped in Chanel, as if they expected to find a Four Seasons Hotel. I can certainly understand that it must be frustrating to try to help a population that has more faith in local herbalists and shamans but, honestly, what did they expect? During dinner, the pair complained non-stop about the conditions, the lack of medical supplies, the behaviour of the people and the food they received.

'One night, people came into my house and stole my hair conditioner,' said Heike, searching round the table for pity. 'I wept and wept.' I suggested she use locally made coconut oil – which is probably the basic ingredient of many western hair products – but she didn't seem to hear. Billy generously gave her a bottle of his own conditioner, but I was more inclined to tell them both to get a grip. They were like babes, suddenly thrust beyond the cradle of consumer comfort, mewing for a metropolis.

Whenever I become this judgemental, I always have to stop and take a look at myself. Do I complain too much?

Friday 21 January 2005

I was supposed to go on a picnic to another side of the lagoon, where there is apparently an island with a stunning inner lagoon, but Billy is in terrible pain from his ears and can barely hear so I stayed behind to nurse him. Teariki says that since his balance and equilibrium are fine he can't have burst an eardrum.

Those who went on the picnic returned in very high spirits, saying it was absolute paradise and that a fantastic day was had by all. I was very upset to have missed it and became determined to get there before we leave. Coincidentally, Fanny missed out on shore fun here as well. It was raining when the *Janet Nichol* arrived and since her rheumatism was very bad she thought it best to remain on board. But the sun soon appeared, and after dosing herself with a tonic she felt better. Anxious to see the island, she hurried to get ready to go ashore and searched for Louis to accompany her. She wasn't too happy when Lloyd pointed him out – already in the dinghy some distance away and headed for the island without her. She wrote:

> I spend a dreary day trying to see what they are doing
> through the open glass and trying to hear the singing which
> the wind occasionally drafts towards me. The sun and opera
> glass combined give me headache, and I spend the rest of the
> day in sulks . . . The boat comes back at dinner time,
> everybody talking together about the curious experiences
> they have had, all quite excited. I feel like a child who has
> missed the pantomime, and listen to them talk with an ill
> grace.

Saturday 22 January 2005

Hina came aboard to go through my photos of Fakaofo and fill in the missing history. During our conversation, it emerged that she had been to Swains. I was shocked to hear she had seen a wooden homestead on the other side of the island from where I spent my time. Charlene had obviously lied to me about its existence (as did the Jennings brothers concerning her presence on the island). She had point blank denied there was any other

old building apart from the church, and now I am intrigued to
know why. Hina also explained the issue with the graves in the
island's far cemetery that I did not visit. One of the biggest
questions about Eli Jennings's occupation of Swains is what
happened to the existing population after he turned up. Some
believe there were Tokelauan people growing food there when
he arrived but that Jennings got rid of them somehow. Were they
relocated? Killed? Enslaved? Did they leave of their own accord?
Have wicked stories been concocted to discredit the Jenningses
in an attempt to reclaim the atoll? The graveyard I missed
probably held some answers. I'm kicking myself.

'What time is church tomorrow?' I asked Hina.

'You're going?' she asked in surprise. I nodded.

'It's funny,' she said, 'that white people came here all those
years ago and told us to cover up and attend church. Now most
of them come here in skimpy clothes and go snorkelling on
Sundays. The people of Nukunonu will be pleased to see you at
tomorrow's service.'

But when I went ashore with Alicia for the 8 am service, I
found that it had been delayed. A baby had died during the
night, so the people were preparing for the funeral. I followed
the path to the graveyard, where most of the men in the village
were digging and cleaning up the surrounding area. Just in time,
I remembered that it is taboo for women to be in the graveyard
at such a time. I stopped short and called for permission to
observe from a distance. The men were working silently,
diligently removing fallen coconuts, leaves and other debris. A
small rectangular hole was being hollowed for the newest little
resident, while the bereaved father, a youth in a trendy shirt and
haircut, stood nearby with his head bowed low. An older man's
hand rested on his shoulder.

I went back to the church where I met Klaus and Heike, who
had been up all night trying to save the infant. They told me that
when he was brought to the hospital he was haemorrhaging and
already unconscious, with a fever of forty-one degrees. The

baby's parents, said Hina, were very young and unmarried. Their families had not accepted their live-in relationship, so they received little support. I now understand that the German volunteers focus on minutiae in order to distract themselves from the overwhelming frustration of trying to provide western medical care here. They are treating wounds that have developed unnecessarily into serious infections, managing diabetes caused by poor diet and lack of education, and losing patients seen too late to be saved.

The entire village was expected to gather for the funeral Mass. Pio led a procession from the family's house to the church, depositing the little white coffin that had been hastily hung with purple and gold decorations, in the centre of the nave. For our benefit, Pio translated his sermon into a single English sentence: 'We are all one.' Afterwards, we walked with the islanders to the graveyard for the final ceremony. I had been hoping to go on my missed picnic, but since the whole village was in mourning I assumed it would be cancelled. But Pio approached me and, very touchingly, presented me with the wreath from around his own neck.

'You have joined us here in our grief, so now you are free to take pleasure in the day,' he proclaimed. 'Luckily, it was only a baby who has died.' That seemed like curious logic. 'It is a joyful day for us,' he smiled, presumably thinking of heaven.

Billy, Kayt, Rolle, Teariki and I joined Hina and others on a local expedition to the special picnic spot. I was so eager to experience what I had missed I foolishly ignored the fact that the weather was changing and that we would have to travel in a rickety fishing boat across an enormous expanse of lagoon in an approaching storm. It was a terrible ride. Torrential rain poured inside the boat on all sides and visibility was reduced to a few feet. After an hour of rain-lashing and wave-thumping, we arrived just as the skies were clearing. The place was, indeed, utterly gorgeous – a horseshoe of an atoll with a perfect, butter beach surrounding a clear, turquoise lagoon. In the centre of the bay a shallow sandbar led to a pea-green, inner lagoon with a statue of the Virgin Mary rising out of its middle depths – a painted, praying, Lady of the Lake.

While Billy fished on the point, the rest of us went snorkelling to view two blowholes, deep coral chasms that had been known to suck people into their swirling guts. When we returned, Hina had grilled fresh mackerel on a beach fire and coconuts had been cut for drinking. We sat beneath a roof of tree-branches while Billy performed an impromptu fashion show with draped seaweed garments. The other men did sensible things, like roasting plump coconut crabs on a roaring beach fire, which were delicious.

Monday 24 January 2005

Fanny described the people of Atafu, the most northern Tokelauan island, as 'the only flatterers I have seen among natives.' If only they had remained so! I went ashore with Teariki and, not being sure of our position, asked the first person I saw if I could speak with the *faipule*. A woman, Moe, came up and sternly asked us to present ourselves immediately to the council of elders, which was sitting at that time. In the upper room of a large, red-roofed *marae*, thirty men were sitting at trestle tables arranged in a square. Moe was our coach and translator. She told me I must face the council, introduce myself, and explain why we are here. This was a daunting command, since my inquisitors looked rather unsympathetic. I stood before the *faipule*, the *aliki* (mayor), and the rest of the elders, and did my best to tell the story of my journey so far. I mentioned my interest in the Stevensons, and expressed my eagerness to know the history and stories of Tokelau, as well as visiting sites that might be relevant to Fanny's visit.

At the end of my impromptu presentation I received a little applause, which encouraged me to believe I would be welcomed from that point but, instead, the men began to argue. Should I be allowed to stay? They were annoyed with their representatives in Samoa, for although it had been broadcast we were coming, they had received no details, probably due to the poor inter-island communications at the time. There were many points of contentiousness, especially from one belligerent specimen in the corner. Was the Samoan office going to keep the landing fees? Shouldn't Atafu get them instead? Was I going to be making money from the book? Was I related to the Stevensons? Then the focus turned to Teariki. Was he related to Dr Emosi F. Puni from Samoa who had been the island's doctor for several years?

'He's my father,' replied Teariki. After that revelation, our situation rapidly improved. The outgoing *faipule* Kelli posited that it was a good thing someone was interested in Tokelauan history. He formally welcomed us, then wondered aloud if, given that it was nearly lunchtime, they had enough food for everybody in the room. I quickly turned to Moe.

'That's no problem,' I said, relieved. 'I've already eaten.'

Moe looked terrified. 'Please don't refuse,' she pleaded under her breath. I pulled up my chair to a bright pink stew and rice on the *faipule*'s table. 'That one making all the noise,' Moe whispered, nodding at the corner antagonist, 'he's my husband.'

I was surprised to discover that the ex-*faipule* Kelli is a PhD student in the Anthropology Department at Oakland University, California, and that both he and the newly elected *faipule* Colloway speak excellent English. After my severe grilling, all through a translator, it was bizarre to suddenly be chatting so amicably. Now they were offering us coconuts, vegetables and medical help. Now they were upset we were not staying longer. It was very confusing. Outside, heavy rain began to fall. When it lightened up a little, we were taken on a tour of the village by a nurse who had known Teariki's father. She showed us where he lived, some coconut trees he planted and the hospital where he once worked. It is interesting to see how small islands deal socially with contagion and disease. In the middle of the inland lagoon was a man-made quarantine island, presumably used in earlier times for sufferers of white men's ills, such as leprosy.

I was taken to the home of a carver, who learned his craft after contracting polio as an adult, and bought some exquisitely carved canoes, all with tiny ropes, paddles and rudders. Sitting on the lino floor haggling over the price, I managed to get a good look round the living space. A huge boom box sat on a low chest. Set against another wall was a tiny stove and a few pots and pans. Several high shelves provided storage for suitcases and bags of clothes, while wooden decorations resembling gingerbread men hung near the ceiling. Four generations lived together in this one large room with a vestibule. An elderly man and woman sat in wheelchairs near the door. She had one leg amputated below the knee, probably from diabetes. From time to time, several children careened in and out of the room, one with a nasty cough. A middle-aged woman was lying on her side in one corner, weaving fine mats from a pile of newly dried pandanus leaves. Two more adults reclined in the centre of the room, fanning themselves in the sweltering heat, while three others and a teenage couple sat upright on wall-side benches. None of the family bothered to move when I arrived.

Tuesday 25 January 2005

This evening we had an unbelievably gorgeous night sail under a full moon. Strong, warm breezes enveloped us as we lay out on the aft deck. Under the Milky Way, I reflected upon our time in the Tokelaus. We are so used to being made welcome in most countries of the world, but isn't it arrogant of us to *expect* it? Unless an island is deliberately courting tourism, why should the people allow foreigners to visit, especially if their purpose is unclear? After such a terrible history of slavery, it is little wonder the Tokelauan people are still wary of strangers arriving in large boats. Perhaps it was significant that even Pio had refused my invitation to dine with us on board.

These thoughts were underscored later this evening when I found an account by a Raratongan called Maka (a letter to a Reverend H. Gee), of a terrible incident that occurred in Atafu on 16 February 1863:

Sir, all the people of this island are carried off. They have taken the chief Oli, who was in Samoa, and thirty-four other men. All that remains here are women and children, and six male adults . . . Such, Sir, has been the cruelty of this ship to the people of this land . . . Had we known the character of the vessel no one would have gone on board. We are startled that such a thing should be done to this people. Two men who were returned to the shore by the Captain, told us that when the people reached the ship with their things for sale . . . But this was the contrivance of the Captain: he placed some things into the hold of the vessel – the best of the cloth, red cloth, and shirts, and trousers, and white and blue calicoes . . . Then the Captain said to the men, 'look to the cloth on deck and that in the hold, and see what to choose' . . . then all went below . . . one of the crew gave them wrappers and shirts, and trousers and hats to put on. So the men rejoiced that they had got such clothing to attend worship in. But some of the crew were hidden in the hold, armed with cutlasses . . . None remained on deck except the chief . . . he called down to his people to return to the deck . . . The chief was standing over the hatchway, when some of the crew seized him and threw him down into the hold . . . Then the hatchway was immediately closed down upon them all. These two men also told me they saw one of the people struck down by the crew with a sword. They saw the blood flow like water. They do not know if he was killed for the ship hastened off.

Sir, there is nothing we do now but mourn and weep for

our island is destroyed. But we think now that they have
taken all the strong people of this land they will return with
the ship to fetch the women and children. This is my
inquiry, what shall we do if the ship comes again? Tell us
what to do . . .

When I read the name of the trusted, Tokelauan-speaking
recruiter, who earned around $10 per head or $1,000 for 'a
goodly number' of people of Atafu stolen as slaves, my hackles
rose; it was Eli Jennings.

Wednesday 26 January 2005

Australia Day.

I sang 'Waltzing Matilda' for anyone who would listen. Dick,
my fellow Australian, celebrated the day right from the start by
eating a Tim Tam for breakfast. He's shortly going to be the best
man at his mate's wedding in Melbourne, so he's trying to write
a speech. Billy has offered him various suggestions, all of which
would clear the room. My husband's ears have much improved
under Teariki's care, thank heavens. He's supposed to be
performing in New York next week.

I am on a no-sugar diet, so Tim Tams are out. I tried to
persuade Kayt to make an artificially sweetened Pavlova for
dessert.

'But I haven't got any fresh fruit,' she wailed.

'Ah,' I said, 'then what about a sugar-free Lamington?' But
even as I uttered that last phrase I knew it was sacrilege.

Kayt eventually came up with a menu of pie floaters
(swimming in mushy peas) followed by barbecued fish. To that
end, Alicia reeled in what she thought was a wahoo, but it
turned out to be a barracuda. We argued about whether or not
it could be eaten. I devoured one once in Gozo, and found it
delicious. Still sceptical, Kayt set aside some fillets then strung

the rest over the stern on a fishing rod. She and Alicia stood with their eyes glued to the end.

'What on earth are you doing? I asked.

'Just chumming for shark,' she replied.

The sea and its inhabitants are always full of surprises. At 5°39.649′ south by 176°55.595′ west, Alicia reported a 5 by 21 (nautical miles) oval patch of sea that suddenly dropped off from 6,000 metres to 8,000 metres.

'I've never seen anything like it,' said the Captain. 'It's like someone took a big scoop outta the sea floor.'

I went into the galley about quarter to five and found Kayt having a disastrous Australia Day galley moment.

'Why?' I asked.

'My pies exploded, my ANZAC biscuits are soft, my barracuda's inedible and now Evan's helping me,' she said. I sympathized, glaring at Evan, who was busy using the food mixer as a weapon against some massive, imaginary foe. In the end, though, we had a delicious dinner, consisting of the planned pie starter, barbecued wahoo with coleslaw and the last of the potatoes, followed by an enormous Lamington cake made by Teariki and Evan under Kayt's supervision. The non-Australians made tired old disparaging remarks, such as 'When exactly did they stop sending convicts to Australia?' Someone even had the gall to ask, 'What IS wrong with Steve Irwin?' after which I decided they'd all gone too far.

'I won't hear a word against the Crocodile Hunter,' I said sternly. 'I mean, crikey! He's my pin-up boy!'

Full as an emu's udder, we stood on the port deck and watched the phosphorescence, huge balls of it, sparkle and pop in our bow wake. At 9 pm the moon rose, a softly glowing orb wrapped in pale organza ribbon, breaking free of dark purple cloud-fingers at the world's beginning. Who cares that we had to fuck off from Fakuofo? We're lucky, lucky people.

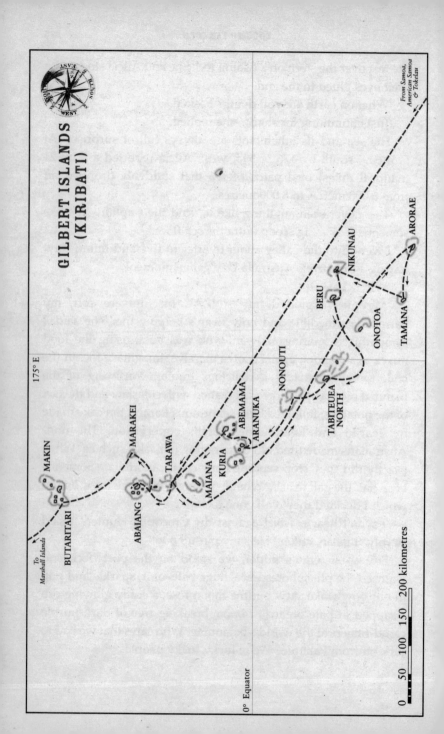

GILBERT ISLANDS (KIRIBATI)

175° E

To
Marshall Islands

From Samoa,
American Samoa
& Tokelau

MAKIN

BUTARITARI

MARAKEI

ABAIANG

TARAWA

MAIANA

KURIA

ABEMAMA

ARANUKA

NONOUTI

TABITEUEA
NORTH

BERU

NIKUNAU

ONOTOA

TAMANA

ARORAE

0° Equator

0 50 100 150 200 kilometres

CHAPTER ELEVEN

SHIPWRECKED!

04°29.9' S
178°35.8' W

Thursday 27 January 2005

We are experiencing wonderfully calm seas again, although there's still a fair swell. Our progress is quite slow, averaging only four or five knots, but it's so pleasant nobody cares. The boys lounged in the saloon playing video games, while the girls were in their bikinis, sunbathing on the foredeck. Later on, Scarlett baked cookies. The sunset was outstanding, its rouge streaks reflected perfectly in a glassy sea. By contrast, the Captain received a distress call from a boat called the *Explorer* that is adrift some distance north of here with 900 passengers on board. Two of the crewmen are injured, but help is on the way.

'What the hell were they doing up there this time of year?' wondered the Captain. At least we are headed beyond the reach of brewing hurricanes. Meanwhile my husband sits happily on the aft deck with a cup of tea and a biscuit. He loves the mysteries of on-board provisioning ('chocolate biscuits that procreate in a cupboard for months on end!') and thinks Kayt is a goddess. 'Three miracles a day, from a kitchen the size of a cardboard box!' He still hasn't learned to say 'galley'.

On 1 February we arrived at Tarawa, the main centre of the Republic of Kiribati (pronounced Ki-ri-bahs). This Micronesian country comprises thirty-three islands (including groups known as the Gilbert, Phoenix and Line Islands) spread out over three and a half million square kilometres in the Central Pacific Ocean. Prior to this trip I had never heard of it, although, as a child, I used to love the stamps I had collected from the once-unified British Crown Colony of Gilbert & Ellice Islands. We anchored in Tarawa harbour, surrounded by ancient, rust-blighted cargo ships, leaky tin dinghies, a disintegrating mariner training ship called the *Moamoa* and a smart grey Australian patrol vessel. We waited around most of the day to clear Customs, which was frustrating because after five days at sea we were all dying to get off the boat. Not that the shore appeared very inviting. A fuel depot surrounded by barbed wire dwarfed a few shacks on one side of the landing, while a couple of cranes loomed above several tin-roofed warehouses on the other. We could see a small marina that had attracted a flotilla of garish, oddly built fishing and transport boats. A putrid smell emanated from the shallows, whenever the wind wafted our way.

Kelly arrived to join the crew, a lean, laid-back, blonde Canadian.

'This is my first Pacific island,' she said, with a brave attempt at enthusiasm.

'Bummer,' I replied.

Wednesday 2 February 2005

Too much dilly-dallying on board this morning. I couldn't stand it any longer, so I went ashore alone in a very bad mood. A long jetty, lined with a steep sea wall of cement bags, serves as one side of a sheltered channel to a crowded dinghy dock. Up close, one could see that many of the boats in the marina had been built in a curious, higgledy-piggledy fashion, with little regard for style or safety. Two of the inter-island passenger boats, both absolutely stuffed with people and ready to depart, featured enclosed toilets built out over the stern so that waste dropped directly into the sea beneath. A dozen or so small, naked, brown boys were swimming nearby, taking it in turns to dive off a stone slipway. Just beyond them, a tall lamp-post topped by a harbour light lay bent over at a 45-degree angle to the water, probably the result of a close encounter with a truck. I leapt out of the tender on to slippery cement steps, up to my ankles in slimy greenish liquid. Ahead of me was a store with *Korekorea's Corner* written on the wall beside a painted can of Victoria Bitter. *Take Away* was written underneath, with a big red arrow pointing round the side of the shed to a serving hole in the wall under a dingy awning. To my left was a four-pump gas station beside a gigantic puddle of grey, filmy rainwater and an ugly communications tower.

I had no phone, no transport and no command of the Kiribati language, so I had to improvise. Two Caucasian men were perched on bikes chatting together on the side of the road, their wheels half-immersed in the puddle. One of them looked unmistakably Scottish, with red hair, pale skin and freckles. Stefan, who indeed hailed from Fife, briefed me on expatriate life here. 'The first thing local women ask is, "Are you married?" and the second is "Do you *want* to be married?"'

The Tarawa economy is tough, so apparently the girls here want white husbands to bring in revenue for their families. Stefan gave me a list of dos and don'ts of negotiating the Tarawa bureaucracy. 'Don't mail anything valuable and don't ask any unnecessary questions, because you're bound to get an answer you don't like.' He took me to lunch at a drab Chinese restaurant with a few other *I-Matang*, as foreigners are called here. We sat down with a long-haired, barefooted New Zealand man, confusingly named Alice, who runs a clean-up and recycling programme. Tarawa, it seems, is home to many volunteers from Australia, New Zealand, Britain and the USA (there are fifty-eight Peace Corps workers alone) whose countries fund an enormous number of aid projects, especially in the areas of security, health, education and environment.

I learned that my eyes had not deceived me; this place is in very bad shape, both environmentally and economically speaking. Nearly 30,000 people are crammed into twelve square miles with little fresh water, inadequate catchments and appalling sanitation (half of them just use the beach). Land has been reclaimed to provide extra living space and link up adjacent islands by causeways, but this was done without the necessary forethought to prevent further problems of over-crowding, food shortages, waste management, lagoon blockages and damage to reefs and marine life. It's a shocking mess. My husband came ashore shortly after I did and immediately pronounced South Tarawa to be the Arsehole of the Pacific. So far, I have to agree.

After lunch, Stefan took Billy and me for a ride on a packed community minibus. Despite the rows of heads blocking my view on all sides, I managed to discern that most people here live in traditional, thatched houses decorated with brightly coloured washing; that there is no shortage of smiling children and that pigs here eat from troughs made of giant clam shells. When we reached the suburb of Bairiki, after negotiating several of the most mountainous speed bumps I've ever seen, Stefan took us to present ourselves at the Australian, British and New Zealand High Commissions. Only the big cheese for New Zealand required an appointment; the other High Commissioners were most welcoming.

The British High Commission in Tarawa is closing down. Its last overseers, John and Sally, are a jovial couple from Hertfordshire who gave us tea in a cosy office while lamenting the withdrawal of the British from this Pacific post – due presumably, to their increased diplomatic presence in more newsworthy areas of the world such as the Middle East. On the other hand, Australia's presence in Kiribati is growing. Annual development assistance arrives here to the tune of 11 million Aussie dollars. Jurek Juszczyk, the Australian High Commissioner, is a bright and charming man of Polish origin. The quintessential 'Our Man in Tarawa', he sports the fashionably crumpled linens of a tropical diplomat that are so admired by my husband. Steve, another Australian in his office, is married to a beautiful girl from the southern island of Abemama. He happily informed us that technically, at least according to Abemama tradition, he is entitled to have sex with her sisters. No wonder *I-Matang* men here look smug.

'So what exactly are you doing here?' I asked businessman John Brown, a British 'Ernest Borgnine' character, complete with round belly, sailor's rolling gait and Singapore tattoos. He came here in 1989 and now takes visitors on Second World War history tours as a sideline. Previously, John spent twelve years in the Royal Navy and five years in the British Foreign Service. When the Powers That Be needed someone in Tarawa, they approached John.

'Where's that?' he said.

'Oh, it's in the middle of the Pacific.'

'What do I have to do?'

'Just take the scientists fishing,' they said.

After John retired, he returned here as a foreign investor. Among other things, he manufactures soft-serve Frosty Boy ice-cream and artificial limbs.

As we began to tour around South Tarawa, it became apparent from the large amount of disintegrating military paraphernalia still lying about – on the beaches, half submerged on reefs and in people's gardens – that this was once the scene of some monumental wartime action. My knowledge of twentieth-century wars was as rusty as the sea-facing mounted guns, searchlight batteries and aircraft parts we passed along the way, so John provided me with a potted history. In 1938, the

Americans and Australians realized the Japanese expansion into the eastern Pacific was becoming threateningly large.

'Big Iron Bob – you'll remember Australian Prime Minister Bob Menzies? He stopped exporting steel to the Japanese, so they were looking for raw materials in the Pacific,' explained John. The Japanese lost the majority of their aircraft carriers at the Battle of Midway, so island atolls such as Tarawa were very important to them in order to maintain surveillance of the US fleet. 'When the Japanese first came here in 1941,' said John, 'they evacuated all of the local population to the end of the island, explaining, "We are now at war with America, Britain and the Dutch East Indies." They came back in early 1942, bringing a thousand soldiers of the elite naval Japanese defence forces, who proceeded to build 500 bunkers on Betio.'

Kwajalein, one of the Marshall Islands northwest of Kiribati, was a strategically important military base. The Japanese had it and the Americans wanted it; but before they could take it (as well as other Pacific prizes such as Truk in the Carolines and Saipan in the Marianas), the Americans had to make a trial invasion landing. They chose Tarawa as the first amphibious assault of an island-hopping campaign code-named Operation Galvanic. Five thousand members of the 2nd Marine Corps invaded on 20 November 1943 and took it in three days, but not without great loss of life. 'They needed close air support, which they didn't have,' said John. 'They needed frogmen to check the underwater obstacles for mines, traps and other obstacles that would hinder their Higgins landing craft. When the marines jumped into deep water their radios got wet and didn't work, so they should have had waterproof ones. They needed a beach master to co-ordinate the stores which were being off-loaded from the ships. Without one, they were getting ponchos and blankets when they really needed plasma, water and ammunition. It was a big learning curve.'

At the time, there was a neap tide (unusually low) so there was far less water over the Betio reef than the four feet they had anticipated. Many of the amtracs, or amphibious tractors, ferrying the marines ashore, were blown apart, or hung up on underwater obstacles. The Japanese had sunk the *Niminar*, a Fijian trading ship, and filled it with machine-gun nests from which they attacked the American troops as they were trying to wade ashore. The men were decimated on the reef, for there was nowhere to hide. Those who made it were stuck on the beach at the end of the first day: 1,500 American troops in about 100 yards of beach and nowhere to dig in.

In all, 1,072 Americans died here, and 2,292 were injured, over the three-day period. The Japanese lost 4,729 men, while only 17 Japanese prisoners of war and 129 Korean labourers were taken. Not a bad little blood-bath, for a dummy run before Kwajalein.

There is a Japanese memorial, a Shinto shrine, in Betio on which is inscribed *The futility of war, may we last in peace forever*.

'With all their manpower, guns and ammunition, why didn't the Japanese manage to repel the Americans back to the sea?' I asked.

'Because their leader, Shibasaki, was already dead,' replied John, leading me to the admiral's bunker. 'He died on the first day with a salvo from an American warship that was out there in the harbour. They spotted him coming out of his command centre with all his high-echelon staff and blew him to pieces. On top of that, their wire communications were all on the surface of the sand, and the Hellcats came in with 500-pound blast bombs and blew them to bits.'

At the bottom of the US Marine Corps monument were the words *Enjoy your independence, and guard it well*. 'They don't maintain it,' scoffed John. 'They don't maintain anything here.'

On the reef in front of the hospital, John pointed out the remains of a landing craft and the engine room of the *Niminar*. To our left was part of a Mark 2 Sherman tank, largely under water.

'It ran into a bomb hole,' explained John. 'It was actually named *Cecilia*, after the driver's little girl. He was from Los Angeles and he later died in Taipan.' The water before us was still full of live ammunition, including 88mm mortars. John finds quite a bit of ordnance himself. 'I put what I accumulate on the top of my water tank where my kids can't get at it,' he said. 'Just before Christmas, an Australian ordnance team came through here and blew up about 30 tons of shells and things that we'd collected: 88mm mortars, 75mm shells, all sorts of stuff. We had a brilliant show on the Sunday night, with all the pyrotechnics going off, all the flares and rockets going off on the beach. The kids loved it!'

'Are there still mines out there?' I asked.

'Oh yeah, there are two mines somewhere in the lagoon in Makin. If you go up there be very careful, OK?'

Along the shore road we passed one of the four 8-inch Vickers guns on the island, manufactured by Sir Armstrong Whitworth Ltd, in Manchester. Weighing twenty tons, it can shoot a Volkswagen a distance of eleven miles. A Mark 1 amtrac, whose driver was probably killed by snipers in the coconut trees, was rusting in long grass, while a searchlight battery generator was a blight on someone's front yard. One man had built his house on top of a Japanese personnel bunker (that now housed his pigs), while in the centre of a crammed family housing compound sat a live shell, decorated by a flourishing wreath of violet bougainvillea.

After viewing all this evidence of battles played out in the Tarawa theatre, hostile events that had had nothing to do with the people of this country (or I-Kiribati as they're known), I finally voiced what had been puzzling me.

'How do the local people feel about the war, all the fighting that took place, all the damage?'

'It doesn't affect them,' replied John, who is married to Molly, an I-Kiribati. 'The war,' he continued, 'was between America and Japan. It was nothing to do with Kiribati.'

'But they just turned up here one day and shot the hell out of the place,' I argued. 'Many of them were enslaved, shot or injured. Surely that was seen as undesirable!'

'Yeah,' he replied, 'but the people really affected were those on Banaba, now known as Ocean Island. The Japanese had originally evacuated all the Banaban women and children to Nauru, Guam and Kwajalein, but they kept 150 young blokes to do their fishing and labour work. Five days after armistice, August 1945, they lined them up blindfolded on a cliff and shot them. Two survived and crawled into a cave underneath. Lieutenant Commander Suzuki was later hanged for that at the war crimes commission.'

Retribution came in many forms, and on both sides. There had been coastal watchers in the Gilbert Islands from 1939 and twenty-two of them – seventeen New Zealanders, two Australian and three British – were rounded up by the Japanese and beheaded Four months later an uprising occurred at a Japanese prisoner-of-war camp at Featherstone in New Zealand. There was a guard there whose brother had been one of the coastal watchers beheaded in Tarawa. When the uprising was in full swing he let loose with his Thompson machine gun and killed forty-two of the Japanese prisoners.

On Friday Jurek very kindly arranged a lunch for me and my husband at his residence. I was thrilled to meet Henry, an elderly man with a walking stick who had been houseboy to Admiral Shibasaki. Henry's master had been good to him, and even promised to take him back to Japan, to raise him as his own son. Just before the American landing, Shibasaki sent Henry away to safety on a nearby island. The boy sat under a coconut tree, trying to avoid being rained on by shell fragments, and watched the battle unfold. When he learned his master's fate, he was devastated and even tried to contact the family back in Japan to inform them of the admiral's promise to welcome him into their bosom. Predictably, they did not respond.

At lunch I sat with Willy Tokataake, who came from the southern Kiribati island of Abemama, or 'land of moonlight'.

Willy is one of the descendants of Tembinoka, the colourful King
of Abemama who hosted Fanny and Louis on his island for
several weeks when they first arrived aboard the *Equator*.

'He was crazy,' said Willy, 'and he died childless. I am
descended from his nephew, who became King after him. The
current King, now only a figurehead, is a man called Don
Tokataake, who still lives on Abemama.'

Natan Teewe, who also comes from Abemama, sat on my left.
'I can't wait to visit your island,' I confessed.

'I'm flying there tomorrow on an official visit,' he said.

'Can I come?' I asked cheekily.

'Well,' he smiled, 'I am the Minister for Transport. I may be
able to find you a spare seat.'

After lunch, Jurek took me aside. 'Here are some things
you're going to need if you fly to Abemama tomorrow,' he said,
handing me a curious collection of objects: a round, pale green
tin of Gallaher's Irish Cake tobacco; a history book about the
construction of the Kiribati *maneaba* or meeting house; and a
pack of spray deodorant. I was most surprised about the latter
and wondered if he'd noticed a personal freshness problem
about which even my best friend had failed to inform me.

'Do tell,' I invited.

'The Irish Cake is a suitable gift for the elders when you
attend the ceremony,' he explained, 'and as an honoured guest
you will be expected to get up and spray the deodorant on the
dancers while they are performing for you.'

I stared at him, a knowing smile crinkling around my mouth.
'Yeah, yeah, yeah,' I said. 'Good one, Jurek. Now, tell me the
truth.'

'I'm serious,' he smiled. 'It is the custom for guests to freshen
the dancers by spraying their underarms with deodorant, or
shaking powder on their necks while they are performing. The
most important guests will go first, government officials for
example. All you have to do is follow their lead.'

We had been invited to attend the Waitangi Day event at the

New Zealand High Commission that same evening. 'I'm not fucking going,' said my husband. 'I don't fancy celebrating Maori-land-rip-off Day.'

'How do you think I feel?' I retorted. 'I'm part-Maori. But Natan's going to meet me there to let me know if I can go to Abemama.'

The evening turned out to be just another ex-pat piss-up, full of Peace Corps workers and church volunteers – although it was also attended by most local dignitaries. Anote Tong, the President of Kiribati, a handsome, charismatic man of Chinese descent, smiled warmly as he shook my hand. 'I understand you'll be travelling to Abemama with me tomorrow,' he said.

The next day I took the 6.30 am Presidential flight to Abemama, Land of Moonlight, as one of the official guests at the opening of a new *maneaba*, or open-sided meeting house that serves as the centre of social, governmental and spiritual life in every village throughout Kiribati. As we took off, the rickety propeller aircraft gave me pause, but it landed neatly along the coral runway and taxied to a clearing outside the small terminal. A couple of wooden benches had been set out for the President and his party. Between the aircraft steps and the benches, a long line of welcomers waited to shake hands with each one of us. I followed the lead of Tebi, Natan's wife, who became my cultural adviser for the day.

'*Mauri!*' With each white-shirted welcoming official, I exchanged a local greeting, shaking hands once with an expansive movement. I learned later that ancestral spirits circle above the *maneaba*, so a large shake is necessary to catch their attention. In Kiribati, it's all about the ghosts.

As we VIPs were parking our sweltering behinds on the benches, a song began, accompanied by rhythmic clapping. A group of female dancers emerged from the airport terminal, jiggling their upper torsos. Once upon a time, before the missionaries informed them that their bodies were hung around with naughty bits that shouldn't be exposed, the dancers would have been charmingly adorned in nothing but grass skirts, amulets and shell jewellery, but today they were covered from neck to ankle in long red outfits over which they'd tied green bushes like ballerinas' tutus. They shuffled out in single file, a group of twenty or so women who ranged from nubile, giggling maidens to gap-toothed, smirking matrons. They lined up facing us. As they paused momentarily, arms outstretched, I caught a sudden movement to my left as Leigh Chen, the wife of the Taiwanese ambassador, suddenly sprang from her seat and darted out towards them, deodorant in hand. In amazement and horror, I watched her deftly squish a stream of vapour under each and every armpit. Tebi followed suit with another atomizer, the two of them trying to weave in and out of the now windmilling dancers, trying to reach their elusive targets. I felt sick with nerves, for I realized it was probably my turn next. I fingered Jurek's spray stick in my bag but I could not bring myself to attempt what seemed then to be an abominable act.

The dancers approached us and placed a floral garland on each of our heads. I noticed that the President's wife, Madame Tong, had coiffed her hair perfectly for this addition, in an elegant chignon. I, on the other hand, was suffering from the lankness of locks that accompanies a humid atmosphere and a dawn rising. We were offered some breakfast, served out of plastic buckets. There was *bero* (fruit with coconut), coconut cake, coconut toddy and milky tea. I nibbled on a bit of cake. Eventually our transport arrived, a car for the President and a council truck for everyone else. I watched the women deftly climb aboard in their lava-lavas and hoped to do the same without flashing my G-string to the good people of the village. Fortunately, I was rescued by Leigh, who bumped her husband on to the flatbed and invited me to ride inside the cab with her. The Ambassador kindly acquiesced, but I'm sure he was irritated. Then began the slow and jarring trek several miles along the narrow island to our destination, an impressive, newly completed *maneaba* that was about to receive its inauguration.

After prayers outside, the President cut a ribbon in the western style and we all traipsed in and sat in our prescribed places on finely woven pandanus mats. Fine mats are used throughout the Pacific Islands, not only as seating for guests, but also as gifts, marriage beds, and currency. They are painstakingly handwoven by women and are often passed down as family heirlooms.

Maneaba ceremonies are long, and the protocol is extremely complex. As an *I-Matang*, I knew I would be forgiven for small mistakes, but I'd had little time for training and was constantly afraid I might give offence. There were prayers, songs, speeches and more dances. Just when I thought I would die if I couldn't get my legs in a more comfortable position, the master of ceremonies blew a whistle and a tower of booming speakers burst into a disco number. One of the council members approached me and bowed with arms outstretched. I stood up happily and followed him to the centre of the *maneaba* where the President and other officials were already boogieing with their host partners. I tried to remember the rules about not giving the wrong signals while dancing; I had learned from a Peace Corps volunteer that I should not under any circumstances look my dance partner in the eye, or move close to him if he held his arms up in a big 'O' shape.

'I know someone who had what she thought was an innocent dance,' he said, 'but by the end of it, she was engaged.'

More speeches followed and Tebi translated as much as she could, so I was able to glean that a white woman had never before arrived with an official party. I was very taken by the relaxed humour with which the speeches were delivered. There was a good deal of sexual innuendo, which I learned was common in Abemama society. I had been forewarned about the folklore joke concerning the 'University of Abemama'. This is not a proper institution but, rather, an accumulation of knowledge concerning sexual practices and techniques that is part of the island's history.

'I am an Associate Professor at a Californian Institute,' I said,

'but I am rather interested in a position at the University here...'
This scored delighted guffaws all round. With each bout of
dancing, people became more relaxed. Even quite elderly people
cavorted in an erotic manner, not something we see much of in
our culture. Only once did the MC, who happened to be a
bishop, decide to intervene when he saw a couple practically
shagging on the dance floor. Later, a middle-aged man got up
and performed a bawdy action song that Tebi's translation
revealed was a variation of the English 'I'm a little teapot, short
and stout' nursery song. The spout was his penis and the
analogy was all about heating up his 'water' so it comes to the
boil and spurts out – not exactly subtle, but hilarious, and very
well received by the audience. I thought it was quite wonderful
to discover a society of people who are so comfortable
expressing their sexuality, even in an official ceremony.

When the dancers and musicians performed their more
serious traditional numbers, I was summoned by Tebi to follow
her with the deodorant spray. I meekly walked into their circle,
head and shoulders bowed as I had been taught to do out of
respect for the sacred space in the centre of the *maneaba*, and
attempted to overcome my culturally bound resistance to this
very personal act of grooming. It wasn't easy to reach their
armpits while they were moving but they seemed grateful for
the service. Tebi did not stop at freshening the performers, but
led me on to squish practically everyone. It was astounding.

In two separate instances during the song and dance displays
a performer broke down and began to cry uncontrollably. I
wondered what was wrong but could only conceptualize these
events in ethnocentric terms as a couple of bad cases of stage
fright.

'On the contrary,' explained Tebi, 'the performers were
simply overcome by the powerful magic of their songs and
dances; in fact, a concert without such an occurrence is
considered lukewarm.'

Lunch was an enormous feast of roast pig, breadfruit,

chicken, fish, clams, taro, coconuts and many foods I did not recognize. We ate in the *maneaba*, and afterwards there were more speeches and more gift-giving, and I was directly asked to supply them with a security perimeter fence to protect the new building. Hell, and I'd already given them Jurek's tobacco, short of a couple of sticks that had been plundered by my husband in desperation to fill his pipe the night before.

As the day wore on, I realized with some trepidation that I was going to have to pee at some point. I finally asked Tebi to take me to a bathroom, and she began leading me towards the beach.

'Er, I think I'm actually OK.' I halted, resolved not to be the owner of one of the glaringly visible bottoms voiding themselves on the nearby sand.

When I arrived back in Tarawa, elated after a truly extraordinary day, I was brought down to earth by the realization that I had no way of contacting the boat because I had forgotten to take a radio. I was forced to hitch a buck-jumping ride on a leaky fishing dinghy. There was a terrible swell. Fearful that the boatman might bang-up the *Takapuna*'s stern, I had him circle while I screamed for assistance. Eventually Rolle came on deck and heard me. My hero launched the tender, came alongside and grabbed me out of the dinghy like a father dragging his child off a runaway horse. I was very, very shaken.

On Sunday, Scarlett, Teariki and I went to church at the Chapel of the Sacred Heart convent, an appealing round building with open wooden fretwork walls that allow the breezes to circulate. The nuns lay on breakfast for the congregation, one of the highlights of the Tarawa weekly calendar. Two sprightly sisters, Aileen and Eileen, welcomed us with tea and a plate of their superb fig jam on toast. At the beginning of the Japanese occupation, the Sacred Heart nuns were issued a stern warning, signed by the Japanese squadron commanders: *If you behave, you will be well treated; if you misbehave you will be severely punished*. Among other treasures in their archives are letters from

pioneer French sisters. They did not have an easy time of it, and
Sister Aileen's own story is fairly typical. She was twenty-eight
years old when she set sail from Sydney Harbour on Anzac Day,
thirty years ago, on an eighty-foot mission vessel captained by a
priest. Also on board were a lay engineer, three young French
priests acting as crewmen and two other sisters with whom
Aileen shared the duties of cook, nurse and stewardess. In their
long black habits and white heart veils the three nuns had signed
on as crew at Circular Quay – lining up with crowds of burly,
tattooed sailors. (Louis thought the stories of those hardy
seamen would make many fine, buccaneering adventure books
and, to that end, he got them talking whenever he visited
Sydney. Perhaps he was talking to the wrong gender.)

A flotilla of small boats followed the mission vessel out of the
harbour to bid God speed; but after two days at sea the engine
broke down and they had to limp back to Sydney. When the
sisters crawled into the convent at five o'clock in the morning,
their Mother Superior put her foot down.

'That's the end of it,' she said. 'They're not going.'

'Oh, Mother,' argued the young priests, 'they're good for
morale.'

On their second attempt, the crew nearly made it to Noumea
before they had another mechanical failure. This time they had
to wait several weeks in the French colony while the boat
underwent repairs. Eventually they set off for Fiji, but soon
found themselves caught in a 'whirlpool' – perhaps some kind
of oceanic anomaly – that span them round and round and
disabled their steering. Or perhaps the steering problem came
first. Aileen laughed as she remembered how seasick the three
sisters were – all fighting over the one basin. They did not arrive
in Kiribati until 10 June, nearly three months after they set out.

'So,' she smiled wanly, 'I have no love for the sea.'

A few visitors came aboard on Sunday afternoon, including
Madame Tong with quite a few children in tow. The kids ate ice-

cream, watched American videos and ran exuberantly all over the boat. The First Lady's ancestors were stolen away from Kiribati by slavers, so she was raised in Fiji. Eager to educate me about Kiribati history and culture, she lent me books from her own library and invited us to a special dance performance on Tuesday.

On Monday I visited the Tarawa Marine Training Centre, an impressive local college where young men are trained to be professional seamen, including deckhands, engineers and cooks. After graduating, they are placed on German ships and are thereafter able to send $1,000 a month home to their families – big money here. The Captain Superintendent was an exceedingly squat Bulgarian with a bad case of flu he'd picked up in Bavaria. Just what I need. I tried not to breathe in his presence.

At 3 pm I went back on board to make sure everything was under way for tonight, since the President and his wife are coming aboard for dinner. Poor Kayt is cooking against great odds; we have very few provisions and there's no running to Marks and Spencer in this corner of the globe. On my way home she telephoned me, wailing: 'If you see any veggies on the way home – *anything* – just get 'em!'

At 4 pm the President's private secretary and a policeman turned up to check over the boat, in case we were planning an assassination. The policeman was surprised we asked him to remove his shoes and the secretary seemed a bit harassed. He is new at the job, and at short notice he'd had to figure out how to get the dock cleared for tonight.

At 7 pm the President and Madame Tong, plus private secretary and attaché (bodyguard), called to say they were on the dock. Rolle appeared on deck looking amazingly smart in pressed shorts and a clean polo shirt, with his hair slicked back. He and the Captain took the tender into the dock. It was quite choppy, so our guests were a little wet when they arrived, and had some difficulty getting on board. Nevertheless, we had a relaxed and informal dinner, just the four of us, while the presidential entourage sat on the aft deck chatting with Teariki.

'Don't mention China!' Jurek had warned (Kiribati has recognized Taiwan), so we talked about normal human issues, such as the pain involved in parenting. You could see the stresses on the pair. Their family life is interrupted because the President travels to islands for ceremonies over most weekends. He needs to address the power of the councils of elders throughout the twenty-two inhabited islands, dotted about over an area as large as the United States.

'Those old men have a lot of power,' he said. 'They can dissolve governments. It's illegal and unconstitutional, but it can happen.' The fact that his own brother is Leader of the Opposition must add an extraordinarily challenging dimension to his presidency.

Staring out into the darkness of the lagoon, the President said he once saw a 15-foot tiger shark – bigger than his dinghy – this side of the pass, so Arthur Grimble's 1930's tale of their lagoon feeding grounds in *A Pattern of Islands* may still hold true. I asked if he had ever seen a black shark. The Stevensons' royal host, Tembinoka of Abemama, was said to have descended from the creature, so Fanny created a flag for him: 'three crosswise stripes for the three Islands, green, red, and yellow, with a large black shark lying across them. The shark has white teeth, and a white eye. A triple crown of yellow is just over him.'

I also inquired about the origins of the deodorant-spraying custom. 'I assume it didn't exist before deodorant sprays were invented?' I asked.

'Ah,' said Madame Tong, 'but earlier on, people probably used the special oils that were made from secret family recipes.'

The couple proudly attested to the power of Kiribati traditional dancing and explained that it was bound up with the ritual and magic of the place. Magic, I learned, was a part of the culture and belief system here. 'When I was a young man,' said the President, 'I came back from being educated in New Zealand

and thought I knew it all. I was soon told "You know nothing." There is magic in everything. Westerners don't understand. It is not part of your vocabulary.'

There was a rather weird moment when he started telling us about a volcanic stone in the *maneaba* in his village of origin that has 'babies'. At that point, Billy decided to give him some advice on how to run the government. 'I know how to solve your over-population problem,' said my husband. 'Cannibalism. Everybody should eat one person.' From that point on we just laughed a lot.

Miraculously Kayt managed to whip up an impressive presidential feast:

Spiced crab salad topped with breaded soft shell crab with a red pepper dressing

Lamb with red wine, rosemary and honey jus served with colcannon & broccoli [colcannon is a mixture of cabbage, potato, bacon & herbs]

Coconut & chocolate cheesecake with Kahlua sauce

At midnight we said our goodbyes and our guests and the Captain jumped into the tender, driven by Rolle.

'Drive as if you're sober,' joked Billy.

As the dinghy approached the channel and we were all just congratulating ourselves on the fact that the evening had run pretty smoothly, Rolle managed to run smack into the reef. It had become exposed at low tide and was barely discernible in the darkness. The rather violent collision broke the propeller and disabled the tender. The President's security man freaked out, but our Captain kept his head. He jumped into the water with the line in his teeth and began to swim. He towed the dinghy thirty metres to shore on the left side of the channel. When they got close to the bank, the President's men tried to raise the police whose depot was nearby, but no one answered.

Then Madame Tong took charge and told them to flash their torches at a passing car. The driver got out and, using a rope, managed to haul his shipwrecked leader up the steep, cement-bagged banks to safety. After that, Rolle stood on the reef steadying the dinghy so it wouldn't float away before help arrived. Most endearingly, the presidential couple requested a couple of chairs so they could sit on the dockside and watch what happened next.

'If I had a couple of beers I'd be really happy,' said the President, who misses his nights of drinking with pals there by the dockside. Eventually, Rolle flagged down a fishing boat, whose driver gave them a tow.

'Enjoy being shipwrecked last night?' I asked the President the following evening. He had thoughtfully included us in a UNICEF reception so we could see an outstanding dance group.

'It was an adventure,' replied Madame Tong with a broad smile.

As is the custom, we received floral headdresses from the dancers. Billy got a lovely pink one.

'Do I look like a dodo?' he whispered.

'Of course not, darling,' I lied.

The male dancers appeared wearing fine mats tied round their bodies with belts of human hair. 'Only your own family's hair can be worn,' explained Madame Tong. The dancing was truly extraordinary, accompanied by powerful, vibrant chanting and songs that began with solo voices answered by a full chorus. Bodies are slapped rhythmically in a fashion I've never seen outside Kiribati. The performers' jerky movements are accentuated by the vibration of their amulets, necklaces and other accessories.

'It is incredible magic,' whispered the President. This troupe displayed great precision, and I was struck by the wide variety of dances, emulating battles, birds and animals, canoe journeys and human relationships. One symbolized an octopus, in which the waved arms of four dancers served as tentacles. For a particularly sacred dance, several women changed their green grass skirts for darker-stranded fibre skirts.

'It's pandanus,' whispered Madame Tong. 'It has been baked and prepared in a special way. Can you smell it?' Indeed, a sweet, charcoal-like scent wafted towards us, released from the ceremonial costumes by the heat of the dancers' bodies. Later I heard that on some islands they are substituting commercial video-tape for the dark pandanus strands of some skirts, which looks remarkably similar but does not please the nostrils.

On Wednesday, I dragged Billy to a Betio reef to see a Sherman tank exposed by the sunrise tide. He was less than thrilled.

'I've always wanted to be woken in stygian darkness to go and look at scrap metal,' he said.

Later in the morning, I toured the Betio copra factory to see how the raw material is processed: via hammer and expeller, to either copra cake or oil. At all stages it was lovely stuff: rich, syrupy and sweet-smelling. Then Scarlett, Alicia, Evan and I visited the school for children with disabilities established by Madame Tong. It is a neat, well-run establishment in a compound near the airport. Once we got over the fact that the classrooms are marked above the doors with labels like 'Welcome to Deaf & Hearing Impaired Children', we were able to appreciate that the school is really quite a miracle – one of the most progressive things about Kiribati. We were utterly transported by the harmonious voices of the children with visual impairments who surprised us with a soulful rendition of 'Walk Right Back' by the Everly Brothers that brought us to tears. This was the treasure of the island of Tarawa.

On Friday, Billy, who can finally hear out of both ears again, left early for New York. I raced to the University of the South Pacific to check out the library, then picked up Jurek who is taking the weekend off to sail with us to Abaiang. Also among our guests will be the Labour Minister and his wife, whom the President suggested we invite. Even though it made excellent sense to take along an Abaiang dignitary, I was nervous about it, for the couple speak little English. Even worse, two additional people, the Head Councillor and the Council Clerk of Abaiang, came with them. I panicked because we had only one cabin left, but I was assured they would all sleep in the *maneaba*. I just wondered how I would explain to Kayt that there were two more mouths to feed from our already terribly depleted provisions. There's no decent fresh food here in any of the few stores, so she is having a very hard time.

We motored to Abaiang because there was no wind. It was not until we arrived at the only suitable anchorage, near the lagoon entrance, that the minister informed us we had to first land at Ribona village which was miles away, on the other side of the uncharted lagoon. It was essential, he said, to be received initially by the elders and council members of that particular village, or misfortune would follow. The Captain shook his head doubtfully, but we set off at a snail's pace, with Rolle up the mast, picking our way between the sudden shallows and ubiquitous coral bommies. To navigate this lagoon safely, we really needed a diver to proceed us, because the changes in depth were extremely sudden and the tides unknown. Meanwhile, the elders were already gathering in the Ribona *maneaba*.

The mood on deck became very tense. At one point, Kelly, who was plotting our position, sighed in exasperation and threw down her pencil.

'That's it!' she exclaimed. 'We're now off the chart!'

The Captain and I watched the depth finder with a great deal of alarm.

'Not many yachts come here,' said Jurek, which surprised no one.

As the afternoon sun fell lower in the sky, Rolle came down from the mast, complaining that he could no longer see. Instead, he got into the tender and took the lead, using information from the tender's depth finder.

We reached Ribona dreadfully late for our reception. The

head man, wearing a 'Proud to be an American' T-shirt, chided us for our tardiness, but after we made profuse apologies our welcome was very warm indeed. In keeping with *maneaba* protocol, every Takapunian stood up and introduced himself. This was carried off with aplomb by most, although Rolle inspired the most giggling. The *maneaba* was beautiful, with a traditional ceiling that resembled one I'd seen among Lloyd's photos. As usual, dancers first performed a garlanding ceremony. This group wore proper grass skirts with two different types of fronds; a yellow-green short layer over a longer, darker skirt. I had to coax the rest of the crew to help with the deodorizing, but amid smirks, outright giggles and much photographic recording, everyone took a turn. Unfortunately, some of our lot sprayed too timidly and failed to get right at the pits, which caused stifled laughter from our hosts. It is considered very inept to miss one's mark, especially if the recipient happens to be singing at the time and winds up with a mouthful of Old Spice. There were many speeches, gift-giving (we provided school supplies) and a generous feast.

'Mmm, those bananas look good,' said Jurek, hinting that we should be careful what we ate. (Caucasian visitors tend to lack the strong stomachs necessary for the local cuisine.) It was too late; Evan was already tucking into all sorts of dodgy fare. I had learned to go for a little rice and to drink only coconut milk in the shell. We all bopped merrily with our host partners, this time to the vocal stylings of the village choir. When there was a call for us to show them dances from our own culture, Scarlett delighted all by performing a Scottish sword dance, using a couple of criss-crossed palm sticks, while Evan led several of our gang in a geeky rendition of 'Do the Hokey-Cokey'. Ah, culture! Whoever said it was about a striving for perfection?

There is a strong belief in magic here. The people are very superstitious, and pedantic about ritual. We were expected back in the *maneaba* the next morning at seven for a breakfast of bananas, pancakes and coconut milk; no excuses. It was also

particularly important to the people of this village that we take
a tour of the islet, hear their oral history and be introduced to
their ancestral spirits. Indeed for *our wellbeing*, we were warned,
we must take the tour, lest punishment, even death should
follow. Those crew members who had considered sneaking
back to the *Takapuna* after breakfast promptly changed their
minds and we meekly followed our designated shaman on a
pilgrimage to three sacred shrines. A handsome, athletic woman
with several children in tow walked swiftly ahead of us, wearing
only one sandal. Her hair was striped with grey, she smoked
incessantly and her teeth were decayed. I tried to guess her
age but, as was usually the case, I was culturally ill-equipped to
do so. Take away dentistry, decent nutrition, hair dye, facial
grooming, cosmetics, plastic surgery – not to mention the
seductive attention of buff young personal trainers – from any of
my LA girlfriends (dare I include myself?) and they'd probably
look similarly, well, world-weary. With a life-expectancy of
barely fifty-six years, our shaman was probably only thirty.

In the first magic site a man had been buried sitting up so he
could see the setting sun. The second was a hideout by the ocean
where a castaway 'black man' had captured and eaten anyone
who strayed too close. Lastly, we were shown a sacred well that
is considered magical because its water level remains constant.
At each of these shrines we were expected to give a stick of Irish
Cake tobacco as an offering to the spirits and pretend not to
notice when it disappeared into little brown fingers. Over the
latter, I had had much soul-searching. Could we in all conscience
promote the continuance of a habit thrust upon the people by
ignorant, early white traders? Unfortunately, we were reliably
informed that spirits and elders alike enjoyed their addiction
and would have no other appeasement.

Our shaman kept referring to a place at the end of the island
where we would soon be met by many others and I was
dreading another long *maneaba* ceremony – until I realized that
the 'others' were ghosts. On a silvery-white beach she anointed

our cheeks with coral sand and adorned us with garlands made of a lime green vine. We were now known to the ancestral spirits, she assured us after a lengthy invocation, and would hereafter be able to move around the island freely, avoiding death or disaster. Good to know.

When we returned to the *maneaba* there was a pop quiz. I was asked to stand and reiterate what I'd seen and learned. Thank heavens I'd been paying attention. It was, in fact, very moving to see how grateful the people were that their oral history had been heard and appreciated by us outsiders. In a place where there is little in the way of material wealth, it is clearly most meaningful to be truly known. I thanked them for their generous hospitality and we went on our way to our next *maneaba* experience in the village of Koinawa.

'I'm on holiday,' said Jurek with a wry smile. 'You'll forgive me if I don't join you this time?'

At lunchtime we were received in a dreadfully humid concrete structure. There was more dancing, more feasting, more gift-giving, more speeches, more disco-bopping and, alas, more hokey-cokey. The local children picked it up immediately and were busy in a circle, 'shaking-it-all-about' as we left.

We retired to the boat quite exhausted. The minister and his wife installed themselves in the guest cabin and asked for some videos. Thereafter, they only emerged for meals.

'Perhaps they have a great sex life,' mused Jurek, whose wife was away in Poland.

'Hmmm,' I smiled, slipping a steamy copy of *Red Shoe Diaries* into the cover of *Sleepless in Seattle* and handing it to them at lunchtime on Sunday.

That evening I overheard Scarlett leaving a voice message for one of her friends in LA: 'Hi, Danny, it's Scarlett. I sent you something but then I remembered you are a vegan so email me and let me know if sharks' teeth are against your religion or whatever. Hope you enjoyed semi-formal. I'm here doing the sword dance and spraying people with deodorant.'

Monday 14 February 2005

No Valentine in sight. We arrived back in Tarawa, where our guests disembarked and I went ashore to run a few errands: trying to find the only bookshop, buying fishing baskets and stocking up on pandanus knives embedded with sharks' teeth. I met up with Linda, a woman from Butaritari whose ancestors were the official dolphin-callers for the King whenever he wanted a special meal. Last week, several members of her current family were lost at sea in their canoe. The New Zealand authorities dispatched a search plane, but when that mission failed, her brother consulted a navigational soothsayer, who assured him they were safe, just off Kuria – which is exactly where they were found. The soothsayer even divined their seating position in the canoe. Perhaps the President was right; there are more things in heaven and hell than the western world dreams of.

At 11 am we left for the northern Kiribati islands, stopping to reel in a tuna on the way. Toaea, a Department of Fisheries employee who came along to supervise our diving forays, was appalled to see Kayt pouring vodka into the gills of the dying fish.

'Why are you doing that?' he asked.

'This is the way we kill them,' she replied.

He grabbed a knife and plunged it into the nerve that runs between pectoral fin and tail, then again right between the eyes. Blood squirted in Kayt's face. He filleted the fish so it bled fast, then cut out the liver and offered it to her.

'Er, no thanks,' she said, watching him scoff half of it raw.

'This stops you going blind,' he said, smacking his lips. 'It's the best part.'

'I'll fry you up the other half for breakfast,' winced Kayt.

At dawn the next day we arrived in Marakei, after putting up with a headwind all night. Our steering is on the blink again, and Rolle is trying to fix it. The lagoon entrance was elusive, even at high tide, so we sailed up and down off-shore, peering through binoculars to try to find a passage. We tried radioing without success. There were people on the beach but the entryway near the government station was under attack by a pounding surf. Finally Teariki and I set off in the tender, driven by Dick. As we neared the shore we suddenly heard a terrible scraping noise from the propeller, a sign that we'd gone too shallow. We jumped out into the midst of swimming children, and were rescued by a fisherman called Matiera who took us to visit Namarou, chief of the village of Buota. We sat on a fine mat with his womenfolk, while a three-week-old baby gurgled in the middle of us all. I introduced myself and asked for permission to look around. Namarou welcomed me but explained that this is not the island of Marakei as we had thought, but Onowa; the atoll is divided into two parts.

By coincidence, the *Casco* party made the same error. In Fanny's diary entry for 17 June she wrote: 'Maraki. We stopped at the wrong settlement.' It's obviously an easy mistake to make. Fanny was not too taken with the population. Previously, when she visited Marakei on board the *Equator*, she found that:

The aspect of the people was more savage and ugly than we had heretofore seen, the faces brutal and unintelligent. Half-grown children, and, indeed, some more than half-grown, were entirely naked. The young boys were like little old men, their faces hard and their eyes haggard and anxious. I saw one with St Vitus's dance, several with hydrocephalus and a number who had affections of the eyes. Many of the little girls had their heads entirely shaved, with the exception of a small tassel at the nape of the neck which gave a very curious effect. The older ones wore their hair brushed out to a great size. Almost all wore necklaces of braided hair with an oval bit of red or white shell hanging to it like a locket. Almost all the women wore a girdle of flat, round beads (made of cocoanut shells) above the ridi [skirt made out of leaves].

Fanny noticed that the island was a republic, governed by the 'old men', and she was quite entertained by a list of the laws they had made that day: 'Dancing, one dollar fine; concealed weapons, five dollars; murder, fifteen; stealing, twenty-five; and telling a lie, fifty dollars.'

Namarou runs a tight ship these days, too, with a total alcohol ban. He imposes a $100 fine on anyone who brings booze into Buota, or enters under the influence. He told us the creation story of his village: once upon a time it was only a reef. Gradually stones built up and trees grew, so that four women, Nantekimam, Nei Reei, Rotebamua and Tangangau, were encouraged to settle here. After a while, the waves caused a large rock to bang against the reef and thus two men were created, Attii and Kaboo, who also settled there. But one day Kaboo complained that there were too many coral boulders on the island, so they all set to work, throwing them into deep water, until it became a small islet called Kabei. Then Attii said: 'Let's explore the whole island.' Kaboo took a left path and Attii went right, intending to meet in the middle of the other side. Kaboo however, died on the way. A broken stone shows where he perished, while an intact one sits on the right-hand side indicating that Attii survived his circuit. Consequently, any visitor who wants to explore the island must travel around to the right. It is very unlucky to go left.

There are no old buildings here, except a copra shed, but I was told there was once a settlement of Chinese people. They brought their own timber and made homes on proper concrete foundations. Matiera took me to see the remains, but unfortunately this quick tour involved going a short way left around the island. Afterwards, as I was jumping from the tender back on board the *Takapuna*, I misjudged the gap and banged up my knee. Ah, the power of suggestion . . . or was it magic?

We reached the island of Butaritari on Thursday evening, but we did not go ashore because we had been warned that the council was very strict about timing and our appointment was

Miss Shredded Wheat, 1965 – Equator-crossing ceremony with Neptune (Captain Mike)

Nikunau survivor of six months adrift in a canoe

Stopping stones – treacherous channel approach, Arorai, Kiribati

Scottish pedicure – Scarlett's
Highland sword dance, Butaritari

'You put your left foot in…'
President of Kiribati and
Madame Tong, Abemama

Kayt and beau in
maneaba courting ritual

Kiribati dancers wearing sacred pandanus skirts, Tarawa

Dance troupe with imposter, Kiribati

Japanese military post, now private residence and pig pen – Jaluit, Marshall Islands

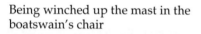

Biker Barbie, Kiribati

Being winched up the mast in the boatswain's chair

Not scared? My foot! From the mast top, Abiang

Head man – Tara by the king's fishpond, Butaritari

New Mother Hubbards – Fanny's favourite dresses

Copra load of this! Modern ship that has replaced vessels like the *Equator* and the *Janet Nichol*

Vaguna with his rain stick,
Nuitau, Tuvalu

Women's Association sewing and craft
workshop, Nanoumea, Tuvalu

There was an old woman who lived in a boat –
with schoolchildren in Beru

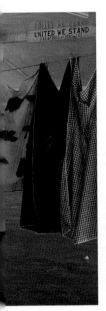

No prescription needed – Dr Puni administering jelly babies in Nanouti

Crazy paving in Kiribati – Fanny's pandanus sweet treat drying in the sun

Just popping out for a soaking – Arorai

Lagi and his devil box, Nuitau, Tuvalu

not until 11 am on Friday. Linda had arranged for us to be received by the elders and council members in the *maneaba*, and to see a performance of Butaritari traditional dancing. She made the proposal in a traditional form called a *bubuti*, meaning an undeniable request which must be honoured. The eleven Takapunians who stepped ashore at the King's Wharf were greeted by sixty villagers in white shirts and red lava-lavas. Women immediately anointed our cheeks with coral sand, in a ceremony called *Te Tetano Bakoa*, and adorned our necks with leis made of the indigenous *Teongo Buangi* plant. Everyone drank water from the same coconut shell; Linda had promised us it would be pre-boiled.

'Do not refuse it,' she warned. After shaking hands all around with an exchange of '*Mauri!*' we walked in procession along a causeway to the *maneaba*, followed by a choir singing lovely harmonies. Along the way we passed a Second World War Japanese plane, rusting in shallow water just off the beach.

Inside the *maneaba*, dancers garlanded us with the local *nikapuputi* plant, while they wore skirts decorated with *tebatatara*, a parsley-like shrub. The chief welcomed us and, as usual, we were asked to introduce ourselves and state the purpose of our visit. We are all becoming accustomed to the *maneaba* protocol and can now begin our speeches in the appropriate style, i.e. addressing the dignitaries first and greeting them with a '*Mauri!*' that is always returned by the throng.

The order and ceremony with which we were greeted in Butaritari was the antithesis of Fanny and Louis's experience. When they first arrived in Butaritari on board the *Equator*, on Sunday 14 July 1889, the kingdom was in an uproar. On the advice of some white traders, the King had lifted the *tapu* (taboo) against liquor, so almost everyone on the island was drunk and disorderly, to the extent that the Stevenson party were at risk for their lives. Fanny, Lloyd and others loaded their pistols and commenced target practice to warn off would-be-attackers. Notwithstanding, rocks were thrown at their rented house, so their plans to stay ashore for a few weeks came into question. Louis appealed to the trader who was responsible for selling alcohol (although, in any case, the local people throughout the region make their own fermented brew called 'sour toddy'); however, the rumour that Louis was a personal friend of Queen Victoria motivated the king to set a *tapu* on any attempt to harm them, for fear the British monarch might send a man of war to reap revenge. Fanny remained indoors during most of the unrest but one day she ventured out to the windward side of the island to look for shells:

> Here a strange man and woman joined me. They were not reassuring companions . . . as they were unkempt, clad in nothing but a small fragment, each, of dirty old gunny sack, and their faces were haggard and anxious. At first they walked with me as I went about my business of gathering shells, but presently, seeming to tire of this amusement, they began to crowd me off the beach toward the land; then seizing me by the arms, one on either side, they boldly marched me into a narrow, crooked path that led through the clustering cocoanut trees . . . As I reluctantly moved along beside my captors, the lady, evidently with a kindly feeling for my comfort, drew a clay pipe from out an enormous hole in her ear, stuffed it with strong, course tobacco, lighted it, puffed a moment, then placed it in my mouth. As I could not guess whether their intentions were hostile or otherwise and all the warnings I had received flashed through my mind, with sublime courage I accepted the situation. But it was a solemn experience. We emerged from the palms to find the town in a turbulent uproar, the street in front of our house filled with a howling, fighting, drunken mob. It was a great relief to find we were just in front of my own door; the two natives held me fast until we were safely in the veranda, when, to my astonishment, the man fell on his knees, and offered up a fervent prayer.

This incident began Fanny's friendship with Butaritari residents Nan Tok and his wife. Eventually, things settled down and the Stevenson party was able to enjoy their stay. They were particularly impressed with the island's traditional dances. 'Of all so-called dancing in the South Seas,' wrote Louis, 'that which I saw in Butaritari stands easily the first.' Fanny's reaction to them was utterly passionate: 'My blood became hot and cold, tears pricked my eyes, my head whirled, I felt an almost irresistible impulse to join the dancers.'

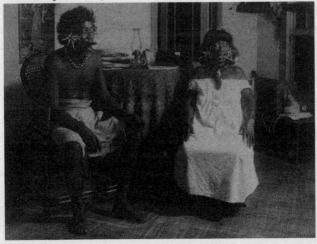

During my speech in the *maneaba*, I told the people of Butaritari that Robert Louis Stevenson thought they had the best dancers anywhere and, naturally, there were nods all round. They had gathered their finest dancers to entertain us and we were not disappointed. The first performance was a *maie* greeting dance; the second was one that in earlier times was performed only for the King. Next, we were aroused by an ancient war dance called the *teietoa* in which two groups of dancers face-off each other with hostile movements, the Kiribati version of *West Side Story*. A northern dance called a *kaimatoa*, or stiff dancing, was followed by a sitting dance called a *tebino*. The best was kept for last, when three highly decorated people, including two girls in the sacred pandanus skirts, performed a wonderful dance about Christmas.

When a bit of sausage flew through the air and nearly landed in my lap, I thought it was the start of a food fight, until someone explained it was an invocation of ancestral ghosts who must be fed first. A man stood in the centre of the *maneaba* with a frankfurter and knife in his hand.

'Spirits of the north!' he called, throwing a piece in their direction. 'That's for you!' He then flipped a piece in the opposite direction. 'Spirits of the south, a piece for you!' He repeated it for east and west, then finally threw some upwards and downwards for heaven and hell. Then the buffet was open and we living VIPs were invited to take our portions first. Linda had instructed us to help ourselves twice, taking just a little each time. After we had finished, the council members and elders ate, then finally everybody else.

I made the mistake of presenting my gifts too early in the proceedings, but there was a graceful cover-up. Scarlett danced, then she and Alicia played a flute duet. These performances were very much appreciated and we were informed that no foreign visitors had ever before reciprocated with offerings from their culture. The people asked questions that revealed their curiosity about our age and marital status. The discovery that

Teariki was a single doctor caused quite a ripple of interest among the available females and, henceforth, wherever he went he was flanked by smiling young women with lowered eyelashes.

'You could be getting a lot of action,' I teased him.

Just after we all piled into a council truck to tour the island, the heavens opened and produced torrential rain, but we pressed on to the northern tip of the island where a large outrigger canoe was waiting. Our guide, and apparently the font of all wisdom concerning the Beginning of the World, was a grubby man wearing a T-shirt inscribed with *Ten Reasons Why Beer is Better than a Woman*.

'I am going to show you the entrance to the underworld,' he said, motoring over transparent, sky-tinged water to a bottomless hole in the middle of the lagoon, while we all fixed our eyes on random pieces of misogyny: Number Seven – *Beer is always wet*, Number Nine – *A beer always goes down easy*, and Number Ten – *You always know you're the first one to pop a beer*. Given this, it was hardly surprising that his explanation of the Creation of Mankind involved the bursting of zits. The God Nareau was apparently born out of a popped pimple on the forehead of the Creator of the World. As a gold-red sunset leached across an other-worldly sky, we peered down into a mysterious circle of fathomless water where the island of Butaritari was pulled out of hell on the end of a fish hook. No wonder the island's name means 'stinky seaweed'.

The following day I went ashore alone at 10 am to continue my tour of the shrines. We followed a long, bumpy road through jungly paths, trying to avoid being whacked by tree branches through the open window of the truck. In several small villages, people were just beginning a lazy Saturday. Two little sisters walked hand-in-hand with matching red hibiscus flowers behind their ears, while a smaller child drove a bicycle wheel with a stick, like a Victorian schoolboy. Families were out on their motorbikes, often with four people on board arranged like acrobats in a circus troupe. The father drives with a toddler in his lap, followed by an older child standing on the pillion with the mother at the rear. It's heart-stopping every time.

Two elders, Tara the Chairman and his assistant Tawita, were waiting to meet me in their northern village *maneaba*. I sat on a fine mat while the elders grouped themselves on the far side with the light behind them. I could see them only in silhouette.

'What are we waiting for?' I asked the Chief Councillor, Tererei, after a few minutes.

'The *unimane* [old men] want you to taste their food before they take you to the shrine,' he explained. 'They are waiting for their women to bring it.'

I fanned myself to mitigate the dreadful humidity. After trying hard to cross my legs, I gave up and tucked them behind instead. This is a no-no, but reasonably acceptable for a white person if she covers the soles of her feet. At last, Tara began to speak and formally welcomed me. A young woman turned up with a large, round plastic box, a kettle, a tray of tea-making things and some fresh coconuts. I reached for a coconut, but was immediately reprimanded by the Chief Councillor who drew my attention to the fact that Tara was saying grace. At the end of the prayer they crossed themselves and then the lid came off the plastic box to reveal thick bread and butter sandwiches. The butter tasted a little rancid.

When I went outside to get in the truck for the next shrine visit, I was able to see Tara in broad daylight. He was wearing a western-style floral shirt and had the most extraordinary 'honest I'm not bald' hair do I've ever seen: a carefully arranged flush of woolly grey back-hair swept forward over his bald crown and held in place by a garland. By comparison, Tawita had a fine head of hair. It was almost as if there was competition between them.

After a few minutes' drive, we found a large well, solidly supported by a wall of stones.

'This is *Teneinimaan*,' said Tara. 'It is the King's fish pond.' I peered in and spotted a lonely black balloon-fish with white spots. 'I am going to tell you a story handed down from our ancestors about how it came to be,' he said. 'There was once a very strong and skilful giant called Auriaria. He was particularly famous because no other giants had ever been able to vanquish him and they were all afraid of him. This giant had two pets, a coconut crab and a swordfish. One day he had to leave them at home and go off to fight. His pets in turn went to fight their own battles, but the crab was not a good fighter and he died on the islet of Bikaati. The swordfish skipped over the sea, rose in the air and vaulted down, sword-first, into this hole. He continued boring a passage underground until he emerged into the sea, but once he surfaced, he was spied by a vicious giant called Naunta who killed him with one blow. When Auriaria returned from his battles, he was eager to see his pets. First of all he was dismayed to see his crab dead on Bikaati islet and then, on top of that, he came here and saw that his swordfish had been destroyed by Naunta. Auriaria wanted revenge. The two giants fought a terrible battle in a place I will show you next.'

He took us to a nearby beach for part two: 'You see the waves?' he continued. 'They do not follow a regular pattern, but go in their own direction.' Indeed the waves did appear to crisscross and smash against each other as if two opposing currents met in one place. This was caused, said Tara, by the battle of the giants. Auriaria prevailed, and the churning water was created by Naunta's legs kicking from beneath as he was slain.

We walked a little way inland, to a large clearing that was quite bare of vegetation. 'This is a *maneaba* of the spirits,' said Tara, pointing at nothing I could see. 'It is used by them for celebration and dancing.' He caught the sceptical look on my face. 'I can prove that it exists,' he said, 'because mentally ill people come here to join the ceremonies and dances. They walk here from all round the island.'

'What do you think causes mental illness?' I asked.

'People break a *tapu*,' replied the councillor.

'Such as?' I asked.

'Oh, women who go to forbidden places when they are menstruating, for example,' he replied.

There is a visible shrine in the centre, consisting of a stone with a small clamshell on top. As usual, I had to lay my Irish Cake beside it with as much reverence and ceremony as I could muster. Tara cleared his throat and began to invoke the spirits.

'Ghosts, this is your smoke from . . . what's her name again?' The council clerk prompted him. 'Pamela. The spirit people here will protect her from evil ghosts during her time of travel.'

We sat down in the nearby physical *maneaba* for lunch. The councillor asked Tara to say grace but, contrary to his behaviour this morning, the elder refused, saying wickedly, 'We *unimane* are not related to Catholic or Protestants. We are *evil* people!' It was the first time I had come across stark evidence of a division between the old beliefs and the new, and it was riveting to witness. When our lunch arrived in the ubiquitous Tupperware boxes I peered at the offered fare and decided my best bet was to break off a piece of coconut crab. I gingerly removed a leg but my host, seeing my preference, grabbed the whole crab and proceeded to prepare it for me with his bare hands. He smashed the shell open on the ground, shoved his whole hand inside, messily extracted the meat, then took out the vein and flipped it away. He ceremoniously held up the remainder of the meat, waved it around for a bit, then loudly blessed it before proffering it to me as a most specially prepared large morsel.

My last appointment that day was an audience with the seventy-year-old sister of the last King, Uraura. Seeing me approach, Kuinii (whose name is appropriately pronounced Queenie) quickly donned a clean black skirt, smoothed her hair and set out a fine mat. She had bright eyes, a low, throaty voice and a rasping cough. The councillor said her late brother had been King when he was a boy in the 60s. I asked what had happened to end the monarchy. 'The King was cancelled' was the translation of her reply.

'Why was he cancelled?' I asked.

'It came from the people,' she explained. 'It was very confusing trying to decide who was going to be King. Many people claimed it was *they* who should be on the throne.'

When the Stevensons met King Tebureimoa, who was the monarch of Butaritari when they were here, he had just relinquished all of his wives but one, under pressure from the missionaries. This not only reduced his sexual opportunities but diminished his puissance with the elders in his kingdom and caused him to lose the copra revenue he'd once gained from his ex-wives' families. When Fanny and Louis arrived he was sulking about all of this, lounging around in dirty pyjamas, and indulging in opium.

Sunday 20 February 2005

I couldn't sleep. Woke at 4.18 am sweating about a number of issues, on both land and sea. Or maybe it's just my hormones. We sailed out of Butaritari at ten, bound for Majuro (we're coming back to visit the southern Kiribati islands in a few weeks) and pretty soon we were in very lumpy seas. The bad weather worsened and it wasn't long before we had 40-knot winds and a 20-mile-wide rainsquall coming at us. Within ten seconds of the rain starting the decks were completely sopping. I wasn't on watch but I might as well have been; I spent much of the night on deck. Quite a few of us were up there, trying to sleep amid all the grinding of winches as the watch keepers tried to reduce sail whenever the worst of the wind came, then pump up our speed where possible. The Captain said it was the worst rain he'd ever seen. I'm dreadfully sick, but not so much from seasickness. I think I've succumbed to food poisoning.

Monday 21 February 2005

It's darn hard to vomit, shit and hang on to something at the same time. Shocking night. Dysentery very bad. All the time I kept my spirits up because I thought we'd be in Majuro at nine this morning. However, it turned out that when Rolle was estimating our arrival time he was looking at the wrong island. If we really get a move on we can make it by nightfall, but I don't think that's going to happen. We're going to have to hang outside the lagoon in this weather all night and enter Majuro harbour in the morning. I absolutely cannot write another word.

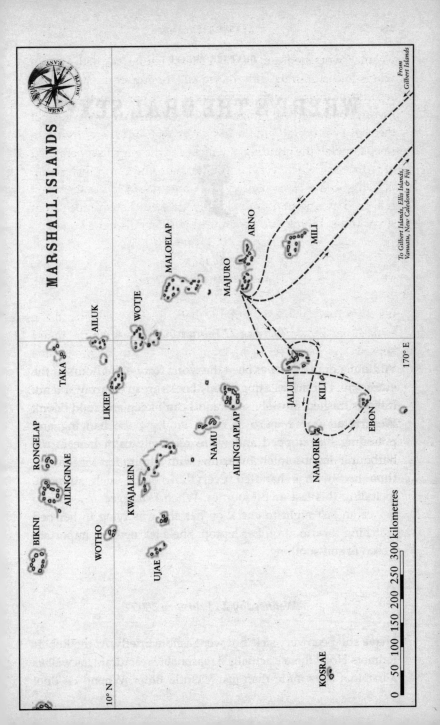

MARSHALL ISLANDS

BIKINI
RONGELAP
AILINGINAE
WOTHO
UJAE
KWAJALEIN
TAKA
AILUK
LIKIEP
WOTJE
NAMU
MALOELAP
AILINGLAPLAP
ARNO
MAJURO
NAMORIK
JALUIT
KILI
MILI
EBON
KOSRAE

10° N
170° E

From
Gilbert Islands

To Gilbert Islands, Ellis Islands,
Vanuatu, New Caledonia & Fiji

0   50 100 150 200 250 300 kilometres

CHAPTER TWELVE

WHERE'S THE ORAL SEX?

07°06.16′ N
171°21.30′ E

Tuesday 22 February 2005

Without a doubt this has been the worst forty-eight hours of the entire trip. I'm sick as a dog, all my books are in disarray and my cabin is trashed. I barely slept and I can't keep any food down. We arrived into Majuro at noon. At least the banging and pounding has stopped and we're relatively calm here in the harbour. I am absolutely overcome with admiration for Scarlett, though. She has handled everything with such strength, including this last awful journey. When I dragged myself into her cabin last night to check on her she was lying in her bed watching a cartoon on her laptop. She's learned the important lesson of self-soothing.

Wednesday 23 February 2005

I have still been very sick, but went ashore briefly. At the Robert Reimers Hotel there's actually a reasonable restaurant, as well as a bar that sells more than just Victoria Bitter. Whoop de doo!

Majuro is a big yachties' community. Quite a few small sailboat owners hang out up here for the cyclone season, and some have been in the vicinity for years. I must say, they were very welcoming and invited us to events on their well-organized social calendar – bowling night, pizza night and even a race round the harbour. Kayt is happy because there are supermarkets here that have fresh food. All right, there's a big part of me that knows this is still a truly horrible, soulless, culture-degraded slice of Americana but, frankly, after Tarawa, I'm just thrilled to see a place where things are a little less chaotic and people actually have toilets.

Fanny thought Majuro was very pretty:

> a pearl of low islands . . . At the entrance it is broken up
> into the most enchanting of small islands . . . all very green
> and soft, and the lagoon clear, and like chrysoprase in colour.
> Mr Henderson offered us a little house to stop in on the
> windward side, so we took our mats and blankets and a
> lantern with us in the boat. The house was the old lookout,
> and consisted of a single room with lattice work running
> along two sides of the wall including the roof: there was no
> other window. The door had a padlock and we locked it
> when we came and went, and had much difficulty in
> keeping track of the key.

Yeah, well, 'a pearl' Majuro most definitely is not. Not any more. The arrival of several thousand American military personnel in the 1940s saw to that. Laura, though, the town at the far western tip of the island, is prettier and breezier. I toured the island with Brad, a lanky fifty-something Californian who has lived here for over twenty years. A dive guide as well as something of a military historian, he lives in a junk yard where he accumulates scrap metal for sale, including entire ships, trucks and buses.

'My kids sleep in a container each!' he said proudly.

We drove down the main drag, past clothing stores, bars and some large government buildings. The Bikini Island Town Hall is one of the smartest buildings on Majuro, a pseudo-Georgian structure with white pillars and fancy gold lettering. Roughly 1,270 Bikinians live on Majuro now – a big jump in population from the 200 who, in 1946, were moved 425 miles south to Kili Island to avoid being zapped. As Bob Hope said, 'As soon as the war ended, we located the one spot on earth that hadn't been touched by the war and blew it to hell.' Brad says that most of the Bikini historical sites have been closed down.

'They're afraid someone's going to grab a dirty bomb and try to guesstimate wind patterns from earlier data,' he said.

We left for Jaluit at noon the next day. As we've come to expect, the entrance to the lagoon was fraught with danger. One must manoeuvre sideways towards the far shore first, a counter-intuitive action, before traversing the pass.

'Imagine going through there without having engine power,' said Brad. There are around twenty known wrecks here, from the early days of arriving European sailing vessels. When we arrived on the main island of Jabwor, Brad insisted we immediately take some boxes of Diet Coke and ramen to the mayor who owns the local store. They were probably peace offerings, for there seemed to be some tension between Brad and the mayor. I have a feeling our new on-board guide has quite a story behind him.

'Yeah, the mayor here accused me of stealing an airplane,' said Brad with a shrug.

'Did you?' I asked suspiciously

Fanny and Louis went ashore here on a blazing hot June day, headed for the commissioner's terracotta-coloured residence. Both of them were dressed up to the nines, although, given the wear and tear of their seafaring life, they had to improvise a little:

Louis with his best trousers, yellow socks, dirty white shoes, and a white linen coat from the trade room that could not be buttoned because of its curious fit. It was hoped, however, that a gold watch and chain would cover all deficiencies. I wore a blue linen native dress, but it was covered by a long black lace cloak. I had on red stockings, and shoes cut to ribbons by coral. On my head I wore a black straw turban, and a spotted veil covered my face: altogether I thought my appearance most respectable. Not having gloves I thought it a good plan to put on all my rings which flashed bravely in the sun.

They ate lunch and drank wine with the German official then walked round his garden. Brad says that in Fanny's time, when the Germans were established in Jaluit, the place was peaceful. They didn't want wars, they preferred commerce. They prevented arms being sold because they wanted the playing field to be kept even between the clans.

At that time Marshallese sailors used 'stick charts', locally devised navigational aids made by tying together flat pieces of wood in patterns that indicated the direction of swells, and the location of the surrounding islands. When Louis expressed interest in owning one, the commissioner promised to have one made for him.

Sunday 27 February 2005

The hymn-singing here is more high-pitched and strident than the soothing harmonies of Samoan church choirs. However, today's church congregation was visually beautiful, the women with bright Mother Hubbards and fresh garlands in their hair. They wear the headdresses further forward on the brow than is the custom in the Gilberts and I think it's more flattering. Men and women sat separately for the service.

'I was hoping the rest of the crew would have come,' smiled Brad, 'because I like to play a little trick and seat the single guys with the single women.' He's a troublemaker, that's for sure.

Valentine, a woman in a green dress and matching flip-flops, insisted on giving up her seat to sit on the floor as I was led to the front row. From my vantage point I could see that decorating the pulpit railing were banknotes and groceries people had brought as gifts for the pastor. After the service a dozen or so Sunday School children sang and squirmed before their proud parents, braving the odd jeer from window-peeping rivals who hadn't made the cut.

When we returned to the *Takapuna*, I found Brad's Marshallese girlfriend, who had followed him here to Jaluit, sitting in the saloon. When I put my hand out to greet her, she surprised me by receiving it with a suspicious frown. Meanwhile, Brad was buzzing nervously around the galley. She followed him in there and spoke unpleasantly to both Kayt and Sarah whom she seemed to consider as competition.

'Marshallese women are very jealous,' explained Brad. It wasn't just that. His girlfriend was leaning on him for money and alcohol, and flew into a rage when (fortunately) he refused to provide the latter. Such an action on a dry island could get us all into trouble.

By contrast, Fanny encountered a sweet and docile young local woman named Topsy, married to a white trader named King. She was so taken with the girl she painted a portrait of her:

a very little creature, thin and small and much given to dress
... At any hour of the day I would find her there, her thick
hair shining with oil and carefully braided, a different
headdress for a different hour, her keys hanging below her
two rows of necklaces, always busy at something: sometimes
it was a necklace she was stringing on shreds of pandanus,
sometimes a new print holaku she was cutting out with a
most capable business like air: or she might be feeding her

WHERE'S THE ORAL SEX?

monkey ('monkaia' she pronounced it), or her gentle eyed dog, or, sorting her possessions into order. She had two pretty large chests quite filled up with prints, coloured handkerchiefs, and various accessories of the toilet . . . On one arm she proudly showed me the word 'Majuro' tattooed, and on the other 'Topsy.' I asked Mr King why she was called Topsy. 'When I first got her,' he said, 'she was just a wild thing . . . So I called her that in fun, but she liked the name so much that I gave it to her, and tattooed it on her arm.' It seems that she was a castaway from another Island, every other soul in the canoe being lost. She was perfectly ignorant, and when something was said about her heart gravely assured Mr King that she had no heart, but was solid flesh all through.

Monday 28 February 2005

We went ashore hoping to find some relics from the German time, such as the remains of the commissioner's house that Louis and Fanny visited, but there was really nothing left.

'When the Japanese came here,' said Brad, as we strolled past a group of teenagers playing volleyball, 'they gave the Germans notice: "Pack your bags. We're the boss, you're not." The Japanese landed a hundred troops. They took over the German administration headquarters and made it theirs. I presume the original German building was destroyed and replaced by this concrete command structure.'

We peered into a two-storeyed house with Japanese windows that is currently inhabited by a Jaluit family. Behind it are the remains of the officers' bath houses, now serving as a series of pig pens.

'The Japanese commander here killed some Marshallese, including two children,' said Brad. 'He knew he would eventually be executed for war crimes. He called himself the "Sun of Jaluit"; thought he was hot stuff. Did the ceremonial sword thing in the end.'

None of the concrete Japanese structures have been repaired since they were attacked by the Americans.

'A couple of months before they invaded Majuro and Kwajalein,' said Brad, 'the USA bombed the crap out of Jaluit. I guess intelligence told them they had way too many pigs and chickens here, and were living too high on the hog. Also, they wanted to practise their new bombs. They worked on their new pathfinder skills, meaning you first drop a purple smoke bomb then get others to try to hit the target. It was also the first napalm attack. They put their wings down so the planes were virtually flying at a stall to slow down, then tried to drop the bombs in a nice pattern. The first aircraft would drop its load, the second overlapped and the third put bombs wherever the others hadn't dropped them. They basically cooked off everything on the island.'

When we departed Jabwor to pick our way across the lagoon to Emidj, the site of the Japanese naval base, it was my turn to go up to the top of the mast to act as lookout. Dick winched me up 120 feet in the bosun's chair, while I tried to stabilize myself by grabbing at the radar casing on the way and kicking myself free of the mainstays and spreaders. I settled myself on the jumpers and tried to overcome my vertigo. I took out my walkie-talkie. 'Hi, Skipper.' I tried to sound calm. 'What can you see?' he asked.

I peered at the surrounding sea. 'Couple of bommies ahead.' It was amazing how well one could see them from up here, brown patches surrounded by pale turquoise. 'There's one fifteen degrees off the port bow, and one about four cables away at thirty degrees off our starboard bow.' I felt the rigging swaying as we rocked in the swell so I gripped the spreader with my right leg and wound my left round the mast. I was thirsty but I didn't dare change my grip to take out my water bottle. It would be a very serious mistake to drop it, or my walkie-talkie. Probably put a terrible hole in the deck, or kill a person. I wound the radio strap tightly round my wrist.

The lagoon was bommie soup, but so far there was enough room to avoid disaster. We travelled eight miles west, then headed north. As we turned, I felt the wind pick up and the mast begin to sway alarmingly through a greater angle. Then, far off to starboard, I got my first glimpse of an ominous sight: a thick, black rain squall creeping in towards us. I tried to ignore it, but eventually the blue sky shrank to nothing and the first raindrops hit my skin like savage pin-pricks. Down came a hard-hitting torrent that soaked me through in seconds and annihilated my sight. I lowered my head, gripped as tight as I could, and told myself 'Breathe. This shall pass.' At least I had a chance to quench my thirst. I angled my open mouth to the sky and drank. As I did so, I gleaned a little hope, for I spied blue sky way off in the distance. I clung there miserably for several long minutes until the rainsquall trundled off to port. 'OK, Captain,' I said. 'I can see a bit now.'

'You're breaking up,' he said. Then my radio stopped transmitting. 'Come down,' he ordered.

'Respect, man,' I said to Dick when I was safely back on the

deck (he frequently does that job). 'I wouldn't like to be up there
in a big blow.'

That afternoon we dived on a wrecked Kawanishi H8K
seaplane lying upside-down at around fifty feet, just off one of
the island's massive Japanese seaplane ramps. Its wings were
intact, as was its nose with a 20mm cannon sticking out of it.
Around the carcass lay left-over machine-gun shells, four sets of
propellers and the gunner's position that had been blown right
off the tail. Goldish coloured coral had grown all over the
aircraft. I thought nature had made it very beautiful, a vibrating,
carpeted sculpture, punctuated with small clumps of saluting
red anemones. We peered through the cockpit window and saw
glass water bottles, a fully loaded magazine for the front cannon
and a school of brilliant blue fish.

Tuesday 1 March 2005

The first of March is Nuclear Survivors' Day in the Marshall
Islands. The Emidj school was on holiday but there were no
ceremonies. We took a deep dive to see another H8K seaplane,
this one quite intact except for a broken tail, lying at 100 feet in
rather murky water. Once used for long-range patrol and
reconnaissance, it was sunk at its mooring so the control cables
were still attached in front. It seemed massive at 30 feet tall, 92
feet long, with a 124-foot wingspan.

After the dive, I met a fisherman on the beach. 'There used to
be one more airplane out there,' he said, scratching his head, 'but
someone took it.' The finger seems to point at Brad.

Late in the afternoon we walked through the jungle to see the
Japanese radio building, behind which was a bunker where
three American prisoners of war were incarcerated. They'd had
engine trouble and landed in the lagoon just west of Majuro
before drifting to Jaluit. All three were eventually executed.
Amid the vines and ferns of the damp and steamy jungle, there

were several Japanese buildings – bunkers and warehouses – now hiding like discreet, high-end resort bungalows. Again, nature has beautified the power station way beyond its functionality, with graceful palms and pandanus flourishing upon its flat roof. One warehouse had some Kanji writing on one wall and a lonely soldier's drawing of a naked Japanese girl.

The next day I went ashore to donate some school supplies. The schoolhouse bell was a wartime Japanese oxygen tank hanging from a tree. Older children sat at traditional desks learning mathematics, while those too young for the classroom were playing under a tree. It was unbearably hot and there was no breeze.

'Why don't they go in the water to cool off?' I asked a man with a baby on his knee.

'They're afraid of sharks,' he replied.

'So when do they start to swim?'

'Oh,' he shrugged, 'not until they're sixteen.'

We sailed on to Imroij, the Jaluit island where the King traditionally lived. In the past it was a trading station because of its convenient location beside a navigable channel. As we approached the main centre, we could see a very beautiful white German church. We went ashore in torrential rain and saw a small German cemetery. The people there were very friendly. They gave us coconuts and wanted to provide a feast for us, but we explained that we couldn't stay long. Our dive party in the late morning descended 80 feet from the edge of the reef and immediately saw the debris of a B25G bomber. While swimming around it, Scarlett found herself beside a 500-pound unexploded bomb. There was also a bandolier, five or six shells in a magazine, two sets of three-bladed propellers and a tyre from the nose gear with a bullet imbedded in it. This aircraft had been on a bombing run about 50 feet above the tree tops when anti-aircraft fire blew off its right wing.

'It rolled over and nosed in at 200 knots,' said Brad. 'That's why it's in so many pieces.' There were twelve Japanese soldiers living on Imroij at the time. 'They ordered the Marshallese to go out and recover the bodies of the airmen,' said Brad. 'They laid them out on the sand like tuna for inspection.' His voice betrayed controlled emotion. 'They didn't have a boat to take them to Jabwor to show them off, so they stripped them of their rings, dog tags and so on, then ordered the Marshallese to row them out to deep water and dump them over the side.' He took a deep breath. 'It took me twelve years to find all that out.'

I've warmed to Brad. He is creating a database of everyone killed in the Marshall Islands during the last war. I asked him what his motivation was for doing so and he said that he had found a deceased aviator not so long ago, with his crashed aircraft, and was thus able to provide closure for the man's grieving family. He seems to have found that very gratifying.

After a very nasty overnight ride, we arrived early at Namorik, a small diamond-shaped atoll that is home to around 600 people. Many of the population have moved to Springdale, Arkansas, in the USA to work for the Wal-Mart company. There may be as many as 4,000 Marshall Islanders in Springdale now, plucking chickens for the well-stocked freezers of American households.

Ketton Jobran, who was born in 1919, remembers the German time and when there was a king here, called Lialan.

'Life beforehand was better,' she said. 'People used to work together, stay together, help each other. Now it's different. The customs are gone, the old rules broken, and people are separated.' She has a fifty-eight-year-old son in Arkansas, to whom she sometimes speaks on the SSB (Single Sideband) radio.

Alden, a fisherman, showed me around. He walked me along the main road of Elmont village, past the volleyball court donated by Australia, and the neat houses, many of which were sporting new solar energy panels provided by the EU. The taro patch, though, was barely flourishing.

'This island used to be the *alele*,' he said, 'the food-basket for the King. Now, eighty per cent of our food comes from the

United States. There is plenty of diabetes here now.'

Fanny's diary entry for Namorik on Friday 27 June says simply that 'Louis went ashore and met a wicked old man.' I asked Alden if he knew of any wicked old man who'd lived on the island.

'My grandmother told me a story about one of my own ancestors,' he said, a little shamefully. 'He was a strange old warrior who used to bail the King's canoe. He was given land at the end of the island where he lived with his wife. He would not allow anyone else to get their share of fish from the traps while he was doing so and people stayed clear of him. One day a fisherman paddled past his house in a canoe, singing a song. "He has a nice voice," remarked his wife. In a fit of jealousy, the warrior went after the fisherman, killed him and brought his head back for his wife to see. "There's your nice voice," he said.'

But Louis's 'wicked old man' was not a native of Namorik; rather, he was an unpleasant white trader, the inspiration for one of the characters in Louis's *Beach of Falesá*. I overheard Brad describing this island as 'a sport-fucking place', so I'm beginning to think the 'wicked old man' is on board with us. Brad claims there was a school in the village of Lungar on the east end of Arno Atoll where young women could go to learn sexual intercourse techniques. They practised with coconut kernels, inserting them in their vaginas and exercising their internal muscles until they could twirl them round and squeeze them out – a bit like modern Kegel exercises. The school's speciality was 'The Helicopter', a woman-on-top position where she performs a circling movement. Brad has been hinting heavily round the *Takapuna* that his own sexual prowess is, well, outstanding.

'Marshallese men don't go down on women,' he said smugly, 'so I have a lot of satisfied customers.'

Saturday 5 March 2005

We arrived at Ebon, after suffering 45-knot winds through the night, and had to wait in lee of the island until it was light. It's a very narrow pass. The German settlement was situated on the right side of the channel entrance. They probably had to send small whalers in to pick up the copra since it was too dangerous an entry for schooners without an engine. You can no longer see the *Hazeltine*, the wreck of an American schooner that Fanny saw from the *Janet Nichol*. It has probably been entirely broken up by now, but an old man on the island verified that it was once visible. I might try searching underwater for remnants, if the current allows.

'When the Americans arrived,' said my designated guide, an elderly Ebon-born dentist who'd lived in Honolulu, 'the Marshallese did not tell them there were a few Japanese hiding on the island, including some civilians who had been digging phosphate. When two marines were ambushed and killed, the Americans rounded up as many Japanese people as they could find and killed nineteen: twelve soldiers and seven civilians.' A Japanese couple who ran the phosphate company gave their two children to a Marshallese family before fighting to the death. 'Those two children came back as adults in 2002,' he said. 'They chartered a plane, then got off and walked to the place where their parents were killed. They showed no emotion, just bowed silently, then turned, got back on the plane and left.'

On Sunday we went to church in heavy rain, a trip that redefined the meaning of 'wet landing', then we left for Majuro at noon. On the way we passed the village of Kiu where the people evacuated from Bikini Atoll are now living. All their lights were on, even though it was late at night.

'It's true,' said Rolle. 'Dey do glow in de dark!'

'Actually,' said Brad, 'they keep their lights on all through the night because they're worried about demons.'

'Demons,' howled my husband when I spoke to him on the

phone. 'Their island was blasted by nuclear bombs and they're frightened of wee bogeymen?'

Monday 7 March 2005

This has been the worst damn ride ever. The minute we got through the pass we found ourselves in a 15–20-foot swell. I wanted to turn back but no one listened. Poor Kayt had to get up at 5 am, when we were in the calmer lee of Jaluit, to cook dinner for tonight. It was her only chance to stay upright in the galley all day. The crew is lying helplessly around the pilot house trying not to puke. I've never seen anything like it. The next day was just as horrible, but thankfully we got in to Majuro harbour at three this afternoon, very relieved, and went ashore for the yachties' Pizza Night. In the morning, Scarlett and Evan were very glad to leave on a plane to LA.

On Thursday evening I went to the Marshall Islands High School to see a production of *Twelfth Night*, performed by the students, played half in English and half in Marshallese. I loved the rustic characters. Revamped to appeal to Marshallese sensibilities, they were a huge hit. On Saturday we took part in the Mieco Beach Yacht Club Race and, taking our handicap into consideration, came in second last.

'I'm shocked,' I joked. 'Apparently people with smaller yachts can sometimes go faster.' The crew thoroughly enjoyed the competition and all participants met for a party in the evening. I had hoped for some customary après-race protests, with attendant brawling, but these were not allowed. Instead, there was a discussion of a pirate attack that occurred last week. An email containing the details awaited me back on board:

On 8 March 2005, two sailing yachts, Mahdi & Gandalf, were moving SW 30 miles off the coast of Yemen . . .
At about 1600 we observed two boats approaching us

head on from the SW. These boats were 25–30 feet long, had higher freeboards and were diesel powered. They were coming very fast directly at us. There were 4 men in each boat. The boats separated at about 200 yards ... coming down Mahdi's port side and firing into the cockpit. The other boat was firing an automatic weapon at both Gandalf and Mahdi ... These guys obviously intended to kill us. The first boat swung around behind Mahdi's stern to come up and board us. At that point, Rod Nowlin, aboard Mahdi and armed with a 12 gauge shotgun loaded with buckshot, and I started shooting into their boat. I forced them to keep their heads down so that they could not shoot at us. After firing 3 shots at them their engine started to smoke and I swung around to shoot at the boat ahead. At that point, I saw Jay Barry on Gandalf ram that boat amidships almost cutting it in two and turning it almost completely over. I turned back around to shoot again at the boat behind Mahdi and that is when they turned away from Mahdi and were heading toward the stern of Gandalf, about 100 feet away.

The bow of the pirate's boat came right up against Gandalf's stern and two men stood up on the bow to board Gandalf ... I shot both of them. That boat then veered away and I shot the driver, although I am not sure of the outcome ... Mahdi and Gandalf kept going at full speed to put as much distance between the pirates and us as possible. As soon as we were out of rifle range we looked back and both boats were drifting and appeared to be disabled.

Thank God someone's finally decided to fight back!

Monday 14 March 2005

I don't know what's wrong with me, but I'm not doing well at all. I'm sad, frustrated, losing the dream. It's hard to admit, but right now I feel that I can't wait to get off the boat. It's Dick's birthday so we had a night out at a bar called the Flame Tree, but I just wasn't into it. In the morning I was still feeling very bad. I stayed in bed late until Teariki insisted I get up, and we drove to Laura in the rain. We walked on the beach, had some dinner at the Outrigger, then shot some pool at the Flame Tree. I'm afraid I partied too hard and ended up singing disgraceful karaoke in the wee small hours. Poor Teariki had to pick up the pieces.

'I'm only twenty-six,' he complained. 'I'm the one who should be getting tipsy, with you the disapproving one, not the other way around.'

Friday 18 March 2005

When Fanny and Louis arrived back at Jaluit they found that, as promised, the commissioner had found some stick charts for Louis. They were ingrigued by them:

> Louis and the commissioner and Captain Brandeis tried to make out the names of the Islands by comparing it with an European chart, but could not . . . A woman who had been 30 years in the Islands was consulted, and afterwards a native but still they were baffled.

I found some stick charts, too. They are quite attractive, but I suspect they were made purely for the tourist market. Dick tried to compare them to Admiralty charts but he, too, was baffled by the system. In fact, unlike conventional western navigational charts, they are mnemonic aids that indicate swell patterns rather than accurate landform positions. I have been told the ancient Marshallese navigational skills are largely lost.

Saturday 19 March 2005

We left for Tarawa with Crowded House ringing round the cockpit: *There is freedom within; there is freedom without. Try to catch the deluge in a paper cup.* The lyrics seemed to match my mood. What is WRONG with me? Perhaps I have just been missing my baby. We arrived back at Tarawa on Monday. In heavy rain with terrible seas and a bad swell at the stern, I managed to get ashore to pick up Scarlett from the airport. I'm happy to have her back.

Wednesday 23 March 2005

A lovely day of pure sailing, averaging a gentle six knots. This is what it's all about. Although, we were pulled a little off course by quite a strong current. I went on deck around 3 pm and found the Captain and Kelly musing about why no sea bottom was registered at that point. They had been skirting Maiana Atoll at round 00.53°2´ north by 172°52´ east. The Admiralty charts said, *Dangerous. Uncharted with shoals and rocks.* They were using the sounder to try to get as close to the southwest corner of the atoll as possible, but the depth just plummeted without their being any explanation. Later, the Captain drew my attention to another unusual phenomenon: off to starboard a narrow band of sea current was going in the opposite direction from that of the surrounding ocean. Extraordinary.

Tonight we had a beautiful moonlight sail, with warm breezes wafting us directly into a golden moon-path. The Captain's voice jerked me out of a deep trance. 'It's mesmerizing, isn't it?'

*

I've been on board the *Takapuna* for seven months and now it's nearly Easter. I wonder where we'll be by then. Right now, we're about a day away from Arorai. I got into my bikini this morning, for a quick sunbathe on top of the pilot house where no one can see and, in remembering how my outfit got its name, felt guilty about all those people displaced by a mushroom cloud.

Scarlett is trying to register to sit her SAT college entrance exams, which is tricky by satellite. She's not happy. One hit of LA and she's mourning the absence of shopping malls. Our new crew member Kelly is in pain of the physical kind. She was thrown violently against the swim ladder when disembarking from the tender and is now suffering from a bad haematoma on her inner thigh. Teariki does not like the look of it. He used the Tempus 2000 to call Medlink for a second opinion. The doctor in Arizona concurred that the haematoma is OK for now, but we'll have to airlift her from Arorai to Tarawa for surgery if it gets worse.

Fanny faced two medical emergencies en route to Arorai. One of the deckhands crushed his fingers between the ship and the tender. 'He has been crying like a child almost continuously since,' wrote Fanny. She was also trying to nurse the Captain. 'I went through the two medical books available, and we, he and I, came to the conclusion he must be suffering from an inflammation of the stomach.'

We arrived at Arorai on Saturday, after one of the nicest journeys we've had. I'm feeling much better. It's a beautiful day and the sea is calm. There is no lagoon here, but we managed to drop anchor off the beach on the leeward side. I was dressing in my cabin when the Captain knocked on my door.

'Hey, you just might score a traditional ride to the beach. There's a couple of guys in an outrigger at the stern!'

I ran up on deck and invited the two fishermen on board for a soda. Teariki showed them round while I put together a gift pack for the local school, tobacco for the elders, my camera, water and radio. Their boat took only three people and they would have preferred to take just Teariki but, in the end, I managed to persuade them to help me into a carefully balanced position in the centre of the canoe, and they rowed me towards a line of surf and a dynamited channel. As we approached the shore I realized that half the village had gathered, the majority of them children.

'The people here have never seen a boat like yours,' said Teeta, the school principal, who happened to be fishing on the rocks where I landed. 'They have seen much bigger ones, like the supply ship that comes every month, but not a sailing boat.'

He told me he is from Beru, but came with his wife four years ago to teach arithmetic to ninety teenagers.

'What did you find different about this island?' I asked.

'A lot more sharing,' he said immediately. 'Everyone contributes, we work in groups.'

At that moment, Dick arrived on shore in a new tin boat we'd picked up in Majuro to save the wear and tear on the *Takapunier* (that's what we've started calling the tender, although Billy prefers 'Love Me Tender'). As soon as he alighted, an impromptu team of children surged forward and lifted the boat up on to the beach. Dick stood watching them in amazement. 'Valet parking!' he whistled.

Bwenateuea, another teacher, introduced herself to me on the walk into the village. While we sat chatting in the shade, four boys played nearby, engrossed in a competitive game that involved climbing on walls and trees. I was startled when I thought I heard one shout: 'Fuck you!' 'No, fuck you!' shouted another.

Dick turned to me. 'Tourette's on the island?' he mused. But Bwena insisted that in fact the boys were chanting 'Bwaka!' which sounds very much like 'fuck' but actually means 'fall'!

As we walked through the village, I was struck by the extensive use of alternative energy. The EU donated solar panels throughout the Marshall Islands and seventy-five were installed here last year.

We came across a commemorative stone with 'LMS 1870' on

it. When people from the London Missionary Society landed here they persuaded the Council of Elders to stop other churches being established, and that has been upheld ever since.

'The government is not happy about it,' said Teeta. 'It's against the constitution, but they've honoured the *unimane*, even though it was wrong.' I heard that on some other islands with similar restrictions, rival missionaries have begun to sue the councils.

When we arrived at the *maneaba*, the chief and three other *unimane* were engrossed in a game of cards. They completely ignored us.

'What are they playing?' I asked Teeta.

'It's called Sorry,' he replied.

We were brought *moi moito* or drinking coconuts, and sat slurping them while a couple of young boys, who were caring for toddlers without any women present, bounced them gently and showered them with kisses as though they were their mothers. I couldn't remember when I had last seen such a thing in my own culture. On the other hand a boy with an unusually short haircut, a new arrival from Tarawa, was dragging around a toy military tank that he'd covered with a leaf for camouflage. The chief, growing ever more passionate about his game of Sorry, continued to ignore us, but through Teeta we were able to obtain permission to visit the famous navigation stones that lie at the very end of the island. I set off with Teeta and Teariki on borrowed bicycles, trying to arrange my skirt as modestly as the local women do. Here it's really *tabuaki* (taboo) to show one's crotch.

A number of standing stones facing in various directions have been placed at strategic points on the promontory. Teeta believed they were so positioned to indicate the direction of other islands and provide other navigational information, but we failed to understand the system.

'Some researchers are working on it,' he said, taking us to his house for tea. Marshallese compounds contain four buildings –

separate huts for sleeping, eating, cooking and bathing. We sat
on his *boti*, a raised platform house with thatched roof, decorated
with garlands of artificial flowers. A hammock was strung from
two of the side beams, while a TV screen took centre stage, along
with a DVD and video player. In his yard a pig and some
chickens roamed freely, and I identified breadfruit, papaya and
pumpkin growing in the garden. In the adjacent house, three
women were reclining on colourful pillows.

'Is one of those women your wife?' I asked.

'Yes,' he said. I was surprised that he had not introduced her
right away.

'Which one is she?' I asked, getting up to greet her.

'The largest one,' he said. I had a quick flash of how I would
respond if my own husband pointed me out to strangers with
such words. I walked over to the women, shook hands, then
returned to the first house. It was an awkward social situation
and I could not decipher it. Was I meant to sit with the women
and leave the men together? Was I being treated like an honorary
man because I am a western woman?

'Do the other people in the village come to watch your
videos?' I asked Teeta.

'Yes, but their tastes are not the same as mine. They like wars
and fighting.'

'What do you like?' I asked.

'Slow movies with stories,' he replied. 'Like *Bend It Like
Beckham*.'

Teeta told me he had a son back on his own island of
Beru. 'Would you like me to take a gift or something to him?' I
offered.

'No,' he said sadly. 'I used to write, but now . . .' he trailed off.

'How long is it since you've seen your boy?'

'Four years,' he replied. 'He was two when my wife and I
left.'

There was a pause. 'Why did you leave him?' I asked gently.

He stared at the floor. 'My father wanted him.'

I was shocked. 'Why?'

'Because there were no other young children.'

I tried to take this in. 'In your culture,' I asked, 'if your father says he wants you to leave your son behind, do you have to do it?'

'You can argue,' he said, 'but it wouldn't do any good.' Obviously the request had been a *bubuti*, an undeniable one. I had not realized it could apply to children.

We sat in silence for a minute or two. I stretched my legs out in front of me, a social 'no no'. 'Please excuse me,' I said. 'White people have difficulty keeping their legs crossed.' That broke the mood; I thought Teariki was going to die with laughter, for he obviously took it the wrong way.

A number of boatmen cruised by the *Takapuna* this afternoon, including three fishermen in a twelve-foot dinghy with four enormous dead grey sharks lying in the bottom. It's hard to believe that they had actually caught and landed them themselves using simple fishing gear. The people here eat fresh shark and also dry it to eat when it's too stormy to go fishing. The fins, however, are passed to the elders, who sell them to an Asian distribution company in Tarawa.

Sunday 27 March 2005

Easter.

I woke at 2 am because the boat was rolling so much. Fanny had bad weather in this vicinity, too, in mid July:

Had a sharp squall last night . . . I put my head out of the port and watched the rain drops strike the sea, each one producing a spark like a star. It seemed as though the heavens were reversed. I often find my bath, when I take it after dark, blazing like liquid fireworks. Once a little fish was swimming about. The weather continues bad and we are rolling a good deal.

Her patients were making slow progress:

> Louis feels much better again, but the Captain the same, very weak and ill. [The crushed] hand looks as though I meant to make a bad job of it. I suppose I should burn it out. I detest surgery of the mildest sort.

Teariki had arranged for his patient to be airlifted to Tarawa from Tamana this afternoon. 'I don't want to go!' complained Kelly. 'I'm scared of hospitals.' When she was small she faked a stomach ache to avoid school and was rushed to hospital for a needless appendectomy. 'Don't worry,' he soothed her. 'I'll come with you.'

We'd arrived at Tamana during the night but had to wait until dawn to try to anchor, pacing up and down off shore in the swell. When daylight broke we pulled in opposite a huge church and anchored in twenty metres. I kept watch to see any signs of people arriving for the Easter service.

'According to our chart plotter, you're already at church,' quipped the Captain. It was certainly strange to see, due to the inaccuracy of the available charts, our position on the screen as being right in the middle of the island itself.

At 8.30, Teariki rowed me ashore in the tin dinghy and found it easy to enter the shallow, dynamited pass. People had gathered on the shore to greet us. Centre stage was the only policeman, Te Biri, a short congenial man in uniform, who informed us the church service was at ten. He led us to a small thatched house to await the hour.

I asked Tieem, the school principal from Onotoa, what differences he noticed between his island and Tamana.

'Well,' he said, 'culture for one thing.'

'You mean there are different cultures on islands so close together?' I asked in astonishment.

'Yes,' he said, looking a little uneasy, 'especially language.'

I did not understand. 'You mean the people here speak a different language than those on Onotoa?'

'No,' he said haltingly, 'just the way they use the language. For example, here they say words in normal greetings that are forbidden everywhere else – except Arorae.'

'Such as?' It sounded so intriguing I had to pursue my line of questioning. After some persuasion, Tieem wrote in my notebook the Kiribati phrase *Te butae k'o na mauri* which means 'Oh shit, hello!' Another popular greeting is *I tatoa atuum* or 'I will split your head!' I've now realized that the boys on Arorae were indeed swearing. Apart from the profane greetings, Tamana is a very proper island, entirely dry of alcohol and no dancing or fishing on Sundays. It was surprising, therefore, to discover the church only a third full for the Easter service. We sat through what seemed like a long, uninspiring sermon but perhaps a boring church experience was preferable to Fanny's story of the island:

> A man from another Island, indignant at being beaten in a wrestling match, watched at the church door and struck a spear into the victim from the effects of which he died. The execution was by hanging. They dragged the man up by the neck, let him down and looked to see whether he was dead, then up with him again, and so on until they were satisfied.

Two people in a canoe are adrift off Nikunau. They went out fishing and never came back. We'll keep a sharp lookout for them on our way north. When the *Janet Nichol* arrived in Nikunau crowds of local people came on board with wares for sale. Fanny wrote:

> A shark's tooth spear was offered to me for a dollar. I also bought . . . for a florin an immense necklace of human teeth. In some of these Islands, but more particularly in Mariki it

was, a little while ago, a dangerous possession to own a good set of teeth, as many people were murdered for them. I trust mine were honestly come by, at least taken in fair warfare . . . A father who possesses good teeth often leaves them as an inheritance to his oldest son. They are worth a great deal, or were . . . [A local trader] has known many murders for teeth. My necklace seems a gruesome possession.

Monday 28 March 2005

Everyone on watch last night kept a careful eye out for the missing people in the canoe, but no sign. We may see them closer to our next stop, Beru, which we will reach before nightfall today. We shall have only a few hours in Nikunau because there is no anchorage. I am dying to ask one of the local people about necklaces made of human teeth, but after Fanny's warning I'm afraid there might be an ensuing crime!

Tuesday 29 March 2005

Lovely overnight sail to Nikunau. Tonight's moon seemed more silver, last evening's more gold. At dawn we found an anchorage, but had some difficulty locating the position of the dynamited pass. We finally located it near an enormous disused Roman Catholic church, opposite a ramp. People here are very good about standing on the beach and guiding you in. I went ashore with the Captain as soon as it was light and found the pass perfectly navigable. Many residents were gathered on the beach when we arrived. We shook hands with everyone as usual, and greeted them with 'Mauri! Mauri!'

A storyteller took us to a grove of buka trees. 'A long time ago,' he said, 'there was a woman living in Makin who was a navigational genius. Her brothers were jealous that she had been given such talent, so one day when they were at sea they pushed her overboard. She drifted here and landed in this place. They called her Mwanganibuka. She married Teman and taught him her navigation skills, so from then on the people on this island had them, too.'

They say the first people here on this island were from Samoa, and they brought their own magic. Tituabine was a Samoan witch on whom many people relied for luck in fishing. She was married to another ghost called Taburitongoun, a demon who walks around whistling at nighttime. If one dreams of a dog, or sees a sooty tern, those are signs of Taburitongoun. The storyteller took us to a grave and rolled away a stone to reveal a skull that still had some teeth in it.

'Tituabine's descendants are buried here,' he said. He then took us to their *maneaba* and shrine. 'There used to be some skulls here,' he said, 'but a while ago, a man from the Catholic church came and took them away because he did not approve of them. He died soon after.'

At the time of Fanny's arrival here people showed their affection to a deceased loved one by putting them up on the rafters and, when their decaying juices dripped down inside, they dipped their food in them before eating. No wonder Nikunau means 'island of flies'. Nowadays funeral ceremonies last for three days, with the biggest *botaki* or feast on the third day. Everyone from the village is invited. The body is laid out for the first two days and the widow sits with it beneath a mosquito net, covering it with cloths and deodorant to improve the smell.

The people I met here denied the tradition of human teeth necklaces, but they do say that everyone owned necklaces made from dolphin teeth that were passed down as heirlooms. There are still a good many customs designed to ward off supernatural malevolence. Pregnant women will rub themselves with a special plant oil to keep away evil spirits, and even babies are massaged and oiled for the same reason. Open wounds are treated by the chanting of magic words, blowing on them three times, or applying beads. When men comb their hair they are very careful about saving any loose strands for burning. It is believed that if someone gets hold of a piece of your hair, they could put a spell on you. These old beliefs sit side by side with Christianity. I heard of a Christian couple whose children have a curable tropical skin condition that causes scaliness. Their parents have told them they have fish skin because their grandfather cast a spell on his fishing boat to improve his catch. 'It was so powerful,' they said, 'even you are fish-like.'

I asked Erica, a Peace Corps worker on the island, what it was like being here alone, as a single woman. 'You can't go out after dusk without being accompanied by male kin,' she replied, 'and you can't go into the bush alone day or night because of ghosts or drunken men. If a woman is attacked or raped in the bushes, it's considered her fault.' It's not all plain sailing for boys, either. Erica said they are often circumcised as late as ten or eleven years old, by a nurse who just turns up one day and does the whole village.

Erica has had her teaching challenges. 'I was making coconut biscuits with my students,' she said. 'I asked for a knife, but instead of requesting a *kabaang*, I asked for a *kabwanga*.' The children screamed with laughter, wondering why, at that precise moment, their teacher needed a penis. She has been very distressed about the corporal punishment that is meted out in her school. 'Kids are hit hard with bits of pipe for anything, even for getting a math problem wrong,' she said. 'I'm from California . . . you don't *do* that . . . we talk about feelings instead.'

The local schoolteacher's father is a remarkable old man who, twenty years ago, drifted out to sea in a canoe and was gone for six months. I sat beside him as he lay on his mat, barely able to move from a sudden illness.

'I went fishing,' he started, 'with thirty other people in a number of different boats. The wind and weather were quite good. I was alone in my canoe, with a sail and paddle. After a few hours, the weather started to get bad and the currents became very strong. Everyone got back except me and three other people who were all together. The other three landed at Beru the following day, but I drifted all the way to PNG.'

'Papua New Guinea?' I was astounded. 'How did you survive?'

'I fed on the small fishes that came close to my canoe, swimming away from larger ones. I had no hook or line so I had to catch them in my hands and dry them in the sun. I had no drink, only rainwater.'

'What was the worst moment?' I asked.

'One day a shark came, a big one, and tried to eat the canoe.' His eyes still held the fear of that moment.

'What was it like when you first saw land?'

'I did not expect to see a huge mountain; that land was not like the islands I knew. After I came nearer to the shore and beached the canoe I saw two brothers approaching me. They spoke to me but I didn't understand them. Then they picked me up and carried me to their canoe. They put me in the middle and paddled me along a river to their home. On the way, I motioned that I need water. The man in front pointed at the water we were paddling in. I was confused – we don't have rivers here – thinking it was salt water which must not be drunk. So then the brother behind me took a cup and showed me the water was fresh.

'They welcomed me into their home. I could not walk for some time, because my legs were too swollen, so I was taken to a clinic and treated there. After a few days I returned to the family. I taught them to make baskets, weave mats, and cut toddy. When I went with them to church the priest realized I was from far away, so he got a message to Honiara and eventually a ship came and brought me back here. I have kept in touch from time to time – two or three letters. But now I think, maybe they have died from the war in Bougainville.'

I turned to his wife. 'What did you think when he was missing for so long?'

'I was sure he was still alive,' she replied with a smile. She'd visited a dream-tender who informed her that her dreams proved he was not dead.

When I returned to the boat I told the Captain the man's story. 'Makes all those people who complain about having to get into life rafts look pretty lame,' he said. 'I mean, get over it!'

We set sail for Beru at 1.30 pm and arrived at the island at 5 pm amid a gorgeous sunset, with a rainbow throwing lovely colours on to the shore. When the *Janet Nichol* came here there was a great deal of copra, but I saw very little produce. It is such a pity Fanny did not see this island, for I think it is really one of the most beautiful I've ever seen, quiet and unspoilt with a stunning lagoon. I went ashore with Alicia.

First we came to a thatched family compound where a smiling man with a coconut crab in his hand used the creature to point us in the direction of the village. When we saw a sign to the primary school off a forked road, we wandered in for a visit. Teachers were gathered under a *maneaba*. We were waved into a classroom by the principal, who asked us if we would like to talk to the children. We found them exuberant, bright and engaging. They were supposed to be receiving religious instruction during that period, but they didn't have a teacher. Alicia drew a map of the world showing the countries we'd visited, decorating it with wonderful cartoon emblems of each place, and then they sang us the Kiribati national anthem. We reciprocated by teaching them Humpty Dumpty.

In the afternoon the local people arranged for a truck to take us around the island. We passed the government station and drove through a boarding school, founded by the missionary Hiram Bingham. The inner lagoon, now divided by a causeway, is a fine place for bone fishing, but one needs the permission of the elders. Just after it we passed the blackened remains of a *maneaba*. Apparently, the people from that village laid claim to its being the first one on the island, but rivals in other villages disputed that. A fight ensued, during which the *maneaba* in question was burnt down.

Fanny may not have been able to visit the island but a Beru trader brought her gifts on board, including:

a large, thick packet of very delicious sweetmeats made from Pandanus, which is first baked in the ground, then scraped – the meaty part of the fruit – and strained through cocoanut cloth (the natural stuff) and spread out to dry for several days on a mat. I think it is dampened a little with cocoanut milk. It is excellent. One way of preparing it is to moisten the sheets with cocoanut milk, place them in layers, and put the dish in the sun for 2 hours.

We are normally very careful about not walking through people's back yards, which sometimes means avoiding the beach altogether, but when Alicia and I went to visit one of the *unimane* we had to walk down the side of his compound. There we saw sheets of pandanus, 'fruit leather' as we call it, drying in the sun. It was much as Fanny had described.

We heard today that the canoeists have been found.

Wednesday 30 March 2005

We arrived early at Tabiteuia North, or 'Tab North' as it's known. Fanny wrote that it was a difficult lagoon to enter and we, too, found it was so shallow and full of coral heads we had to anchor quite a way out. There is a lovely variation of colour, according to depth, in the lagoon. I set off for shore with Dick to pick up Kelly and Ricky, who will be arriving off the plane from Tarawa. At first we could find neither the channel nor the landing. Then we saw two men lifting their canoe a long way off shore until it was deep enough to float. We knew then we were in for a long reef walk.

At the government station we met Tata on his motor scooter, a retired man who now teaches in the primary school. He took me along a potholed road, through lovely, sleepy villages, with kids calling out *I-Matang* as I passed. Eventually I heard a whistle and saw both doctor and patient, looking rather glad to see me. Kelly had some horror stories of the Tarawa hospital, including the fact that she had to intervene when someone mislabelled her X-ray. The first doctor they were supposed to see, an Estonian volunteer, had not turned up.

'Sorry,' said his assistant. 'He drinks a bit.'

The people here in Tab North make beautiful traditional swords and shark's teeth knives. Fanny liked them:

> I have bought three pretty good shark's teeth spears, one
> for a striped undershirt, the other two for a couple of
> fathoms of fine cotton print apiece. They have been made
> for sale, but the wood is coconut – one very handsome,
> hardwood – the teeth very white and sharp and regular,
> and all neatly worked together with fibre hair and pandanus
> leaf strips.

The knives are not just ornamental. According to the Peace Corps worker I met on Aranuka, they don't station a volunteer here on Tab North because it's too dangerous. They even refer to the island as 'Stab North' because there are frequent knife attacks. Moreover, the people deal out a swift, idiosyncratic form of justice that avoids the complications of red tape and trials. It was strange to hear of bloodshed occurring in such a beautiful, ostensibly peaceful place, but this island is notorious throughout Kiribati. Apparently, the Tab North soccer team was in Tarawa for the inter-island games last summer and one of them walked into a bar and stabbed a member of the opposing team – precipitating retaliation by other bar customers, who immediately killed the aggressor.

*

We left for Nanouti (pronounced Nah-noose) and arrived just after nightfall. Fortunately it's an easy anchor. I had heard that this island was known for the practice of magic, and was particularly interested in locating a 'devil box', a kind of shaman's bag of tricks mentioned by both Louis and Fanny after visiting these parts. They bought one on their first visit to Abemama, and Fanny described the aftermath:

> All the head women had their devil boxes, taking the greatest care of them. They consulted me about ours through every interpreter they could find. They always referred to the box indirectly; the interpreter would be told first to ask if I had not carried away from Abemama something very precious. Upon my answering that I had, questions were then put as to its whereabouts, etc. Louis and I were talking to the King on a different matter in which the escaping of steam was mentioned. His Majesty jumped to the conclusion that we were speaking of the devil box, and assured us that we need feel no alarm when the shell inside (representing the devil, Tiaporo) made a noise. We had only to give it a very small bit of tobacco and that would settle him.

Dick took us ashore in the tender, but we left too late and the tide was very far out, leaving extremely shallow water. Eventually we landed in the village of Umantewenei, inhabited by around 200 people, where we found the oldest Catholic church in Kiribati, built in 1898. The pastor Father Iona met us wearing a 'King of the Road' T-shirt. I asked around about magic stories, and if there was a devil box anywhere nearby, and was directed to the village of Temotu to find an *unimane* called Maio. We got back in the tender and zoomed to the far end of the island, until it got so shallow Teariki and I had to get out and wade. The sand was unusually soft and clay-like. We sank into it so deeply that I kept getting stuck. Most embarrassingly, Teariki had to haul me, like a useless, half-drowned cow, for about a mile in to the shore.

Hot and exhausted, we approached a bunch of kids and a couple of fisherman. 'This is the part,' I said cynically, 'where I ask: "Is this Temotu?" and they point even further south . . .' Which is exactly what happened. When we did finally get to the village, Maio was away in Tarawa; however, we were taken to his brother. I stooped low under his *buia* and asked him if he could tell me any old stories.

'No,' he said.

'Legends?'

'No.'

'Magic stories?'

'No.'

'Do you have a devil box?'

'No.'

It was a disaster.

We trudged back to the tender and began the tricky task of attempting to find a navigable channel back to the boat. The sun was facing us, which made it impossible to see colour variation in the water. Exasperated, Dick called the *Takapuna* for help, since there was a better vantage point on board with the sun behind. Luckily, the Captain was able to guide us across the reef before nightfall.

Fanny too had a frustrating day on Nanouti. On 7 July she went ashore after breakfast with Lloyd but, while they were exploring, one of their fellow passengers took the tender back to the ship, leaving them stranded for the entire day:

> We were tired, hungry, and very angry at being so deserted.
> Lloyd finally went off to try and get back somehow in a
> canoe that he might fetch me something to eat. I was afraid
> to venture in a canoe after my attack of rheumatism at one of
> the other Islands, caused by a wetting, and preferred the
> discomforts I know of to possible pain in the future. I had
> already got pretty wet crossing the surf in our own boat, and
> was dressed in a filthy gown and chemise lent me by a native

woman. I asked when I arrived for the loan of a dress, and the woman gave me her cast off one. I did not know what to do, as it was transparent and could not come out of the inner room. [Before going off with the tender] Mr Buckland . . . demanded a chemise for me. The woman removed her own in a dark corner, folded it up, then pretended to take it from a trunk which she opened. After this piece of either pride or delicacy (the latter, I believe) I felt bound to put it on, although it was reeking with sweat. As my head ached I lay down on a mat with an incredibly filthy pillow under my head, and tried to sleep. The people of the house, some 20, came in every few minutes to look at me, and if the children made a noise they were promptly smacked, thereupon bawling enough to raise the roof; and every little while a crowd of outside children would be beaten out of the house with yells and howlings. I never saw so much discipline administered before on any of the Islands. Outside my window a child was steadily smacked for crying for at least half an hour . . . In the meantime . . . Lloyd had found a canoe, and a native willing to take him off for the high price of 10 sticks of tobacco. Mr Buckland awaking to a sense of the enormity of his behaviour had already dispatched a canoe with some sandwiches, a tin of sardines, useless for want of an opener – and two bottles of stout with a corkscrew. When Lloyd discovered this, not liking to leave me alone for the entire day, he tried to return to me, but in spite of all he could do was land in the surf some two miles from where I was. He struggled along the reef, sometimes thrown down by the surf, and sometimes up to his arm pits in water. He had on shoes of leather, but they became soaked through, and the nails coming loose tore the sole of his foot, adding to the difficulty of walking. He also cut his ankle on the reef, and grazed his leg, both serious things to have happen to one here . . . It was quite dark when we got off, and the night very chill, so that I feared I should have

my rheumatism after all. Mr Buckland, who came in the
boat was proper in his apologies, but I told him to wait until
I was in a better temper.

Friday 1 April 2005

On the island of Aranuka I met an *unimane* called Tawita who is
also a magistrate.

'Do you have a devil box?' I asked.

'I had one,' he said, 'but a French person took it, along with
my books. I had sacred oils in it.'

'Do you still do devil work?' I asked.

He sighed a little regretfully. 'I have tried to change to the
new life.'

We left at noon, as it was imperative we reach Abemama
before nightfall. I went below and was just enjoying a snooze
when a heavy box flew across my cabin and hit me on the head.
This was accompanied by a massive tipping of everything
around me and a sense that my porthole was underwater for
quite a few seconds. The Captain had been cranking up the
speed when a sudden squall hit us with winds that were too
strong for the amount of sail we had put out, and the rudder
went haywire for a moment. It was a virtual 'knockdown', and
the mast was pretty much horizontal for a short time. A huge
ceramic jar of Milo smashed in the galley causing a terrible mess.
It was almost like magic.

Louis and Fanny's first visit to Abemama, during their *Equator*
trip, was on 1 September 1889. Although Tembinoka the King had
no love for white men, he allowed the Stevensons to stay ashore
for a number of weeks on his own land. He built a compound for
them that they named Equator Town. Fanny wrote:

We have been now a month on the island of the redoubtable
Tembinoka, an absolute monarch, who holds the lives of his

subjects (our own also) in the hollow of his hand. He says:
'I kill plenty men, him 'praid (afraid) now. I no kill any
more.' That he does not mean to kill any more his subjects
do not believe, nor I, quite, myself . . . we chose a spot where
we thought it would be pleasant to live, and Tembinoka
ordered his men to carry houses and set them up there for us.
The Captain and Lloyd stayed at the King's palace all
night; the next morning they were alarmed to see Tembinoka
shooting into the village with a rifle. He explained that his
men were lazy and should be at work, so he was reminding
them that accidents were possible.

On Saturday we moored off Binoinano village, a hop, step
and jump from where Fanny and Louis stayed. We went ashore
in the tin dinghy because it seemed sensible to prepare for a
shallow approach. I asked a man repairing the *maneaba* where I
could find Don Tokataake, the current King. He told me he lived
some distance away in the village of Temarama, and offered to

drive Teariki and me there in his truck. Unfortunately, Don was not at home, but we met his cousin who runs a nearby store. Leslie Schutz is a man of German descent whose grandfather, William Reiher, came here from the Marshall Islands as a shipwright and local navigator. He built a boat called the *Santa Teresa* for the Catholic mission.

'Abemama is the only island that still has a king,' he said, 'but he's just a figurehead now.'

'What does he do?' I asked.

'Oh, he attends a few functions, opens Telecom buildings and so on – and he's had a few wives.'

'How does he make his living?'

'By selling his land.'

'Is there much of it left?'

'Very few plots,' replied Leslie. 'He's just sold one, though.'

'Where is he now?' I asked.

'In Tarawa,' he replied. 'Off to spend the proceeds getting himself a new wife, I suppose,' he added with a snigger.

I asked Leslie what Tembinoka had been like. 'Very cruel,' he said. 'He used to shoot people or have them killed just because he felt like it. And he used to choose a "human rooster". He'd see a man and say, "You are the rooster for a week. Go up into the rafters." So the man would go up there and have sex with any women he wanted because they were chickens to him. It was for Binoka's entertainment. All the females used to hide.' I doubt that Fanny and Louis saw any such thing. Louis wrote about the king's predilection for wearing women's frocks, as well as bizarre naval uniforms of his own design. With his beaked nose, long hair and piercing eyes, Louis thought the monarch could have made a fortune on the West End stage.

Leslie advised me to talk to David Brecktefield in Kabangaki, the last village on the island. We hired a motorbike and raced to the end of the island as the sun began to set.

'What was Tembinoka like?' I asked David. 'I've heard stories . . .'

'Ah, Binoka was a notorious king,' he said. 'He was above the law. I never heard of him killing people himself, but he would order others to do it. He had many wives.'

'That wasn't unusual for that time, was it?' I asked.

'But he had them on all of the three islands he owned: here, Kuria and Aranuka.'

Across the road from Equator Town, I had seen Tembinoka's crumbling tomb, an unmarked concrete eyesore that was half-covered in weeds.

'What happened to Tembinoka after Robert Louis Stevenson left Abemama?' I asked David.

'He went in his ship to invade Nanouti,' he replied, 'but when he came back he stopped at Kuria where he contracted smallpox. The British warship *HMS Royalist* took him on board from Kuria to be court-martialled for attacking Nanouti. The interpreter at that trial was Robert Louis Stevenson. The British returned Binoka home, however, because they saw he was sick with smallpox. He died soon after.' I had previously been told that Tembinoka died of syphilis. That would have provided one explanation for his mental state.

I asked David why he called him 'Binoka' rather than Tembinoka.

'"Tem" means "Mr", so "Tembinoka" means "Mr Binoka".'

'So,' I said, 'when Robert Louis Stevenson wrote "King Tembinoka" that really meant "King Mister Binoka"?'

'Yes,' he smiled.

David's grandfather was a German trader and ship owner who settled here long ago. David is now the presiding magistrate of the island, so he was the perfect person to ask about the tantalizing stories I'd heard concerning local marriage arrangements.

'According to Abemama law, you have the right to play around with your wife's sisters,' confirmed David. 'It still applies today.'

When I asked him about the 'University of Abemama', David

squirmed and looked away. 'It is actually the University of Tuangaona,' he said. 'King Binoka was the first to learn . . .' he struggled with the word . . . 'cunnilingus. He learned it from the whalers. Before that no one practised that here. At first it was kept a secret, so only Binoka's family clan knew about it, then eventually they taught it to others.' I clarified that it was taught to both men and women, and included fellatio.

'Where did all this happen?' I asked.

'In the next village of Tbanga,' David replied. 'There is a shrine there . . .'

Apparently it was shaped like a tongue. We raced to Tbanga as twilight fell. Seeing a man outside his house, I hopped off the motorbike and excitedly accosted him. 'Where is the Tuangaona?' I cried. He laughed loudly and summoned his friends.

'What was that again?' he asked in amusement.

'Where's the Tuangaona?' I repeated, little knowing I had just asked about the location of the oral sex.

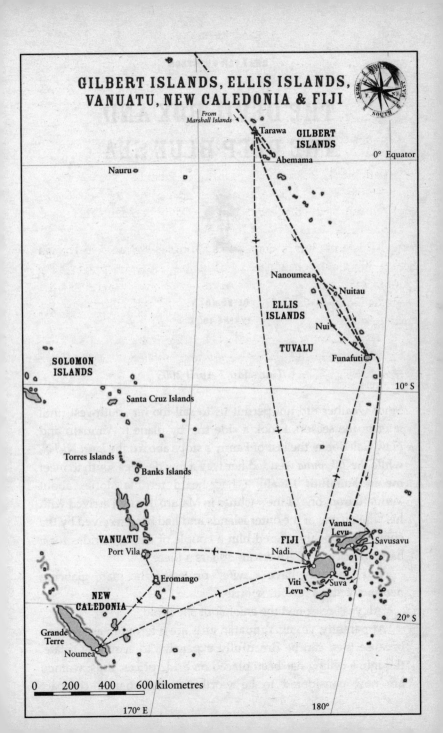

GILBERT ISLANDS, ELLIS ISLANDS, VANUATU, NEW CALEDONIA & FIJI

From Marshall Islands

Tarawa

GILBERT ISLANDS

0° Equator

Abemama

Nauru

Nanoumea

Nuitau

ELLIS ISLANDS

Nui

TUVALU

Funafuti

SOLOMON ISLANDS

10° S

Santa Cruz Islands

Torres Islands

Banks Islands

Vanua Levu

Savusavu

VANUATU

FIJI

Nadi

Port Vila

Eromango

Viti Levu

Suva

NEW CALEDONIA

20° S

Grande Terre

Noumea

0   200   400   600 kilometres

170° E

180°

CHAPTER THIRTEEN

THE DEVIL BOX AND THE DEEP BLUE SEA

01°22.36′ N
172°56.10′ E

Thursday 7 April 2005

Since weather did not permit us to sail too far southwest until later in the season, I took a side trip by plane to Vanuatu and New Caledonia, the last of Fanny's stops aboard the *Janet Nichol*, while the *Takapuna* wended her way a few degrees south to meet me in Funafuti, Tuvalu. I had heard terrible stories about Vanuatu from one of the yachties in Majuro. He had arrived with his wife on one of the outer islands and had been received by the chief, who openly offered him a couple of teenage brides for a bargain price of 90 American dollars a piece.

'But I already have a wife,' protested the man, glancing nervously at his furious spouse.

'Ah yes,' reasoned the chief, 'but she is old.'

Apparently, young Vanuatan girls are referred to as Toyotas, because they can be dreadfully expensive to acquire. Of late, though, a ceiling has been placed on bride prices; thus, women are now considered to be worth far less than a compact

Japanese ride. Women are curfewed, downtrodden, the recipients of ubiquitous domestic violence and are banned from drinking kava, a local drug. Looking on the bright side, they are no longer put to death for viewing a male kava ceremony. But it was not only the prospect of being a commodity and barred from many activities I take for granted in my own country that bothered me: malaria, dengue fever and all forms of hepatitis are rife throughout all the islands. Needless to say, I decided that Teariki should accompany me on this trip, not only because of his medical qualifications – nor even to protect me from being sold for a rusty old tricycle – but more particularly because he can speak Bislama (a kind of pidgin English spoken in Vanuatu).

When we landed in Port Vila, I was pleasantly surprised by the town. It is picturesque, and has become quite developed without the loss of its natural charm, sporting coffee shops, boutiques, nightclubs and a nice hotel. Our taxi driver was surprisingly forthcoming about his own marital arrangements. He was recently hitched and had been lucky enough to get his bride for half price.

'Most cost $100,000 vatu (500 sterling) now,' he said smugly, 'but I joined the Church and found a woman there. See, the Protestants frown on bride prices, so I went to her father and did a deal for fifty grand.'

'How's it going so far?' I asked.

'Not bad,' he said. 'I have a four-month-old daughter.'

'Nice,' I said savagely. 'Future investment.'

Trevor and Basil, the emergency room doctors at the local hospital, are Teariki's best friends from their med school days. They agreed to take me to a local kava bar when they got off work. Western woman are allowed to patronize such an establishment but only if they are accompanied by a male. Kava is a mild, foul-tasting root-based soup that tingles on one's tongue and induces a soporific state wherein all one wants to do is laze under a coconut tree. Teariki had warned me, though, that

Vanuatu kava is a far more powerful concoction than the stuff I'd
tried in Fiji. I pooh-poohed this warning and it was to my peril.

When I first heard about the kava bars, I was imagining
places a little like cocktail bars, possibly quite chic, with stools
and tables – perhaps a bit like the oxygen bars in New York. In
anticipation of this evening I felt excited, yet quite wicked to be
going out on the town with three young doctors.

'What should I wear?' I pondered, deciding on high heels and
a tight, low-cut outfit that would have landed a local woman in
jail. Perhaps I have spent too much time lately trying to be a
model of multicultural awareness. Perhaps that is why I
snapped on this particular evening.

When Trevor and Basil arrived to meet us at the hotel bar,
they were shocked that Teariki and I had just eaten dinner, and
that we were downing our second cocktail.

'You should have the kava on an empty stomach,' said Trevor
disapprovingly, 'and drink alcohol *afterwards*.' I was afraid to ask
why.

We took off in a taxi for a kava bar and I soon wondered why
we seemed to be travelling away from the lights of the main
township into the suburbs. It suddenly occurred to me that I
might be about to experience more the crack-den level of kava-
imbibing.

'Lot of people here with hepatitis?' I nervously asked Basil.

'Around eighty per cent,' he replied.

'And do they, I mean, the bowls they serve the kava in . . . do
they, er, wash them at all?'

'I doubt it,' he smiled. The cab pulled up on the corner of a
dimly lit street, outside a small house with a dingy light on the
roof, its sole trade signal. We got out and walked into the dark
driveway. A few shadowy forms slunk about in the garden and
the desperately unappealing sounds of retching filled the air. My
heels sunk into the muddy grass. Oh yes, I was dressed for the
occasion all right. I followed the boys to the back door and
climbed a couple of concrete stairs into a bare room with a trestle

table on which were placed some large bowls covered with cling film, a ladle and a pile of dripping, smaller glass bowls. Two grubby, stoned women, eyelids at half-mast, stood ready to fill our order.

'Large or medium?' asked Trevor.

I took a deep breath. 'I'll go for the large,' I said foolishly, deciding then and there I had to just surrender to the experience, come what may. These guys were *doctors*, after all, although the number of calls they were getting on their cell phones suggested to me they might actually be on duty. The older of the women carefully ladled out four bowls of beige liquid. We filed out into the front garden and lined up facing the hedge with our bowls in front of us. A couple of nasty, loud retches and a full-throttle vomit resounded out of the shadows to our right. I longed for the ceremonial circles, the endless speeches, the hand-clapping ritual of the Fijian ceremonies.

'Ready? One, two, three . . .' We all downed our bowls in as few gulps as possible. I froze for a moment, reeling at the disgustingness of taste and texture, then followed the boys to a seat on the veranda. We waited for the first hit to take effect.

'Why is it so dark?' I asked.

'To protect people from the light,' replied Basil. 'This stuff makes you photosensitive.'

Over the next few minutes, my three companions receded into a relaxed . . . I would almost use the word *comatose* . . . state, and it would have been very nice if the same thing had happened to me. Unfortunately, it didn't. Instead, I began to spiral upwards into a frighteningly manic mood, in which I was inspired to babble like an afternoon television host whose main guest has failed to appear. I know about this kind of unforeseen reaction; it is called a paradoxical effect, when a drug does the opposite to what is expected. I believe there shortly came a moment when the boys very much regretted allowing me to accompany them to this bastion of male mojo-moving, and probably revisited the advantages of female prohibition.

Anyway, for reasons best known to them, they tolerated my behaviour and even offered me a second bowl of kava – which I accepted because I no longer had the ability to reason. Soon after, we took off for a proper bar with cocktails and pool tables, and it was here that I became bravely experimental, attempting to reduce my mania with various different kinds of alcoholic beverages. It was around this time that I began to feel sick, but even more worrying was the mounting paranoia that began after my fourth white Russian. It didn't help that I was the only woman in the room, that the atmosphere was filled with tobacco smoke, and that a trip to the bathroom that involved a glimpse in a cracked mirror led me to believe that I was nothing but a haggard crone with no hope for any future happiness and a nasty accident just waiting to happen. Oh yes, I was on my way down. Fortunately, I didn't burden anyone else with this information.

'I need some air,' I announced, and strode outside where I became the focus of attention for scores of Vanuatan men who could not afford the drink prices inside and hung around to snigger at the Caucasian matron dressed as a teeny-bopper who couldn't handle the local grog. I had half-expected one of my doctor-companions to follow me out, but I guess they don't do that sort of thing. I was dying to go back to the hotel, but I felt duty-bound to keep up with my buddies who, by contrast, seemed to be having a very good time. Eventually we went on to a busy nightclub where the sight of bloated ex-pats gyrating to old Olivia Newton-John numbers led me even closer to a good chunder than the kava had done. I begged for a reprieve and was eventually whisked back to the hotel for a long sleep. As my husband would have said, 'Pamela, what *possessed* you?'

The next day, we took an early flight on a decrepit, eight-seater prop plane to Eromango (which means mango-land, since five different varieties of mango are found there). If the outer islands of Vanuatu can be seen as the offspring of the main island, then the one we were about to visit is the weird kid they never talk about. We landed on a grass runway in the middle of nothing. A shed served as both the airport terminal, and a warehouse for fly-covered fish destined for the big-smoke markets. The person who was supposed to meet me for a cultural tour was nowhere in sight; in fact, no one was in sight and the two Australian honeymooners who'd got off the plane with us suddenly realized their mistake and re-embarked for the more tourist-friendly island of Tanna. We sat alone on a bench for a few minutes, swatting at flies and dodging mosquitoes, watching the young New Zealand pilot in the silent plane fill out his paperwork. I desperately wanted to rush up to his cockpit window and scream: 'You ARE coming back for us at 1.30 pm, aren't you? PROMISE!' He taxied off over the weeds and was soon a wobbly dot in a hazy topaz sky.

Still no tour guide. When a truck pulled up in front of the terminal, I approached the driver. 'Could you take us to Dillon Bay?' The man looked blank, until Teariki entered his sightline. With a man in my vicinity I was accommodated and we were soon bumping our way through the jungle to the nearest village, a scene of many vile acts of violence and cannibalism against missionaries in the early nineteenth century. Well, it was just retaliation for the fact that outsiders had brought pestilence to the island and that many of those who survived had been stolen away to work the Queensland sugarcane fields. The population was reduced from 10,000 to 400 within just a few years.

Jonah, who showed us round the village at Port Dillon, seemed quite proud of the carnage that had taken place here. He kept repeating it over and over again: 'Yes, we killed very many missionaries here.' John Williams, James Harris, James Gordon and James MacNair perished, as well as George and Eileen Gordon whom Jonah said were stabbed inside their home. He did not address me at all, but relayed everything via Teariki. I was forced to follow several paces behind the two of them and tried not to seethe. At times I became quite rebellious. 'I had a little too much kava last night,' I taunted Jonah, knowing he would be shocked that I'd had any at all. When he referred to me as Teariki's wife, I came close to losing the plot altogether. I suppose the concept of a man having a female boss is an alien one here. On second thoughts, being mistaken for a twenty-six-year-old man's wife, rather than his mother, was really quite a compliment.

Fanny had more fun by *not* landing at Eromango:

> a good deal of amusement was got from discussions concerning the mango and the proper way to eat it. Mr Stoddard said it should be eaten with a spoon, which is impossible. We soon discovered that he had confused the mango with the barbadine, although he would not confess it. One evening when the bread was under baked and new, I pressed the crumb with the semblance of a spoon and solemnly presented it to him as a mango spoon; he accepted it as gravely as it was offered. I discovered this morning that a large pumpkin that had been hanging up to ripen, was to be cooked; begging the loan of it from the cook, Mr Hird and I tied it up in an enormous parcel, and Louis wrote out a card in printing letters, which was attached to it . . .

> For Walter Stoddard
> —one Mango—
> with the fond love of the
> inhabitants of Eromango
> (This is gathered, with a spoon, from the finest mango-swamp in the Island. But beware of the fate of the martyr, Williams, who died from trying to eat one with too short a spoon. O Mango and do likewise!)

On Sunday, when we arrived in the late evening on the island of Grande Terre in New Caledonia, it was immediately apparent that its capital Noumea is no longer 'a city built from Vermouth boxes', as Louis once dubbed it. Ritzy and expensive, it has earned instead the title 'Paris of the Pacific'. I missed having the pleasure of arriving by boat. The mere fact that we immediately found ourselves on a dual carriageway was enough to thoroughly unnerve me; well, it's been eight months since my last one. Fanny was luckier. She had the advantage of seeing the beauty of Noumea's shoreline:

> A succession of the most lovely small bays began to open
> out as we neared the Island. The reef runs out some forty
> miles, and is studded with small islands, some high, like
> small hills, some what I call high-low, and some like low
> Islands we have just left. A strip of coral topped by a fringe
> of cocoa palms. The magnificence of the mountains. The
> mountains I will leave to an abler pen than mine to describe
> the incredible beauty of the entrance.

On arrival in our first French territory for some time, Fanny and I both had the same idea: 'Naturally our first object was to find a good meal,' wrote Fanny ... 'So off we all started, all in the best clothes we could find ... At the hotel we had a delightful meal ... and an excellent bottle of fine wine.' Following her lead, I, too, wasted no time finding a fine French restaurant, although I felt terribly guilty, thinking of everyone aboard the *Takapuna* putting up with the meagre provisions available in Tarawa. Oh well, *c'est la vie*! Louis left the *Janet Nichol* in Noumea, and took a different ship to Australia. They met up in Sydney, where, on their previous visit, they are reported to have received an icy reception at the first hotel they tried. After so many months at sea, they were a raggedy bunch, and unrecognizable as the famous Robert Louis Stevenson and family.

On Monday, we visited the stone jetty where, from May 1864, convicts once came ashore to start a new life in the French penal colony. Nowadays, the University is situated in one of the early arrival buildings, so along the wharf scores of students were eating lunch and sunbathing. In Fanny's time:

the wharf was crowded with the usual sort of people one sees in such places, only the odd thing was they did not look French, nor did the convicts we saw in the town and on the roads. These latter all looked bad and vicious, some absolutely devilish, but no more French than English, or German, or American. They seemed to belong to a race of their own – the criminal race.

In total, 21,000 convicts were shipped here, so no wonder Fanny saw so many. She also noticed a prevalence of indigenous Kanak people: 'Mixed with them were a great many natives, some of them strapping fellows, and most of them dressed with regard for the colour effect that one finds in all the dark people.' New Caledonians are still recovering from the trouble that occurred when French–Kanak relations turned ugly in the 80s. Unfortunately, a few echoes of those days were evident in the demonstrations at McDonald's and outside my hotel on Friday. On the other hand, the Tjibaou Cultural Centre I visited, a miracle of design by Renzo Piano, is a thrilling tribute to Kanak traditions and art.

Saturday 16 April 2005

While I was en route to Nadi (having spent a week conducting *mahu* research in New Caledonia), Kayt phoned to say the *Takapuna* had arrived safely in Funafuti, but that the provisioning situation there was dire. An influx of people from surrounding islands for an inter-island children's sports carnival had severely depleted the island's resources and there was no fresh food available. Charged with trying to take back some provisions to ward off scurvy from hungry Takapunians, Teariki and I ran around trying to find a grocery store. Unfortunately, all we could find on a Saturday evening was a dozen questionable tomatoes, some sweetcorn from New Zealand and a pineapple.

In the morning we supplemented our pitiful supply at an airport coffee shop, whose owner allowed us to purchase, besides coffee beans, a few lettuces and a crate of oranges and apples. We boxed it all up and paid an exorbitant excess baggage charge, not knowing if we'd be allowed to take it through Customs. Luckily, the Funafuti officials were flexible. They inspected my measly produce, then released to us what will now be the most expensive couple of salads in the history of the universe.

It was lovely to be back on board, and after all that air travel I couldn't wait to go sailing again. On Monday, the Captain applied for permission to go to the outer islands visited by Fanny: Nuitao, Nanoumea and Nui. Unfortunately, Funafuti is awash with civil servants; I hope our letter doesn't sit in someone's in-tray for too long. In the meantime, I explored the island. Fanny and Louis were surprised by several aspects of Funafuti:

> To begin with the fact of the poisonous fish being outside the reef is contrary to what one has reason to expect . . . There was much marsh and green stagnant pools, and there was a fever smell in the air. The Island seemed unusually wide, but what was our astonishment when we pushed through the bushes and trees to find ourselves not on the ocean beach, as we expected, but on the margin of a large lagoon emptied of its water almost entirely by low tide. The lagoon was everywhere enclosed, but the traders told us that there was a blow hole outlet into which the natives had thrown piles of coral, hoping to block it up . . . I wandered away from Louis, gathering shells, but was recalled by a wild shout. I found Louis bending over a piece of the outer reef that he had broken off. From the face of both fractures innumerable worms were hanging like a sort of dreadful thick fungi.

Louis and Fanny could not possibly have predicted that Tuvalu would one day pay for the fine roads in Funafuti with money generated from selling its 'dot TV' (for 'dot Tuvalu') internet address to wealthy television companies. A quick drive along the narrow island revealed that these people have a monumental waste disposal crisis. The natural beauty of one end has been annihilated by a trash dump. Worse, in the centre there are large holes, now filled with water and rubbish, where the American military excavated soil to make the airport runway in the 1940s. I sat down with Mataio Tekinene, the Director of the Environment.

'Waste management is a major problem here,' he said, stating the glaringly obvious. 'We have already put in place a waste management unit with assistance from Australia.'

'How much did they give you?' I asked.

'About one and a half million.'

'What did you do with the money?' I asked, picturing all the kids I'd seen swimming round in littered swamps. He turned out to be a master of bureau-speak.

'Project implementation,' he replied. 'The EU also provided some different components which – we, er, have yet to implement.'

'Give me a million and a half,' said Rolle when I returned to the Takapuna, 'and I'll clean it up myself.'

Sadly, I have to look to my own culture to explain the environmental and bureaucratic mess in which the Tuvaluans now find themselves. Western societies created the junk food, disposable nappies and other goods in non-biodegradable packages that have made this place such an environmental disaster. We created the advertising that made them believe they needed it all, when in fact it gives them diabetes, hypertension and other illnesses. We provided the model of government and administration that means nothing gets done, not to mention the model of corruption in high places. On top of that, our contributions to global warming are making it rather likely that Tuvalu will entirely disappear beneath the surface of the ocean before too long. It all seems so hopeless.

'We're not putting any of our rubbish ashore here, Captain,' I said. It was a weak gesture, but the best I could come up with.

Fanny too, heard of terrible actions by outsiders that had shaped the behaviour of the Funafuti inhabitants:

In 1866 . . . two American vessels under the Peruvian flag came to the Island, and distributed presents right and left to all who came to receive them. Naturally the people were delighted, and when it was proposed that as many as liked should go to Peru to be educated by these kind people, they flocked aboard in crowds. The King anxious that all should participate in this good fortune blew his horn which was the royal summons. By the time the trader arrived two thirds of the population were gone, and the King was in the very act of blowing his horn to gather the remaining subjects, now reduced to the very young and the very old. It is needless to say that the vessels were slavers, and the entrapped Islanders were never seen again. Throughout the Islands . . . there are not 150 inhabitants altogether. They have a bad name, and are said to be a dirty, rough, dishonest lot. Dishonest, that is, so far as cheating goes, for they do not steal. No wonder they are dishonest, for they learned in a good school . . .

I heard that there was going to be a traditional dance show, at a Government do in honour of the Belgian Ambassador.

'Could I please see the Minister?' I asked a woman in the Foreign Affairs Office, hoping to wangle an invitation.

'He's also the Prime Minister,' frowned the woman in the office. 'What do you want with him?'

'Just to ask him a few questions,' I replied, which is never a good way to secure an audience with a head of state. In the end, I received my invitation and duly appeared at 7 pm dressed in 'island style' i.e. long floral print dress with covered shoulders. The government officials I met were charming and welcoming, and the Belgian Ambassador a hoot. A lively Buddhist and poet, he willingly joined the dancers, as is the custom here for the most important guests, allowing himself to be draped in a flowery headdress and skirt. His jerky, thrusting gyrations caused a great deal of mirth.

'Why were you doing that?' asked the Prime Minister.

'I was imagining there was a female spirit in front of me,' replied the Ambassador. When the PM went on to inquire how Belgium managed to persuade the European Community to have its headquarters in Brussels, he replied: 'With wine, women and chocolates.'

Monday 25 April 2005

Having waited nearly a week for permission to visit the outer islands (all the while running out of food), I stormed into the impressive government building donated by the People's Republic of China (Taiwan) to see the immigration people and try to clear us to visit the outer islands. When I explained my concerns face-to-face with the head man, Charles, he turned things round within a few minutes. I can't wait to get out of here.

Friday 29 April 2005

We arrived at Nui around 9 am. We could not enter the lagoon for there is no pass, but two men came to pick me up in a tin dinghy. This was just as well because, just as Fanny found it, the line of pounding surf around the reef was extremely daunting. One of the boatmen was quite Caucasian in appearance, for he was descended from Martin Kleis, one of the early German traders. This is a neat island with a very beautiful inner lagoon. Half the population, though, is away in Funafuti for the inter-island school games. It is strange to see so few children around.

Fanny noted that the people here speak a Gilbert Island tongue, similar to that spoken in Kiribati, and this is still true, athough one might have expected to hear a Tuvaluan language on Nui. An *unimane* called Litangi told me the story of how this occurred. In the past, he said, the people of Nui spoke the same language as the rest of Tuvalu until some of them went off on a long trip to the island of Nanomanga to get some fresh food. While they were away, some travellers set off from Kiribati in their *paulua*, or canoes, tied together. They sighted Nui and decided to go ashore, where they found that there were mostly women on the island, performing traditional *fatelele* dances. The newcomers decided to stay. They married the local women and established their own language. The story seemed unfinished but no one seems to know the rest. Were some of the newly married women previously married to the men who went off to Nanomanga? Was it consensual? What happened when the first lot returned?

It's always the small details and incidents that are the most intriguing. My husband, who is on a concert tour in Scotland, called to say a young man stopped him yesterday at the stage door and asked him if he would sign his grandfather's artificial leg. 'I'll bring it over to you,' he said. He reappeared a couple of minutes later, pointing out the old man who was sitting across the road, waving delightedly. Billy obligingly signed the leg.

'It had a sock and shoe on it!' he said.

We reached Nanoumea early Saturday morning and I was lucky enough to get a ride in with local fishermen at nine. It was another treacherous pass, but they surfed it expertly. The day Fanny arrived, the conditions at the reef were so terrible that a boat containing traders and missionaries capsized, several canoes were smashed and many bags of copra were lost overboard.

This is one of the prettiest islands I've seen, with an absolutely gorgeous, shallow lagoon, a neat settlement of around 700 people and a very picturesque church with turrets and an intricately decorated tower in a sort of Bavarian style. I asked Tekapu, an eighty-year-old man, if he knew of any traders who had been here in the early days. He did not, but he wanted to talk about the Second World War. He remembered the time when the Americans arrived and sent all the people in the main settlement to the nearby islet of Lakena, in order to protect them from Japanese attack, should it come. It eventually did.

'In one bomb-hole where a big gun once sat,' said Tekapu, 'there were no whole bodies left at all, just pieces.'

Once again, wartime debris, including two rusty transport vessels and a fighter plane, have marred the beauty of the island. I wish the nations involved would clean up their mess.

While touring the island I sat in the back of the council truck with Lopati, the secretary of the Nanoumea *kaupule* or council. A single parent, he is struggling with finding good treatment for his seventeen-year-old son who has schizophrenia.

'Is he on medication?' I asked.

'They sent me some on the supply ship,' he answered, 'but it was out of date.'

Lopati took us to a Women's Association event in the *maneaba*, the finale of a two-week sewing and craft workshop. Ruta, the President, welcomed Scarlett, Teariki and me to their feast and showed us the deftly sewn pillow cases and lava-lavas they had printed and embroidered. I was struck by the beauty of the people who had gathered there, with fresh garlands in their hair and all in brightly coloured outfits, some of which had been tie-dyed during the week. Even the pastor's wife was resplendent in a tie-dyed Mother Hubbard in rainbow hues.

Fanny's appearance was a focus of admiration by local women when they came on board the *Janet Nichol*:

> they first examined my clothes, and then myself. First they tried to unfasten my dress, but I would not let them do that, so they turned up my sleeves. Their taste differed from mine, for, while I was thinking what a cold, ugly colour a white arm looked beside their warm brown ones, they were crying

out in admiration. One woman touched her nose to my feet, and rubbed it all over my arms, sniffing softly . . . 'She is just like a pickaninny.'

Sunday 1 May 2005

When Fanny arrived at Nuitau she found it 'The only one of the Ellices I have seen gave me such an unpleasant impression that I shall not be disappointed if I do not go ashore.' I had the opposite impression of this island. Yes, there was a heavy surf at the reef, but in the early light, the small island of Nuitau was an incandescent green, with wide creamy beaches met by rows of healthy palms. A couple of fishermen came to the stern to say they'd take us in if we moved adjacent to a safer channel. After watching their boat being buffeted like a see-saw on the reef, I told Scarlett to stay behind and leapt with Teariki inside the slippery fishing dinghy. It's been ten years or so since a yacht came here. Vaguna, the secretary of the Nuitau *kaupule*, greeted me at a steep part of the beach where a concrete wharf lies broken, due to the erosion of its foundations and the onslaught of a large wave.

The people here are trying hard to preserve their culture. A new chief was inaugurated last week, amid traditional ceremonies that included displays of *lima*, martial arts forms (wrestling, knife-fighting and combat with spears and coconut whips) that are unique to Nuitau. Vaguna showed me the island's new *maneaba*, which has an ancient chief's seating-stone, now painted in black, red and white stripes, embedded in its floor. It also has a central pit of broken coral stone that is used as a drum during dancing ceremonies. The upper walls are decorated with fine miniature examples of the material culture of Nuitau, including some instruments of healing and sorcery. Vaguna pointed out a magic fishing lure used to catch tuna, as well as a magic summoning device.

'There was once a chief who ran out of tobacco,' he said. 'A man skilled in magic used one of these to reroute a ship that was on its way to Australia. It stopped here, and the chief got his smoke.'

'Is magic still practised here?' I asked.

'Yes,' he said. 'I have a special stick in my house that makes rain.'

'May I see it?' I asked. We walked to his new concrete home, where he unwrapped an oval piece of dark wood preserved with a sweet-smelling oil.

'When the Prime Minister came here recently,' he said, 'he wanted to try it out. The first-born woman in the family is the one who must use it, so my father's oldest sister placed it outside in the sun to draw far-off rain clouds over here. The rain came the following day and it continued for four days, with raindrops larger than usual.'

'Have you ever heard of a devil box?' I asked. I had really given up hope of ever finding one.

'There are some devil boxes on this island,' said Vaguna. 'I will ask some people about it after they come out of church.'

Within half an hour I was sitting in the home of Lagi, a medicine man who had agreed to show me his own devil box. Lagi's wife greeted Teariki with hugs and tears, for she had known his grandparents who were Seventh Day Adventist missionaries here. We were invited into a back room, where Lagi pulled out an old, carved sandalwood box, probably Asian in origin. He opened it with some ceremony and allowed us to peer inside. There were three bottles containing magic potions, a few tuna lures on which spells had been placed and some magic string. Beside the box was a woman's handbag, a modern, portable devil box that Lagi takes with him when he makes house calls. It, too, contained a bottled potion that looked like coconut oil with some large, dark flakes in the bottom. I asked Lagi for permission to photograph the devil box and he smiled in agreement. I pressed the power button on my digital camera.

Strangely, the battery was dead, although it had been fine a moment ago.

'Teariki,' I said, 'did you bring a camera?'

'Yes, Scarlett's,' he replied, taking it out. Most frustratingly, my daughter's camera would not work either. Teariki fiddled with it for a while, but could not bring it to life.

'Is that battery dead too?' I asked.

'It can't be.' He shook his head. 'Scarlett said it had just been recharged.'

'Hmm,' I said, quite perplexed at catching an odd smirk on Lagi's face. Teariki and I looked at each other uneasily. This was really weird. I swallowed hard and put away the camera. 'Strong magic,' I acceded.

EPILOGUE

Thursday 26 May 2005

Fiji

We left Niutau on the evening of 1 May. The hurricane season appeared to be leaving the South Pacific, so the Captain headed the *Takapuna* down to Fiji. We hung around Savusavu for a while, enjoying such treats as the White Wall (a ravishing underwater cliff entirely covered in pearly coral), then cruised to Taveuni and the main island of Viti Levu. The *Takapuna* will soon undergo an overhaul and refit, so I shall leave the boat in Nadi, then return after the northern hemisphere summer for her onward journey west.

Fanny finished up her *Janet Nichol* cruise with a horribly stormy passage from Noumea to Sydney, where she and Lloyd were reunited with Louis. The Sydney climate was never good for Louis' health, so in September, they returned to Samoa and pitched themselves into the hard work of developing the Vailima estate.

On 2 December 1894, after four charmed years at Vailima, Louis was at home goading the family into playing a game of charades, which involved performing wicked pantomimes of some of their friends. The following morning he wrote some more of his latest book, *The Weir of Hermiston*.

'It will be my best work,' he said to Belle, to whom he was dictating. Just before lunch, he stopped work, rode into town to mail some letters, then took a swim to cool off. After announcing to Fanny that he was ravenous, he helped her prepare a salad then went to the wine cellar for a bottle of burgundy. Upon his return, he suddenly experienced a terrible pain in his head. Fanny managed to get him into a chair just before he fell unconscious. Lloyd raced into town to bring the doctors, but Louis was dying of a cerebral haemorrhage and nothing could be done. It was not long before he breathed his last, and his body was placed on the dining table in the Great Hall, covered with a Union Jack. Soon, local people began to arrive to pay their respects to *Tusitala*. They placed fine mats over him, lit candles, then sat vigil: praying, chanting and singing hymns until the morning. Early the next day, hundreds of men arrived to cut a path to the top of Mount Vaea and to dig Louis's grave at the summit. It was a chief's burial.

Last January, with the *Takapuna* lying in Apia harbour, I saw Louis' death certificate on the writing desk in his old study. It was signed by an Apia health officer: 'Cause of death: apoplexia'. I stared transfixed at the cold, official document. It was sad to think he had only four years at Vailima. 'But what a finale,' I told myself, 'surrounded by such beauty of both nature and people.' I decided to make a pilgrimage up the beautiful, rain-forested Mount Vaea to visit his tomb, and set off early the following morning, wearing stout footwear as the guidebooks suggest. The heavy panting of robust rugby players on their way down from the summit should have been a bit of a hint that I was facing a thoroughly challenging climb; nevertheless, doused from head to toe in insect repellent, I attempted to charge straight up the short, steep path. After only a few minutes, I was anticipating a massive heart attack and had to slow my ascent to a snail's pace. Fortunately there were plenty of natural resting places. I fancy Louis, too, must have needed to sit during his regular climbs to the spot he had chosen for his own burial. Birds sang above, ferns flourished at my feet and I was grateful for the canopy of Tahitian chestnuts, broad-leafed *maota* fruit trees and Samoan ebony that filtered the harsh sunlight from my over-heated body.

At the summit there is a small oval of flat land with a view of the harbour beyond. A yellow rubbish bin draws the eye, while a coloured picture of Jesus adorns a nearby tree; *Iesu ou te talitonu ia te oe*, it says, 'Jesus I trust in you'. Louis' tomb is of white, cracking plaster, defaced here and there with graffiti. His famous poem is misquoted on the plaque, with an added 'the' between 'from' and 'sea':

> Home is the sailor home from the sea,
> And the hunter home from the hill.

Three years after Louis' death, Fanny sold Vailima and returned to California. There, as the widow of Robert Louis Stevenson, she enjoyed a certain celebrity. Long ago she had given up trying to maintain conventional standards when it came to her behaviour, lifestyle, or appearance. Europeans who visited Fanny in Samoa described her as wild-looking, like a half-Mexican person, clothed in a grubby native dress, with a guitar slung over her shoulder like a travelling player. In widowhood, Fanny continued to defy convention. She eventually sought the companionship of young male protégés, notably the writer Ned Field, who was forty years her junior. Ned was Fanny's secretary and household member for ten years until, on 18 February, 1914, at nearly seventy-four years old, Fanny died from a stroke. The final, suitably unusual, twist in Fanny's story is that, in the same year of her death, Belle and Ned Field were married. Belle was then 56, and Ned twenty years younger.

In 1915, Belle and Ned took Fanny's ashes to Samoa, to be placed with Louis, in his grave on Mount Vaea. Her plaque on Louis' tomb is inscribed with her initials, F-V-DE-G-S and, underneath, her Samoan name, AOLELE. Below that, right and left, are two circles that each contain an engraved flower:

frangipani for the island and Fanny's personal emblem, the tiger lily. Louis's poem to her is inscribed in English on one side and in Samoan on the other:

> Teacher, tender comrade, wife
> A fellow-farer true through life
> Heart-whole and soul free
> The august Father gave to me.

My husband wrote me a very different kind of verse. As a Glaswegian renegade with a monumental dose of class-consciousness, he is never one hundred per cent sure that sailing on a yacht is an acceptable activity for a working-class hero, especially since the yacht happened to have a few creature comforts like showers, a washing machine and a coffee-maker. All right, it was actually a cappuccino machine, but we could only use it when it was dead calm – not too frigging often, I can tell you. Anyway, to show his disapproval, Billy came up with the following sea shanty, intended to take the piss out of yours truly:

I am the jolliest sailor boy to sail the raging main,
I've sailed in searing heat, me boys, and I've sailed in hurricanes;
I always wear a sailor's smile, as spinnakers I hoist –
But my air conditioner's broken and I'm feeling very moist.

Chorus
Yo ho sailor boys climbing up the mast,
Yo ho sailor boys shouting 'Aye avast!'
Yo ho sailor boys sailing round the horn –
But there's always time for a cup of tea, and a nice wee buttered scone.

The life of a modern yachtie's not a doddle as you know;
Last night I tripped on something, and I nearly hurt my toe.

The thunder crashed, the lightning flashed and lit the mighty
sea –
Well I think it did, because of interference on TV.

Repeat Chorus

This from a man who became adept at jumping ship before any
of the long, squall-ridden sea passages! But it's true that, unlike
the vessels in which the Stevensons travelled, we had the luxury
of modern navigation and safety equipment that eliminated
some of the guesswork, a water-maker to convert seawater into
drinking water, hydraulic winches, a global satellite communications system and, yes, air-conditioning. The latter is essential
in the tropics; Fanny and the crew were very often forced
to sleep on mats on the deck (aboard *Janet Nichol* she was the
sole woman among fifteen men) because the heat below
was unbearable.

I was sad after leaving Nuitau, the last Pacific island in my quest
to follow in Fanny's wake. At the same time, I felt elated to have
completed such a unique, albeit demanding voyage. It was a rare
challenge for any sailor, and our route was beyond the scope and
opportunity of most. Since leaving Florida we have travelled
19,000 nautical miles in nine months, almost three-quarters of
the way around the world if we'd followed a flying crow at the
Equator. Although we never had a shoot-out with pirates on the
open seas, we have cheated hurricanes, treacherous reefs,
sudden squalls, dangerous landings, fire, accidents at sea,
inaccurate charts and nefarious human beings.

Having now completed the same journeys as Fanny and
Louis, there is no doubt in my mind that the Stevensons were
utterly brave, pioneering and intrepid seafarers, visiting places
that, even in the heyday of the copra business, were unknown to
the world at large. In particular, Fanny was unique as a female
explorer, a travelling woman who was attached to neither

Church nor trader; although at this point I feel bound to applaud the bravery of any women who, for whatever reason, made similar voyages. They were never easy – and nor are they today. Fanny, of course, was a reluctant seawoman; but her very ambivalence about the ocean was one of the elements that made her journey such a triumph of will over water.

One must not be fooled by the fact that Fanny and Louis appeared to travel in style, at least aboard the *Casco*; no fancy food, furniture or frock makes up for the discomfort, the confinement, dangers, the terror of such extensive sailing, especially as they (and we) were often in poorly charted waters attempting precarious landings on sweltering, unfamiliar islands. Fortunately, our two parallel experiences had in common skilled captains and crews who could keep us all safe, and an entire ship's company with the constitution to put up with a great deal: bad weather, seasickness, terrible heat, cramped conditions, lack of sleep, the constant threat of disaster and long separations from loved ones.

Frankly, I was surprised at how similar our passages truly were. For me, the journey began to wear thin at around the same place as it did for Fanny; after spending so much time on either side of the Equator, we both began to long for a large dose of our own culture's definition of developed civilization. But that is not to decry in any way the power of the experience, nor the wondrousness of those regions and their admirable people.

Since the dawn of European contact the inhabitants of Pacific Islands have been cheated, killed, enslaved, disenfranchised, depopulated, colonized and relocated. I certainly had a first-hand education in the cultural and environmental desecration of those fragile populations – and, unfortunately, it continues today. There are a number of ways Western nations cause them injury, through our trade, industry, politics and lifestyle. In particular, the world's major industrial countries seem prepared to sacrifice Pacific people and their islands by failing to address the causes of global warming. Water levels are rising, islands are disappearing, and I pray it will soon be understood that a people so spiritually and ancestrally connected to their environment cannot simply be resettled.

Louis' book *Treasure Island* is one of the best-loved adventure stories ever written, and it appeals primarily because it holds for the reader the sense of letting go, a satisfying casting off of encumbrances; likewise, during my own search for the treasure in each one of the many islands I visited, I experienced a blissful shedding of the trappings and complications of my busy life ashore, and an unearthing of my own true self. I have emerged healthier, stronger, less spoiled and more resilient. I have become accustomed to life at sea – and wonder just how I'll fare ashore, once more at the mercy of highways, hairdressers and high-heeled shoes.

The thing about the ocean is: you have to face your self. I have never in my life felt so alive, so humble, so moved, or so terrified, as I have in the past year. Yet I cannot wait to head off again, through the glorious Indian Ocean and beyond. I guess it's in my blood. My great, great grandfather sailed the seas in his own ship. For years he whispered to me in my dreams. I've finally listened.

BIBLIOGRAPHY

NPD: No publishing date

Adams,   John Q., *South Seas Memories*, The Desert News, 1919

Alexander,   Caroline, *The Endurance* – Shackleton's Legendary Antarctic Expedition, Alfred A. Knopf, 2000

Anshen,   Ruth Nanda, *Letters From the Field 1925–1975* – Margaret Mead, Harper & Row, 1977

Apelu,   Teagai, *Tala O Funafuti*, Manuela Tolua, 2002

Balfour,   Graham, *The Life of Robert Louis Stevenson*, Volume 2, Charles Scribner's Sons, 1901; *The Life of Robert Louis Stevenson*, Methuen and Co., 1911

Balfour,   Marie Clothilde (ed.), *From Saranac to the Marquesas*, Methuen and Co., 1903

Bathurst,   Bella, *The Lighthouse Stevensons*, Perennial, 2000

Beavis,   Bill, McClosky Richard, *Salty Dirty Talk* – The Nautical Origins of Everyday Expressions, Sheridan House, 1995

Bell,   *In Search of Tusitala*, NPD

Bell,   Ian, *Dreams of Exile*, Henry Holt and Company Inc, 1992

Bergreen,   Laurence, *Over the Edge Of the World* – Magellan's Terrifying Circumnavigation of the Globe, HarperCollins Publishers, 2003

Bermann,   Richard A., *Robert Louis Stevenson in Samoa*, Mutual
             Publishing Company, 1939

Bird,   Isabella L., *Six Months in the Sandwich Islands* –
             Among Hawaii's Palm Groves, Coral Reefs, and
             Volcanoes, Mutual Publishing, 1998

Bissell,   Harvey, *Cruising with the Wanderluster*, Saturday
             Night Publishing Company, 1931

Booth,   Bradford A., Mehew, Ernest, *The Letters of Robert
             Louis Stevenson* – Volume Seven and Eight, Yale
             University Press, 1995

Borofsky,   Robert (ed.), *Remembrance of Pacific Pasts* – An
             Invitation to Remake History, University of Hawaii
             Press, 2000

Boulay,   Roger, *Vanuatu Arts* – The Artefacts tell their Story,
             Editions Grain de Sable, 2004

Brewis,   Alexandra, *Lives on the Line* – Women and Ecology
             on a Pacific Atoll, Harcourt Brace College
             Publishers, 1996

Brooks,   Charles Morris, *Guarding the Crossroads* – Security
             and Defense of the Panama Canal, P and P Group,
             Inc, 2003

Browne,   J. Ross, *A Peep at Washoe* – Sketches of Virginia
             Nevada Territory, Stanley Paher, 1986

Buzacott,   Aaron, *Mission Life in the Islands of the Pacific*,
             University of the South Pacific, NPD

Cahill,   Emmett, *Yesterday at Kalaupapa*, Editions Ltd, 2000

Cairney,   John, *The Quest for Robert Louis Stevenson*, Luath
             Press Ltd, 2004

Callow,   Philip, *Louis*, Ivan R. Dee Publisher, 2001

Calder,   Jenni (ed.), *Tales of the South Seas*, Canongate
             Classics, 1996

Campbell,   I., C., *Worlds Apart* – A History of the Pacific Islands,
             Canterbury University Press, 2003

Carpenter,   Angelica and Shirley, Jean, *Robert Louis Stevenson* –
             Finding Treasure Island, Lerner Publications Co.,
             1997

Carre,   Marie Jean, *The Frail Warrior* – A Life of Robert
                  Louis Stevenson, Greenwood Press, 1973

Castle,   Alan, *The Robert Louis Stevenson Trail* – A Walking
                  Tour in the Velay and Cevennes, Southern France,
                  Cicerone Press, 1992

Cenci,   Diogenes Cedeno, *The Panama Canal Strait Sought
                  after by Christopher Columbus in the route of the Storms
                  (The Fourth Trip of the Oceana Sea Admiral)*, Edicion
                  del Circulo de Lecture de la USMA, 2001

Chesterton,   G. K., *Robert Louis Stevenson*, House of Stratus, 2000

Childress,   David Hatcher, *Ancient Tonga and The Lost City of
                  Mu'a Including Samoa, Fiji, and Rarotonga*,
                  Adventures Unlimited Press, 1996

Christensen,   Chris, *American Samoa In the South Seas*, Robert
                  Boom Co., NPD

The City of Edinburgh Council, *Edinburgh* – Robert Louis
                  Stevenson, Edinburgh, 2001

Clare,   Maurice, *A Day with Robert Louis Stevenson*, Hodder
                  and Stoughton, NPD

Clark,   Blake, *Hawaii* – The 49th State, Doubleday and
                  Company, Inc., 1947

Clark,   Sydney, *All the Best in the South Pacific* – Tahiti,
                  Samoa, Fiji, New Caledonia, New Zealand,
                  Australia, Dodd, Mead & Co., 1961

Colvin,   Sidney (ed.), *Robert Louis Stevenson* – Letters,
                  Charles Scribner's, 1918

Conrad,   Joseph, *Typhoon*, Gallimard, 1991

Conte,   Eric, *L'archeologie En Polynesie Francaise* – Esquisse
                  D'un Bilan Critique, Au Vent Des Iles, 2000; *Tereraa*,
                  Collection Survol, 1992

Convis,   Charles L., *Frontiersmen* – True Tales of the Old
                  West, Volume 12, Pioneer Press, Nevada, 1999

Crocombe,   Ron (ed.) and Crocombe, *Marjorie Tuainekore*,
                  Freedom and Training For Pacific Media, Pacific
                  Islands Communication Journal Vol. 15 No. 2,
                  University of the South Pacific, 1988

Crose,   Commander W. M., *American Samoa* – A General
                Report by the Governor, Washington, 1913

Cummings,   David W., *Mighty Missionary of the Pacific*,
                Bookcraft, Inc, 1961

Curran,   Harold, *Fearful Crossing* – The Central Overland
                Trail Through Nevada, Nevada Publication, 1987

Daiches,   David, *Robert Louis Stevenson and His World*,
                Thames and Hudson, 1973

Dark,   Sidney, *Robert Louis Stevenson*, Hodder and
                Stoughton, NPD

Darwin,   Charles, *The Origin of Species By Means of Natural
                Selection or The Preservation of Favoured Races in the
                Struggle for Life*, Penguin Books, 1985; *Voyage of the
                Beagle*, Penguin Books, 1989

Davanzati,   M. Forges, *Polynesie* – Islas De Ensueno Trauminsel,
                Aprile, 1991

Davidson,   James D. G., *Scots and the Sea*, Mainstream
                Publishing, 2003

Davies,   Hunter, *In Search of Robert Louis Stevenson* – The
                Teller of Tales, Interlink Books, 1996

Daws,   Gavan, *Holy Man* – Father Damien of Molokai,
                University of Hawaii Press, 1973

Dening,   Greg, *Marquises 1774–1880*: Reflexion Sur Une Terre
                Muette, Editions De L'association 'Eo Enata, 1999

Denoon,   Donald, *The Cambridge History of The Pacific
                Islanders*, Cambridge University Press, 1997

Deschamps,   Emmanuel et Aiu, *L'Archipel Des Marquises*, Les
                editions Le Motu, NPD

Dieudonne,   Fran (ed.), *The Pacific Islands and the Sea*, Neptune
                House Publications, 2002

Dryden,   Linda, *The Modern Gothic and Literary Doubles*,
                Palgrave Macmillan, 2003

Eigner,   Edwin, *Robert Louis Stevenson and Romantic
                Tradition*, Princeton University Press, 1969

Ellison,   Joseph W., *Tusitala of the South Seas*, Hasting House
                Publishers 1953

Faaniu,   Simati [et al], *Tuvalu* – A History, University of the South Pacific, 1983

Field,   Isobel, *This Life I've Loved*, Longmans, Green and Co., 1938

Findlay,   J. Patrick, *In the Footsteps of Robert Louis Stevenson*, Edinburgh, 1911

Fischer,   Roger, Steven, *A History of the Pacific Islands*, Palgrave, 2002

Fitter,   Julian and Daniel, Hosking, David, *Safari Guides* – Galapagos, HarperCollins Publishers, 2000

Fitzpatrick, Judith M. (ed.), *Oceania* – Struggles to Survive and Thrive, Greenwood Press, 2001

Fitzpatrick, Elayne Wareing, *A Quixotic Companionship*, Old Monterey Preservation Society, 1997; *Robert Louis Stevenson's Ethics for Rascals*, Xlibris Corporation, 2000

Flood,   Bo, Beret E. Strong, William Flood, *Pacific Island Legends* – Tales from Micronesia, Melanesia, Polynesia, and Australia, The Bess Press, 1999

Fontain,   Pierre [et al], *Manu* – Les Oiseaux De Polynesie, Collection Survol, 1999

Fraser,   Bashabi (ed.), Elaine Greig (ed.), *Edinburgh* – An Intimate City, Edinburgh, 2000

Freeman,   Derek, *Margaret Mead and Samoa*: The Making and Unmaking of an Anthropological Myth, Harvard University Press, 1983

Froude,   James Anthony, *Oceania or England and Her Colonies*, Charles Scribner's Sons, 1904

Furnas,   J. C., *Anatomy of Paradise* – Hawaii and the Island of the South Seas, William Sloane Associates, Inc, 1947; *Voyage to Windward*, William Sloane Associates, 1951

Gallimore,   Ronald (ed.), Alan Howard (ed.), *Studies in a Hawaiian Community* – Na Makamaka O Nanakuli: No. 1, Bernice P. Bishop Museum, 1969

Garrett,   John, *Where Nets Were Cast* – Christianity in Oceania

Since World War 2, University of the South Pacific, 1997

Gibbings, Robert, *Over the Reefs*, J. M. Dent and Sons Ltd, 1948

Gill, William Wyatt, *From Darkness to Light in Polynesia*, University of the South Pacific, 1995; *Jottings from the Pacific*, The Religious Tract Society, 1885

Gilson, Richard, *The Cook Islands*, Victoria University Press, 1980

Goodwin, Bill, *South Pacific Frommer's*, Wiley Publishing Inc, 2002

Gotz, *Polynesian Tattoos* – Past and Present, A Pacific Promotion Tahiti S. A. Production, NPD

Grattan, F. J. H., *An Introduction to Samoan Custom*, Samoa Printing and Publishing Co. Ltd, 1948

Gravelle, Kim, *Fiji Times* – A History Of Fiji, The Fiji Times Ltd, 1979

Grimshaw, Beatrice, *In the Strange South Seas*, Hutchinson and Co./J. B. Lippincott Company, 1908

Gugelyk, Ted, Bloombaum, Milton, *The Separating Sickness*, Separation Sickness Foundation, 1996

Gunson, Niel (ed.), Scarr, Deryck (ed.), Terrel, Jennifer (ed.), *Echoes of Pacific Wars*, Target Oceania, 1998

Hall, James Norman, Nordhoff, Charles Bernard, *Faery Lands of the South Seas*, Garden City Publishing Co., 1926

Hanley, Sister Mary Laurence, O.S.F, *Pilgrimage and Exile* – Mother Marianne of Molokai, University of Hawaii Press, 1991

Harman, Claire (ed.), *Essays and Poems* – Robert Louis Stevenson, Everyman, 1992; *Robert Louis Stevenson* – A Biography, HarperCollins Publishers, 2005

Harper, Graeme, *Colonial and Postcolonial Incarceration*, Continuum, 2001

Hart, John Williams, *Samoan Culture*, Ati's Samoan Print Shop, 1996

Hawaii Historical Society, *74th Annual Report of the Hawaiian Historical Society* – 1965, Hawaii, 1966

Hawaii Mission Children's Society, *Missionary Album* – Sesquicentennial Edition 1820–1970, Hawaiian Mission Children's Society, 1969

Heiser, Victor, *An American Doctor's Odyssey* – Adventures in Forty-five countries, W. W. Norton and Co. Inc., 1936

Hellman, George S., *The True Stevenson*, Little, Brown, and Company, 1925

Henry, Brother Fred, *Samoa* – An Early History, American Samoa Department of Education, 1980

Henry, Richard, Dana, Jr, *Two Years Before The Mast* – A Personal Narrative of Life at Sea, Penguin Books, 1981

Heyerdahl, Thor, *Kon–Tiki*, Washington Square Press, 1973

Hezel, Francis X., S. J., *The First Taint of Civilization* – A History of the Caroline and Marshall Islands in Pre-Colonial Days, 1521–1885: Pacific Islands Monograph Series, No 1, University of Hawaii Press, 1983

Hill, Robin A., *Pure Air and Good Milk* – Robert Louis Stevenson at Swanston, 1995; (ed.), *Robert Louis Stevenson in a South Seas World*, 2002; *Robert Louis Stevenson in Germany*: Robert Louis Stevenson's Earliest Travels in Europe, Alphagraphics, Edinburgh, 2001

Hockings, John, *Traditional Architecture in the Gilbert Islands* – A Cultural Perspective, University of Queensland Press, 1989

Holmes, Lowell D., *Quest for the Real Samoa* – The Mead/Freeman Controversy & Beyond, Bergin & Garvey Publishers, Inc, 1987; Holmes, Ellen Rhoads, *Samoan Village* – Then and Now, Harcourt Brace College Publishers, 1992; *Treasured Islands*, Sheridan House, 2001

Hooper   Antony (ed.), Britton, Steve (ed.), Crocombe, Ron
              (ed.), Huntsman, Judith (ed.), Macpherson, Cluny
              (ed.), *Class and Culture in the South Pacific*,
              University of Auckland, University of the South
              Pacific, 1987; Huntsman, Judith, *Matagi Tokelau*,
              Office for Tokelau Affairs and University of the
              South Pacific, NPD

Horwell   David, Oxford, Pete, *Galapagos WildLife* – A Visitor's
              Guide, Bradt Publications, 1999

Horwitz,   Tony, *Blue Latitudes* – Boldly going where Captain
              Cook has gone before, Picador, 2003

Huet,   Karin, *A Meme La Mer*, Editions Glenat, 2001

Humann,   Paul, Deloach Ned, *Reef Fish Identification* –
              Galapagos, New World Publication, 2003

Huntsman,   Judith (ed.), Chowning, Ann (ed.), *The Journal of the
              Polynesian Society*, Polynesian Society, 1999

Issler,   Anne Roller, *Stevenson at Silverado*, James Stevenson
              Publishers, 1996

Jackson,   Frances (ed.), *The Hawaiian Journal of History*:
              Volume 12, Hawaiian Historical Society, 1978

Jackson,   Geoff and Jenny, *An Introduction to Tuvaluan*,
              Oceania Printers, 1999

Jackson,   Micheal H., *Galapagos* – A Natural History,
              University of Calgary Press, 1993

Japp,   A. H., *Robert Louis Stevenson* – A Record, An
              Estimate, A Memorial, IndyPublish.com, NPD

Jolly,   Margaret (ed.), Macintyre Martha (ed.), *Family and
              Gender in the Pacific* – Domestic Contradictions and
              the Colonial Impact, Cambridge University Press,
              1989

Jolly,   Roslyn (ed.), *South Sea Tales* – Robert Louis
              Stevenson, Oxford University Press, 1999; (ed.), *The
              Cruise of the Janet Nichol*, University of New South
              Wales Press Ltd, University of Washington Press,
              2004

Judd,   Gerrit P., *A Hawaiian Anthology* – Portraits of

Paradise: the Hawaii of History, Legend, and
Literature by Mark Twain, Robert Louis Stevenson,
Jack London, Herman Melville and many
others . . ., The Macmillan Company, 1967

Kasarherou,   Emmanuel, *Jinu* – The Spirit of Oceania, Agence de
Developpement de la Culture Kanak, 2003; (ed.),
Mwakaa – The Pathway of Kanak Tradition, Tjibaou,
2000

Kay,   Robert F., *Hidden Tahiti and French Polynesia*, Ulysses
Press, 2003

Kelman,   John, *The Faith of Robert Louis Stevenson*, Fredonia
Books, 2003

Kennedy,   Melvin D. (ed.) [et al], *Providing Passage into the
Twenty-first Century*: The Panama Canal, Panama
Canal Commision, 1994

Kent,   Harold Winfield, *Dr Hyde and Mr Stevenson*, Charles
E. Tuttle Company, 1973

Kiely,   Robert, *Robert Louis Stevenson and the Fiction of
Adventure*, Harvard University Press, 1965

Kilgallin,   Anthony Raymond, *Napa* – Images of America: An
Architectural Walking Tour, Arcadia, 2001

Kirch,   Patrick Vinton, *On the Road of the Winds* – An
Archaeological History of the Pacific Islands Before
European Contact, University of California Press,
2002

Knight,   Alanna (ed.), Warfel Elizabeth Stuart (ed.), *Robert
Louis Stevenson* – Bright Ring of Words, Balnain,
1994; *The Passionate Kindness* – The Love Story of
Robert Louis Stevenson and Fanny Osbourne, The
Molendinar Press, 1980

Knudsen,   Eric, *Teller of Hawaiian Tales*, Mutual Publishing,
1946

Koch,   Gerd, *Songs of Tuvalu*, University of the South
Pacific, 2000; *The Material Culture of Kiribati*,
University of the South Pacific, 1986

Koenig,   Robert et Denise (ed.) [et al], *Voyage Pittoresque –
               Autour Du Monde*, Haere Po No Tahiti, 1988

Kowata,   Kinuko (ed.) [et al], *Inqn in Majol* – A collection of
               Marshallese Folktales, Alele Museum, Library, and
               National Archives, 1999

Kramer,   Dr Augustin, *The Samoa Islands* – An Outline of a
               Monograph with Particular Consideration of
               German Samoa, University of Hawaii Press, 1995

Langmore,   Diane, *Missionary Lives* – Papua, 1874–1914: Pacific
               Islands Monograph Series, No.6, University of
               Hawaii Press, 1989

Lapierre,   Alexandra, *A Romance with Destiny* – Fanny
               Stevenson, Carroll and Graf Publishers, Inc, 1995

Latorrie,   Octavio, *The Curse of the Giant Tortoise* – Tragedies,
               Crimes, and Mysteries in the Galapagos Islands,
               Quito, 2003

Leib,   Amos P., *The Many Islands of Polynesia*, Charles
               Scribner's Sons, 1972

Leon,   Vicki, *Uppity Women of Ancient Times*, Conari Press,
               1995

Levy,   Robert I., *Tahitians* – Mind and Experience in the
               Society Islands, University of Chicago Press, 1988

Lewis,   Roger C. (ed.), *The Collected Poems of Robert Louis
               Stevenson*, Edinburgh University Press, 2003

Linkels,   Ad and Lucia, *Hula, Haka, Hoko* – An Introduction
               to Polynesian dancing, Mundo Etnico Foundation,
               1999

Lockwood,   Victoria S. (ed.), *Globalisation and Culture Change in
               the Pacific Islands*, Pearson Prentice Hall, 2004

Logan   Leanne, Geert Cole, *New Caledonia* – Kanak Culture,
               French Flavor, Lonely Planet Publications, 2001

Loti,   Pierre, *Tahiti* – The Marriage of Loti, KPI Ltd,
               1986

MacArthur,   Ellen, *Taking on the World*, Penguin Books, 2003

Macdonald,   Barrie, *Cinderellas of the Empire*, University of the
               South Pacific, 2001

Mackay,   Margaret, *The Violent Friend* – The Story of Mrs
               Robert Louis Stevenson, J M Dent and Sons Ltd,
               1969

Mackenzie,   Donald A., *Myths and Traditions of the South Sea
               Islands*, The Gresham Publishing Co Ltd, NPD

Maclellan   Nic, Chesneaux Jean, *After Muroroa France in the
               South Pacific*, Ocean Press, 1998

Mageo,   Jeannette Marie, *Theorizing Self in Samoa* –
               Emotions, Genders, and Sexualities, The University
               of Michigan Press, 1998

Maixner,   Paul (ed.), *Robert Louis Stevenson* – The Critical
               Heritage, Routledge and Kegan, 1981

Manguel,   Alberto, *Stevenson Sous Les Palmiers*, Actes
               Sud/Lemeac, 2001

Maude   H. E. (ed.) and H.C. (ed.), *An Anthology of Gilbertese
               Oral Tradition*, University of the South Pacific, 1994;
               The Evolution of the Gilbertese Boti, University of the
               South Pacific, 1991; *The Gilbertese Maneaba*,
               University of the South Pacific, 1980

Meleisea,   Malama, *Lagaga* – A Short History of Western
               Samoa, University of the South Pacific, 1987; *The
               Making of Modern Samoa* – Traditional Authority and
               Colonial Administration on the Modern History of
               Western Samoa, University of the South Pacific,
               1987

McCullough,   David, *The Path Between the Seas* – The Creation of
               the Panama Canal 1870–1914, Simon and Schuster,
               1977

McDonald,   Douglas, *Nevada* – Lost Mines and Buried
               Treasures, Stanley W. Paher, 1981

McGaw,   Sister Martha M., *Stevenson in Hawaii*, Greenwood
               Press, 1978

McLaren,   Moray, *Stevenson and Edinburgh*, Chapman and
               Hall, 1950

McLaughlin,   Mark, *Western Train Adventures*: The Good, the Bad,
               the Ugly, Mic Mac Publishing 2003

McLynn,   Frank, *Robert Louis Stevenson* – A Biography, Random House, New York, 1993

McNally,   Raymond T., Florescu, Radu R., *In Search of Dr Jekyll and Mr Hyde*, Renaissance Books 2000

McQuarrie,   Peter, *Conflict of Kiribati*, University of Canterbury, 2000; *Strategic Atolls*, University of Canterbury and University of the South Pacific, 1994

Mead,   Margaret, *Coming of Age in Samoa*, Perennial Classics, 2001

Mebane,   John Cummins, *The April Of Her Age*, Windward Publishing Company, 1994

Mehew,   Ernest (ed.), *Selected Letters of Robert Louis Stevenson*, Yale University Press, 2001

Melville,   Herman, *Typee* – A Peep at Polynesian Life, The Modern Library, 2001

Middleton,   Dorothy, *Victorian Lady Travellers*, E. P. Dutton and Co., Inc., 1965

Mighall,   Robert (ed.), *Robert Louis Stevenson* – The Strange Case of Dr Jekyll and Mr Hyde and other Tales of Terror, Penguin Books, 2002; Lucky Mike; *Dancing on Raindrops* – Extreme Adventures, M42 Corp, 2004

Miller,   Korina, Jones Robyn, *Pinheiro Leonardo*, Fiji, Lonely Planet Publications, 2003

Moitessier,   Bernard, *La Longue Route* – Seul Entre Mers et Ciels, Arthaud, 1986

Montgomery,   Helen Barrett, *Christus Redemptor* – An Outline Study of the Island World of the Pacific, The Macmillan Company, 1907

Moore,   W. G., *Family in Samoa* – This is Their Life, Hulton Educational Publication, 1961

Moors,   Harry J., *With Stevenson in Samoa*, NPD

Morris,   Aldyth, *Robert Louis Stevenson* – Appointment on Moloka'i, University of Hawaii Press, 1995

Murphy,   Jim, *Across America on an Emigrant Train*, Clarion Books, 1993

Neider, Charles (ed.), *The Complete Short Stories of Robert Louis Stevenson* – With a Selection of The Best Short Novels, Da Capo Press, 1998

Nickerson, Roy, *Robert Louis Stevenson in California*, Chronicle Books, 1982

Noble, Andrew (ed.), *From the Clyde to California* – Robert Louis Stevenson's Emigrant Journey, Aberdeen University Press, 1985

O'Brien, Frederick, *Atolls of the Sun*, The Century Co., 1922

Oliver, Douglas, *Black Islanders* – A Personal Perspective of Bougainville 1937–1991, Hyland House, 1991; *Oceania* – The Native Cultures of Australia and the Pacific Islands, Vol. 1 & 2, University of Hawaii Press, 1989; *The Pacific Islands*, University of Hawaii Press, Honolulu, 1989

Pager, Sean, *Off the Beaten Path* – Hawaii: A Guide to Unique Places, The Globe Pequot Press, 1997

Panoff, Micheal, *La Terre Et L'organisation Sociale En Polynesie*, Payot Paris, 1970

The Pasifika Library, *Robert Louis Stevenson* – A Footnote to History, Pasifika Press, 1996

Peattie, Mark R., *Nan'yo*, University of Hawaii Press, 1988

Peltzer, Louise, *Chronologie des evenements politics*, sociaux et culturels de Tahiti et des archipels de la Polynesie francaise, Au Vent Des Iles, 2000

Poole, Adrian (ed.), *The Master of Ballantrae* – A Winter's Tale: Robert Louis Stevenson, 1996

Prince, Jan, *Tahiti and French Polynesia Guide*, Open Road Publishing, 2002

Ralston, Caroline, *Grass Huts and Warehouses*, Australian National University Press, The University Press of Hawaii, 1978

Rankin, Nicholas, *Dead Man's Chest* – Travels after Robert Louis Stevenson, Phoenix Press, 2001

Rehbock, Philip F. (ed.), Chaplin, Helen G. (ed.), *The Hawaiian*

Journal of History: Volume 18, 1984, Hawaiian Historical Society, 1984

Reinstedt, Randall A., *The Strange Case of the Ghost of the Robert Louis Stevenson House*, Ghost Town Publication, 1988

Rennie, Neil (ed.), *In the South Seas*, Penguin Books, 1998

Rigo, Bernard, *Alterite Polynesienne* – Ou les metamorphoses de l'espace–temps, CNRS Editions, 2004

Robertson, Ailsa, *The Cook Islands*, Heinemann Education, 1989

Robinson, Roger (Selection, Introduction, Commentaries), Wendt, Albert (Foreword), *Robert Louis Stevenson – His Best Pacific Writings*, Bess Press, 2003

Robson, R. W., F.R.G.S., *The Pacific Islands Year Book – 1942*, Pacific Publications, 1942

Rogers, Hilary, Carillet, Jean-Bernard, Wheeler, Tony, *Tahiti and French Polynesia*, Lonely Planet Publication, 2003

Russell, Joe, *Exploring the Marquesas Islands*, Fine Edge Productions, 2000

Russell, Rev. M., L.L.D. and D.C.L., *Polynesia or Historical Account of the Principle Island in the South Sea including New Zealand*, Oliver & Boyd, 1842

Ryan, Paddy, *The Snorkeller's Guide to the Coral Reef* – From the Red Sea to the Pacific Ocean, Crawford House Press, 1994

Sahlins, Marshall, *How "Natives" Think*, The University of Chicago Press, 1995

Sanchez, Nellie Van de Grift, *The Life of Mrs Robert Louis Stevenson*, James Stevenson Publishers, 2001

Saquet, Jean-Louis, *The Tahiti Handbook* – Tefenua, Editions Avant et Apres, 2003

Sawyers, June Skinner (ed.), *Dreams of Elsewhere* – The Selected Travel Writings of Robert Louis Stevenson, The In Pinn, 2002

Scemla, Jean-Jo, *Le Voyage En Polynesie*, Bouquins, 1994

Seagraves, Anne, *High-spirited Women of the West*, Wesanne, 1992; *Roses of the West*, Wesanne Publication, 2002;

Women of the Sierra, Wesanne Publication, 1992; *Women Who Charmed The West*, Wesanne Publication, 1991; *Soiled Doves* – Prostitution in the Early West, Wesanne Publication, 1994

Shineberg,   Dorothy, *The People Trade* – Pacific Island Laborers and New Caledonia, 1865–1930, University of Hawaii Press, 1999

Sissons,   Jeffrey, *Nation and Destination*: Creating Cook Islands Identity, University of the South Pacific, 1999

Skinsnes,   Anwei (ed.), Wisniewski, Richard A. (ed.), *Kalaupapa and the Legacy of Father Damien* – National Historical Park, Pacific Basin Enterprises, 1988

Slocum,   Joshua, *Sailing Alone Around the World and The Voyage of the Liberdade*, National Geographic Adventure Classics, 2003

Smith,   Ali, *Laws of the Bandit Queens* – Words to Live by from 35 of Today's Most Revolutionary Women, Three Rivers Press, 2002

Smyth,   Admiral W. H., *The Sailor's Book* – The classic source for over 14,000 nautical and naval terms, Conway Maritime Press, 2005

Spennemann,   Dirk, Etto, *Ennaanin* – A Collection fo Essays on the Marshallese Past, Historic Preservation Office, Republic of Marshall Islands, 1993

Stall,   Edna Williamson, *The Story of Lauhala*, Petroglyph Press, Ltd, 1974

Stanton,   Ken, *Mount St. Helen and Robert Louis Stevenson State Park* – A History and Guide, Bonnie View Books, 1998

Steuart,   J. A., *Robert Louis Stevenson* – Man and Writer, Sampson Low, Marston and Co, Ltd, NPD

Stevenson,   Fanny, *The Cruise of the Janet Nichol*, NPD

Stevenson,   Robert Louis, *The Amateur Emigrant*, Carrol and Graf Publishers, 2002; *The Black Arrow*, Tom Doherty Associates Book, 1998; *The Body Snatcher and Other Tales*, Dover Publication, 2001; *The Bottle Imp*, Tree Garden Workshop, 1994; *Catriona*, The Harvill Press, 1995; *A Child's Garden of Verses*, Charles Scribner's Sons, NPD; Van De Grift, Fanny, *The Dynamiter*, Books for Libraries Press, 1971; *Island Nights Entertainments* – The Misadventures of John Nicholson, William Heinemann, Ltd, 1926; *The Silverado Squatters*, Quiet Vision Publishing Inc., 2000; *Travels With A Donkey In the C'evenes and The Amateur Emigrant*, Penguin Classics, 2004; *Treasure Island*, NPD; Osbourne, Lloyd, *The Wrong Box*, Amereon House, 1989

Stone,   Donna K. (ed.) [et al], *Jabonkonnaan in Majel* – Wisdom from the Past: A collection of Marshallese Proverbs, Wise Saying, and Beliefs, Alele Museum, Library and National Archives, 2000

Suggs,   Robert C., *The Island Civilizations of Polynesia*, The New American Library of World Literature Inc., 1960

Talmage,   Rev. T. DeWitt, D. D., *The Pathway of Life*, Historical Publishing Company, 1894

Talu,   Sister Alaima [et al.], *Kiribati*, University of the South Pacific, Kiribati Government, 1985

Tarte,   Daryl, *Island of the Frigate Bird*, University of the South Pacific, 1999

Taylor,   Albert P., *Under Hawaiian Skies*, Advertiser Publishing Co., 1922

Taylor,   N. J., *The Legend of Simoneau Plaza* – Monterey, California 1879, N. J. Taylor, 2001

Terry,   R. C. (ed.), *Robert Louis Stevenson* – Interviews and Recollections, 1996

Thomas,   Nicholas, *Cook* – The Extraordinary Voyages of Captain James Cook, Walker and Co., 2003

Thomson,   Jeff, *Point Lobos State Reserve*, Walkabout Publications, 1997

Toullelan,   Pierre-Yves, Gille Bernard, *Le Marriage Franco–Tahitien*: Histoire de Tahiti du 18th Siecle a Nos Jours, Editions Polymages – Scoop, 1991

Tregaskis,   Moana, *Hawaii*, Fodor's Travel Publication, 2001

Troost,   J. Maarten, *The Sex Lives of Cannibals*, Broadway Books, 2004

Tseng,   Wen–shing (ed.), McDermott, John F. Jr (ed.), Maretzki, Thomas W. (ed.), *People and Cultures in Hawaii* – An Introduction for Mental Health Workers, University of Hawaii – School of Medicine, 1974

Tuiteleleapaga, Napolene A., *Samoa Yesterday, Today and Tomorrow*, Todd and Honeywell, Inc., 1980

Universite De La Polynesie Francaise, D. E. A. Imagol Mundi, *Elogue du Metissage* – Myths et realites en Polynesie, Haere Po, 2003

University of the South Pacific, *In Search of a Home*, University of the South Pacific, 1987; *Polynesian Missions in Melanesia*, University of the South Pacific, 1982

Vanderburg,   William O., *Mines of Lander and Eureka Countries*, Stanley Paher, 1988

Verne,   Jules, *Around the World in Eighty Days*, The Modern Library, 2004

Weber,   Lin, *Old Napa Valley* – The History to 1900, Wine Venture Publishing, 1998

Wendt,   Albert, *Leaves of the Banyan Tree*, University of Hawaii Press, 1994

Whistler,   Dr W. Arthur, *Flowers of the Pacific Island Seashore* – A guide to the littoral plants of Hawaii, Tahiti, Samoa, Tonga, Cook Island, Fiji and Micronesia, Isle Botanica, 2002

William,   Glyndwr, *The Great South Sea*, Yale University Press, 1997

Winegar,   James S., *The Robert Louis Stevenson Museum* – Vailima, The Robert Louis Stevenson Museum/ Preservation Foundation Inc., NPD

Wisniewski,   Richard A., *Hawaiian Monarchs and their Palaces (A Pictorial History)*, Pacific Basin Enterprises, 1987
Wooley,   John G., G., Mary D., *South Sea Letters*, The New Voice Press, 1906

www.janesoceania.com
www.janeresture.com